Computer-Assisted Music Analysis (1950s-1970s)

Methodology of Music Research
Methodologie der Musikforschung

Edited by / Herausgegeben von Nico Schüler

Vol. / Bd. 8

PL ACADEMIC RESEARCH

Nico Schüler

Computer-Assisted Music Analysis (1950s-1970s)

Essays and Bibliographies

PL ACADEMIC RESEARCH

Bibliographic Information published by the Deutsche Nationalbibliothek
The Deutsche Nationalbibliothek lists this publication in the Deutsche Nationalbibliografie; detailed bibliographic data is available in the internet at http://dnb.d-nb.de.

Published with financial support from
Texas State University.

Library of Congress Cataloging-in-Publication Data
Schüler, Nico.
Computer-assisted music analysis (1950s-1970s) : essays and bibliographies / Nico Schüler.
pages cm -- (Methodology of music research ; Bd. 8)
Includes bibliographical references.
ISBN 978-3-631-39764-0
1. Musical analysis--Data processing--History. I. Title.
ML74.S388 2014
780.285--dc23
2014024049

ISSN 1618-842X
ISBN 978-3-631-39764-0 (Print)
E-ISBN 978-3-653-04860-5 (E-Book)
DOI 10.3726/978-3-653-04860-5

PL Academic Research is an Imprint of Peter Lang GmbH.

Peter Lang – Frankfurt am Main · Bern · Bruxelles · New York · Oxford · Warszawa · Wien

This publication has been peer reviewed.

www.peterlang.com

To my loving wife, Sunnie.

Contents

Preface

> "I should like to suggest that computer analysis will become one of the most important directions in musicology for the next generation. One hears frequently the comment that computers will make musicology mechanistic. Bear in mind, however, that the computer does what it is told: even its most sophisticated procedures depend on the imagination of the researcher for instructions; and the final results always require further interpretation. In these two functions – instruction and interpretation – the researcher controls the fundamental musicality of the investigation. If the results are mechanistic, he cannot blame the computer." (Jan LaRue 1970a, 197.)

Computer-assisted music analysis, which emerged about 60 years ago, provides analytical tools that help solve problems, some of which may be unsolvable without the assistance of the computer. Unfortunately, most research in the area of computer-assisted music analysis has been carried out, again and again, without any explicit review of preceding attempts and accomplishments. Even the most recent research bears traces of two fundamental flaws that have plagued most research carried out to date: there is no comprehensive historical framework of computer-assisted analytical methods, and there is no critical evaluation of those methods.

A series of articles in several volumes, this being the first volume, will attempt to overcome some of these shortcomings. I will provide a historical account and framework of methods of computer-assisted music analysis; to a limited degree, I will also attempt to critically reflect on these methods and approaches. The source materials for the historical account through today consist of over 2,500 published and unpublished writings, including dissertations and internal research papers from many countries, that were collected and analyzed over many years, starting with an article I wrote in 1996, but especially with my dissertation (Schüler 2000) and several subsequent articles (Schüler 2002b, 2003, 2005, 2006, 2007, 2013). The essays and bibliographies have been corrected and expanded. Each essay contains a thorough bibliography, and ultimately an alphabetical bibliography as well as a chronological bibliography are provided within the scope of the volume.

This particular volume (through the 1970s) contains essays on developments of music encoding, on measurements derived from statistics and information theory (as those were the primary measurements applied to computer-assisted music analysis through the 1970s), on the development of computing technology, on the beginnings of computer-assisted music analysis (through the 1950s), on the 1960s, and finally on the 1970s. While the quantity of research grew dramatically over time, in each decade, through today, we can find specific developments. It is also interesting to compare the bibliographies on each decade; and even more interesting is the chronological bibliography (by year) at the end of the volume, which shows the change in quantity and topics over the years. We can see increases in scholarly output in 1964, 1967, and 1970; of course, they correlate with the publication of particular books and journals. We can also observe a decline in the late 1970s (before renewed interest, a new generation of scholars, and new directions are responsible for an increase in scholarly output in the 1980s, as we will discover in the next volume).

Of course, many scholars have contributed to this historical and bibliographic account of computer-assisted music analysis, most notably Stephan M. Kostka (1974), Deta S. Davis (1988, 1992 and 1993), and Bo H. Alphonce (1980 and 1989a). And I would especially like to thank some of my teachers for their encouragement to work on this topic since the late 1980s: Manfred Vetter, Gerd Rienäcker, Reiner Kluge, Rosalie Schellhous, Mark Sullivan, and Bruce Campbell.

Although I have been striving for completeness in terms of the bibliographies, I am certain that there are writings that I have either not heard of or was unable to retrieve. And thus I would kindly ask the readers to point out the shortcomings, so this research area can continue to improve.

References

Alphonce, Bo H. 1980. "Music Analysis by Computer – A Field for Theory Formation," *Computer Music Journal* IV/2 (Summer): 26-35.

_________. 1989a. "Computer Applications: Analysis and Modeling," *Music Theory Spectrum* XI/1 (Spring): 49-59.

Battier, Marc, and Jacques Arveiller. 1978. *Musique et informatique: une bibliographie indexée*, réédition augmentée. Paris: Elmeratto.

Bent, Ian D. 1980. "Analysis," *The New Grove Dictionary of Music and Musicians*, edited by Stanley Sadie, vol. 1. London: Macmillan. 340-388.

_________. 1987. *Analysis*, with a glossary by William Drabkin. London: Macmillan.

Bent, Ian, and John Morehen. 1978. "Computers in the Analysis of Music," *Proceedings of the Royal Musical Association* CIV (1977-78): 30-46.

Berlind, Gary. [n.d.]. Writings on the Use of Computers in Music. Compiled by Gary Berlind in collaboration with Barry S. Brook, Lejaren A. Hiller Jr., Jan P. LaRue, and George W. Logemann. New York: New York University, Institute for Computer Research in the Humanities. Mimeographed.

Cope, David. 2008. *Hidden Structure: Music Analysis Using Computers*. Wisconsin: A-R Editions.

Davis, Deta S. 1988. *Computer Applications in Music: A Bibliography*. Madison, WI: A-R Editions.

_________. 1992. *Computer Applications in Music: A Bibliography, Supplement 1*. Madison, WI: A-R Editions.

_________. 1993. *Computer Applications in Music: A Bibliography, Supplement 1*. Oxford: Oxford University Press.

Dunsby, Johnathan, and Arnold Whittall. 1988. *Music Analysis in Theory and Practice*. London: Faber Music.

Jesser, Barbara. 1991. *Interaktive Melodienanalyse. Methodik und Anwendung computergestützter Anaylseverfahren in Musikethnologie und Volksliedforschung: Typologische Untersuchung der Balladensammlung des DVA*. Studien zur Volksliedforschung 12. Bern: Peter Lang.

Kluge, Reiner. 1974a. *Faktorenanalytische Typenbestimmung an Volksliedmelodien*. Beiträge zur musikwissenschaftlichen Forschung in der DDR 6. Leipzig: Deutscher Verlag für Musik.

Kostka, Stephan M. 1974. *A Bibliography of Computer Applications in Music*. Hackensack, NJ: Joseph Boonin.

LaRue, Jan. 1970a. "New Directions for Style Analysis," *Musicology and the Computer: Three Symposia*, edited by Barry S. Brook. New York: The City University of New York Press. pp. 194-197.

Schnell, Christoph. 1985. *Die Eingabe musikalischer Information als Teil eines Arbeitsinstrumentes. Ein Beitrag zur Computeranwendung in der Musikwissenschaft*, Bern, Frankfurt/M., New York: Peter Lang.

Schüler, Nico. 1996. "Methoden computerunterstützter Musikanalyse - ein historischer Überblick," *Zum Problem und zu Methoden von Musikanalyse*, edited by Nico Schüler. Hamburg: von Bockel. pp. 51-76.

_________. 2000a. "Towards a General Methodological Classification of Computer-Assisted Music Analysis," *Proceedings of the 2000 International Computer Music Conference in Berlin*, ed. by Ioannis Zannos. San Francisco, CA: The International Computer Music Association. pp. 221-224.

_________. 2000b. "Towards a Methodological View on (Computer-Assisted) Music Analysis," *Bridges: Mathematical Connections in Art, Music, and Science*, ed. by Reza Sarhangi. Winfried, Kansas: Southwestern College, 2000. pp. 99-104.

_________. 2000c. Methods of Computer-Assisted Music Analysis: History, Classification, and Evaluation. Ph.D. dissertation. East Lansing, MI: Michigan State University.

_________. 2001. "On Methods and Methodology of (Computer-Assisted) Music Analysis," *Musikkonzepte - Konzepte der Musikwissenschaft*, vol. 1, ed. by Kathrin Eberl and Wolfgang Ruf. Kassel: Bärenreiter. pp. 380-385.

_________. Ed. 2002a. *Computer-Applications in Music Research: Concepts, Methods, Results*. New York: Peter Lang.

_________. 2002b. "Music Analysis of the Next Generation? Recent Development in Computer-Assisted Music Analysis," *New Sound. International Magazine for Music* 20: 34-47.

_________. 2003. "Towards a History of Computer-Assisted Music Analysis: Developments since 1989," *Journal of the Institute for Music Research at Kyunghee University* [South Korea] I (October): 325-342.

_________. 2005. "Reflections on the History of Computer-Assisted Music Analysis I: Predecessors and the Beginnings," *Musicological Annual* [Ljubljana, Slovenia] XXXXI/1: 31-43.

_________. 2006. "Reflections on the History of Computer-Assisted Music Analysis II: The 1960s," *Musicological Annual* [Ljubljana, Slovenia] XLII/1: 5-24.

_________. 2007. "From Musical Grammars to Music Cognition in the 1980s and 1990s: Highlights of the History of Computer-Assisted Music Analysis," *Rationalism of a Magic Tinge: Music as a Form of Abstract Perception* [Bergamo Festschrift], ed. by

Leon Stefanija and Katarina Bogunovic Hocevar. [*Musicological Annual* XLIII/2] Ljubljana, Slovenia. pp. 371-396.

_________. 2013. “Computerunterstützte Mozartanalyse: Geschichte, Methoden, Kritik und Ausblick,” *Mozartanalyse heute*, ed. by Gernot Gruber. Laaber: Laaber Verlag. pp. 69-100.

Steinbeck, Wolfram. 1982. *Struktur und Ähnlichkeit. Methoden automatisierter Melodienanalyse*. Kieler Schriften zur Musikwissenschaft 25. Kassel: Bärenreiter.

Uhrlandt, Dirk, and Nico Schüler. 1992. “Informationsmaße in der computergestützten Musikanalyse.” *Kammermusik Heute* 2: 102-112.

On Developments of Music Encoding

Computers can be employed as a tool in composition, in bibliographic research, to create thematic indices, and to scan, transcribe, print, and analyze music, and so forth. Historically, the first computer applications in music spanned two areas, composition and analysis, but in all the applications that subsequently developed one thing was required: a representation of the music in a digital form.[1] Since the first use of computers in the field of music, different digital codes for representing musical relationships have been developed, and recurrent problems relating to encoding have emerged. F. P. Brooks et al. (1957), for instance, used a simple numeric representation of pitch and tone duration. On the other hand, MUSIC V[2], which developed in several different "dialects," used several kinds of representations, many of which are still in use today. These include the file format of SCORE, which substituted spatial placement parameters for time-ordered parameters. MUSIC V's differentiation of global parameters and its event list also prefigured the Standard MIDI file format.

The several hundred codes, developed over the last four decades, correspond to a wide range of demands: from simple statistical applications to complex cognitive ones. However, most of them suffer from one or more kinds of problems: technical problems of their implementation, problems in the flow of information, problems inherent in a certain type of notation, or the problems in the limitations of the relation between the system and the user. (Schnell 1985, 289 f.) Fortunately, the means of entering the digital representation into the computer are independent of the purpose of the code and has posed few prob-

1 Christoph Schnell (1985) and Eleanor Selfridge-Field (1997a, 1997b) presented a detailed description of the problem. Their studies are the main sources of information for this essay.

2 Generating sound samples was part of a research project carried out in the mid-1950s at Bell Telephone Laboratories. (The goal of this research project was the transmission of telephone conversations in a digitized form.) The Bell engineer Max Mathews explored the calculation and generation of sound, coming up with the two experimental programs MUSIC I (1957) and MUSIC II (1958), which were able to synthesize simple sounds via a limited number of triangle-wave functions. For this, Mathews used an IBM 704 computer. The first comprehensive synthesis program, MUSIC III, was completed on an IBM 7094 in 1960. Soon after, James Tenney became involved in the project, followed by Hubert Howe, Godfrey Winham, and Jim Randall. In the mid-1960s, MUSIC IV was re-written in the high-level language FORTRAN, and re-organized and extended as MUSIC V in 1969 at Bell Laboratories, featuring more global sound-control, the possibility of representing individual notes and note-patterns, and supporting the simulation of performance nuances (such as ritardando, crescendo, etc.).

lems. Christoph Schnell (1985, 44) distinguished the following fundamental, most frequent input possibilities:

- input from a special keyboard,
- input with the help of a mechanized music editor,
- input from a conventional computer keyboard,
- input from a piano keyboard,
- input from a direct recording of analog acoustical information, and
- input from direct scanning of optic-musical information.

These alternatives relate to two basic goals: first, encoding acoustical information as completely as possible, and, second, to encoding abstract musical information. The latter usually involves converting the graphical information (symbols of acoustical events, the notation) into a digital representation. In most cases, musical information outside the score is not converted, but sometimes – depending on the application – even notated parameters, such as dynamics or phrasing, are omitted.

Another factor that has often been a problem, particularly in any complicated analysis, is related to the amount of computer memory needed for carrying out any complex analysis. If, for instance, the analysis involved several parameters of musical events (i.e., not only pitch and tone duration), a relatively large amount of memory was necessary. In the past, the amount needed was often more than common computers had available.[3] Until smaller computers with large amount of memory and higher computation capacities were available (i.e., until about the mid-1980s), most applications were developed on mainframe computers or workstations. Using these computers for musical purposes required a high degree of technical understanding, which meant that the musicologists or music theorists could not use their native methodology, but instead, had to use methods native to the computer and only *adapted* to musical purposes.

Finally, understanding several key and related problems and solutions require a brief discussion of some of the most widely used codes for digital representation of music.

The Plaine and Easy Code was initially developed by Murray Gould (sometime before 1964), and then expanded and improved by Gould and Berry S. Brook. It was intended to enable the transfer of musical bibliographic data to electronic data-processing equipment (see Brook and Gould 1964, 142). The Plaine and Easy Code enabled the replacement of conventional, purely monolinear notation with ordinary typewriter characters. Thereby, not only tempo, key

3 See the essay on developments of computing technology in this book.

signature, meter, pitches, and durations could be encoded, but also some phrasing marks and embellishments.

Starting in 1962, Jerome Wenker developed the comprehensive music description code MUSTRAN (see Byrd 1984, and Wenker 1972b, 1974, 1978). It included all common symbols of traditional music notation and assigned them an alphanumeric code, which was translated by the computer into an internal machine-oriented notation. MUSTRAN was mainly used for the analysis of (single-voice) folk songs and went through various developments on a number of platforms.

In the middle of the 1960s, Murray Gold also co-authored the ALMA code (Alphanumeric Language for Music Analysis) together with George W. Logemann (see Gould and Logemann 1966 and 1970). ALMA evolved from the Plaine and Easie Code and was based on characters available on the IBM 029 Keypunch. It enabled the encoding of data relating to the following categories: composer, title, instruments, movement, tempo, clef, key signature, time signature, dynamics, expressions (e.g., morendo), pitches, durations, texture markings, and instrumental techniques. ALMA influenced the development of other early musical codes and, later, was absorbed into the object-oriented program *MScore*.

The Digital Alternative Representation of Musical Scores (DARMS) begun being developed in 1963 by Stefan Bauer-Mengelberg under the name "Ford-Columbia Input Language" (see Bauer-Mengelberg 1970) and was developed further by Raymond Erickson and others. DARMS is strongly print-oriented, and it includes all information of traditional music notation written for any number of voices. DARMS "is the earliest encoding language still in use. . . . DARMS offers a paradigm that is rarely present in the other codes discussed here: namely, that all files stored in DARMS code may be converted to an unambiguous 'canonical' version." (Selfridge-Field 1997a, 163.) It is entirely based on relative spatial placement and not on sounding pitches. Today, DARMS exists in several different dialects (see Selfridge-Field 1997a).

In the 1960s, Michael Kassler developed IML (Intermediary Musical Language), together with the programming language MIR (Musical Information Retrieval). IML represented common music notation and accompanying text on punched cards, and it was designed to represent and solve problems of music theory.

MIDI (Musical Instrument Digital Interface) was developed in the mid-1980s as the result of collaborations between several synthesizer companies. MIDI filled the need for a universal digital representation of performed music. It originally was intended to be a real-time protocol enabling communication between different digital hardware devices. Its format is described in detail in Selfridge-Field 1997b. Since MIDI was exclusively designed for the creation of performances of sound, MIDI is limited when used for music theoretical applications. To overcome certain insufficiencies (e.g., MIDI's failure to represent rests), MIDI extensions have been developed which provide both performance information and score information. (See ibid.)

In recent years, many analytical approaches are based on digital audio.

Musical representations were usually developed with regard to specific tasks. Even though musical encoding is one of the bases for computer-assisted music analysis, there are close relationships between the development of digital encoding of music and the development of methods of computer-assisted music analysis (as one of the many computer applications in music).

Literature

Bauer-Mengelberg, Stefan. 1968. "'The Truth, the Whole Truth, and Nothing but the Truth'," *Computer Studies in the Humanities and Verbal Behavior* I/2: 52-54.

_________. 1970. "The Ford-Columbia Input Language," *Musicology and the Computer: Three Symposia*, edited by Barry S. Brook. New York: The City University of New York Press. pp. 48-52.

_________. 1974. "Digital Alternate Representation of Musical Scores (DARMS)," *Computers and the Humanities* VIII/4 (July): 255.

Brook, Barry S., and Murray Gould. 1964. "Notating Music with Ordinary Typewriter Characters," *Fontes Artis Musicae* XI/1 (January-April): 142-159.

Brooks, Frederick P., A. L. Hopkins, P. G. Neumann, and W. V. Wright. 1957. "An Experiment in Musical Composition." *IRE Transactions on Electronic Computers* VI: 175-182. (An errata see in vol. 7 (1958): 60.) Reprinted in *Machine Models of Music*, edited by Stephen M. Schwanauer and David A. Levitt. Cambridge, MA: The MIT Press, 1993. pp. 23-40.

Byrd, Donald Alvin. 1970a. "Music Notation by Computer," *Computers and the Humanities* V/2 (November): 111.

_________. 1970b. "Transcription by Plotter," *Random Bits* V/9 (May): 6-8.

_________. 1971. "Humanities Programming for Creative Work," *Random Bits* VI/5 (January): 1, 8-12.

_________. 1974. "A System for Music Printing by Computer," *Computers and the Humanities* VIII/3 (May): 161-172.

_________. 1975. "Music Programs at Indiana University," *Computational Musicology Newsletter* II/1: 2-4.

_________. 1976. "Music Notation by Computer," *Computers and the Humanities* X/1 (January-February): 51-52.

_________. 1977. "An Integrated Computer Music Software System," *Computer Music Journal* I/2 (April): 55-60.

_________. 1984. Music Notation by Computer. Ph.D. dissertation. Bloomington, IN: Indiana University.

Cantor, Don. 1971. "A Computer Program that Accepts Common Musical Notation," *Computers in the Humanities* VI (November): 103-109.

Erickson, Raymond F. 1969. "A General Purpose System for Computer Aided Musical Studies," *Journal of Music Theory* XIII/2 (Winter): 276-294.

_________. 1970b. "A Syntax-Directed, Changeable System for Processing Data for Music Analysis," *Computers and the Humanities* IV/5 (May): 343.

_________. 1970c. "Music and the Computer in the Sixties," *AFIPS Conference Proceedings* 36: 281-285.

_________. 1971b. "DUPACK (DARMS Utility Package)," *Computers and the Humanities* V/5 (May): 313.

_________. 1971c. The Ford-Columbia Music Representation (DARMS). [New York: IBM Systems Research Institute].

_________. 1972a. "The Computer and Music," *Journal of the American Musicological Society* XXV/1 (Spring): 102-107.

_________. 1972b. Abstract of *Rhythmic Problems and Melodic Structure in Organum Purum: A Computer-Assisted Study* by R. F. Erickson, *Computers and the Humanities* VI/4 (March): 254.

_________. 1972c. "The Uses of Computers in Music: A State of the Art Report," *First USA-Japan Computer Conference Proceedings: October 3-5, 1972, Tokyo, Japan.* Montvale, NJ: American Federation of Information Processing Societies. pp. 124-129.

_________. 1975a. "'The DARMS Project': A Status Report," *Computers and the Humanities* IX/6 (November): 291-298.

_________. 1975b. "'The Darms Project': A Status Report," *Computational Musicology Newsletter* II/1: 7-8.

_________. 1976. DARMS: A Reference Manual. New York: Department of Music, Queens College.

_________. 1977. "MUSICOMP 76 and The State of DARMS," *College Music Symposium* XVII/1 (Spring): 90-101.

Gomberg, David Aaron. 1975. A Computer-Oriented System for Music Printing. D.Sc. dissertation. Saint Louis, MO: Washington University.

Gould, Murray. 1967. "A Keypunchable Notation for the Liber Usualis," *Elektronische Datenverarbeitung in der Musikwissenschaft*, edited by Harald Heckmann. Regensburg: Gustav Bosse. pp. 25-40.

Gould, Murray, and George W. Logemann. 1966. ALMA: An Alphanumeric Language for Music Analysis. New York University: Institute for Computer Research in the Humanities. [Los Angeles: University of California Library / Music Library, calling no. ML 432 G 734a]

Gould, Murray J., and George W. Logemann. 1970. "ALMA: Alphanumeric Language for Music Analysis," *Musicology and the Computer: Three Symposia*, edited by Barry S. Brook. New York: The City University of New York Press. pp. 57-90.

Hanzelin, Fred Lee. 1978. The Software for Computer Assisted Graphical Representation of Single Instrument Melodic Lines and Harmonic Spectra Using DARMS Encoding and Acoustical Data. Ph.D. thesis, University of Illinois at Urbana-Campaign.

Harris, Mitch, Alan Smaill, and Geraint Wiggins. 1991. "Representing Music Symbolically," *IX Colloquium on Musical Informatics*, edited by Antonio Camurri and Corrado Canepa. Genova 1991. pp. 55-69.

Kassler, Michael. 1964. MIR – A Simple Programming Language For Musical Information Retrieval. Technical Report No. 3, Project 295D, March 1964. Princeton, New Jersey: Princeton University, Department of Music. [University of California at Berkeley: Music Library, calling no. ML 74 .4 M4 K 35 1964 MUSI]

_________. 1966. "Toward Musical Information Retrieval," *Perspectives of New Music* IV/2 (Spring-Summer): 59-67.

__________. 1968. A Trinity of Eassays. Ph.D. dissertation. Princeton, NJ: Princeton University.
__________. 1970a. "An Essay Toward Specification of a Music-Reading Machine," *Musicology and the Computer: Three Symposia*, edited by Barry S. Brook. New York: The City University of New York Press. pp. 151-175.
__________. 1970b. "MIR – A Simple Programming Language for Musical Information Retrieval," *The Computer and Music*, edited by Harry B. Lincoln. Ithaca: Cornell University Press. pp. 299-327.
Kostka, Stephan M. 1984. The M-PARC System for Musical Encoding (Mnemonic Pitch and Rhythm Code, Version 3). Unpublished Manuscript. Austin, TX: The University of Texas at Austin, Department of Music.
Mathews, Max. V. 1969. *The Technology of Computer Music*. Cambridge, MA: The M.I.T. Press.
Pape, U. 1969. "Ein Verfahren zur Verschlüsselung und Symbolisierung von Kompositionen in Hinblick auf eine Musikanalyse mit EDV-Anlagen," *Elektronische Datenverarbeitung* XI (July): 342-345.
Schaffer, John Wm. 1994. "Threader: A Computer Interface for the Graphic Entry, Encoding, and Analysis of Musical Material," *Computer Music Journal* XVIII/1 (Spring): 21-29.
Schnell, Christoph. 1985. *Die Eingabe musikalischer Information als Teil eines Arbeitsinstrumentes. Ein Beitrag zur Computeranwendung in der Musikwissenschaft*, Bern, Frankfurt/M., New York: Peter Lang.
__________. 1986a. Die Eingabe musikalischer Information in den Computer," *Output* XV/1: 37-49.
__________. 1986b. Eingabe musikalischer Information in den Computer. Ein Neues Verfahren," *Output* XV/5: 51-60.
__________. 1989. *Ein System zur computergestützten Forschung in den Geisteswissenschaften. Konzeption, Implementierung, Anwendungsbeispiele*. Bern: Peter Lang.
Selfridge-Field, Eleanor. 1993. "Music Analysis by Computer," *Music Processing*, edited by Goffredo Haus. Madison, WI: A-R Editions. pp. 3-24.
__________. 1997a. "DARMS, Its Dialects, and Its Uses," *Beyond MIDI. The Handbook of Musical Codes*, edited by Eleanor Selfridge-Field. Cambridge: The MIT Press. pp. 163-174.
__________. Ed. 1997b. *Beyond MIDI. The Handbook of Musical Codes*. Cambridge: The MIT Press.
Wenker, Jerome R. 1970. "A Computer Oriented Music Notation Including Ethnomusicological Symbols," *Musicology and the Computer: Three Symposia*, edited by Barry S. Brook. New York: The City University of New York Press. pp. 91-129.
__________. 1972a. "A Music Compiler for Musicologists and Ethnomusicologists," *Computers and the Humanities* VII/2 (November): 124.
__________. 1972b. "MUSTRAN II - An Extended *MUS*ic *TRAN*slator," *Computers and the Humanities* VII/2 (November): 125.
__________. 1973. "Music Encoding - Keypunch," *Computational Musicology Newsletter* I/1: 6-7.
__________. 1974. "MUSTRAN II: A Foundation for Computational Musicology," *Computers in the Humanities*, edited by J. L. Mitchell. Edinburgh: Edinburgh University Press. pp. 267-280.
__________. 1978. A Computer-Aided Analysis of Anglo-Canadian Folktunes. Ph.D. dissertation. Bloomington, IN: Indiana University.

Wittlich, Gary, Donald Byrd, and Rosalee Nerheim. 1978. "A System for Interactive Encoding of Music Scores Under Computer Control," *Computers and the Humanities* XII/4: 309-319.

Wolff, Anthony B. 1972. "Development of a DARMS-to-Canonical DARMS Translator," *Computers and the Humanities* VI/5 (May): 316.

__________. 1977. "Problems of Representation in Musical Computing," *Computers and the Humanities* XI/1 (January-February): 3-12.

Overview of Measurements Derived from Statistics and Information Theory

As a basis for the understanding of specific methodological discussions in this book, some measurements derived from statistics and information theory will be briefly explained here. The measurements most frequently mentioned in this text are listed in alphabetical order. For more detailed information or mathematical formulas see such standard works as Glass and Hopkins 1996, Goulden 1952, Shannon and Weaver 1949, or Goldman 1968.

Arithmetic Mean (Average)
The arithmetic mean (sometimes called 'average') is calculated by dividing the sum of all elements (e.g., pitches, coded as a numerical value) by the number of elements.

Auto-Correlation
Auto-correlation gives information about the relation of one characteristic (e.g., pitch) to itself, shifted in time. – See also Correlation.

Chi Square Test for Goodness of Fit
The Chi Square Test for Goodness of Fit can calculate whether two samples (e.g., melodies) are equal or not. Thus, it compares observed and expected frequencies.

Correlation and **Regression**
Correlation gives information on the relationship between two (or more) characteristics, e.g. if two characteristics such as pitch and tone duration are dependent on one another linearly or not. The correlation coefficient is a statistical measure for linear dependence of characteristics.

For example, if the melodic contour of a song tends to move in a certain direction (ascending or descending), then there is a strong linear correlation of pitch and direction. In this case, the correlation coefficient would be either close to the positive maximum, one (ascending), or to the negative maximum, minus one (descending).

If two characteristics are correlated approximately in a linear fashion, it is often useful to estimate the progress of the characteristics through a progression line. The increase of this progression line (regression line) is determined by the regression coefficient.

Discriminant Function
The discriminant function uses multiple measurements to discriminate between two groups (e.g., to disciminate between two groups of folk songs that originate in different areas).

Entropy[1]
Entropy is a form of measurement found in the conceptual methodology of information theory and is not related to semantics but to syntax. It is an index of the degree of 'information' found by analyzing single elements (e.g., pitches or tone durations) or groups of elements taken as a unit. In the latter case, the entropy is of 'higher order'. The entropy is specifically the negative sum of all logarithms of the probability of each event multiplied by the probability of each event. (See Shannon and Weaver 1949, 49 f.) The average entropy of a melody, for instance, is the negative sum of all logarithms of the probability of each note multiplied by the probability of each note. In case of calculating the entropy of the second order, the specific succession of two notes, for example, are seen as *one* element.

Entropy Profile[2]
The entropy profile is a measurement for the degree of average 'information' found by analyzing a class of elements (i.e., all occurrences of the pitch c' taken as a unit). For example, the entropy profile of pitches would determine the average degree of 'information' of all c' in a piece of music.

Factor Analysis
Factor analysis is a mathematical tool, which can be used to examine a wide range of data sets. The goal is to find factors that can be used to characterize a group of objects (e.g., songs), i.e. to find a group of objects with common characteristics.

Frequency
There are two types of frequencies: absolute frequency and relative frequency. Absolute frequency is the exact number of a specific class of elements (e.g., pitch class c), while relative frequency is the absolute frequency of a specific element related to the total number of elements. The relative frequency is always smaller or equal to one, because the denominator is always larger than or equal

1 Entropy, in information theory, was first defined by Claude E. Shannon in 1949. See Shannon and Weaver 1949, 49 f.

2 For the mathematical basis of the entropy profile see Bandt and Pompe 1993. First applications of the entropy profile in music analysis was described in detail by Uhrlandt and Schüler 1992.

to the numerator. The quotation in percent results from the multiplication with the factor 100.

Kurtosis
Kurtosis refers to the flatness or peakedness of a (distribution) curve, relative to the size of the standard deviation.

Markov Chains
A Markov Chain is a model for a sequence of events in which the probability of a given event (or grouping of events, i.e. event of 'higher orders') is dependent only on the preceding event (or event of 'higher orders'). For instance, the probability of a sequence of five pitches, i.e. a group of pitches of order five, would be dependent only on the preceding group of five pitches.

Monte Carlo Method
The Monte Carlo Method is a method of obtaining an approximate solution to a numerical problem by the use of random numbers. In music, this method was first applied to composition by Hiller and Isaacson (1959). Here, random sequences of integers were equated to notes, durations, dynamic values and playing techniques. These random integers were then screened by applying various rules and rejected or accepted, depending on the rules.

Probability
Probability is a measurement for the likelihood of occurrence of a chance event (element).

Redundancy
Redundancy is a measurement, taken from information theory, that gives information about the partial (or complete) repetition of 'message content', i.e. elements. (See also **Entropy**.) For instance, if there is an increasing number of a certain pitch or a certain melodic phrase, the entropy of this pitch or melodic phrase decreases and the redundancy increases.

Regression
See **Correlation**.

Skewness
Skewness refers to a (distribution) curve, which is asymmetrical.

Standard Deviation
The standard deviation is the square root of the **variance** (see also there). It refers to the average distance of elements (e.g., pitches) from their mean value.

Transition Frequency
Transition Frequency is the frequency with which certain elements (e.g., pitches) occur in some places when it is known that certain others occur in previous places.

Transition Probability
Transition probability is the probability of an element (e.g., a note or a group of notes) which follows another specific element (note or group of notes).

Variance and **Standard Deviation**
Variance and standard deviation give information about the distribution of the elements (e.g. pitches, tone durations, or intervals) around the mean, i.e. the average distance of all elements from the mean. The variance is calculated by permanently subtracting the mean from each element, squaring all results, adding them together and dividing them by the total number of all elements minus one. The standard deviation is the square root of the **variance**.

Literature

Bandt, Christoph, and Bernd Pompe. 1993. "The Entropy Profile – A Function Describing Statistical Dependencies," *Journal of Statistical Physics* 70/3-4 (February): 967-983.

Glass, Gene V., and Kenneth D. Hopkins. 1996. *Statistical Methods in Education and Psychology*, 3rd edition. Boston: Allyn and Bacon.

Goulden, Cyril H. 1952. *Methods of Statistical Analysis*, 2nd edition. New York: Wiley.

Goldman, Stanford. 1968. *Information Theory*. New York: Dover.

Hiller, Lejaren A., and Leonard M. Isaacson. 1959. *Experimental Music. Composition with an electronic computer*. New York: McGraw-Hill.

Shannon, Claude E., and W. Weaver. 1949. *The Mathematical Theory of Communication*. Urbana: University of Illinois Press.

Uhrlandt, Dirk, and Nico Schüler. 1992. "Informationsmaße in der computergestützten Musikanalyse." *Kammermusik Heute* 2 (1992): 102-112.

The Development of Computing Technology Through the 1970s and Its Influence on the Development of Music-Analytical Approaches

Introduction

This essay will not outline developments of computer-assisted music analysis, but instead summarize the development of computing technology from the 1940s through the 1970s and draw parallels to its influence on the development of music-analytical methods. The history of computers and computing cannot be seen as merely a history that starts with electronic calculators in the 1940s. The history of calculating machines and the science of computational strategies go back hundreds of years. However, a comprehensive history of computing cannot be provided with this essay. Only a short overview of the developments of electronic computers and computing shall be given here, to help understand the history of computer-assisted music analysis.[1] The emphasis on how the developments of computing and computers influenced the development of computer-assisted music analysis is related to the fact that this knowledge is often absent in contemporary discussions of computer applications in music analysis.

1. Developments of Computing and Computing-Supported Music Analysis in the 1940s

During the 1940s, several electro-mechanical and the first electronic computers were developed, starting with the "Z3" in 1941 by the German Konrad Zuse and the IBM Automatic Sequence Controlled Calculator, usually known as "Harvard Mark I", during the early 1940s. The Harvard Mark I was constructed for Harvard University between 1937 and 1944, and its main designer was the Harvard researcher Howard H. Aiken. Other computers of the 1940s were the "ENIAC" (Electronic Numerical Integrator and Calculator; 1946), the "EDVAC" (Electronic Discrete Variable Automatic Computer; 1949), and the "EDSAC" (Electronic Delay Storage Automatic Calculator; 1949), the latter of which became the first full-scale universal digital computer with saved programs based on John von Neumann's computer architecture.[2]

Although these early developments were very exciting at the time, those early computers were not easily accessible and not used for any music projects.

1 The overview of developments of computers and computing is based on Campbell-Kelly & Asprey 1997, Rechenberg 2000, Nash 1990, Ceruzzi 2003, and O'Regan 2008.

2 John von Neumann (1903-1957) was a Hungarian-American mathematician and polymath. His saved-program architecture includes a processing unit, a control unit, a memory to store data and instructions, external mass storage, as well as input and output mechanisms.

Some scholars did use, however, electro-mechanical calculating machines. For example, in 1949, Bertrand Bronson described a procedure for using an electro-mechanical calculator to carry out a comparative study of British-American folk-tunes. He used punched cards for encoding general information (publication, collector, singer, etc.), regional information, and musical characteristics, such as range, mode, time signature, number of phrases, phrasal scheme, final tone, initial interval between the upbeat and the first strong accent, etc. Then, the sorting machine was able to automatically pick out cards with desired characteristics. Thereby, certain musical characteristics could be matched with certain geographical origins, etc. Results of this theoretical procedure were published ten years later (Bronson 1959).

2. Developments of Computing Technology and the First Use of Computers for Music Analysis in the 1950s

In the second half of the 1940s, IBM became the leading company in the computer industry. The "Card Programmed Calculator" became – in the late 1940s and early 1950s – the most often sold calculating tool. However, by the end of the 1940s, IBM had also developed several full-scale computers. In addition, IBM developed the magnetic drum for the main memory (instead of mercury delay lines or electrostatic storage tubes). Another private company developed the UNIVAC (UNIVersal Automatic Computer) by 1951. It was the world's first commercially available, fully electronic computer, and it became a market leader for its type. The UNIVAC was eventually the first computer the broader public had been introduced to during election night in the USA in 1952, when it accurately predicted Eisenhower's win over Stevenson. After that, 'UNIVAC' became a generic name for computers.

The prediction of the election outcome also showed the great potential for computers in data processing for many business areas. Thus, in the early 1950s, there was a change of the main use of computers: a change from mathematical calculations to data processing. Thus, the first music applications date from the mid-1950s. Dozens of computer businesses – mainly in the United States – emerged. Most of them were eventually acquired by bigger office-machine firms. But IBM re-entered the market with its IBM model 701 in 1952. The first real data processing computer was announced one year later: the IBM 702. This computer used a more reliable and faster tube technology (memory) and a modular construction; but most importantly, its magnetic tape systems made the UNIVACs obsolete. IBM's superior marketing and its customer service helped gain the leadership in this area. The low-cost Magnetic Drum Computer (IBM 650; 1953) was acquired by many institutions of higher education. It reflected IBM's total-system view, i.e. the combination of computer development, programming, field service, customer transition, and training, which led to the eventual replacement of the electro-mechanic punched-card accounting machine in the early 1960s. IBM developed the 1401 model with transistors (instead of tubes) and core memory (instead of the magnetic drum); peripherals were new card readers, punchers, high-speed printers, and magnetic tape units. To avoid the high cost of machine replacements, IBM developed the programming system RPG (Report Program Generator) – a business data processing language designed for analysts familiar with punched-card machines. This programming language is still in use today. Also, IBM itself developed software solutions.

The first extensive, systematic use of an electronic computer for music-analytical purposes was described by the mathematician Frederick P. Brooks (et al.) in 1957. Brooks conducted an analysis-synthesis-project at the Computation Laboratory at Harvard University[3], using a Harvard MARK IV computer – a computer built in 1952 by Harvard University for the United States Air Force. For this project, high-order probabilities of 37 hymn tunes were calculated. Those probabilities were then used for the synthesis of new melodies, using Markov chains of orders one through eight. Even though this experiment was limited to (melodic) samples that were not structurally complex, this procedure "permitted the production of a significant number of acceptable tunes within a reasonable time" (ibid., 180).[4]

While Brooks' experiment is rarely mentioned in the literature, the work of Lejaren A. Hiller and Leonard Isaacson has been extensively noted, specifically their work on the *Illiac Suite* (String Quartet No. 4) is mentioned in almost every textbook on electronic music.[5] The *Illiac Suite* was composed with the ILLIAC I computer in 1956 at the University of Illinois. ILLIAC stands for "ILLInois Automatic Computer", and the ILLIAC I was developed and built at the University of Illinois in 1952. The computer had 2,800 vacuum tubes, measured 3m by 0.6m by 2.6m, and weighed 4.5 tons.[6] ILLIAC I was very powerful for its time; in 1956, it had more computing power than all of the Bell Telephone Laboratories. Even though the computer was, in this composition project, not used for analysis but for the generation and selection of random values in a type of stochastic modeling (known as the "Monte Carlo Method")[7], Hiller's and

3 Youngblood 1960 also mentioned an unpublished term paper from 1955 by F. P. Brooks, which lets assume that Brook's project was already realized in 1955. See Youngblood 1960, 23, footnote 42. In addition, see Neumann and Schappert 1959.

4 For sample melodies see ibid. Neumann and Schappert 1959, which contains the description of the project in German, also reprinted some of the melodies.

5 Brooks' paper was not widely available, whereas Hiller's and Isaacson's book (1959) became available in almost every library.

6 See http://www.economicexpert.com/a/ILLIAC:I.htm (last accessed on December 12, 2013).

7 The Monte Carlo Method is a method of obtaining an approximate solution to a numerical problem by the use of random numbers. In music, this method was first applied to composition by Hiller and Isaacson (1959). Here, random sequences of integers were equated to

Isaacson's importance for computer applications in music goes beyond composition. In their book (Hiller and Isaacson 1959), they suggest several computer applications to music analysis:

- statistical and information theoretical applications,
- analysis of musical similarity,
- pattern search,
- analysis of sounds and their physical constitution,
- optical music recognition,

and based on analytical results:

- realization of *continuo* and figured bass and to complete part writing,
- missing parts could be reproduced based on statistical style analysis,
- systematic generation of musical materials for teaching purposes.

(See ibid., 165-170.) Most or all of these suggestions were launched during the late 1950s and early 1960.

Already by 1953, programming had become a serious research project at IBM. There, John Backus proposed a higher-level programming code, called Formula Translator (FORTRAN). His goal was to develop an automatic programming system which could produce machine code as good as that written by an experienced programmer with only short and logical commands. Finalized in 1957, FORTRAN became the first successful scientific programming language and is still in use today in certain dialects. An improved version, FORTAN II, followed in 1959. By the end of the 1950s, several other languages had been developed by other computer manufacturers or research groups: MAD, IT, ALGOL, etc. However, FORTRAN continued to dominate scientific applications. Last but not least, 'standardizing' FORTRAN made it possible to exchange programs, even if different makes of computers were used. ALGOL was, for several years, more common in Europe; eventually, even there FORTRAN took over a dominating position. In music analysis, especially FORTRAN was used from the 1960s on, and such an example will be summarized further below.

3. Developments of Computing Technology and Computer-Assisted Music Analysis in the 1960s

In the early 1960s, IBM continued with a standardization process to achieve compatibility among all their computer components as well as their software components. The result was their System/360 in 1964. However, programming turned out to be more costly than the hardware itself. Further developments were fully integrated circuits, giant number-crunching computers, and time-sharing computer systems (which allowed more than one user to execute programs concurrently).

---

notes, durations, dynamic values, and playing techniques. These random integers were then screened (by applying various rules) and rejected or accepted, depending on the rules.

The military had also played an important role in the emerging computer industry since World-War II. For their needs, the idea of real-time computing for a flight simulator at MIT was most important. For the purpose of real-time computing, computers with a much higher speed and a much higher reliability were needed than existing technology had to offer. Important developments were the core-memory, printed circuits, mass-storage devices, and CRT-graphical displays. Military projects also provided a 'platform' for further developments in software engineering.

The first large civilian *real-time* project was the airline reservation system SABRE (Semi-Automatic Business Research Environment) in the 1950s and early 1960s, and the Universal Product Code (UPC) in the early 1970s. First scanners were manufactured by IBM and NCR. These developments were of great economic importance: the entire manufacturing-distribution-network became involved in electronic data tracking and automatic ordering, etc.

While in the early 1950s software was still supplied at no additional cost by the computer manufacturer, 'software contracting' soon developed. In the early 1960s, the software industry was booming. However, in the late 1960s, a software crisis emerged because of the much faster growing hardware industry and the incapability of exploiting the new hardware effectively (since large programs were needed). It took many years before programming became a real engineering discipline with its 'structured design methodology' and its development model as an organic process that would never really be 'finished'. The concept of 'software packages' emerged in the late 1960s; these packages were much more cost-effective than custom software. At the same time, large computer manufacturers decided to price their software and hardware separately.

The possibility of quickly processing a large amount of data with new computer techniques was recognized in the 1960s, especially by US-scholars in musicology and music theory. In 1966, Gerald Lefkoff (1967b) and Allen Forte (1967) addressed this topic at the "West Virginia University Conference on Computer Applications in Music". Forte gave 'good' reasons for applying the computer to music analysis: "The computer can be programmed to deal with complex structures – such as musical composition – very rapidly. . . . A second reason for using the computer derives from the requirements of completeness and precision that form the basis of every computer program. . . . The design of an algorithm, the formulation of a decision-structure to solve a problem, the careful checking out of a malfunctioning program – all these activities provide clarifications and insights which would be difficult, perhaps impossible, to obtain otherwise." (Ibid., 33-34.) Without going into details, Forte also described a computer project[8] for the determination of similarities and differences of sets, for the interpretation of those with respect to characteristics of the environments

8 His set of computer programs was written in MAD.

in which they occur, and for the design of a structural model in terms of set-complex theory (ibid., 39).[9] Gerald Lefkoff (1967b), on the other hand, described a system "for the study of computer-residing, score-derived musical models" (ibid., 45). Written in FORTRAN, Lefkoff's 'model' saved musical information in time-indexed arrays: pitch, rhythmic values, vocal text, figured bass symbols, dynamics, articulations, and editorial comments. Lefkoff then extracted, along with data relating to other relationships, "a complete list of melodic fragments from a group of compositions, with frequency distribution data for the fragments within each composition and . . . [then] compare[d] the relative frequency of occurrence of each fragment in selected groups of compositions." (Ibid., 55.) The value of Lefkoff's model can be seen in its ability to generalize such analytical procedures and thereby discover stylistic trends.

Other analytical methods during the 1960s involved the application of statistical and information-theoretical measurements. For example, the East-German Reiner Kluge (1974a)[10] analyzed similarities among Altmark[11] folk songs. More than 130 syntactic characteristics were discovered and then used to determine similarities of pairs of melodies (out of random samples with each about 40 melodies[12]). Kluge's research was outstanding, because he developed a similarity measurement. Using factor analysis, Kluge identified pseudo-individuals, out of which 12 different types and mixed types were derived. Kluge's study showed that a successful comparative analysis is only possible if many musical characteristics are analyzed in relation to each other.

4. Developments of Computing Technology and Computer-Assisted Music Analysis in the 1970s

The 1970s brought faster, and more reliable, integrated circuits, random-access disk storage units, semiconductor memory, more effective time-sharing, communication-based on-line computing, and virtual memory. In 1971, the 4004 microprocessor was announced by INTEL; it was the first "computer on a chip". The microprocessor was initially used for simple control applications and for (emerging) minicomputers, but soon it was used for full-scale computers. The first personal computer came on the market in 1977: the Apple II. The personal computer included a central processing unit, a screen, a keyboard, floppy disk drives, and a printer.

---

9 A similar program, written in the computer language SNOBOL 3, was described in Forte 1966.

10 Even though his dissertation was published in 1974, the (dissertation) research was conducted between 1965 and 1968, and defended in 1968.

11 Altmark is an area in Southeastern Germany.

12 The restrictions to limited samples were necessary because of on the low efficiency of the computer used (ZRA1).

With the personal computer, new programming languages became important. BASIC (Beginners All-purpose Symbolic Instruction Code) was developed in 1964. It superseded FORTRAN not only in its simplicity, but also in its speed (of translation). It became the introductory language for many students, and in the mid-1970s, it became the first widely available programming language for new personal computers. PASCAL (1971) as well as the systems programming language C (1970; originally developed for the implementation of Unix) became more sophisticated and are still two of the most commonly used higher-level programming languages. The Unix operating system, developed between 1969 and 1974 by Bell Laboratories, became the – for several decades – most widely used operating system for multi-user environments. And while LISP (LISt Processing) was developed already in 1961, it became important decades later, especially in artificial intelligence research.

However, as early as the 1960s, the research of MIT psychologist and computer scientist J. C. R. Licklider suggested that computers could be used to augment the human intellect, but not to supersede it, as AI researchers at the time hoped. Licklider argued that computers should enhance the every-day-work of researchers, since computers spent most of the time not 'thinking', but calculating and referencing. Licklider's theories promoted the development of interactive computing with graphical user interfaces, software engineering, and – years later – text processing (1980) and refined calculating software, etc.

From its beginning, computer-assisted music analysis was frequently used in folk song research. The statistical methods used to analyze art music did not differ from those that were most commonly applied to the analysis of folk songs. However, folk music is smaller in scope and less complex, often involving only a single voice. These are the main reasons computer-assisted analysis continued to be centered on folk songs up to the end of the 1970s, even though computers became more and more powerful, easily capable of handling the greater complexity of multi-part art music.

But there were indeed projects of computer-assisted analysis of *art music* during the 1970s, one important project of which was Dorothy Susan Gross' dissertation research and her subsequent investigations. Her "set of computer programs to aid in music analysis" had the goal "to duplicate the more routine aspects of analysis" (Gross 1975a, 165). The CAL SNOBOL programs were written for a CDC 6600 computer. The CDC 6600 was the first successful supercomputer, which was the world's fastest computer between 1964 and 1969. The music for this project was encoded with MUSTRAN; besides tone duration and pitch, this alphanumerical code also included all the dynamic and articulation markings as well as descriptive words. The 'dialog' between user and computer was realized mostly via punched cards. A later version was developed in SPITBOL for an IBM 370 computer.

Since Gross' research was not primarily directed at analyzing a great number of compositions, the value of her research should be seen in her methodological ideas and in the potentials as well as the structure of the programs. The following lists of procedures and "switches"[13] also show the great variety of characteristics analyzed. The software included the following programs:

- a Linear Grouping Program – looking for linear patterns formed by up to 12 consecutive events in the same voice,
- a Vertical Grouping Program – listing and counting the vertical structures in a piece of music without identifying them,
- a Program for Thematic Analysis – searching for themes submitted by the user,
- a Program for Harmonic and Set Analysis – labeling the chords (roots and quality)[14] and / or sets in a piece, using the list of groups from the Vertical Grouping Program as reference, and
- Program for cumulative counting – accumulating data from two or more pieces.

Each program used switches for specifying and 'individualizing' the analytical process. These user-controlled switches represent a feature, developed mainly in the 1970s for a rather controlled dialog between analyst and computer program.

In 1974, Bo Alphonce presented a computer-assisted foundation of set theoretical analyses and provided, with it, a basis for later approaches in this field. And Norbert Böker-Heil (1974a, 1974b) developed forms of graphical representation for interpretative analysis, building upon new developments in screen and printing technology.

In the 1970s, the search for a musical grammar was probably the most important development in computer-assisted music analysis. The basis for this search was provided by the insight that specific compositions could be represented in terms of a list of grammatical production rules. One of these forms of representation is the parse tree, which graphically represents the syntactic structure of a composition. One of the first attempts of applying Schenker's theory of tonality to computer-assisted analysis of music was made by Michael Kassler (1975a, 1975b, 1975c, 1977; see also Kassler 1964). He explicated the middleground of Schenker's theory and programmed[15] the decisions procedures for formalized languages that constitute this explication (see Kassler 1975b, 7). A LISP-based system for the study of Schenkerian analysis was developed by Robert E. Frankel, Stanley J. Rosenschein, and Stephen W. Smoliar (1974, 1976a. 1976b, 1978).

---

13 Those "switches" would select one of two sets of instructions.

14 Incomplete chords, which could not be identified, were labeled "ambiguous". (Gross 1975, 109.)

15 Kassler wrote his programs in the APL programming language and used IBM 360/50 and CDC Cyber 72 computers.

Already in the early 1970s, Otto Laske's search for a grammar of music was an exploration of a "generative theory of music" (Laske 1972, 1973, 1974a, 1975a, 2004). But Laske's grammar concept was based not on notated music, but on a formal model of empirically acquired musical *activity*. Thus, Laske's studies were early studies in musical cognition. He was interested in formal properties of cognitive tasks that process musical input. "Instead of producing a taxonomic analysis of musical structures, Laske has turned to what is essentially a project in cognitive psychology." (Roads 1979, 52) Laske's understanding of 'sonology' expressed "the relationship between the syntactic structure of a music and its physical representation in so far as this relationship is determined by grammatical rules" (Laske 1975a, 31). Laske tried to explicate musical grammars as computer programs in so far as they, more or less, relate to musical activity, such as composing or listening.

Reflecting the development of powerful computing technology, the 1970s were a rich decade for computer-assisted music analysis. Existing (statistical and information-theoretical) methods were refined, separate measurements were converted into complex, multi-factor analyses, and, most importantly, the core of computer-assisted, analytical methods was extended by psychological and set theoretical approaches as well as approaches drawing on Schenkerian analysis and generative grammars.

Considering the developments of computing technology, it is interesting to note that the 1970s also saw the development of mass-market home computers. However, these computers had such a low capacity that no noteworthy music-analytical project was using such computers.

Final Remarks

The first fully electronic computer was developed by 1946, and music scholars soon began adopting ideas from computing to music analysis. Subsequent developments of computing technology as well as of higher-level programming languages spurred almost countless music-analytical (albeit not always useful or successful) experiments by either music scholars or computer scientists. On average, computer-applications in music analysis seem to lag about 5 to 10 years behind the developments in computer hardware and the developments in software engineering.

Literature:

Alphonce, Bo H. 1974a. The Invariance Matrix. Ph.D. dissertation. New Haven, CT: Yale University.

__________. 1974b. "The Invariance Matrix as an Analytical Tool," *International Musicological Society: Report of the Eleventh Congress, Copenhagen 1972*, edited by Henrik Glahn, Søren Sørensen, and Peter Ryom. Copenhagen: Edition W. Hansen. pp. 228-235.

Böker-Heil, Norbert. 1974a. "Der Zustand polyphoner Strukturen: Ein Beispiel Automatischer Stilbeschreibung," *International Musicological Society: Report of the Eleventh Congress, Copenhagen 1972*, edited by Henrik Glahn, Søren Sørensen, and Peter Ryom. Copenhagen: Edition W. Hansen. pp. 108-120.

_________. 1974b. "Musikalische Stilanalyse und Computer. Einige grundsätzliche Erwägungen," *International Musicological Society: Report of the Eleventh Congress, Copenhagen 1972*, edited by Henrik Glahn, Søren Sørensen, and Peter Ryom. Copenhagen: Edition W. Hansen. pp. 45-50.

Bronson, Bertrand H. 1959. "Toward the Comparative Analysis of British-American Folk Tunes." *Journal of American Folklore* LXXII: 165-191.

Brooks, Frederick P., A. L. Hopkins, P. G. Neumann, and W. V. Wright. 1957. "An Experiment in Musical Composition." *IRE Transactions on Electronic Computers* VI: 175-182. (An errata see in vol. 7 (1958): 60.) Reprinted in *Machine Models of Music*, edited by Stephen M. Schwanauer and David A. Levitt. Cambridge, MA: The MIT Press, 1993. pp. 23-40.

Campbell-Kelly, Martin, and William Aspray. 1997. *Computer. A History of the Information Machine*. New York: BasicBooks.

Ceruzzi, Paul E. 2003. *A History of Modern Computing*, 2nd edition. London (England) and Cambridge, MA: MIT Press.

Cope, David. 1991. *Computers and Musical Style*. Madison, Wisconsin: A-R Editions.

_________. 1996. *Experiments in Musical Intelligence*. Wisconsin: A-R Editions.

_________. 2000. *The Algorithmic Composer*. Wisconsin: A-R Editions.

_________. 2001. *Virtual Music: Computer Synthesis of Musical Style*. Cambridge, MA: MIT Press.

_________. 2005. *Computer Models of Musical Creativity*. Cambridge, MA: MIT Press.

_________. 2008. *Hidden Structure: Music Analysis Using Computers*. Wisconsin: A-R Editions.

Forte, Allen. 1966. "A Program for the Analytic Reading of Scores," *Journal of Music Theory* X/2 (Winter): 330-364. Reprinted in *Machine Models of Music*, edited by Stephen M. Schwanauer and David A. Levitt. Cambridge, MA: The MIT Press, 1993. pp. 55-81.

_________. 1967. "Computer-implemented Analysis of Musical Structure," *Papers from the West Virginia University Conference on Computer Applications in Music*, edited by Gerald Lefkoff. Morgantown: West Virginia University Library. pp. 29-42.

Frankel, Robert E., Stanley J. Rosenschein, and Stephen W. Smoliar. 1974. The Modeling of Musical Perception on a Digital Computer Via Schenkerian Theory. Music Report No. 4, April 1975. Philadelphia: Moore School of Electrical Engineering, University of Pennsylvania.

Frankel, Robert E., Stanley J. Rosenschein, and Stephen W. Smoliar. 1976a. Schenker's Theory of Tonal Music: Its Explication Through Computational Processes. Music Project Report No. 7. Philadelphia: University of Pennsylvania, Department of Computer and Information Science.

Frankel, Robert E., Stanley J. Rosenschein, and Stephen W. Smoliar. 1976b. "A LISP-Based System for the Study of Schenkerian Analysis," *Computers and the Humanities* X/1 (January-February): 21-32.

Frankel, Robert E., Stanley J. Rosenschein, and Stephen W. Smoliar. 1978. "Schenker's Theory of Tonal Music - its Explication through Computational Processes," *International Journal of Man-Machine Studies* X: 121-138.

Gross, Dorothy Susan. 1975a. A Set of Computer Programs to Aid in Music Analysis, Ph.D. dissertation. Bloomington, IN: Indiana University.

Hashagen, Ulf, Reinhard Keil-Slawik, and Arthur L. Norberg. Eds. 2002. *History of Computing: Software Issues: International Conference on the History of Computing, ICHC 2000, April 5-7, 2000, Heinz Nixdorf Museums-Forum, Paderborn, Germany*. Berlin and New York: Springer.

Hiller, Lejaren A., and Leonard M. Isaacson. 1959. *Experimental Music. Composition with an Electronic Computer*. New York: McGraw-Hill.

Huron, David. 1993. *The Humdrum Toolkit: Software for Music Researchers*. [computer disks and installation guide.] Stanford, CA: Center for Computer Assisted Research in the Humanities.

_________. 1995. *The Humdrum Toolkit: Reference Manual*. Menlo Park, CA: Center for Computer Assisted Research in the Humanities.

_________. 1999. *Music Research Using Humdrum: A User's Guide*. Stanford, CA: Center for Computer Assisted Research in the Humanities.

Honing, Henkjan. 1990. "POCO: An Environment for Analysing, Modifying, and Generating Expression in Music," *Proceedings of the 1990 International Computer Music Conference*. San Francisco: Computer Music Association. pp. 364-368.

Kassler, Michael. 1964. A Report of Work, Directed Toward Explication of Schenker's Theory of Tonality, Done in Summer 1962 as the First Phase of a Project Concerned with the Applications of High-Speed Automatic Digital Computers to Music and to Musicology. Princeton, NJ: Princeton University Music Department. (Mimeographed.)

_________. 1975a. "Explication of Theories of Tonality," *Computational Musicology Newsletter* II/1: 17.

_________. 1975b. *Proving Musical Theorems I: The Middleground of Heinrich Schenker's Theory of Tonality*. Technical Report No. 103. Sydney: The University of Sydney, Basser department of Computer Science.

_________. 1975c. "Explication of Theories of Tonalities," *Computers and the Humanities* IX/4 (July): 192-193.

_________. 1977. "Explication of the Middleground of Schenker's Theory of Tonality," *Miscellanea Musicologica* 9: 72-81.

Kluge, Reiner. 1974a. *Faktorenanalytische Typenbestimmung an Volksliedmelodien*. Beiträge zur musikwissenschaftlichen Forschung in der DDR 6. Leipzig: Deutscher Verlag für Musik.

Laske, Otto. 1972. "On Musical Strategies With a View to a Generative Grammar for Music," *Interface* I/2: 111-125.

_________. 1973. "On the Methodology and Implementation of a Procedural Theory of Music," *Computational Musicology Newsletter* I/1: 15-16.

_________. 1974a. "In Search of a Generative Grammar for Music," *Perspectives of New Music* XII/1-2 (Autumn-Summer): 351-378. Reprinted in *Machine Models of Music*, edited by Stephen M. Schwanauer and David A. Levitt. Cambridge, MA: The MIT Press, 1993. pp. 214-240.

_________. 1975a. *Introduction to a Generative Theory of Music*. Sonological Reports. Utrecht: Institute for Sonology.

_________. 1984. "KEITH: A Rule-System for Making Music-Analytical Discoveries," *Musical Grammars and Computer Analysis*, edited by Mario Baroni and Laura Callegari. Florence: Leo S. Olschki. pp. 165-199.

_________. 2004. *Musikalische Grammatik - Musikalisches Problemlösen: Schriften 1970-1974*, editied by Nico Schüler. Frankfurt / New York: Peter Lang.

Lefkoff, Gerald. Ed. 1967a. *Papers from the West Virginia University Conference on Computer Applications in Music*. Morgantown: West Virginia University Library.

_________. 1967b. "Computers and the Study of Musical Style," *Papers from the West Virginia University Conference on Computer Applications in Music*, edited by Gerald Lefkoff. Morgantown: West Virginia University Library. pp. 43-61.

Leman, Marc. 1992. "Artificial Neural Networks in Music Research," *Computer Representations and Models in Music*, edited by Alan Marsden & Anthony Pople. London: Academic Press. pp. 165-301.

_________. 1995a. *Music and Schema Theory. Cognitive Foundations of Systematic Musicology*. Berlin: Springer.

Mazzola, Guerino. 1985. *Gruppen und Kategorien in der Musik*. Berlin: Heldermann.

_________. 1990. *Geometrie der Töne - Elemente der Mathematischen Musiktheorie*. Basel: Birkhäuser.

Mazzola, Guerino, Thomas Noll, and Emilio Lluis-Puebla. 2004. *Perspectives in Mathematical and Computational Music Theory*. [Osnabrück, Germany]: Electronic Publishing Osnabrück.

Nash, Stephen G. Ed. 1990. *A History of Scientific Computing*. New York: ACM Press.

Neumann, P. G., and H. Schappert. 1959. "Komponieren mit elektronischen Rechenautomaten," *Nachrichtentechnische Zeitschrift* VIII: 403-407.

O'Regan, Gerard. 2008. *A Brief History of Computing*. London: Springer.

Rechenberg, Peter. 2000. *Was ist Informatik? eine allgemeinverständliche Einführung*, 3rd edition. München, Germany: Hanser.

Roads, Curtis. 1979. "Grammars as Representations for Music," *Computer Music Journal* III/1 (March): 48-55.

Schaffer, John Wm. 1992. "A Prolog-Based Program for the Interactive Analysis of Atonal Scores," *Musikometrica 4*, edited by Moisej G. Boroda. Bochum: Brockmeyer. pp. 145-180.

_________. 1994. "Threader: A Computer Interface for the Graphic Entry, Encoding, and Analysis of Musical Material," *Computer Music Journal* XVIII/1 (Spring): 21-29.

Schüler, Nico. 1999. "A Composer's Cognitive Musicology," *Otto Laske: Navigating New Musical Horizons*, edited by Jerry Tabor. Westport, Connecticut: Greenwood. pp. 135-150.

_________. 2000c. Methods of Computer-Assisted Music Analysis: History, Classification, and Evaluation. Ph.D. dissertation. East Lansing, MI: Michigan State University.

_________. Ed. 2002a. *Computer-Applications in Music Research: Concepts, Methods, Results*. New York: Peter Lang.

_________. 2003. "Towards a History of Computer-Assisted Music Analysis: Developments since 1989," *Journal of the Institute for Music Research at Kyunghee University* [South Korea] I (October): 325-342.

_________. 2005. "Reflections on the History of Computer-Assisted Music Analysis I: Predecessors and the Beginnings," *Musicological Annual* [Ljubljana, Slovenia] XXXXI/1: 31-43.

_________. 2006. "Reflections on the History of Computer-Assisted Music Analysis II: The 1960s," *Musicological Annual* [Ljubljana, Slovenia] XLII/1: 5-24.

_________. 2007. "From Musical Grammars to Music Cognition in the 1980s and 1990s: Highlights of the History of Computer-Assisted Music Analysis," *Rationalism of a Magic Tinge: Music as a Form of Abstract Perception* [Bergamo Festschrift], edited by Leon Stefanija and Katarina Bogunovic Hocevar. [*Musicological Annual* XLIII/2] Ljubljana, Slovenia. pp. 371-396.

Tatnall, Arthur. Ed. 2010. *History of Computing: Learning from the Past: IFIP WG 9.7 International Conference, HC 2010, held as part of WCC 2010, Brisbane, Australia, September 20-23, 2010: Proceedings*. New York, NY: Springer.
Youngblood, Joseph E. 1958. "Style as Information." *Journal of Music Theory* II/1 (April): 24-35.
__________. 1960. Music and Language: Some Related Analytical Techniques. Ph.D. disseration. Bloomington, IN: Indiana University.

Predecessors and the Beginnings of Computer-Assisted Music Analysis (Through the 1950s)

Introduction

The first part of this essay focuses on the philosophical basis of computer-assisted music analysis, i.e. the application of information theory to aesthetics. The second part describes representative applications of statistical and information-theoretical measurements to music analysis and other computational approaches to music analysis which did not include the use of electronic computers[1]. In most cases, those approaches were direct models for computer-assisted applications, and an understanding of the development of computer-assisted analysis is not possible without the knowledge of these early approaches that used no computer. The third part of this essay provides a short historical account of the development of early computers and summarizes the earliest computer-applications to music analysis, carried out during the 1950s.

1. The Philosophical Foundation: Information Theory and Aesthetics

Richard Pinkerton wrote already in 1956: "Information Theory may well prove generally useful for studying the creative process of the human mind. I don't think we have to worry that such analysis will make our art more stilted and mechanical. Rather, as we begin to understand more about the property of creativeness, our enjoyment of the arts should increase a thousandfold." (Richard C. Pinkerton 1956, 86) The results predicted by Richard C. Pinkerton have hardly been realized. But especially with regard to certain developments in the area of Artificial Intelligence during the 1990s, research has produced results that came much closer to Pinkerton's vision of the usefulness of information theory for studying creative processes.

Pinkerton was one of the first to explore the application of information theory to music, specifically to music analysis. The philosophical rationale, however, was ultimately provided by several people: George D. Birkhoff (1931, 1950), Abraham Moles (1956a, 1956b, 1958, 1962, 1966), and by Max Bense (1954, 1966a, 1966b, 1969) and his disciples Helmar Frank (1964, 1968), Rul Guntzenhäuser (1962), Siegfried Maser (1971), and Frieder Nake (1974). Using information theory, all of those scholars sought either to explain some aspects of

1 Joseph Schillinger (1948) provided detailed descriptions of mathematical relationships in music, but he was not primarily trying to provide a methodology for music analysis or for composition. For that reason, Schillinger's work will not be discussed here.

aesthetic reflection and artistic cognition, or both, or to analyze or synthesize 'artistic artifacts'.

Information theory itself was based on a model, partly mathematical and partly physical, relating to the transmission and reception of messages ('information'). In this context, information was related to the potential variety of messages in contexts and the probabilities of messages. For instance, if a melodic phrase in a piece of music occurs for the first time, it is an unexpected event, i.e. it has a probability of zero; hence, it has a high degree of originality and it "modifies the behavior of the receptor" (Moles 1966, 22). If a melodic phrase occurs many times, its probability increases and the originality, the degree of 'information,' decreases. In 1949, Claude E. Shannon defined a measure of information, called 'entropy,' as a logarithmic function of the statistical probabilities of different messages. (See Shannon and Weaver 1949, 49 ff.) Thus, information was considered measurable to the extent that it could determine how predictability and unpredictability relate to the variety of a system.

Taking a different tact, Bense's aesthetics had its origin in the theory of signs. His attempts to create a mathematical notion of aesthetics, a quantitative, descriptive notion he called 'information aesthetics' ['Informationsästhetik'], came out of his interest in cybernetics, and was based on the analytical procedures described by the US-mathematician and physicist George David Birkhoff. In the 1920s, Birkhoff had tried to develop a formula for dealing with aesthetics, defining *aesthetic measure* (M) as a quotient of the *order* (O) of an 'aesthetic object' and its *complexity* (C): M=O/C. (See Birkhoff 1950, 288-306, and 320-333.)

Moles, on the other hand, in his 'aesthetic perception theory', based his theory on the evaluation of experimental data and statements, an evaluation in which the relation of innovation and redundancy was very important. (See Moles 1958.) Moles distinguished between semantic information and aesthetic information, a distinction based on the insight that Shannon's information theory was hardly applicable to the analysis of art works in terms of their artistic value ('aesthetic information'), but instead was related to what he called the 'inner structure' of these art works ('semantic information').[2]

Responding to the aesthetic theories of Bense and Moles, Helmar Frank proposed an 'exact information theory' (Frank 1964, 1968). He combined automata theory, system theory, and sign theory, with information theory and theories drawn from experimental psychology. To define his 'subject model' mathematically, using theories of automata (i.e., the subject is viewed as the addressee of the message, which is the work of art), he needed such categories as 'surprise value' ['Überraschungswert'] and 'conspicuousness value' ['Auffäl-

2 An overview of "Aesthetics of Music and Information-Theory," mainly based on Moles' theory, was also given by Jan L. Broeckx (1979, 105-125).

ligkeitswert']. Frank's integration of empirical research and experimental psychology in his theory is even more important than his theory per se. In this sense, his theory can be seen as an early case of cognitive research like that done in the 1980s and 1990s.

A follower of Bense, Siegfried Maser (1971), proposed the creation of a 'numerical aesthetics' ['Numerische Ästhetik'], derived from Baumgarten's definition of aesthetics as the science of the critical assessment of beauty. Maser interpreted Baumgarten's model of aesthetics as an objective, scientific aesthetics, based on three sciences: the 'science of the real' ['Realwissenschaft'], the 'science of the formal' ['Formalwissenschaft'], and the 'science of the intellect' ['Geisteswissenschaft']. He proposed distinctions between 'macro aesthetics'[3] ['Makroästhetik'] and 'micro aesthetics'[4] ['Mikroästhetik'] in the process of formulating a 'complete aesthetic analysis'[5] ['vollständige ästhetische Analyse'] (Maser 1971, 91). Maser's method of an 'aesthetics by measurement' ['Maßästhetik'] is based on the precise quantitative description of objects, which he sees as the 'rational basis' for an 'aesthetics of value' ['Wertästhetik']. He thinks that the more rigorously the rational basis for the formulation of values is defined, the more convincing will be the speculations and conceptions derived from this basis.[6]

All of the attempts mentioned above, which tried to describe aesthetic artifacts with mathematical methods, specifically with methods derived from information theory, were relatively unsuccessful in formulating meaningful philosophical generalizations about works of art. The failure to distinguish different levels of aesthetic information contained in art works was one of the main reasons for the lack of success (see, for instance, Kasem-Bek 1978). Although the mathematical description of complex aesthetic processes and attempts to calculate aesthetic values produced few significant results, the application of information theory to the analysis of structural norms of art works, specifically of motives and phrases, did produce some significant results.[7] Since repetition of musical structures is responsible for creating musical form, the analysis of musi-

---

3 The formula for calculating the 'Macro Aesthetics' is: Macro Aesthetic Measure (MAE) = Order / Complexity.

4 The formula for calculating the 'Micro Aesthetics' is: Micro Aesthetic Measure (Mae) = Entropy / Redundancy.

5 The formula for calculating the 'Complete Aesthetic Measure' is: Macro Aesthetic Measure (AE) = [(MAE + Mae) / 2] birk.

6 "Je präziser aber diese rationale Basis formuliert wird, desto überzeugender wirken die darauf begründeten Spekulationen und Wertkonzeptionen." (Maser 1971, 125).

7 Regarding aesthetic perception, Coons and Kraehenbuehl (1958, 128) call this the level of concept formation. It goes beyond the level of simple perception. In the same article, they also suggest defining information as a quotient of 'nonconfirming tests of predictions' and 'predictions tested' (ibid., 139). See also Kraehenbuehl and Coons 1959.

cal structures based on the measurement of redundancy was fruitful, particularly when it was embedded in observations of musical form.[8]

2. On Predecessors and 'Relatives' of Computer-Assisted Music Analysis

Otto Ortmann was an important pioneer of statistical analysis of music. His article from 1937, still virtually unnoticed, involved an analysis – certainly conducted without an electronic calculator – that was restricted to interval frequencies of song melodies by Robert Schumann (48 songs), Johannes Brahms (38 songs), and Richard Strauss (40 songs). No distinction was made between ascending and descending intervals; intervals of equal distance but different nomenclature (e.g., augmented second and minor third) were grouped together. Ortmann calculated the interval distributions of each song and an interval average for all the songs by each composer, the percentage of songs by each composer in which every specific interval was present, and the range of positions which every interval holds – with regard to its frequency – in most of the songs. No matter what the specific results[9] may be worth, and no matter how the question of what validity these results hold generally for songs written by these composers, Ortmann must be given credit for initiating a new form of analysis and for being self-critical enough to point out the disadvantages of disregarding other musical (and non-musical) parameters.

In 1949, Bertrand Bronson used an electro-mechanical calculator – not a 'computer' – to carry out a comparative study of British-American folk-tunes. He used punched cards for encoding general information (publication, collector, singer, etc.), regional information, and musical characteristics, such as range, mode, time signature, number of phrases, phrasal scheme, final tone, initial interval between the upbeat and the first strong accent, etc. Then, the sorting ma-

8 This notion was already supported in the theoretical articles (i.e. with no practical analyses of music) by Leonard B. Meyer (1957) Joel E. Cohen (1962), Fritz Winckel (1964), and later by Alfred Huber (1974) and others.

9 Some parts of each distribution, based on songs by different composers, were similar to each other. Others were different, and thus interpreted as "characterizing" for the composer's style. For Schumann, the predominance of unisons, the relative absence of wide intervals and of chromatic inflection, and the consistency with which the frequency order unison - major second - minor second is found (in 65 % of the songs) was characteristic (Ortmann 1937, 7). Characteristics of Brahm's songs were the relative absence of unisons, the preference for thirds (especially minor thirds), the frequency order major second - minor second - unison (in 45 % of the melodies), and – "not very pronounced" – the preference for chromatic inflection (ibid., 6 ff.). Finally, characteristics in Strauss' melodies based on interval frequency (except a slightly predominant use of sixths) were not found (or, in other words: a uniformity is typical); in different ways, the distributions were similar to the songs by both of the other composers, Schumann and Brahms (ibid., 8 f.). This certainly shows the limitations of this approach, which Ortmann himself was aware of. – In general, Ortmann concluded a "chronological tendency towards an increase in pitch-motion" (ibid., 9).

chine was able to automatically pick out cards with desired characteristics. Thereby, certain musical characteristics could be matched with certain geographical origins, etc. Results of this theoretical procedure were published ten years later (Bronson 1959).

A similar, but much more sophisticated, system called *cantometrics* was developed by Alan Lomax. It is a system for rating song performances by qualitative judgements.[10] Rhythmic, melodic, instrumental, tempi, and other performance characteristics, as well as text characteristics, were initially encoded with a 37-digit rating scale, i.e. the number of slots on an IBM punch card. The system became, later, the model for further computer-assisted studies (as, for instance, described in Grauer 1965).

Even though Pinkerton (1956, 84) claimed that Allen I. McHose (1950) was one of the first to use "modern techniques" for analyzing music, McHose did not mention any use of computers in his analyses. However, his statistical analyses of the chord structure of Bach chorales are of importance for later computer applications in harmonic analysis. In his study from 1950, McHose calculated the frequency of chord types, harmonic functions, inversions, etc., as well as the frequency of non-harmonic tones. He also compared root movements and types of chords in works by Johann Sebastian Bach, Georg Friedrich Händel, and Carl Heinrich Graun. But while computer technique, at the time, was not advanced enough to handle McHose's calculations, this kind of study became the direct predecessor of a type of computer-assisted harmonic analysis which evolved in the 1960s.

H. Quastler reported in 1956[11] that Fred and Carolyn Attneave had analyzed cowboy songs and obtained the transition probabilities for every note preceding a particular note. Based on the analytical results, they tried to synthesize "a few dozen" new songs in the same style, but only two of them were "perfectly convincing" (ibid., 169).

Until the mid-1950s, only simple statistical calculations were applied to music analysis, but Linton C. Freeman and Alan P. Merriam in 1956 used a more complex statistical method for the differentiation of two bodies of music: the discriminant function. The discriminant function uses multiple measurements to discriminate between two groups of music. In this case, the two groups

---

10 Lomax' system is based on the hypothesis that "music somehow expresses emotion; therefore, when a distinctive and consistent musical style lives in a culture or runs through several cultures, one can posit the existence of a distinctive set of emotional needs or drives that are somehow satisfied or evoked by this music." (Lomax 1962, 425) See also Lomax 1976. However, Lomax's theory is not undisputed; see, for instance, Kongas-Maranda 1970, Henry 1976, Kolata 1978, Berrett 1979, Locke 1981, and Oehrle 1992.

11 Quastler's report is part of the discussion, following the article of Fucks 1955, pp. 168-169. For F. and C. Attneave themselves, the results were probably not satisfactory enough for publication.

of music were songs of Trinidad Rada and of Brazilian Ketu. Three characteristics were examined: the mean values of frequencies of (1) major seconds and (2) minor thirds in proportion to the lengths of the song, as well as (3) the total interval use. While each separate characteristic showed insufficient discrimination of the two groups of songs,[12] the use of the discriminant function reduced the probability of misclassifying a single song. However, only 3 measures each of interval use from a very small sample of only 20 songs diminished the statistical value of the results. Nevertheless, using a complex statistical method was innovative in that it provided a method useful for a more sophisticated, computer-assisted analysis of music that took place in the following decade.

In 1956, Richard C. Pinkerton published a study on "Information Theory and Melody." In this article, he discussed entropy analysis (i.e., the analysis of the statistical degree on 'information' in music) and redundancy analysis[13] and how each related to the analysis of 39 nursery songs. Even though all calculations were done manually, his approach was already designed to make use of computer assistance (see Pinkerton 1956, 86). Based on the analytical results of pitch and rhythm probabilities, Pinkerton designed a network of tone relations that enabled him to define a compositional procedure to create similar tunes. (However, his 'composed' melodies were "highly monotonous" [ibid., 84].) Pinkerton's network and transition patterns could be seen as early implementations that relate to concepts that have emerged recently in neural network research: "Thinking of our network scheme, it is fun to speculate that a composer's individual style may reflect networks of nerve pathways in his brain." (Ibid., 86.)

Joseph E. Youngblood's applications of information theory to music analysis (Youngblood 1958, 1960) were probably the most extensive studies of all those that could be called the direct 'predecessors' of computer-assisted music analysis. His ambitious calculations showed the need for computer-assistance. Youngblood's attempts to identify and define musical styles was based on the assumption that musical style can be characterized by a stochastic process, specifically a process that can be characterized using a "Markov chain" (Youngblood 1960, 14-15). Youngblood selected song melodies by Franz Schubert, Robert Schumann, and Felix Mendelssohn, and calculated frequencies and probabilities of each scale degree, tone entropies and redundancies, as well as first-order-transition-probabilities for each melody. Some of the results showed, for example, that Mendelssohn used chromatic tones less frequently than Schubert or Schumann, and that Mendelssohn's music was more redundant.

12 The mean differences for major seconds and minor thirds were each significant beyond the one percent level of confidence, but not in the total interval use. However, the overlaps between the two groups of songs in each separate characteristic were too large.

13 Pinkerton calculated specifically entropy and redundancy of single tones as well as transition probabilities.

Youngblood also compared those results to analyses of samples of Gregorian Chant. Almost all of Youngblood's results did not show statistical differences clearly enough. Due to the number of songs sampled and due to the false assumption that redundancies of melodies alone could characterize a musical style, Youngblood's results were not very significant.[14]

The analyses of musical rhythm by John G. Brawley (1959) were intended to provide a means to characterize style. Assuming music to be a discrete system of communication and assuming that music is an ergodic stochastic process that has the structure of a stationary Markov chain, Brawley calculated entropy and redundancy of selected pieces from different time periods. However, Brawley stated himself – with regard to an analysis of a Bach invention – "that this analysis employing information theory is not very valuable. At best, it may tell us a little about this particular invention, but hardly more than we could arrive at by a less exhaustive and less painstaking analysis." (Brawley 1959, 33.) The number of samples used was too small to warrant drawing general conclusions. However, Brawley's conceptual approach became the basis for more successful rhythm research that followed years later.

Just as philosophical generalizations derived from information theory were applied in a highly limited way (see 1.), mathematical (statistical) approaches were applied to the analysis of simple 'aesthetic objects' in a similar limited manner:

Wilhelm Fucks' "mathematical analyses of the formal structure of music"[15] became an important precedent for the devenlopment of computer applications (although Fucks' calculations were still made without the computer)[16], as well as for the elaboration of the application of information theory to aesthetics (see, e.g., Bense 1969). Fucks' music-analytical attempts were connected with his attempts to analyze language (e.g., Fucks 1955, 1956, 1964). His analyses of musical compositions were usually limited to the analysis of pitch and tone duration in selected voices. Even though his list of publications is long, most of Fucks' writings are based on the same, or similar, data. Fucks usually calculated probabilities, transition probabilities, averages, standard deviations, kurtosis and skewness of distribution curves, as well as entropies. In Fucks' analysis from 1958, for instance, his musical materials were limited to the first violin parts of some concertos, symphonies and symphonic poems, and to the soprano parts of

14 In comparison with Youngblood, Joel E. Cohen (1962, 152) applied the same analytical methods to the analysis of two Rock and Roll songs. However, the critique given here for Youngblood's research is especially true for Cohen's.

15 See, for instance, Fucks 1957, 1958, 1962, 1963, 1964 and 1968, as well as Fucks and Lauter 1965.

16 Even though Lejaren Hiller (1964, 10) mentioned that Fucks used already a computer for his study in 1958, there is no indication for the use of computers in any of Fucks' writings themselves.

some masses (Fucks 1958, 9 f.). While results of his earlier research showed a correlation between composer, time of composition, and frequencies of pitch and tone duration, later publications, especially Fucks' analyses from 1963, demonstrated that standard deviation and entropy of pitches (independent of each other) increases monotonously with the time of composition. Transition matrixes of pitches and transition matrixes of intervals provided information on the probabilities of pitches and intervals following each other. Based on the transition matrixes, Fucks calculated correlation ellipses. Finally, W. Fucks and J. Lauter (1965) calculated auto-correlations of pitches and intervals.

At the time, Fucks' methodological approach was already quite complex in its mathematical form, especially with regard to the comparison of different frequency distributions (pitches, tone durations, intervals, and tone pairs) and its comparison to stochastically-generated music. As such, Fuck's approach revealed the significant potential of mathematical analysis of style. However, Fucks' conclusions were very restricted to specific selections of compositions, and his generalizations of epoch characteristics were far-fetched. An important factor for the restricted analytical outcome was the missing distinction between genre characteristics and personal style in music.

Fucks' methods and analytical results were harshly criticized and shown to be erroneous by Günther Wagner (1976). Wagner noticed "that relative interval-frequencies of consecutive tones cannot be seriously considered either for the question of authenticity or for the proof of a historical development" (ibid., 67)[17]. He pointed out "that the standard deviation in compositions of the same genre and the same composer might vary as much as between compositions of different genres by composers, which belong to different epochs" (ibid.)[18]. And finally, he showed "that the relative pitch distribution is completely ruled out as a method for answering questions about authenticity or chronology" (ibid., 69).[19]

A more reliable music-theoretical foundation was provided by Walter Reckziegel (1967a, 1967b, 1967c), a disciple of Fucks, in an extension of Fucks' notion of 'exact scientific' ['exaktwissenschaftlichen'] methods. In his analyses, Reckziegel included the calculation of metrical units and of musical intensity. For this purpose, Reckziegel defined formulas for calculating the entropy of the metrical unit and the 'total entropy', which is the product of the entropy value (H) of u different pitches and v different tone durations [H(u,v)] and of the dif-

17 ". . . daß relative Intervallhäufigkeiten konsekutiver Töne weder für Echtheitsfragen noch für den Nachweis einer historischen Entwicklung ernsthaft in Frage kommen können."

18 ". . . daß die Sigmawerte [Standardabweichung, N.S.] in Werken ein und derselben Gattung des gleichen Komponisten ähnlich schwanken können, wie zwischen Werken unterschiedlicher Gattungen von Komponisten, die unterschiedlichen Epochen angehören."

19 ". . . daß die relative Tonhöhenverteilung als Mittel zur Lösung von Fragen der Echtheit oder Chronologie gänzlich ausscheidet."

ferent pitches u: $u \cdot H(u,v)$.[20] Furthermore, he calculated the 'Bewegtheit' [kind of motion] out of the impulse frequency per metrical unit, 'intensity' and 'density' (arithmetic mean of metrical units). Sound structures and 'complexities' were analyzed (deliberately) without considering harmonic progressions. Reckziegel's attempts show the desire to formulate methods that can deal with a musical complexity greater than that attempted by Fucks' analyses. However, Reckziegel's analyses were still limited with regard to the number and kind of mathematical calculations.

About ten years later, Christian Kaden (1978) discovered an interesting connection between statistical (not computer-assisted) and traditional music analysis, including psychological and sociological aspects. Analyzing the second movement (Allegretto scherzando) of Beethoven's symphony No. 8 op. 93, Kaden tried to verify his intuitive analytical judgment by statistically calculating dependencies of elementary structures (*Gestalt* units), mathematically describable as tone probabilities of higher orders.[21] Kaden's approach was very successful, and his methodology could have been easily adopted for computer-assisted analyses.

Generally, researchers interested in non-computer-assisted approaches to music analysis drawing on mathematics, statistics, and information theory developed an important repertoire of analytical methods that could easily be formalized in computer programs. From today's point of view, most of these approaches have to be evaluated very critically, but without them computer-assisted music analysis could not have emerged.

3. Computer-Assisted Music Analysis During the 1950s

Even in the beginning of the 'computer age' of music analysis, communication between scholars was very slow. At one of the first conferences on computer applications in music (1965), Edmund Bowles phrased this problem as follows: "There exists no clearinghouse, no center of information, no means of intercommunication between scholars in the humanities using the tools of data processing. Currently existing journals and learned societies are reluctant to assume this additional burden, especially outside their own discipline. We need more scholarly convocations such as this one. We need to avoid needless duplication of effort." (Bowles 1970a, 38.) Since then, some journals have come into being, and more and more conferences on the topic have been organized. However, after looking at the publications in the area of computer-assisted music analysis, it seems that not much has changed since the 'beginning': scholars know little about the history of their area, previous successes and failures are hardly known.

20 The exact formulas can be found in Reckziegel 1967a, 16-17.

21 The basis for this approach, the structural segmentation of music, was already described and explained in detail by Kaden in 1976.

Thus, mistakes are duplicated, and prejudices florish. Ultimately, a detailed history of computer-assisted music analysis is needed. The following paragraphs will summarize the earliest project on computer-assisted music analysis – the only one completed during the 1950s.

The first extensive, systematic use of an electronic computer for music-analytical purposes was described by the mathematician Frederick P. Brooks et al. in 1957. Brooks conducted an analysis-synthesis-project at the Computation Laboratory at Harvard University[22]. For this project, high-order probabilities of 37 hymn tunes were calculated. Those probabilities were then used for the synthesis of new melodies, using Markov chains of orders one through eight. Even though this experiment was limited to (melodic) samples that were not structurally complex, this procedure "permitted the production of a significant number of acceptable tunes within a reasonable time." (Ibid., 180.)[23]

While Brooks' experiment is rarely mentioned in the literature, the work of Lejaren A. Hiller and Leonard Isaacson has been extensively noted, specifically their work on the *Illiac Suite* (String Quartet No. 4) is mentioned in almost every textbook on electronic music.[24] The *Illiac Suite* was composed with the ILLIAC computer in 1956 at the University of Illinois. Even though the computer was, in this composition project, not used for analysis but for the generation and selection of random values in a type of stochastic modeling (known as the "Monte Carlo Method")[25], Hiller's and Isaacson's importance for computer applications in music goes beyond composition. In their book (Hiller and Isaacson 1959), they suggest several computer applications to music analysis:

- statistical and information theoretical applications,
- analysis of musical similarity,
- pattern search,
- analysis of sounds and their physical constitution,
- optical music recognition,

and based on analytical results:

- realization of *continuo* and figured bass and to complete part writing,

---

22 Youngblood 1960 also mentioned an unpublished term paper from 1955 by F. P. Brooks, which lets assume that Brook's project was already realized in 1955. The computer used was the Harvard MARK IV. See Youngblood 1960, 23, footnote 42. In addition, see Neumann and Schappert 1959.

23 For sample melodies see ibid. Neumann and Schappert 1959, which contains the description of the project in German, also reprinted some of the melodies.

24 Brooks' paper was not widely available, whereas Hiller's and Isaacson's book (1959) became available in almost every library.

25 The Monte Carlo Method is a method of obtaining an approximate solution to a numerical problem by the use of random numbers. In music, this method was first applied to composition by Hiller and Isaacson (1959). Here, random sequences of integers were equated to notes, durations, dynamic values and playing techniques. These random integers were then screened by applying various rules and rejected or accepted, depending on the rules.

- missing parts could be reproduced based on statistical style analysis,
- systematic generation of musical materials for teaching purposes.

(See ibid., 165-170.) Most or all of these suggestions were launched during the late 1950s and and early 1960. Their results have been described, for example, in Hiller 1962 and 1964.

Concluding Remarks

With the applications described above, the history of computer-assisted music analysis goes far back to applications of information theory to aesthetics, which provided the philosophical basis of statistical and mathematical music analysis, as well as to (practical) mathematical approaches to music analysis that were not completed with a computer. The approaches that did not use computers continue to this day. The first real computer-application was completed between 1955 and 1957 by a team around the mathematician Frederick P. Brooks. While Hiller and Isaacson used pre-determined "rules" for their *Illiac-Suite* from 1956, Brooks et al. derived the compositional rules automatically. As such, the project by Brooks et al. was the only completed project of computer-assisted music analysis of the 1950s, and it was part of an analysis-synthesis-approach, i.e. the main purpose of analytical calculations was to compose. One needs to keep in mind that computers were, at the time, rarely available for music research. However, the many statistical analysis projects that did not use computers as well as Hiller's and Isaacson's vision of future research on computer-assisted music analysis gave directions for more sophisticated computer-assisted music analysis of the 1960s.

Literature Through the 1950s and Other Relevant Literature

Bense, Max. 1954. *Aesthetica*. Stuttgart: Deutsche Verlags-Anstalt.

__________. 1966a. "Ästhetik und Programmierung." *IBM-Nachrichten* 16: 294-296.

__________. 1966b. "Projekter til en generativ aestetik," *Dansk Musiktidsskrift* XLI: 179-82.

__________. 1969. *Einführung in die informationstheoretische Ästhetik*. Reinbek bei Hamburg: Rowohlt.

Berrett, Joshua. 1979. "Alan Lomax: Some Reconsiderations," *Journal of Jazz Studies* VI/1 (Fall-Winter): 54-63.

Birkhoff, George David. 1931. "A Mathematical Approach to Aesthetics," *Scientia* (September): 133-146.

__________. 1950. *Collected Mathematical Papers*, vol. 3. New York: American Mathematical Society.

Bowles, Edmund. 1970a. "Discussion," *Musicology and the Computer: Three Symposia*, edited by Barry S. Brook. New York: The City University of New York Press. pp. 37-38.

Brawley, John Gray. 1959. An Application of Information Theory to Musical Rhythm. M.M. thesis. Bloomington, IN: Indiana University.

Broeckx, Jan L. 1979. *Contemporary Views on Musical Style and Aesthetics*. Antwerp: Metropolis.

Bronson, Bertrand H. 1949. "Mechanical Help in the Study of Folk Song." *Journal of American Folklore* LII/244 (April-June): 81-86.

_________. 1959. "Toward the Comparative Analysis of British-American Folk Tunes." *Journal of American Folklore* LXXII: 165-191.

Brooks, Frederick P., A. L. Hopkins, P. G. Neumann, and W. V. Wright. 1957. "An Experiment in Musical Composition." *IRE Transactions on Electronic Computers* VI (September): 175-182. (An errata see in vol. 7 (1958): 60.) Reprinted in *Machine Models of Music*, edited by Stephen M. Schwanauer and David A. Levitt. Cambridge, MA: The MIT Press, 1993. pp. 23-40.

Cohen, Joel E. 1961. "Some Relationships Between Music and Mathematics," *Music Education Journal* 48/1 (September): 104-109.

_________. 1962. "Information Theory and Music," *Behavioral Science* VII/2 (April): 137-163.

_________. 1964. "Teorie informací a hudba," *Nové Cesty Hudby: Sborník studií o novodobých skladebných smerech a vedeckých názorech na hudbu*, edited by Eduard Herzog. Praha: Státní hudební vydavatelství. pp. 180-215.

Coons, Edgar, and David Kraehenbuehl. 1958. "Information as a Measure of Structure in Music," *Journal of Music Theory* II/2 (November): 127-161.

Freeman, Linton C., and Alan P. Merriam. 1956. "Statistical Classification in Anthropology: An Application to Ethnomusicology," *American Anthropologist* 58/3 (June): 464-472.

Frank, Helmar. 1964. *Kybernetische Analysen subjektiver Sachverhalte*. Quickborn bei Hamburg: Schnelle.

_________. 1968. *Informationsästhetik. Grundlagenprobleme und erste Anwendungen auf die mime pure*, 3rd ed. Quickborn bei Hamburg: Schnelle.

_________. 1997. *Ästhetische Information : eine Einführung in die kybernetische Ästhethik.* Berlin: Institut für Kybernetik.

Fucks, Wilhelm. 1955. *Mathematische Analyse von Sprachelementen, Sprachstil und Sprache*. Köln: Westdeutscher Verlag.

_________. 1956. "Mathematical Theory of Word Formation." *Information Theory: Papers Read at a Symposium on Information Theory Held at the Royal Institution, London, September 12th to 16th, 1955*, edited by Colin Cherry. London: Butterworths Scientific Publications. pp. 154-170.

_________. 1957. "Gibt es mathematische Gesetze in Sprache und Musik?" *Umschau in Wissenschaft und Technik* 1957/2: 33-37.

_________. 1958. *Mathematische Analyse der Formalstruktur von Musik*. Köln: Westdeutscher Verlag.

_________. 1962. "Mathematische Musikanalyse und Randomfolgen. Zufall und Musik." *Gravesaner Blätter* VI: 132-145.

_________. 1963. *Mathematische Analyse von Formalstrukturen von Werken der Musik.* Köln: Westdeutscher Verlag.

_________. 1964. "Gibt es mathematische Gesetze in Sprache und Musik?" *Kybernetik*, edited by Helmar Frank, 4th ed. Frankfurt am Main: Umschau Verlag. pp. 175-187.

_________. 1968. *Nach allen Regeln der Kunst. Diagnosen über Literatur, Musik, bildende Kunst - die Werke, ihre Autoren und Schöpfer*. Stuttgart: Deutsche Verlags-Anstalt.

Fucks, Wilhelm, and Josef Lauter. 1965. *Exaktwissenschaftliche Musikanalyse*. Köln: Westdeutscher Verlag.

Goldman, Stanford. 1953. *Information Theory*. New York: Dover.

Grauer, Viktor A . 1965. "Some Song-Style Clusters – A Preliminary Study," *Ethnomusicology* IX/3 (September): 265-271.

Guntzenhäuser, Rul. 1962. *Ästhetisches Maß und ästhetische Information. Einführung in die Theorie G. D. Birkhoffs und die Redundanztheorie ästhetischer Prozesse*. Quickborn bei Hamburg: Schnelle.

Henry, Edward O. 1976. "The Variety of Music in a North Indian Village: Reassessing Cantometrics," *Ethnomusicology* XX/1 (January): 49-66.

Hiller, Lejaren A., Jr. 1962. Information Theory and Musical Analysis. Mimeographed. Urbana: University of Illinois, Experimental Music Studio. Technical Report No. 5, July 1962. 40 p. (University of Cincinnati Library, MUS ML 3817 .I4 no. 5).

_________. 1964. *Informationstheorie und Computermusik*. Darmstädter Beiträge zur Neuen Musik 8. Mainz: B. Schott's Söhne.

Hiller, Lejaren A., and Leonard M. Isaacson. 1959. *Experimental Music. Composition with an Electronic Computer*. New York: McGraw-Hill.

Huber, Alfred. 1974. "Informationstheorie und Musikanalyse," *Melos* XLI/4 (July-August): 207-210.

Kaden, Christian. 1976. "Strukturelle Segmentierung von Musik - Probleme, Schwierigkeiten, Möglichkeiten," *Beiträge zur Musikwissenschaft* 18: 149-162 and 293-334.

_________. 1978. "Ludwig van Beethoven, Sinfonie Nr. 8, zweiter Satz, Allegretto scherzando. Ansätze zu einer statistischen Strukturanalyse." *Bericht über den Internationalen Beethoven Kongreß 20. bis 23. März 1977 in Berlin*, edited by H. Goldschmidt, K.-H. Köhler, and K. Niemann. Leipzig: Deutscher Verlag für Musik. pp. 113-130.

Kasem-Bek, Jan. 1978. "Informationstheorie und Analyse musikalischer Werke," *Archiv für Musikwissenschaft* 35: 62-75.

Kolata, Gina Bari. 1978. "Singing Styles and Human Cultures: How are They Related?" *Science* CC/4339 (April): 287-288.

Kongas-Maranda, Elli. 1970. "Deep Significance and Surface Significance: Is Cantometrics Possible?" *Semiotica* II/2: 173-184.

Kraehenbuehl, David, and Edgar Coons. 1959. "Information as a Measure of the Experience of Music," *Journal of Aesthetics & Art Criticism* XVII/4 (June): 510-522.

LaRue, Jan. 1970a. "New Directions for Style Analysis," *Musicology and the Computer: Three Symposia*, edited by Barry S. Brook. New York: The City University of New York Press. pp. 194-197.

LaRue, Jan, and Murray Gould. 1969. "Correlational Analysis to Establish Authenticity of 18th-Century Symphonies," *Computers and the Humanities* III/5 (May): 311.

Lauter, Josef, and Roland Mix. 1967. "The Information Content of Music," *Nachrichtentechnische Zeitschrift* XX/2: 86-89.

Locke, David. 1981. "Cantometrics: An Approach to the Anthropology of Music by Alan Lomax [Book Review]," *Ethnomusicology* XXV/3 (September): 527-529.

Lomax, Alan. 1962. "Song Structure and Social Structure." *Ethnology* I/4 (October): 425-451.

_________. 1968. *Folk Song Style and culture*. Washington, D.C.: American Association for the Advancement of Science.

_________. 1976. *Cantometrics: An Approach to the Anthropology of Music*. Berkeley, CA: The University of California Press.

Mandelbrot, B. 1957. "[Review of] W. Fucks, Mathematische Analyse von Sprachelementen, Sprachstil und Sprache," *Word: Journal of the Linguistic Circle of New York* 13: 159-160.

Maser, Siegfried. 1971. *Numerische Ästhetik. Neue mathematische Verfahren zur quantitativen Beschreibung und Bewertung ästhetischer Zustände*, 3rd edition. Stuttgart: Krämer.

McHose, Allen I. 1950. "Musical Research in the Definition of Bach's Contrapuntal Harmonic Style," *Proceedings of the Music Teachers National Association* 42: 126-150.
Meyer, Leonard B. 1957. "Meaning in Music and Information Theory." *Journal of Aesthetics & Art Criticism* XV/4 (June): 412-424.
Moles, Abraham A. 1956a. "Informationstheorie der Musik." *Nachrichtentechnische Fachberichte* 3: 47-55.
_________. 1956b. "Informationstheorie und ästhetische Empfindung." *Gravesaner Blätter* VI (December): 3-9.
_________. 1958. *Théorie de l'information et perception esthétique*. Paris: Flammarion & Cie. American edition: *Information Theory and Esthetic Perception*, translated by Joel E. Cohen. Urbana: University of Illinois Press, 1966.
_________. 1962. "Das neue Verhältnis zwischen Musik und Mathematik," *Gravesaner Blätter* VI: 98-103.
_________. 1964. "Uvedení do soucasného stavu hudby," *Nové Cesty Hudby*: 36-53.
_________. 1966. *Information Theory and Esthetic Perception*, translated by Joel E. Cohen. Urbana: University of Illinois Press.
_________. 1973. *Kunst & Computer*. Köln: M. DuMont Schauberg.
_________. 1986. "Approche informationnelle de la perception et de la creation Musicale," *International Review of the Aesthetics and Sociology of Music* (Croatia) XVII/2 (December): 273-297.
Nake, Frieder. 1974. *Ästhetik als Informationsverarbeitung. Grundlagen und Anwendungen der Informatik im Bereich ästhetischer Produktion und Kritik*. Wien: Springer.
Nathan, Hans. 1958. "The Twelve-Tone Compositions of Luigi Dallapiccola," The *Musical Quarterly* 44 (July): 289-310.
Nettl, Bruno. 1958. "Some Linguistic Approaches to Musical Analysis," *Journal of the International Folk Music Council* X: 37-41.
Neumann, P. G., and H. Schappert. 1959. "Komponieren mit elektronischen Rechenautomaten," *Nachrichtentechnische Zeitschrift* VIII: 403-407.
Norman, Philip B. 1945. *A Quantitative Study of Harmonic Similarities in Certain Specified Works of Bach, Beethoven and Wagner*. New York, NY: Carl Fischer.
Oehrle. Elizabeth. 1992. "Cantometrics: An Approach to the Anthropology of Music," *British Journal of Music Education* IX/1: 83-86.
Ortmann, Otto. 1937. "Interval Frequency as a Determinant of Melodic Style," *Beabody Bulletin* (December): 3-10.
Pinkerton, Richard C. 1956. "Information Theory and Melody." *Scientific America* 194/2 (Febuary): 77-86.
Quastler, H. 1956. Discussion, following Mathematical Theory of Word Formation, by W. Fucks, *Information Theory: Papers Read at a Symposium on Information Theory Held at the Royal Institution, London, September 12th to 16th, 1955*, edited by Colin Cherry. London: Butterworths Scientific Publications. pp. 168-169.
Reckziegel, Walter. 1967a. *Theorien zur Formalanalyse mehrstimmiger Musik*. Köln: Westdeutscher Verlag.
_________. 1967b. "Musikanalyse - eine exakte Wissenschaft?" *Elektronische Datenverarbeitung in der Musikwissenschaft*, edited by Harald Heckmann. Regensburg: Bosse, pp. 203-224.
_________. 1967c. "Musikanalyse und Wissenschaft." *Studia Musicologica Academiae Scientiarum Hungaricae* IX/1-2: 163-186.
Schillinger, Joseph. 1948. *The Mathematical Basis of the Arts*. New York: Philosophical Library.

Schüler, Nico. 1996. "Methoden computerunterstützter Musikanalyse - ein historischer Überblick," *Zum Problem und zu Methoden von Musikanalyse*, edited by N. Schüler. Hamburg: von Bockel, 1996. 51-76.

_________. 2000c. Methods of Computer-Assisted Music Analysis: History, Classification, and Evaluation. Ph.D. dissertation. East Lansing, MI: Michigan State University.

_________. 2002c. "The Philosophical Rationale of Computer-Assisted Music Analysis: Information Theory and Aesthetics," *Computer-Applications in Music Research: Concepts, Methods, Results*, edited by Nico Schüler. Frankfurt: Peter Lang, 2002. pp. 19-30.

_________. 2005. "Reflections on the History of Computer-Assisted Music Analysis I: Predecessors and the Beginnings," *Musicological Annual* XXXXI/1: 31-43.

_________. 2006. "Reflections on the History of Computer-Assisted Music Analysis II: The 1960s," *Musicological Annual* [Ljubljana, Slovenia] XLII/1: 5-24.

Shannon, Claude E., and W. Weaver. 1949. *The Mathematical Theory of Communication*. Urbana: University of Illinois Press.

Springer, G. P. 1956. "Language and Music: Parallels and Divergencies," *For Roman Jakobson*, edited by M. Halle, H. G. Lunt, H. McLean, and C. H. Van Schooneveld. Den Haag: Mouton. pp. 504-513.

Wagner, Günther. 1976. "Exaktwissenschaftliche Musikanalyse und Informationsästhetik." *International Review of Aesthetics and Sociology of Music* VII/1 (June): 63-76.

Winckel, Fritz. 1964. "Die informationstheoretische Analyse musikalischer Strukturen," *Die Musikforschung* XVII/1: 1-14.

Youngblood, Joseph E. 1958. "Style as Information." *Journal of Music Theory* II/1 (April): 24-35.

_________. 1960. Music and Language: Some Related Analytical Techniques. Ph.D. disseration. Bloomington, IN: Indiana University.

Reflections on the History of Computer-Assisted Music Analysis: The 1960s

Introduction

This specific essay[1] focuses on developments of computer-assisted music analysis during the 1960s. While the first real computer-application date as far back as 1955 (see an earlier essay in this book): a team around the mathematician Frederick P. Brooks developed an analysis-synthesis-approach, in which Brooks et al. derived the compositional rules automatically. As such, the project by Brooks et al. (1957) was the only completed project of computer-assisted music analysis of the 1950s, although Lejaren Hiller (1962, 1964) developed ideas that gave directions – for several of his students as well as others (see below) – for the more sophisticated approaches to computer-assisted music analysis of the 1960s.

Representatives of Computer-Assisted Music Analysis in the 1960s

Available hardware severely restricted the computer applications of the 1960s. However, early applications of statistics and of information theory to music analysis – especially in the US – as well as music-philosophical reflections – especially in Europe –, spurred the boom of computer-assisted methods of music analysis. To show specific tendencies of those methods, some trendsetting applications will be discussed.

In his studio for experimental music at the University of Illinois, Lejaren A. Hiller collaborated in several analytical research projects. Three of these projects are described in Hiller 1964.[2] The first project (Bean 1961; see also Hiller and Bean 1966) involved a comparison of four sonata expositions (by Mozart, Beethoven, Hindemith, and Berg), mainly based on first-order entropies of pitches and intervals as well as on the "speed of information" (i.e., of entropy), which was calculated via note density and tempo. But while Bean's project was not computer-assisted, Baker's research (Baker 1963) – the second project mentioned in Hiller 1964 – was partly carried out with the assistance of ILLIAC, the first electronic computer at the University of Illinois.[3] (Thus, this study is the first dissertation project in the area of computer-assisted music analysis.) Modu-

1 Explanations of the basic terminology used in this article and definitions of commonly used terms in this area of methods of computer-assisted music analysis can be found earlier in this book.

2 There, Hiller gives the impression that those projects were mainly his own research projects. However, he rather supervised the dissertation research of his students Calvert Bean (1961), Robert A. Baker (1963), and Ramon C. Fuller (1965).

3 However, exactly how the computer was used was not described in Baker's dissertation.

lation-free passages of 16 string quartets by Mozart, Haydn, and Beethoven were analyzed with regard to transition probabilities of harmonies and of pitches as well as their relationships.[4] Finally, the third project discussed in Hiller 1964 (Fuller 1965; see also Hiller and Fuller 1967) involved the analysis of the first movement of Anton Webern's Symphony op. 21. Here, entropy and redundancy calculations (of higher orders) of pitches and intervals revealed, among others, the formal structure of the piece.

William J. Paisley chose a quite different approach to computer-assisted music analysis. Based on communication theory, Paisley (1964) made a fundamental contribution to identifying authorship (and with it, stylistic characteristics) by exploring "minor encoding habits", i.e. details in works of art (which would be, for instance, too insignificant for imitators to copy).[5] To take an example from a different field, master paintings can be distinguished from imitations by examining details like the shapes of fingernails. Similarly, Paisley showed that there are indeed significant minor encoding habits in music. He analyzed note-to-note pitch transitions in the first six notes of each of the 320 themes by Bach, Haydn, Mozart, Beethoven and Brahms. He chose the parameter 'pitch', because pitches can be easily coded for computer processing and because some research on tonal transitions had already been reported.

In his first analysis[6], Paisley calculated interval frequencies of up to six semitones within the first 6 notes of two 160-theme-samples. Furthermore, he calculated the Chi Square Test for Goodness of Fit of those interval distributions for the two samples. While these results could not significantly distinguish Haydn, Mozart, and Beethoven, Paisley claimed a successful distinction between these composers with his second analysis, in which he calculated frequencies and chi squares of two-note transitions between the classes tonic, third, fifth, all other diatonic tones and all chromatic tones. In both analyses, the results of the chi square test were then compared with results from "unknown samples" (Mozart, Beethoven, Händel, and Mendelssohn). The results from analyzing themes by Mozart and Beethoven could (in the second analysis) be successfully matched with the "known" Mozart- and Beethoven-samples, while Händel and Mendelssohn were significantly different. But even though only a modest amount of data was involved in this investigation, and even though a reduction of the number of possible intervals to seven (based on inversions as well as on neglecting the direction) seems to be questionable, Paisley's study was well documented and its results were, considering the time of the study, very impressive. Several other authors referred later to Paisley's approach.

---

4 However, the harmonic analysis itself was done traditionally, not computer-assisted.

5 For a general discussion on this topic, especially with regard to text analysis, see also Paisley 1969.

6 Paisley performed the analyses on the Stanford University 7090 computer.

In 1969, Stefan M. Kostka wrote a set of FORTRAN-programs[7] for analyzing string quartets by Paul Hindemith[8], following William J. Paisley's definition of "minor encoding habits". His task was "to test the hypothesis that Hindemith's style shows a consistency in his use of certain 'hidden communicators' of which Hindemith himself may or may not have been aware. On the other hand, since Hindemith's style did not remain unchanged throughout his life, it was considered worthwhile to see if his employment of some of these communicators showed a noticeable and consistent change from the early quartets to those written in the 1940s." (Kostka 1969a, 173) Kostka analyzed roots and classes of chords[9], treating each vertical event equally (regardless of their duration or regardless of whether they contained non-harmonic tones etc.). In his explanations, Kostka referred to Gabura (1965), who found – analyzing music by Brahms and Bartók – only small differences in the result of weighting chords by frequency as opposed to weighting chords by duration. Kostka tried to verify this for Hindemith's music on the example of the first movement of his Fifth String Quartet[10] by letting the computer calculate frequencies and percentages of chords. Other algorithms counted frequencies of all chords (both by treating inversions as independent chords and by dealing with "normal forms") and their harmonic contexts. Finally, in horizontal analyses, various kinds of melodic intervals were calculated[11], and the program searched for melodic patterns that had been defined by the analyst, including permutations. Even though Kostka found stringent regularities in the interval frequencies and frequencies of chord classes in all quartets, one can hardly interpret these distributions as "Hindemith's melodic style" (Kostka 1969a, 263); analyses of other genres used by Hindemith or other quartets by other composers would be necessary for a verification. The inconsistencies Kostka found in other analyses (e.g. root movements, tonality,

7 These programs were implemented on a CDC 3600 computer.

8 The music was coded in ANON, an alphanumeric coding system developed in the course of a seminar at the University of Wisconsin, conducted by Roland Jackson. Since the code originally remained unnamed and untested, Kostka named it for his study. (See Kostka 1969a, 112 ff.)

9 Here, the definition of "roots" and "chords" goes back to Hindemith's theoretical system itself, described in Hindemith 1945, 94 ff. Another system of chord classification, which Kostka applied, was based on the distinction between Intervallic, Tertian, Quartal and Whole-Tone chords.

10 The number of pieces for such a verification remained certainly questionable.

11 These included: A) every single interval; B) minor with major intervals combined; C) minor with major and their inversions combined (e.g. descending second and ascending seventh); D) all inversions combined: all seconds with all sevenths etc.; E) intervals with their mirror inversions combined (minor seconds up and down, major seconds up and down, etc.); F) all major and minor seconds, all major and minor thirds, etc., combined.

etc.) led to the conclusion that either those characteristics are not important for Hindemith's style or the analytical method would need to be modified.

Kostka's study (1969a) also showed a limitation of his computer-aided approach to music analysis: the enormous volume of data (the huge number of punched cards) made it impossible to extract, examine, and compare the data "for every theoretical question that came to mind" (ibid., 250). But Kostka's dissertation is very important in so far as it is based on the study of former approaches as well as on ('traditional') music-theoretical and musicological writings pertaining to the style in the music by Paul Hindemith. Some 'traditional' explorations of Hindemith's style could be verified by Kostka's computer-aided study.

The possibility of quickly processing a large amount of data with new computer techniques was recognized in the 1960s, especially by US-scholars in musicology and music theory. In 1966, Gerald Lefkoff (1967b) and Allen Forte (1967a) addressed this topic at the "West Virginia University Conference on Computer Applications in Music". Forte gave 'good' reasons for applying the computer to music analysis: "The computer can be programmed to deal with complex structures – such as musical composition – very rapidly. . . . A second reason for using the computer derives from the requirements of completeness and precision that form the basis of every computer program. . . . The design of an algorithm, the formulation of a decision-structure to solve a problem, the careful checking out of a malfunctioning program – all these activities provide clarifications and insights which would be difficult, perhaps impossible, to obtain otherwise." (Ibid., 33-34.) Without going into details, Forte also described a computer project[12] for the (set theoretical) determination of similarities and differences of sets, for the interpretation of those with respect to characteristics of the environments in which they occur, and for the design of a structural model in terms of set-complex theory (ibid., 39).[13] Gerald Lefkoff (1967b), on the other hand, described a system "for the study of computer-residing, score-derived musical models" (ibid., 45). Written in FORTRAN, Lefkoff's 'model' saved musical information in time-indexed arrays: pitch, rhythmic values, vocal text, figured bass symbols, dynamics, articulations, and editorial comments. Lefkoff then extracted, along with data relating to other relationships, "a complete list of melodic fragments from a group of compositions, with frequency distribution data for the fragments within each composition and . . . [then] compare[d] the relative frequency of occurrence of each fragment in selected groups of compositions." (Ibid., 55.) The value of Lefkoff's model can be seen in its ability to generalize such analytical procedures and thereby discover stylistic trends.

---

12 His set of computer programs was written in MAD.

13 A similar program, written in the computer language SNOBOL 3, was described in Forte 1966.

However, Lefkoff did not describe any concrete analyses; and thus, it is questionable if his theoretical model was indeed functioning and reaching the envisioned goals.

Milton Babbitt (1955, 1960, 1961), with his analytical approaches to dodecaphonic and set structures, was of outstanding importance for music theoretical developments in the US. His research provided the basis for the manifold (US-) discussions on the use of logic-mathematical procedures in music analysis (and likewise in composition). Since the mathematical part in set-theoretical analyses is very suitable for implementations in computer programs, many computer applications in music theory and musicology after the mid-1960s (Babbitt 1965) are related to set theory.

Donald M. Pederson (1968), for instance, described a computer-assisted, analytical project that used set-theoretical and statistical approaches. After the transformation of the musical data (contained in the scores) into a suitable code for music analysis[14], a program computed subset and superset relations of a given set within the score. All set types found were also examined with regard to interval vector and number of occurrences. Finally, another program computed frequencies of pitch classes and generated graphic displays that showed pitch patterns within specific voices and showed the interaction between them; it also found instances of fixed registration, found other pitch patterns, and displayed the registral use of each pitch-class. Pederson analyzed Anton Webern's string quartet op. 28 in two ways: at first, 'traditionally' "to provide a description of the structure and the use of the twelve-tone set and to establish the formal sectioning of the composition" (ibid., 73), and then, after this contextual analysis, non-traditionally, using a computer-aided analysis of the harmonic content applying the methods described above. Pederson concluded, that "even though the two approaches examine different aspects of the music, the relationship found between sections in the contextual analysis are born out by the result of the computer processing" (ibid., 75). Even though the weaknesses of Pederson's approach were the – more or less unexplained – segmentation of the score by the program (to find subsets or supersets of the one set which was identified by himself) and the use of only very basic statistical measurements, Pederson did not only combine traditional and computer-aided analysis in general, but also set theoretical and statistical approaches.

While Allen Forte, in 1965, hypothesized about a computer program that could calculate set complex relations, he described, in 1970, described a computer program that calculated set class memberships for arbitrary sets of pitch classes.

---

14 Pederson used the "Ford-Columbia Digital Alternate Representation of Musical Scores" (DARMS), which was developed by Stefan Bauer-Mengelberg. Since this code was not specifically developed for music analytical investigations, Pederson modified it slightly. (See Pederson 1968, especially pp. 5-16.)

A pilot study that began as an attempt to automate the collection of bibliographic data from five percent of the 17th century chanson repertory (about 300 pieces) by Lawrence F. Bernstein and Joseph P. Olive (1969) ended up as a computer-assisted project in stylistic analysis.[15] Eleven types of stylistic data were calculated, each falling into one of the three categories: routine analysis, statistical analysis, and numeric representation. While routine analysis included standard harmonic analysis (determination of the roots of all triads)[16], measurement of the rate of harmonic rhythm, and determination of the range of the vocal parts, the statistical calculations – also designed to aid in harmonic analysis – were directed at the number of relatively strong or weak root movements, the degree to which inversions were used, the ratio of complete and incomplete chords, and the frequency of recurrent harmonic adjacencies (ibid., 158). Numeric and graphic representation involved ascertaining textural complexity by analyzing the interaction of several (weighted) parameters of style (number of voices, the amount of coordinated rhythmic activity among the voices, the number of separate rhythmic attacks across the polyphony, duration of the notes; ibid., 159). The authors also expressed the need for improving the computer program for further research: The program should determine more than just the roots of complete triads and it should also distinguish between structural and ornamental harmonic motion.

Astonishing for such a project in the 1960s was the (positive) reservation towards the possibilities of using computers for analyzing music: The authors were never "deluded into believing that the computer was in any way capable of analyzing a piece of music. Rather, we used the information made available by the computer as a means of substantiating or explaining the insights into a given composition that we gained by means of a direct confrontation with the music." (Ibid., 160)[17] Thus, the analyses were indeed 'only' computer-*assisted*! The information, which was electronically derived, was only 'helpful' for setting up stylistic profiles of the composers. Even though all analytical operations could have been done without the assistance of a computer, the compilation of the sta-

15 For the music representation of this project, the Chicago Linear Music Language was developed, which especially takes notational necessities of the 16th century chanson into account. The program was written in FAP for an IBM 7094 computer.

16 "In the performance of harmonic analysis, the chords had to be examined each time a note changed in any of the voices. A chord was rejected for either of the following reasons: (1) if it contained less than three notes; or (2) if it included intervals other than thirds and fifths. If neither of these conditions prevailed, the root of the chord was determined by examining the intervals, concentrating on the interval of the fifth, and designating its lower member the root." (Ibid., 159.)

17 It continues: "In this way, the data supplied by the computer proved to be very useful in explaining why a particular portion of a chanson generates a sense of tension, while another section of the same piece creates a feeling of rest." (Ibid.)

tistical data would have taken too much time to be considered feasible. (See ibid.)

Michael Kassler (1966) developed a special-purpose programming language named MIR – an acronym for "musical information retrieval". Since MIR is both a programming language and a language for musical information retrieval, music theoretical functions are directly expressible within the program; at the same time, the program functions as an evaluation tool. MIR was usually used in connection with the IML (Intermediate Music Language) music code. As such a connection between music code and information retrieval language, the acronym IML-MIR was used.[18]

Arthur Mendel (1969) applied, together with Lewis Lockwood[19], the IML-MIR system to the analysis of the style of Josquin des Prez. This included primarily calculations of frequencies of all simultaneities.[20] Using the ratio between the percentages of all the four-part simultaneities that constitute complete triads and the percentages of complete triads, Mendel tried to show that one mass subsection was not composed by Josquin des Prez, as scholars originally assumed. However, the main problem with Mendel's project was the machine-dependent implementation: Because the author had to switch computers, the project could not be continued as planned.

Maurita P. Brender and Ronald F. Brender (1967) developed a program for the transcription and analysis of the Bamberg Codex, notated in Franconian notation. The digital representation of the music included pitch and tone duration. The output of the transcription program, punched cards, was used as input for the analytical programs.[21] The analyses focused on occurrences of part or voice crossing[22], on melodic intervals in each part, on the "average rate of movement"[23], and on vertical intervals occurring in the three positions: strong, weak, and off beats. The output of the program also included a graphic descrip-

18 For a relatively detailed introduction see Robison 1967.

19 Lockwood already presented a progress report on this project at a »Musicology and the Computer I« conference in 1965 (see Brook 1970a), which was published five years later (Lockwood 1970).

20 Future plans included calculations of interval frequencies and of correlations between the primary accent of a Latin word and the duration of the note set to the syllable that is immediately following. (See Mendel 1969, 51.)

21 But here, only five motets with Portare tenors from the Bamberg Codex were analyzed.

22 Thus, parts of the analyses were aimed at the determination "to what extent the motets, tenor, and triplum could be associated with a fixed position in the chord structure" (ibid., 206).

23 "Each melodic interval is divided by the duration of the first note of each pair and the average taken over the whole melodic line." (Ibid., 206.) A surprising result was that decreasing intervals were used more commonly than increasing intervals, i.e. "that descending lines tend to change or move faster and over larger intervals than ascending lines. The motetus was normally the most negative, followed by the triplum, then the tenor." (Ibid.)

tion of the chord usage in every piece. With regard to existing theories of musical practice of the Middle Ages (and specifically, during the time of the Bamberg Codex), Brender and Brender tried to verify traditional assertions, concerning the usage of consonances and dissonances.[24] In addition to the analytical attempts, a formal (context free and only right branching) grammar of Franconian notation was formulated. Successful translations (transcriptions) verified the grammar.

Benjamin Suchoff selected transcriptions of Bartok's Serbo-Croatian Folk Songs (a small collection of 75 women's songs) as a pilot project for lexicographical orderings by computer. After dividing and numbering the melodies in accordance with Bartók's determination of the content structure in every melody section, and after coding[25], the computer extracted string interval sequences[26] coded as sequences of positive and negative integers, and sorted and compared the derived sequences.[27] This made further statistical analyses possible. However, in several short articles (Suchoff 1967a, 1968a, 1968b, 1969, 1970a), the analytical part was mentioned only briefly and only the indexing approach was described in detail. The purpose of using the computer for the analysis remained unclear, at least with regard to the identification of melodic variants, since they were probably realized 'traditionally'. Only in Suchoff's 1968a article, the "machine analysis of a string content for frequency occurrences" (ibid., 6) is mentioned, but without further details. Later, Suchoff (1969) suggested the use of 'skeleton models' in the search for variants and orders. In the explanation of a melodic skeleton, Suchoff referred to Bartók; but it remains unclear in Suchoff's writings if the skeleton models were actually derived with the computer or by hand. In Suchoff 1970a, some analytical results were included, e.g., prevalent types of identical interval sequences, interval frequencies, and frequencies of phrases with a certain interval structure. Suchoff's research certainly provided an important impulse for folksong research on the American continent.

Richard E. Joiner (1969) conducted comparative analyses of eleven Gregorian chants from the early period (approximately 600-1000 A.D.) and twelve from the late period (approximately 1000-1300 A.D.). His analyses were based on frequency counts and relative frequencies of the notes, intervals, and phrases,

---

24 Even though, the assertions could be verified, "the most general fact . . . is that the number of exceptions is considerable. In particular, the assertion that a consonance should begin every perfection is, at best, true only in a simple majority of cases." (Ibid., 207.)

25 The calculations were executed by an IBM 1130 computer (Suchoff 1967a), later by an IBM 360 computer (Suchoff 1968). Most programs of this project were written in FORTRAN, some in PL/1, and the music was encoded in the Ford-Columbia code. The indexing system was devised by Harry B. Lincoln (see Lincoln 1967a, 1967b, 1968a, 1968b, 1969a, 1969b).

26 Repeated notes, interval quality, and rhythmic character were omitted from consideration.

27 Thus, a melodic section of a Serbo-Croatian folk song could be presented, for instance, as "-2 +2 -2 +2 -2 -2".

and on the average length of phrases per chant. The computer program also examined each chant for repeated patterns with the length of two to eight notes. Even though the results – in general formulated by the author himself – 'sounded' characteristic of the music,[28] the standard deviations of all results were too large for a computational model of authentication based on the statistical calculations mentioned above. Furthermore, no validity check was described in Joiner's paper.

In Europe, Roland Mix (1967) extended Wilhelm Fuck's methods of entropy analysis. Having chosen the first movement of Haydn's string quartet, op. 76 No. 3, and the first movement of Schoenberg's third string quartet, op. 30, Mix analyzed entropy dependencies of higher orders of pitches, harmonies, dynamics and rhythm. Among others, Mix discovered that the values of entropies of chords and pitches are much higher in Schoenberg's composition than in Haydn's. However, the relative 'contribution' of the rhythm to the total entropy is larger in Haydn's piece than in Schoenberg's. The dependencies among the parts are larger in Haydn's string quartet than in Schoenberg's. In a different experiment, Mix calculated entropies of pitches (up to order six) of the first violins of three Haydn quartets and compared them. But even though Mix's approaches represent great enhancements of information-theoretical analyses in their complex application to several musical parameters, his results were limited by the computer hardware. Methodologically, Mix's approaches showed the limits of using only one measurement for comparative analyses. But while Fucks and Reckziegel[29] focussed on only one voice of multi-voice compositions, Mix had already attempted a 'vertical' analysis.

The East-German Reiner Kluge (1974a)[30] analyzed similarities among Altmark[31] folk songs. More than 130 syntactic characteristics were discovered and then used to determine similarities of pairs of melodies (out of random samples with each about 40 melodies[32]). Kluge's research was outstanding, because he developed a similarity measurement, based on the formula r = -cos A/N, "whereby A is the number of the coincidences of two elements j, k within N characteristics, relating to the totality of elements"[33] (Kluge 1974a, 31). Using

28 "On the basis of this limited study, Early chant as opposed to Late chant can be said to be shorter, have more phrases, shorter phrases, be more limited in range (of notes), use smaller intervals, and have less shorter repeated patterns but more longer patterns." (Joiner 1969, 213)

29 See the previous essay in this book.

30 Even though his dissertation was published in 1974, the (dissertation) research was conducted between 1965 and 1968, and defended in 1968.

31 Altmark is an area in Southeastern Germany.

32 The restrictions to limited samples were necessary because of on the low efficiency of the computer used (ZRA1).

33 ". . . wobei A die Anzahl der Koinzidenzen zweier Individuen j, k in N betrachteten Merkmalen in bezug auf die betrachtete Individuengesamtheit ist."

factor analysis, Kluge identified pseudo-individuals, out of which 12 different types and mixed types were derived. The results of Kluge's analyses were limited in several ways:

- the hardware available for his research was too limited in speed and memory,
- the number of musical characteristics was not large enough,
- the definition of his measurement of similarity was insufficient,
- the criteria to describe melodic types were insufficient, and
- the number of random samples was too small.

However, Kluge's work became very valuable for further research in this area, because he found several characteristics and groups of characteristics as suitable for comparative analyses of folk songs.[34] Furthermore, Kluge's study showed that a successful comparative analysis is only possible if many musical characteristics are analyzed in relation to each other.

The Major Sources of Computer-Assisted Music Analysis of the 1960s

Besides numerous articles, partly reviewed above, sources of computer-assisted music analysis of the 1960s include also three major publications on the use of computers in music research – Heckmann 1967a, Lincoln 1970a, and Brook 1970a –, each containing several analytical articles.

Harald Heckmann's book on "Elektronische Datenverarbeitung in der Musikwissenschaft" contained five articles on (computer-assisted) music analysis. George W. Logemann (1967a), for instance, described a system for finding the positions in which the second voices of Bach canons from the *Musical Offering* begin; he tried all possible entry points and matched arising interval structures. Eric Regener (1967a) introduced a transcription system as the basis for analytical research[35]; however, this system was not fully in operation at the time. Tobias D. Robison's (1967) article introduced IML-MIR, but did not include any practical application of MIR. Walter Reckziegel (1967b) wrote on the use of measurements for inner tempo and individual tempo[36], and Nanna Schiødt and Bjarner Svejgaard (1967) reported an analysis of Byzantine Sticherarion melodies. The latter project is of special importance and will be discussed here in more detail. It is of special importance, because it was, together with the re-

---

34 Those valuable musical characteristics include, for instance, 'inner melody shape', 'melodic incipits', 'pitch repertory contains the leading tone', 'the lowest pitch occurs after the highest', 'number of changes of melodic direction in the first melodic line', 'unusual melodic intervals', 'unusual transition of tone durations', and 'time signature'. See Kluge 1974a, 155-157.

35 His system was called SAM, "System for Analysis of Music", and was specifically written for the IBM 7090 computer. The transcription code used was LMT (Linear Music Transcription).

36 Thus, Reckziegel's research included further developments of his measurements; see Schüler 2005.

search by Brender and Brender (1967; see above), one of the first projects of computer-assisted music analysis aimed at Medieval music. The task was to find musical formulas in Gregorian chant, whereby neumes were encoded with a special alphanumerical code. The computer program found all commonly used formulas, whereby the authors verified the results via conventional analytical methods. However, one of the most important results of this study relates to the proportion of expenditure to benefit. In most computer applications to music analysis – to this day – the coding and input process takes much too long, i.e. the proportion of expenditure to benefit is unsatisfactory. On the contrary, the analysis of Byzantine neumes seems to be much faster with the help of a computer: "After half an hour you have learned the code so well that you can type the code symbols a little faster than you can write the neumes out by hand. If you want to study the hymns 'by hand' they have to be written out in different ways in any case. Sometimes you may have to write them out in a new way for each new detail you want to study. Working with the computer you only need to write the hymns out once. Afterwards you put the punched paper tape in the machine and you can ask whatever question concerning the encoded material that might enter your mind. . . ." (Ibid., 194.)

Harry B. Lincoln's edition (1970a) of many papers on computer-assisted music analysis[37] include several statistical and combinatorial approaches to the analysis of atonal music. Mary E. Fiore (1970), Ramon Fuller (1970), and Roland Jackson (1970a) made use of frequency counts of pitches, intervals, types of dissonances, and chord types (with a certain interval structure). Gerald Lefkoff (1970) analyzed twelve tone rows and computed the 48 permutations as well as similar segments within these permutations. A computer program by Ian Morton and John Lofstedt (1970) calculated frequencies of chordal roots (in tonal music) and their relation to certain beats of a measure. Joseph Youngblood (1970) tried to determine whether a composer's style is characterized by the distribution of root progressions; mathematical measurements applied were frequency, probability, redundancy, and chi-square probability. However, the most important paper in Lincoln's volume with regard to computer-assisted music analysis was probably the paper on analyzing Javanese music by Fredric Lieberman (1970)[38]. This research is a classic example of dissatisfaction with results that are only partially acceptable. While the synthesis of Javanese-style melodies on the basis of analytical results retained by a 'nearest-neighbor Markov process' was not completely satisfactory, a complex system of interacting variables was developed, which could characterize Javanese music much better than just Markov chains by themselves. This complex system of variables in-

37 They all used either FORTRAN or SNOBOL as programming languages.

38 See also Hood 1967.

cluded, among others, frequencies of pitches, transition frequencies of higher orders, and various (melodic) cadence forms.[39]

Barry S. Brook's book (1970a) is of importance in so far as it is a collection of papers presented at three Greater New York Chapter meetings[40] of the American Musicological Society, two of which were on the topic "Musicology and the Computer". There, Allen Forte, Lewis Lockwood, Barry S. Brook, Murray J. Gould, and many others presented research on new developments in computer-assisted music analysis.[41] These two conferences as well as the "West Virginia University Conference on Computer Applications in Music" in 1966 (Lefkoff 1967a) were the only conferences in the 1960s specifically on the topic of computer applications in music.

Concluding Remarks

A passage in Jan LaRue's article in the volume "Musicology 1960-2000" (Brook 1970a) represents a common way of thinking during the 1960s in the area of computer-assisted music analysis: "May I recommend the computer to you as an instrument without human prejudices. It has its own prejudices, numerical and procedural. But these often act as stimulants and correctives, as healthy balances and supplements to human attitudes. With this new aid, the coming generation of musicologists should develop a style analysis that is comprehensive rather than selective, broad rather than personal, and rich in musical insight." (LaRue 1970a, 197.) LaRue was certainly right in his implication that, at least up to the end of the 1960s, computer-assisted analysis of style was anything but comprehensive and rich in musical insight. Moreover, the goal of a comprehensive and inter-personal, computer-assisted analysis could not even be reached in the following decade.

Literature Published in the 1960s and Other Relevant Literature

Abraham, Gerald. 1967. "Musical Scholarship in the 20th Century," *Studies in Music* I: 1-10.

Andrus, Donald George. 1968. An Analysis of the Acoustics of Tamtam Sounds. D.M.A. dissertation. Urbana, IL: University of Illinois.

Anonymous. 1966. "Computer Programs Designed to Solve Humanistic Problems," *Computers and the Humanities* I/2 (November): 39-55.

Anonymous. 1967a. "Directory of Scholars Active," *Computers and the Humanities* I/5 (May): 178-241.

Anonymous. 1967b. "Directory of Scholars Active," *Computers and the Humanities* II/2 (November): 71-93.

---

39 Other articles in this volume (Lincoln 1970a) referring to computer-assisted music analysis (in one way or the other) are by Frederick Crane and Judith Fiehler (1970), James Gabura (1970), Barton Hudson (1970), W. Earle Hultberg (1970), Theodore Karp (1970), and Michael Kassler (1970b).

40 Two meetings took place in 1965, and the third one in 1966.

41 This research has been discussed already earlier in this essay.

Anonymous. 1968a. "Directory of Scholars Active," *Computers and the Humanities* II/5 (May): 223-250.
Anonymous. 1968b. "Directory of Scholars Active," *Computers and the Humanities* III/2 (November): 105-118.
Anonymous. 1969a. "Directory of Scholars Active," *Computers and the Humanities* III/5 (May): 280-320.
Anonymous. 1969b. "Directory of Scholars Active," *Computers and the Humanities* IV/2 (November): 125-141.
Ashford, Theodore H. A. 1967. "Analysis of Musical Relationships in Contemporary Music," *Computers and the Humanities* I/5 (May): 224.
Babbitt, Milton. 1955. "Some Aspects of Twelve-Tone Composition," *The Score and I.M.A. Magazine* 12: 53-61.
_________. 1960. "Twelve-Tone Invariants as Compositional Determinatns," *The Music Quaterly* 46: 246-259.
_________. 1961. "Set-Structure as a Compositional Determinant," *Journal of Music Theory* V/1 (Spring): 72-94.
_________. 1965. "The Use of Computers in Musicological Research," *Perspectives of New Music* III/2 (Spring-Summer): 74-83.
Baker, Robert Allen. 1963. A Statistical Analysis of the Harmonic Practice of the 18th and Early 19th Centuries. Ph.D. thesis. Champaign, IL: University of Illinois.
Baroni, Mario. 1969. "Linguaggio Musicale della Sonata a Quattro Italiana del Secolo XVI,"*Computers and the Humanities* III/5 (May): 312.
Bauer-Mengelberg, Stefan. 1968. "'The Truth, the Whole Truth, and Nothing but the Truth'," *Computer Studies in the Humanities and Verbal Behavior* I/2 (August): 52-54.
_________. 1970. "The Ford-Columbia Input Language," *Musicology and the Computer: Three Symposia*, edited by Barry S. Brook. New York: The City University of New York Press. 48-52.
Bauer-Mengelberg, Stefan, and Melvin Ferentz. 1965. "On Eleven-Interval Twelve-Tone Rows," *Perspectives of New Music* III/2 (Spring-Summer): 93-103.
Bean, Calvert. 1961. Information Theory Applied to the Analysis of a Particular Formal Process in Tonal Music. Ph.D. dissertation. Champaign, IL: University of Illinois.
Beauchamp, James W. 1967. A Computer System for Time-Variant Harmonic Analysis and Synthesis of Musical Tones. Technical Report No. 15, Electrical Engineering Publication No. 992. Urbana, IL: University of Illinois School of Music Experimental Music Studio.
Bebbington, Brian. 1968. "Folkmusic and Computers," *African Music* IV/2: 56-58.
Bengtsson, Ingmar. 1967a. "On Melody Registration and 'Mona'," *Elektronische Datenverarbeitung in der Musikwissenschaft*, edited by Harald Heckmann. Regensburg: Gustav Bosse. pp. 136-174.
_________. 1967b. "Numericode – A Code System for Thematic Incipits," *Svensk Tidskrift för Musikforskning* 49: 5-40.
_________. 1970. "Studies with the Aid of Computers of 'Music As Performed'," *IMS: Report on the Tenth Congress, Lubljana 1967*, edited by Dragotin Cvetko. Kassel: Bärenreiter. pp. 443-444.
_________. 1971. "Analysis of Rhythmic Performance," *Computers and the Humanities* V/5 (May): 310.
Bengtsson, Ingmar, Alf Gabrielsson, and Stig-Magnus Thorsén. 1969. "Empirisk Rytmforskning. En Orientering om Musikvetenskaplig Bakgrund, Utveckling och Några aktuella Projekt," *Svensk Tidskrift för Musikforskning* 51: 49-118.

Bense, Max. 1954. *Aesthetica*. Stuttgart: Deutsche Verlags-Anstalt.
__________. 1966a. "Ästhetik und Programmierung." *IBM-Nachrichten* 16: 294-296.
__________. 1966b. "Projekter til en generativ aestetik," *Dansk Musiktidsskrift* XLI: 179-82.
__________. 1969. *Einführung in die informationstheoretische Ästhetik*. Reinbek bei Hamburg: Rowohlt.
Berger, Arthur. 1964. "New Linguistic Modes and the New Theory," *Perspectives of New Music* III/1 (Autumn-Winter): 1-9.
Berlind, Gary. 1966. "Writings on the Use of Computers in Music," *College Music Symposium* 6 (1966): 143-152.
__________. 1967. "GRIPHOS: An Interim Report," *Current Musicology* V: 149-152.
__________. [n.d.]. Writings on the Use of Computers in Music. Compiled by Gary Berlind in collaboration with Barry S. Brook, Lejaren A. Hiller Jr., Jan P. LaRue, and George W. Logemann. New York: New York University, Institute for Computer Research in the Humanities. Mimeographed.
Berlind, Gary, Barry S. Brook, Charles M. Dollar, Dee F. Green, Kenneth Janda, Richard Jensen, Louis T. Milic, and Robert Zemsky. 1967. "Annual Bibliography for 1966," *Computers and the Humanities* I/4 (March): 143-156.
Berlind, Gary, and George W. Logeman. 1969. "An Algorithm for Musical Transposition," *Computer Studies in the Humanities and Verbal Behavior* II (August): 102-108.
Bernstein, Lawrence F. 1964. "Data Processing and the Thematic Index," *Fontes Artis Musicae* XI/1 (January-April): 159-165.
__________. 1967. "University of Chicago Chanson Project," *Computers and the Humanities* I/5 (May): 221.
Bernstein, Lawrence F. and Joseph P. Olive. 1969. "Computers and the 16th-century Chanson: A Pilot Project at the University of Chicago," *Computers and the Humanities* III/3 (January): 153-160.
Bernzott, Philip. 1968. Musical Analysis with Computer: Some Programs and Descriptions. M.M. thesis. Chicago Musical College.
Binkley, Thomas E. 1967. "Electronic Processing of Musical Materials," *Elektronische Datenverarbeitung in der Musikwissenschaft*, edited by Harald Heckmann. Regensburg: Gustav Bosse. pp. 1-20.
Bowles, Edmund. 1965. "Computers and Musicology," *Computers for the Humanities: A Record of the Conference Sponsored by Yale University on a Grant from IBM, January 22-23, 1965*. New Haven, CT: Yale University Press. pp. 103-108.
__________. 1970a. "Discussion," *Musicology and the Computer: Three Symposia*, edited by Barry S. Brook. New York: The City University of New York Press. pp. 37-38.
__________. 1970b. "Musicke's Handmaiden: Or Technology in the Service of the Arts," *The Computer and Music*, edited by Harry B. Lincoln. Ithaca: Cornell University Press. pp. 3-20.
__________. 1970c. "Musicology and Computers" [A Review of Harald Heckmann, *Elektronische Datenverarbeitung der Musikwissenschaft*], *Computers and the Humanities* IV/3 (January): 207-219.
Braun, P. 1964. "On a Human Movement Analyzer," *Computational Linguistics* 3: 189-204.
Brender, Maurita P., and Ronald F. Brender. 1967. "Computer Transcription and Analysis of Mid-Thirteenth Century Musical Notation," *Journal of Music Theory* XI/2 (Winter): 198-221.
Brincker, Jens. 1966a. "Kvantitativ musikanalyse," *Dansk Musiktidsskrift* XLI: 175-178.
__________. 1966b. Review of *Informationstheorie und Computermusik* by Lejaren A. Hiller, *Dansk Musiktidsskrift* XLI: 186.

_________. 1970. "Statistical Analysis of Music: An Application of Information Theory," *Svensk Tidskrift för Musikforsking* 52: 53-57.
Brook, Barry S. 1965a. "The Simplified 'Plaine and Easy Code System," *Fontes Artis Musicae* XII: 156-160.
_________. 1965b. "Utilization of Data Processing Techniques in Music Documentation," *Fontes Artis Musicae* XII (May): 112-122.
_________. 1967. "Music Bibliography and the Computer," *Papers from the West Virginia University Conference on Computer Applications in Music*, edited by Gerald Lefkoff. Morgantown: West Virginia University Library. pp. 9-27.
_________. 1969. "Style and Content Analysis in Music: The Simplified 'Plaine and Easy Code'," *The Analysis of Communication Content*, edited by George Gerbner et al. New York: John Wiley & Sons. pp. 287-296.
_________. Ed. 1970a. *Musicology and the Computer: Three Symposia*. New York: The City University of New York Press.
_________. 1970b. "Music Documentation of the Future," *Musicology and the Computer: Three Symposia*, edited by Barry S. Brook. New York: The City University of New York Press. pp. 28-36.
_________. 1970c. "The Plaine and Easie Code," *Musicology and the Computer: Three Symposia*, edited by Barry S. Brook. New York: The City University of New York Press. pp. 53-56.
Brook, Barry S., and Murray Gould. 1964. "Notating Music with Ordinary Typewriter Characters," *Fontes Artis Musicae* XI/1 (January-April): 142-159.
Brooks, Frederick P., A. L. Hopkins, P. G. Neumann, and W. V. Wright. 1957. "An Experiment in Musical Composition." *IRE Transactions on Electronic Computers* VI (September): 175-182. (An errata see in vol. 7 (1958): 60.) Reprinted in *Machine Models of Music*, edited by Stephen M. Schwanauer and David A. Levitt. Cambridge, MA: The MIT Press, 1993. pp. 23-40.
Brown, Charles T. 1968. "To Determine the Melodic Contour of a Melody," *Student Musicologists at Minnesota* III : 87-92.
Brown, Charles T., and Robert D. Oudal. 1969. "The 1968 Introductory Seminar in the Use of Computers in Musical Projects," *Student Musicologists at Minnesota* 3 (1968-1969): 87-92.
Bukharov, R. G., and M. S. Rytvinsskaya. 1962. "Simulating a Probabalistic Process Connected with a Melody," *Kazan Universitet Uchenyia Zapiski* 122: 82.
Citron, Jack. 1966. "MUSPEC," *Computers and the Humanities* I/2 (November): 52.
Cohen, Joel E. 1961. "Some Relationships Between Music and Mathematics," *Music Education Journal* 48/1 (September): 104-109.
_________. 1962. "Information Theory and Music," *Behavioral Science* VII/2 (April): 137-163.
_________. 1964. "Teorie informací a hudba," *Nové Cesty Hudby: Sborník studií o novodobých skladebných smerech a vedeckých názorech na hudbu*, edited by Eduard Herzog. Praha: Státní hudební vydavatelství. pp. 180-215.
Collins, Walter S. 1965. "A New Tool for Musicology," *Music & Letters* XLVI/2 (April): 122-125.
Crane, Frederick. 1968. "Statistical Comparison of Musical Styles," *Computers and the Humanities* II/5 (May): 244.
Crane, Frederick, and Judith Fiehler. 1970. "Numerical Methods of Comparing Musical Styles," *The Computer and Music*, edited by Harry B. Lincoln. Ithaca: Cornell University Press. pp. 209-222.

Csébfalvy, Károly, and Miklós Havass. 1965. "A Direct Computer Processing of Folk Tunes," *Computational Linguistics* 4: 125-129.

Csébfalvy, Károly, Miklós Havass, Pál Járdányi, and Lajos Vargyas. 1965. "Systematization of Tunes by Computers," *Studia Musicologica Academiae Scientiarum Hungaricae* VII/1-4: 253-257.

Curry, Jerry L. 1969. A Computer-Aided Analytical Study of Kyries in Selected Masses of Johannes Ockeghem. Ph.D. dissertation. Iowa City, IA: University of Iowa.

Czekanowska, Anna. 1969. "Zastosowanie polskicg metod statystycznych do klasyfikacji melodii ludowych," *Muzyka* [Poland] XIV/1: 3-18.

Czekanowska-Kulinska, Anna. 1970. "Polish Mathematical Methods in the Classification of Slavic Folk Songs," *IMS: Report on the Tenth Congress, Lubljana 1967*, edited by Dragotin Cvetko. Kassel: Bärenreiter. pp. 440-443.

Detlovs, Vilnis K. 1968. "O statisticeskom analize muzyki," *Latvijskij matematiceskij ezegodnik* [Riga] 3: 101-120.

Draeger, Hans Heinz. 1964. "Analysis and Synthesis of Musical Structures on the Basis of Information Theory," *Bericht über den neunten internationalen Kongress Salzburg 1964*, edited by Franz Giegling, vol. 1. Kassel: Bärenreiter. pp. 261-268.

_________. 1967. "A Quantitative Analysis of Music as Exemplified by Beethoven's Sketches for his Opus 131," *Festschrift für Walter Wiora zum 30. Dezember 1966*, edited by Ludwig Finscher and Christoph-Hellmut Mahling. Hamburg: Bärenreiter. pp. 79-85.

Egeland Hansen, Finn. 1967a. "Det gregorianske repertoire i Codex H 159 Montpellier," *Dansk Arbog for Musikforskning* V (1966-67): 181-182.

_________. 1967b. "Investigation of Tonal Properties of the Gregorian Repertory," *Computers and the Humanities* I/5 (May): 226.

_________. 1970. "Musikalsk analyse ved hjaepl af modeller," *Svensk Tidskrift för Musikforskning* 52: 50-53.

Elscheková, Alica. 1965. "General Considerations on the Classification of Folk Tunes," *Studia Musicologica Academiae Scientiarum Hungaricae* VII/1-4: 259-262.

_________. 1966. "Methods of Classification of Folk Tunes," *Journal of International Folk Music Council* XVIII: 56-76.

_________. 1969. "Technologie der Datenverarbeitung bei der Klassifizierung von Volksliedern," *Methoden der Klassifikation von Volksliedweisen*, edited by Oskár Elschek. Bratislava: Verlag der Slowakischen Akademie der Wissenschaften. pp. 93-122.

Erickson, Raymond F. 1968a. "Music Analysis and the Computer," *Journal of Music Theory* XII/2 (Winter): 240-263.

_________. 1968b. "Music Analysis and the Computer: A Report on Some Current Approaches and the Outlook for the Future," *Computers and the Humanities* III/2 (November): 87-104.

_________. 1969. "A General Purpose System for Computer Aided Musical Studies," *Journal of Music Theory* XIII/2 (Winter): 276-294.

_________. 1970a. Rhythmic Problems and Melodic Structure in Organum Purum: A Computer-Assisted Study. Ph.D. dissertation. New Haven, CT: Yale University.

_________. 1970b. "A Syntax-Directed, Changeable System for Processing Data for Music Analysis," *Computers and the Humanities* IV/5 (May): 343.

_________. 1970c. "Music and the Computer in the Sixties," *AFIPS Conference Proceedings* 36: 281-285.

Evarts, John. 1970. "Stockholm," *World of Music* XII/3: 52-56. [Report on the UNESCO meeting "Music and Technology"]

Fennelly, Brian. 1967. "A Descriptive Language for the Analysis of Electronic Music," *Perspectives of New Music* VI/1 (Autumn-Winter): 79-95.

Ferentzy, Eors N. 1965. "On Formal Music Analysis-Synthesis: Its Application in Music Education," *Computational Linguistics* 4: 107.

__________. 1966. Progress Report on the Project Analysis of Musical Styles by an Electronic Computer, Sponsored by Washington State University. Unpublished Report. Pullman, WA: Washington State University Pullman.

__________. 1967. "A Syntax-Directed Compiler to Analyze Musical Compositions and Text," *Computers and the Humanities* I/5 (May): 225.

Ferentzy, Eors N., and Miklós Havass. 1964. "Human Movement Analysis by Computer: Electronic Choreography and Composition," *Computational Linguistics* 3: 129-188.

Filip, Miroslav. 1964. "Zákonitosti vyvoja harmónie vo svetle základnych myslienok teórie informácie," *Nové Cesty Hudby* (1964): 216-233. [Summary in German: "Entwicklungsgesetzed er Harmonie im Lichte der Grundgedankend er Informationstheorie," pp. 276-277.]

Fiore, Mary E. 1967. "Harmonic Structure in Variation Movements by Anton von Webern," *Computers and the Humanities* I/5 (May): 225.

__________. 1968. "Harmonic Structure in Variation Movements by Webern," *Computers and the Humanities* II/5 (May): 243.

__________. 1970. "Webern's Use of Motive in the Piano Variations," *The Computer and Music*, edited by Harry B. Lincoln. Ithaca: Cornell University Press. pp. 115-122.

Forte, Allen. 1964. "A Theory of Set-Complexes for Music," *Journal of Music Theory* VIII/2 (Winter): 136-183.

__________. 1965. "The Domain and Relations of Set-Complex Theory," *Journal of Music Theory* IX/1 (Spring): 173-180.

__________. 1966. "A Program for the Analytic Reading of Scores," *Journal of Music Theory* X/2 (Winter): 330-364. Reprinted in *Machine Models of Music*, edited by Stephen M. Schwanauer and David A. Levitt. Cambridge, MA: The MIT Press, 1993. pp. 55-81.

__________. 1967a. "Computer-Implemented Analysis of Musical Structure," *Papers from the West Virginia University Conference on Computer Applications in Music*, edited by Gerald Lefkoff. Morgantown: West Virginia University Library. pp. 29-42.

__________. 1967b. "Music and Computing: The Present Situation," *Computers and the Humanities* II/1 (September): 32-35.

__________. 1967c. "Structure of Atonal Music," *Computers and the Humanities* II/2 (November): 86.

__________. 1967d. *Analytic Reading of Musical Scores*. Cambridge: Massachusetts Institute of Technology, April 1967.

__________. 1967e. "The Programming Language SNOBOL3: An Introduction," *Computers and the Humanities* I/5 (May): 157-163.

__________. 1967f. "Structure of Atonal Music," *Computers and the Humanities* I/5 (May): 224-225.

__________. 1970. "The Structure of Atonal Music: Practical Aspects of a Computer-Oriented Research Project," *Musicology and the Computer: Three Symposia*, edited by Barry S. Brook. New York: The City University of New York Press. pp. 10-18.

__________. 1973. *The Structure of Atonal Music*. New Haven: Yale University Press.

Frank, Helmar. 1964. *Kybernetische Analysen subjektiver Sachverhalte*. Quickborn bei Hamburg: Schnelle.

_________. 1968. *Informationsästhetik: Grundlagenprobleme und erste Anwendungen auf die mime pure*, 2nd ed. Quickborn bei Hamburg: Schnelle.

Freedman, M. David. 1967. "Analysis of Musical Instrument Tones," *Journal of the Acoustical Society of America* XLI (April): 793-806.

Fucks, Wilhelm. 1955. *Mathematische Analyse von Sprachelementen, Sprachstil und Sprache*. Köln: Westdeutscher Verlag.

_________. 1956. "Mathematical Theory of Word Formation." *Information Theory: Papers Read at a Symposium on Information Theory Held at the Royal Institution, London, September 12th to 16th, 1955*, edited by Colin Cherry. London: Butterworths Scientific Publications. pp. 154-170.

_________. 1957. "Gibt es mathematische Gesetze in Sprache und Musik?" *Umschau in Wissenschaft und Technik* 1957/2: 33-37.

_________. 1958. *Mathematische Analyse der Formalstruktur von Musik*. Köln: Westdeutscher Verlag.

_________. 1962. "Mathematische Musikanalyse und Randomfolgen. Zufall und Musik." *Gravesaner Blätter* VI: 132-145.

_________. 1963. *Mathematische Analyse von Formalstrukturen von Werken der Musik*. Köln: Westdeutscher Verlag.

_________. 1964. "Gibt es mathematische Gesetze in Sprache und Musik?" *Kybernetik*, edited by Helmar Frank, 4th ed. Frankfurt am Main: Umschau Verlag. pp. 175-187.

_________. 1968. *Nach allen Regeln der Kunst. Diagnosen über Literatur, Musik, bildende Kunst - die Werke, ihre Autoren und Schöpfer*. Stuttgart: Deutsche Verlags-Anstalt.

Fucks, Wilhelm, and Josef Lauter. 1965. *Exaktwissenschaftliche Musikanalyse*. Köln: Westdeutscher Verlag.

Fuller, Ramon Conrad. 1965. An Information Theory Analysis of Anton Webern's 'Symphonie,' opus 21 (with) 'Music for Two Channel Tape and Two Percussionists'. D.M.A. thesis. University of Illinois at Urbana Champaign.

_________. 1970. "Toward a Theory of Webernian Harmony, via Analysis with a Digital Computer," *The Computer and Music*, edited by Harry B. Lincoln. Ithaca: Cornell University Press. pp. 123-131.

Gabura, A. James. 1965. "Computer Analysis of Musical Style," *Proceedings of the 20th National Conference: Cleveland, Ohio, August 24-26, 1965*. New York: Association for Computing Machinery. pp. 303-314.

_________. 1967. Music Style Analysis by Computer. M.Sc. thesis, University of Toronto.

_________. 1970. "Musical Style Analysis by Computer," *The Computer and Music*, edited by Harry B. Lincoln. Ithaca: Cornell University Press. pp. 223-276.

Gilbert, Steven E. 1970. The Trichord: An Analytic Outlook for Twentieth-Century Music. Ph.D. dissertation. New Haven, CT: Yale University.

Goller, Gottfried. 1969. "Zur Bezeichnung der Neumen in der germanischen Choralnotation des 12. bis 14. Jahrhunderts," *Kirchenmusikalisches Jahrbuch* [Germany] LIII: 99-100.

_________. 1970. "Zur Bezeichnung der Neumen in der germanischen Choralnotation," *Bericht über den Internationalen Musikwissenschaftlichen Kongress, Leipzig, 1966*, ed. by Carl Dahlhaus, Reiner Kluge, Ernst H. Meyer, and Walter Wiora. Kassel: Bärenreiter. pp. 173-175.

Gould, Murray. 1967. "A Keypunchable Notation for the Liber Usualis," *Elektronische Datenverarbeitung in der Musikwissenschaft*, edited by Harald Heckmann. Regensburg: Gustav Bosse. pp. 25-40.

_________. 1968. “An Introduction to Computing in Music” [Review of *Papers from the West Virginia University Conference on Computer Applications in Music* by Gerald Lefkoff (Ed.)], *Computers and the Humanities* II/5 (May): 262-263.
Gould, Murray, and George W. Logemann. 1966. ALMA: An Alphanumeric Language for Music Analysis. New York University: Institute for Computer Research in the Humanities. [Los Angeles: University of California Library / Music Library, calling no. ML 432 G 734a]
Gould, Murray J., and George W. Logemann. 1970. “ALMA: Alphanumeric Language for Music Analysis,” *Musicology and the Computer: Three Symposia*, edited by Barry S. Brook. New York: The City University of New York Press. pp. 57-90.
Grauer, Viktor A . 1965. “Some Song-Style Clusters – A Preliminary Study,” *Ethnomusicology* IX/3 (September): 265-271.
Guntzenhäuser, Rul. 1962. *Ästhetisches Maß und ästhetische Information. Einführung in die Theorie G. D. Birkhoffs und die Redundanztheorie ästhetischer Prozesse*. Quickborn bei Hamburg: Schnelle.
Hanson, Jens L. 1969. An Operational Approach to Theory of Rhythm. Ph.D. dissertation. New Haven, CT: Yale University.
Hartmann, Karl L. 1962. Versuch einer mathematischen Musiklehre. Wien: Karl L. Hartmann.
Hatano, Giyoo. 1968. “Ongaku eno johoron-teki sekkin,” *Ongaku Gaku. Journal of the Japanese Musicological Society* XIV: 54-64.
Havass, Miklós. 1964. “A Simulation of Music Composition. Synthetically Composed Folkmusic,” *Computational Linguistics* 3: 107-128.
Heckmann, Harald. 1964. “Neue Methoden der Verarbeitung musikalischer Daten,” *Die Musikforschung* XVII/4: 381-383.
_________. Ed. 1967a. *Elektronische Datenverarbeitung in der Musikwissenschaft*. Regensburg: Gustav Bosse.
_________. 1967b. “Elektronische Datenverarbeitung in der Musikwissenschaft: Eine Einleitung,” *Elektronische Datenverarbeitung in der Musikwissenschaft*, edited by Harald Heckmann. Regensburg: Gustav Bosse. pp. VII-XVII.
_________. 1970. “Elektronische Datenverarbeitung in der Musikwissenschaft,” *IMS: Report on the Tenth Congress, Lubljana 1967*, edited by Dragotin Cvetko. Kassel: Bärenreiter. pp. 424-427.
_________. 1971. “Katalog ‘Deutsches Tenorlied des 16. Jahrhunderts,” *Computers and the Humanities* V/5 (May): 313-314.
_________. 1972. “Informationstheorie und Computer,” *Informatik. Vorträge anläßlich der Jahresversammlung vom 14. bis 17. Oktober 1971 zu Halle (Saale)*, edited by Joachim-Hermann Scharf. Nova Acta Leopoldina vol. 37/1, no. 206. Leipzig: Barth. pp. 619-627.
_________. 1973a. “Musik - Dokumentation, Musik - Information,” *Neue Zeitschrift für Musik* 134/8: 479-482.
_________. 1973b. “Musikwissenschaft, Dokumentation, Information,” *Musicae Scientae Collectanea. Festschrift Karl Gustav Fellerer zum 70. Geburtstag*, edited by Heinrich Hüschen. Köln. pp. 219-224.
Heike, Georg. 1961. “Informationstheorie und musikalische Komposition,” *Melos* XXVIII/9: 269-272.
Hill, George R., and Murray Gould. 1970. *A Thematic Locator for Mozart’s Works, as Listed in Koechel’s Chronologisch-Thematisches Verzeichnis*, 6th edition. Hackensack, NJ: Boonin.

Hill, George R., Murray Gould, David Noon, Hans-Rudolf Diirrenmatt, and Jan LaRue. 1969. "*A Thematic Locator for Mozart's Works as Listed in Köchel's Chronologischthematisches Verzeichnis*," *Computers and the Humanities* III/5 (May): 311-312.

Hiller, Lejaren A., Jr. 1962. Information Theory and Musical Analysis. Mimeographed. Urbana: University of Illinois, Experimental Music Studio. Technical Report No. 5, July 1962. 40 p. (University of Cincinnati Library, MUS ML 3817 .I4 no. 5)

__________. 1964. *Informationstheorie und Computermusik: Zwei Vorträge, gehalten auf den "Internationalen Ferienkursen für Neue Musik" Darmstadt 1963*. Darmstädter Beiträge zur Neuen Musik 8. Mainz: B. Schott's Söhne.

__________. 1967. Analysis and Synthesis of Musical Sounds by Analog and Digital Techniques. An Interim Progress Report to The National Science Foundation (Contract US-NSF-GK-594).

__________. 1968. Music Composed with Computer – An Historical Survey. Technical Report No. 18. Urbana, IL: University of Illinois, Experimental Music Studio.

Hiller, Lejaren A., and Calvert Bean. 1966. "Information Theory Analyses of Four Sonata Expositions," *Journal of Music Theory* X/1 (Spring): 96-137.

Hiller, Lejaren A., and James W. Beauchamp. 1965. "Research in Music with Electronics," *Science* CL: 161-169.

Hiller, Lejaren A., and James W. Beauchamp. 1968. Review of Completed and Proposed Research on Analysis and Synthesis of Musical Sounds by Analog and Digital Techniques. Technical Report No. 19. Urbana, IL: University of Illinois, Experimental Music Studio.

Hiller, Lejaren A., and Ramon Fuller. 1967. "Structure and Information in Webern's Symphonie, Op. 21," *Journal of Music Theory* XI/1 (Spring): 60-115.

Hiller, Lejaren A., and Leonard M. Isaacson. 1959. *Experimental Music. Composition with an Electronic Computer*. New York: McGraw-Hill.

Hindemith, Paul. 1945. *The Craft of Musical Composition*, translated by Arthur Mendel. rev. ed. New York, NY: Associated Music Publishers.

Hood, Mantle. 1967. "Improvisation and Music Theory of the Javanese Gamelan," *Computers and the Humanities* II/2 (September): 88.

Hoshovskyj, Vladimir. 1965. "The Experiment of Systemizing and Cataloguing Folk Tunes following the Principles of Musical Dialectology and Cybernetics," *Studia Musicologica Academiae Scientiarum Hungaricae* VII/1-4: 273-286.

Howe, Hubert S. 1965. "Some Combinatorial Properties of Pitch Structures," *Perspectives of New Music* IV/1 (Fall-Winter): 45-61.

__________. 1966. "Music and Electronics: A Report," *Perspectives of New Music* IV: 68-75.

Hudson, Barton. 1970. "Toward a Comprehensive French Chanson Catalog," *The Computer and Music*, edited by Harry B. Lincoln. Ithaca: Cornell University Press. pp. 277-287.

Hughes, Matt. 1965. Tonal Orientation in Skiabin's Preludes: An Analysis on the Basis of Information Theory. M.A. thesis. University of Texas at Austin.

Hultberg, W. Earle. 1970. "Transcription of Tablature to Standard Notation," *The Computer and Music*, edited by Harry B. Lincoln. Ithaca: Cornell University Press. pp. 289-292.

Jackson, Roland. 1966. "Harmonic Analysis," *Computers and the Humanities* I/2 (November): 52.

__________. 1970a. "Harmony before and after 1910: A Computer Comparison," *The Computer and Music*, edited by Harry B. Lincoln. Ithaca: Cornell University Press. pp. 132-146.

_________. 1970b. “The Computer as a ‘Student’ of Harmony,” *IMS: Report on the Tenth Congress, Lubljana 1967*, edited by Dragotin Cvetko. Kassel: Bärenreiter. pp. 435-440.

Jackson, Roland, and Philip Bernzott. 1966. “Harmonic Analysis with Computer – A Progress Report,” *ICRH Newsletter* I/9 (May): 3-4.

Jackson, Roland, and Philip Bernzott. 1970. “A Musical Input Language and a Sample Program for Musical Analysis,” *Musicology and the Computer: Three Symposia*, edited by Barry S. Brook. New York: The City University of New York Press. pp. 130-150.

Jammers, Ewald; Bielitz, Matthias; Bender, Iring; Ebenhoh, Wolfgang. 1970. “Das Heidelberger Programm für die elektronische Datenverarbeitung in der musikwissenschaftlichen Byzantinistik,” *Sitzungsberichte der Heidelberger Akademie der Wissenschaften, naturwissenschaftliche Klasse* II (1969-70): 3-23.

Joiner, Richard E. 1969. “Gregorian Chant,” *Computer Studies in the Humanities and Verbal Behavior* II/4 (December): 213-219.

Kamien, Roger Jaques. 1964. The Opening Sonata-Allegro Movements in a Randomly Selected Sample of Solo Keyboard Sonatas Published in the Years 1742-1774. Ph.D. dissertation. Princeton, NJ: Princeton University.

Karlina, T. P., and Vilnis K. Detlovs. 1968. “Statisticeskij analiz sekvencij v melodii,” *Latvijskij matematiceskij ezegodnik* 4: 165-173.

Karp, Theodore. 1970. “A Test for Melodic Borrowings among Notre Dame *Organa Dupla*,” *The Computer and Music*, edited by Harry B. Lincoln. Ithaca: Cornell University Press. pp. 293-295.

Kassler, Michael. 1964a. A Report of Work, Directed Toward Explication of Schenker’s Theory of Tonality, Done in Summer 1962 as the First Phase of a Project Concerned with the Applications of High-Speed Automatic Digital Computers to Music ana Musicology. Princeton, NJ: Princeton University Music Department. (Mimeographed.)

_________. 1964b. MIR – A Simple Programming Language For Musical Information Retrieval. Technical Report No. 3, Project 295D, March 1964. Princeton, New Jersey: Princeton University, Department of Music. [University of California at Berkeley: Music Library, calling no. ML 74 .4 M4 K 35 1964 MUSI]

_________. 1966. “Toward Musical Information Retrieval,” *Perspectives of New Music* IV/2 (Spring-Summer): 59-67.

_________. 1968. A Trinity of Essays. Ph.D. dissertation. Princeton, NJ: Princeton University.

_________. 1970a. “An Essay Toward Specification of a Music-Reading Machine,” *Musicology and the Computer: Three Symposia*, edited by Barry S. Brook. New York: The City University of New York Press. pp. 151-175.

_________. 1970b. “MIR – A Simple Programming Language for Musical Information Retrieval,” *The Computer and Music*, edited by Harry B. Lincoln. Ithaca: Cornell University Press. pp. 299-327.

Kawano, Hiroshi. 1969. “Ongaku-teki komyunikeishon no joho-bunseki,” *Ongaku gaku: Journal of the Japanese Musicological Society* XV/3-4: 1-21.

Kiefer, Thomas M. 1969. “Continuous Geographical Distributions of Musical Patterns: A Test Case from the Northwest Coast,” *American Anthropologist* 71/4 (August): 701-705.

Kirschenbaum, Howard. 1967. “Music Analysis by Computer,” *Music Educators Journal* 53 (February): 94-97.

Kluge, Reiner. 1967. “Faktorenanalytische Typenbestimmung an einstimmigen Volksmelodien,” *Computers and the Humanities* II/2 (November): 88-89.

_________. 1970a. "Volksliedanalyse und -systematisierung mit Hilfe eines Rechenautomaten," *Bericht über den Internationalen Musikwissenschaftlichen Kongress Leipzig 1966*, edited by Carl Dahlhause et al. Kassel: Bärenreiter. pp. 158-465.

_________. 1970b. "Zur Automatischen Quantitativen Bestimmung Musikalischer Ähnlichkeit," *IMS: Report on the Tenth Congress, Lubljana 1967*, edited by Dragotin Cvetko. Kassel: Bärenreiter. pp. 450-457.

_________. 1974a. *Faktorenanalytische Typenbestimmung an Volksliedmelodien*. Beiträge zur musikwissenschaftlichen Forschung in der DDR 6. Leipzig: Deutscher Verlag für Musik.

_________. 1974b. "Was kann die Kybernetik der Musikwissenschaft helfen?," *Report of the Eleventh Congress, Copenhagen, 1972*, edited by Henrik Glahn, Søren Sørensen, and Peter Ryom. Copenhagen: Edition W. Hansen. pp. 486-495.

Knopoff, Leon. 1965. " Some Technological Advances in Musical Analysis," *Studia Musicologica Academiae Scientiarum Hungaricae* VII/1-4: 301-307.

_________. 1966. "A Progress Report on an Experiment in Musical Synthesis," *Selected Reports* I/1: 49-60 [Los Angeles: University of California, Institute of Ethnomusicology].

Kobrin, Edward G., and Theodore H. A. Ashford. 1968. "A Solution to the Problems of Vertical Serialization," *Perspectives of New Music* VI/2 (Spring-Summer): 119-124.

Kolinski, Mieczyslaw. 1965a. "The General Dierction of Melodic Movement," *Ethnomusicology* IX/3 (September): 240-264.

_________. 1965b. "The Structure of Melodic Movement - A New Method of Analysis (revised version)," *Studies in Ethnomusicology* 2: 96-120.

Kostka, Stephan M. 1969a. The Hindemith String Quartetts: A Computer-Assisted Study of Selected Aspects of Style. Ph.D. dissertation. Madison, WI: University of Wisconsin.

_________. 1969b. "Statistics in Style Research," *Computers and the Humanities* III/5 (May): 310.

_________. 1971. "Recent Developments in Computer-Assisted Musical Scholarship," *Computers and the Humanities* VI/1 (September): 15-21.

_________. 1974. *A Bibliography of Computer Applications in Music*. Hackensack, NJ: Joseph Boonin.

_________. 1984. The M-PARC System for Musical Encoding (Mnemonic Pitch and Rhythm Code, Version 3). Unpublished Manuscript. Austin, TX: The University of Texas at Austin, Department of Music.

Kupper, Hubert. 1966. "Computer and Musikwissenschaft," *IBM Nachrichten* XVI/180 (December): 297-303.

_________. 1970a. *Statistische Untersuchungen zur Modusstruktur der Gregorianik*. Regensburg: Bosse.

_________. 1970b. *Computer und musikalische Kompositionen*. Braunschweig: Vieweg.

Lachartre, Nicole. 1969. "Les musiques artificielles," *Diagrammes du Monde* 146 (April): 1-96.

Ladner, Robert, Jr. 1968. "Computer Analysis of Music Forms," *Music Journal* 26 (October): 33, 58.

LaRue, Jan. 1966. "The Computer Seminar at Binghamton: A Report," *Notes* XXIII: 236-240.

_________. 1967. "Two Problems in Music Analysis: The Computer Lends a Hand," *Computers in Humanistic Research*, edited by Edmund A. Bowles. Englewood Cliffs: Prentice Hall. pp. 194-203.

_________. 1968. "Two Options for Input of Thematic Incipits," *Institute for Computer Research in the Humanities Newsletter* IV/3 (November): 3-6.

_________. 1970a. "New Directions for Style Analysis," *Musicology and the Computer: Three Symposia*, edited by Barry S. Brook. New York: The City University of New York Press. pp. 194-197.
_________. 1970b. "Some Computer Aids to Musicology," *Bericht über den Internationalen Musikwissenschaftlichen Kongress Leipzig 1966*, edited by Carl Dahlhause et al. Kassel: Bärenreiter. pp. 466-469.
_________. 1970c. "Future Technological Directions," *IMS: Report on the Tenth Congress, Lubljana 1967*, edited by Dragotin Cvetko. Kassel: Bärenreiter. pp. 457-460.
LaRue, Jan, and Marian W. Cobin. 1967. "The Ruge-Seignelay Catalogue: An Exercise in Automated Entries," *Elektronische Datenverarbeitung in der Musikwissenschaft*, edited by Harald Heckmann. Regensburg: Gustav Bosse. pp. 41-56.
LaRue, Jan, and Murray Gould. 1969. "Correlational Analysis to Establish Authenticity of 18th-Century Symphonies," *Computers and the Humanities* III/5 (May): 311.
LaRue, Jan, and George W. Logemann. 1966. "EDP for Thematic Catalogues," *Notes* XXII: 1179-1186.
Lauter, Josef, and Roland Mix. 1967. "The Information Content of Music," *Nachrichtentechnische Zeitschrift* XX/2: 86-89.
Lefkoff, Gerald. Ed. 1967a. *Papers from the West Virginia University Conference on Computer Applications in Music*. Morgantown: West Virginia University Library.
_________. 1967b. "Computers and the Study of Musical Style," *Papers from the West Virginia University Conference on Computer Applications in Music*, edited by Gerald Lefkoff. Morgantown: West Virginia University Library. pp. 43-61.
_________. 1970. "Automated Discovery of Similar Segments in the Forty-eight Permutations of a Twelve-Tone Row," *The Computer and Music*, edited by Harry B. Lincoln. Ithaca: Cornell University Press. pp. 147-153.
Lehr, Mangham D. 1968. "Canon One," *Computers and the Humanities* II/5 (May): 244.
Lewin, David. 1968. "Some Applications of Communication Theory to the Study of Twelve-Tone Music," *Journal of Music Theory* 12/1 (Spring): 50-84.
Lewis, David Sheldon. 1968. Two Parameters of Melodic Line as Stylistic Discriminants. Ph.D. dissertation. Morgantown, WV: West Virginia University.
Lieberman, Fredric. 1970. "Computer-Aided Analysis of Javanese Music," *The Computer and Music*, edited by Harry B. Lincoln. Ithaca: Cornell University Press. pp. 181-192.
Lincoln, Harry B. 1966. "Incipit Interval Sequence Program," *Computers and the Humanities* I/2 (November): 52.
_________. 1967a. "Musicology and the Computer: The Thematic Index," *Computers in Humanistic Research*, edited by Edmund A. Bowles. Englewood Cliffs: PrenticeHall. pp. 184-193.
_________. 1967b. "Some Criteria and Techniques for Developing Computerized Thematic Indices," *Elektronische Datenverarbeitung in der Musikwissenschaft*, edited by Harald Heckmann. Regensburg: Gustav Bosse. pp. 57-62.
_________. 1967c. "Thematic Index of Sixteenth-Century Italian Music," *Computers and the Humanities* II/2 (November): 86.
_________. 1968a. "The Thematic Index: A Computer Application to Musicology," *Computers and the Humanities* II/5 (May): 215-220.
_________. 1968b. Development of Computerized Techniques in Music Research with Emphasis on the Thematic Index. Final Report, Project No. 7-8276, Grant No. OEG 1-7-078272-3898. Washington, DC: Office of Education, U.S. Department of Health, Education, and Welware.

__________. 1968c. "Thematic Index of Sixteenth-Century Italian Music," *Computers and the Humanities* II/5 (May): 243.

__________. 1969a. "A Computer Application in Musicology: The Thematic Index," *Information Processing 68. Proceedings of the IFIP Congress 1968*, edited by A. J. H. Morrel. Amsterdam: North Holland. pp. 957-961.

__________. 1969b. Development of Computerized Techniques in Music Research with Emphasis on the Thematic Index. Washington: Office of Education, U.S. Department of Health, Education, and Welware.

__________. 1969c. "The computer and music research: Prospects and problems," *Bulletin of the Council for Research in Music Education* 18 (Fall): 1-9.

__________. 1969d. "A Computer Application in Musicology: The Thematic Index," *Information Processing* 68: 957-961.

__________. Ed. 1970a. *The Computer and Music*. Ithaca: Cornell University Press.

__________. 1970b. "The Current State of Music Research and the Computer," *Computer and the Humanities* V/1 (September): 29-36.

__________. 1970c. "Thematic Indexing by Computer, Including Development of Necessary Hardware to Permit Printing of Music by Computer," *Computers and the Humanities* V/2 (November): 109-110.

__________. 1970d. A Study of Computer Techniques for Music Research. Final Report, Project No. 9-B-101, Grant No. OEG-2-9-420101-1067. Washington, DC: Office of Education, U.S. Department of Health, Education and Welware, Office of Education, Bureau of Research.

__________. 1970e. "Teaching Computer Applications in Musicology," *IBM Symposium on Introducing the Computer into the Humanities* [Document G 320-1044-0]. Poughkeepsie, NY: IBM. pp. 67-71.

Lockwood, Lewis. 1966. "MIR ('Musical Information Retrieval')," *Computers and the Humanities* I/2 (November): 51.

__________. 1970a. "A Stylistic Investigation of the Masses of Josquin Desprez with the Aid of the Computer: a Progress Report," *Musicology and the Computer: Three Symposia*, edited by Barry S. Brook. New York: The City University of New York Press. pp. 19-27.

__________. 1970b. "Computer Assistance in the Investigation of Accidentals in Renaissance Music," *IMS: Report on the Tenth Congress, Lubljana 1967*, edited by Dragotin Cvetko. Kassel: Bärenreiter. pp. 444-449.

Logemann, George W. 1966a. "Prepare Music Input Data," *Computers and the Humanities* I/2 (November): 51.

__________. 1966b. "Harmonic and Time-line Input and Statistics," *Computers and the Humanities* I/2 (November): 51-52.

__________. 1967a. "The Canons in the Musical Offering of J. S. Bach: An Example of Computational Musicology," *Elektronische Datenverarbeitung in der Musikwissenschaft*, edited by Harald Heckmann. Regensburg: Gustav Bosse. pp. 63-87.

__________. 1967b. "MUSE: A Syntax-Directed System for Music Analysis," *Computers and the Humanities* I/5 (May): 224.

Lomax, Alan. 1962. "Song Structure and Social Structure." *Ethnology* I: 425-451.

__________. 1968. *Folk Song Style and culture*. Washington, D.C.: American Association for the Advancement of Science.

Lombardi, Carlo. 1967. "Investigation of Style of Keyboard Composition of Ruttini and Haydn," *Computers and the Humanities* I/5 (May): 226-227.

Lott, William Loyd. 1968. Arabic 1620: An Analysis and Procedure for Composing Computer Music. M.M. thesis. Denton, TX: North Texas State University.

Mala, Hana. 1967. "Statistická srovnávací analyza sboru Leose Janácka a moravskych lidovych písní," *Hudebni Veda* IV/4: 602-627.

Mason, Robert M. 1969a. "An Encoding Algorithm and Tables for the Digital Analysis of Harmony I," *Journal of Research in Music Education* 17/3 (Autumn): 286-300.

_________. 1969b. "An Encoding Algorithm and Tables for the Digital Analysis of Harmony II," *Journal of Research in Music Education* 17/4 (Winter): 369-387.

Mathews, Max. V. 1969. *The Technology of Computer Music*. Cambridge, MA: The M.I.T. Press.

Mendel, Arthur. 1969. "Some Preliminary Attempts at Computer-Assisted Style Analysis in Music," *Computers and the Humanities* IV/1 (September): 41-52.

Mendel, Arthur, and Lewis Lockwood. 1967. "Music Information Retrieval," *Computers and the Humanities* I/5 (May): 226.

Meylan, Raymond. 1965. "Utilization des Calculatrices Electroniques pour la comparaison Interne du Repertoire des Basses Danses de Quinzi," *Fontes Artis Musicae* 12 (May): 128-134.

_________. 1966. "Recherche de Parents parmi les Basses Danses du Quinzi," *Acta Musicologica* 38 (January): 46-66.

_________. 1967. "Symbolisierung einer Melodie auf Lochkarten," *Elektronische Datenverarbeitung in der Musikwissenschaft*, edited by Harald Heckmann. Regensburg: Gustav Bosse. pp. 21-24.

_________. 1968. *L'enigme de la musique des basses danses du quinzième siècle*. Publications de la Societe Suisse de Musicologie. Bern: Haupt.

_________. 1970. "Teorie de la Centonisation," *IMS: Report on the Tenth Congress, Lubljana 1967*, edited by Dragotin Cvetko. Kassel: Bärenreiter. pp. 427-430.

Mix, Roland. 1967. "Die Entropieabnahme bei Abhängigkeit zwischen mehreren simultanen Informationsquellen und bei Übergang zu Markoff-Ketten höherer Ordnung, untersucht an musikalischen Beispielen," *Theorien zur Formalanalyse mehrstimmiger Musik*, by Walter Reckziegel. Köln: Westdeutscher Verlag. pp. 39-80.

Moles, Abraham A. 1962. "Das neue Verhältnis zwischen Musik und Mathematik," *Gravesaner Blätter* VI: 98-103.

_________. 1964. "Uvedení do soucasného stavu hudby," *Nové Cesty Hudby*: 36-53.

_________. 1966. *Information Theory and Esthetic Perception*, translated by Joel E. Cohen. Urbana: University of Illinois Press.

Morton, Ian A. 1967. "FORTRAN Music Programs Involving Numerically Related Tones," *Computers and the Humanities* II/2 (November): 87-88.

Morton, Ian, and John Lofstedt. 1970. "FORTRAN Music Programs Involving Numerically Related Tones," *The Computer and Music*, edited by Harry B. Lincoln. Ithaca: Cornell University Press. pp. 154-162.

Oudal, Robert D. 1969. "The 1968 Introductory Seminar in the Use of Computers in Musical Projects: A Summary Report of Reactions, Frustrations, and Achievements," *Student Musicologists at Minnesota* III (1968-69): 66-109.

Pape, U. 1969. "Ein Verfahren zur Verschlüsselung und Symbolisierung von Kompositionen in Hinblick auf eine Musikanalyse mit EDV-Anlagen," *Elektronische Datenverarbeitung* XI (July): 342-345.

Paisley, William J. 1964. "Identifying the Unknown Communicator in Painting, Literature and Music: the Significance of Minor Encoding Habits," *Journal of Communication* XIV/4 (December): 219-237.

_________. 1969. "Studying 'Style' as Deviation from Encoding Norms," *The Analysis of Communication Content. Developments in Scientific Theories and Computer Techniques*, edited by George Gerbner, Ole R. Holsti, Klaus Krippendorff, William J. Paisley and Philip J. Stone. New York: Wiley & Sons. pp. 133-146.

Pederson, Donald Margedo. 1968. Some Technique for Computer-Aided Analysis of Musical Scores. Ph.D. dissertation. Iowa City, IA: The University of Iowa.

Pikler, Andrew G. 1960. "Automatische Bewertung von Musikaufführungen," *Gravesaner Blätter* V: 137-139.

Piotrowska, Maria. 1968. Wybrane aspekty problematyki Jeux venitiens jako wstep do badan strukturalnych nad tworczoscia Witolda Lutoslawskiego. M.A. thesis. Warszawa, Poland: University of Warszawa.

Pruett, James W. 1966. "The Harpur College Music-Computer Seminar: A Report," *Computers and the Humanities* I/2 (November): 34-38.

_________. 1968. Review of *Papers of the West Virginia University Conference on Computer Applications in Music* by Gerald Lefkoff (Ed.), *Computer Studies in the Humanities and Verbal Behavior* I/3 (October): 155.

Pruslin, Dennis Howard. 1966. Automatic Recognition of Sheet Music. Sc.D. dissertation. Boston, MA: Massachusetts Institute of Technology.

Pulkert, Oldrich. 1967. "Hudba, samocinne pocitace a jine novinky" ["Music, Computers, and Other Novelties"], *Hudebni veda* 3: 479-484.

Randall, J. K. 1964. "A Report from Princeton," *Perspectives of New Music* III (Spring): 84-92.

_________. 1967. "Three Lectures to Scientists," *Perspectives of New Music* V/2 (Spring-Summer): 124-140.

Raskin, Jeffrey F. 1967. A Hardware Independent Computer Drawing System Using List Structured Modeling: The Quick-Draw Graphics Systems. M.S. thesis. State College, PA: Pennsylvania State University.

Reckziegel, Walter. 1967a. *Theorien zur Formalanalyse mehrstimmiger Musik*. Köln: Westdeutscher Verlag.

_________. 1967b. "Musikanalyse - eine exakte Wissenschaft?" *Elektronische Datenverarbeitung in der Musikwissenschaft*, edited by Harald Heckmann. Regensburg: Bosse, pp. 203-224.

_________. 1967c. "Musikanalyse und Wissenschaft." *Studia Musicologica Academiae Scientiarum Hungaricae* IX/1-2: 163-186.

_________. 1967d. "Die Notenschrift im Computer dargestellt," *Studia Musicologica Academiae Scientiarum Hungaricae* IX/3-4: 395-406.

_________. 1968. "Musik im Datenspeicher," *Die Musikforschung* XXI/4 (October-December): 427-438.

_________. 1970. "Ein Subjektives Tempomaß," *Bericht über den Internationalen Musikwissenschaftlichen Kongress Leipzig 1966*, edited by Carl Dahlhause et al. Kassel: Bärenreiter. pp. 457-458.

Regener, Eric. 1967a. "A Multiple-Pass Transcription and a System for Music Analysis by Computer," *Elektronische Datenverarbeitung in der Musikwissenschaft*, edited by Harald Heckmann. Regensburg: Gustav Bosse. pp. 89-102.

_________. 1967b. "Layered Music-Theoretic Systems," *Perspectives of New Music* VI/1 (Autumn-Winter): 52-62.

Robison, Brian. 1995. "Category Structures and Fuzzy Sets," *Music Theory Online* I/5.

Robison, Tobias D. [n.d.]. A Short Description of the MIR Compiler. Princeton, NJ: Princeton University Music Department.

__________. 1967. “IML-MIR: A Data-Processing System for the Analysis of Music,” *Elektronische Datenverarbeitung in der Musikwissenschaft*, edited by Harald Heckmann. Regensburg: Bosse. pp. 103-135.

Roller, Gilbert H. 1964. The Development of the Methods for Analysis of Musical Composition and for the Formation of a Symmetrical Twelve-tone Row Using the Electronic Digital Computer. Ph.D. dissertation. East Lansing, MI: Michigan State University.

__________. 1965. “Development of a Method for Analysis of Musical Compositions Using an Electronic Digital Computer,” *Journal of Research in Music Education* XIII/4 (Winter): 249-252.

Robison, Tobias D. 1967. “IML-MIR: A Data-Processing System for the Analysis of Music,” *Elektronische Datenverarbeitung in der Musikwissenschaft*, edited by Harald Heckmann. Regensburg: Gustav Bosse. pp. 103-135.

Rothgeb, John. 1966. “Some Uses of Mathematical Concepts in Theories of Music,” *Journal of Music Theory* X/2 (Winter): 200-215.

__________. 1967. “Theories of Tonal Bass Harmonization,” *Computers and the Humanities* II/2 (November): 87.

__________. 1968a. “Theories of Tonal Bass Harmonization,” *Computers and the Humanities* II/5 (May): 243.

__________. 1968b. Harmonizing the Unfigured Bass: A Computational Study. Ph.D. dissertation. New Haven, CT: Yale University.

__________. 1969. “Simulating Musical Skills by Digital Computer,” IEEE Transactions on Computers. Reprinted in *Machine Models of Music*, edited by Stephen M. Schwanauer and David A. Levitt. Cambridge, MA: The MIT Press, 1993. pp. 156-164.

Rubenstein, Nancy Ordelheide. 1969. A Fortran Computer Program for Transcribing Franconian Rhythm. Ph.D. dissertation. St Louis, MO: Washington University.

Sands, Alyce E., et al. 1968. “Annual Bibliography for 1967,” *Computers and the Humanities* II/4 (March): 159-176.

Sands, Alyce E., et al. 1969. “Annual Bibliography for 1968,” *Computers and the Humanities* III/4 (March): 211-224.

Schiødt, Nanna. 1965. “Data Processing Applied to Byzantine Chant,” *Fontes Artis Musicae* XII/2-3: 122-123.

Schiødt, Nanna, and Bjarner Svejgaard. 1967. “Application of Computer Technique to the Analysis of Byzantine Sticherarion Melodies,” *Elektronische Datenverarbeitung in der Musikwissenschaft*, edited by Harald Heckmann. Regensburg: Gustav Bosse. pp. 187-201.

Schot, Joanna Wood. 1962. “Review of *Experimental Music Composition with an Electronic Computer*, by Lejaren Hiller, Jr., and Leonard M. Isaacson,” *Mathematics of Computation* 16/80 (October): 507-508.

Schüler, Nico. 2005. “Reflections on the History of Computer-Assisted Music Analysis I: Predecessors and the Beginnings,” *Musicological Annual* XXXXI/1: 31-43.

__________. 2006. “Reflections on the History of Computer-Assisted Music Analysis II: The 1960s,” *Musicological Annual* [Ljubljana, Slovenia] XLII/1: 5-24.

Sellek, John. 1968. “Music Information Retrieval,” *Computers and the Humanities* III/2 (November): 112.

__________. 1969. “Music Information Retrieval,” *Computers and the Humanities* III/5 (May): 310.

__________. 1970. “Musical Information Retrieval (MIR),” *Computers and the Humanities* V/2 (November): 110.

Sellek, John, and Roger Bakeman. 1965. "Procedures for the Analysis of Form: Two Computer Applications," *Journal of Music Theory* IX/2 (Winter): 281-293.
Simon, Herbert A., and Richard K. Summer. 1968. "Pattern in Music," *Formal Representation of Human Judgement*, edited by B. Kleinmuntz. New York: Wiley. pp. 219-251. Reprinted in *Machine Models of Music*, edited by Stephen M. Schwanauer and David A. Levitt. Cambridge, MA: The MIT Press, 1993. pp. 83-110.
Stacy, William B. 1969. Style and Register as Correlated Factors in the Horn Parts of Selected Symphonies by Joseph Haydn. M.A. thesis. Chapel Hill, NC: University of North Carolina.
Stahl, V. 1964. Informationswissenschaft und Musikanalyse," *Grundlagenstudien aus Kybernetik und Geisteswissenschaft* 5: 51-58.
Stockmann, Doris. 1969a. "Elektronische Datenverarbeitung in der Ethnologie und den ihr nahestehenden Wissenschaften," *Deutsches Jahrbuch für Volkskunde* XV: 134-158.
_________. 1969b. "Zur Arbeit der Study Group of Folk Music Systematization des IFMC," *Analyse und Klassifikation von Volksmelodien : Bericht über die 3. Arbeitstagung der Study Group of Folk Music Systematization beim International Folk Music Council vom 24. bis 28. Oktober 1967 in Radziejowice*, edited by Doris Stockmann and Jan Steszewski. Krakow : Polskie Wydawnictwo Muzyczne. pp. 9-30.
Strang, Gerald. 1966. "Computer Music: Analysis, Synthesis, and Composition," *Journal of the Acoustical Society of America* XXXIX: 1245.
Suchoff, Benjamin. 1967a. "Computer Applications to Bartók's Serbo-Croatian Material," *Tempo* 80 (Spring): 15-19.
_________. 1967b. "Computer Applications to Béla Bartók's Serbo-Croatian Material," *Computers and the Humanities* II/2 (November): 88.
_________. 1968a. "Bartók, Ethnomusicology, and the Computer," *Institute for Computer Research in the Humanities Newsletter* IV/4 (December): 3-6.
_________. 1968b. "Computerized Folk Song Research and the Problem of Variants," *Computers and the Humanities* II/4 (March): 155-158.
_________. 1969a. "Some Problems in Computer-Oriented Bartokian Ethnomusicology," *Ethnomusicology* XIII/3 (September): 489-497.
_________. 1969b. "A Computerized Data Bank of Musical and Textual Information on Bartok's Six String Quartets," *Computers and the Humanities* III/5 (May): 311.
_________. 1970a. "Computer-Oriented Comparative Musicology," *The Computer and Music*, edited by Harry B. Lincoln. Ithaca: Cornell University Press. pp. 193-206.
_________. 1970b. "Aplicarea calculatorelor elektronice la etnomuzicologia Bartokiana," *Musica* XI (November): 10-14.
_________. 1970c. "A Bartoki nepzenekutatas es az elektronikus szamitogepeg," *Muzsika* XIII (July): 6-8; (August): 4-6.
_________. 1971. "The Computer and Bartók Research in America," *Journal of Research in Music Education* XIX/1 (Spring): 3-16.
Suchoff, Benjamin, and Jack Heller. 1970. "Studies Relating to Automation of Bartók Archives," *Computers and the Humanities* V/2 (November): 110.
Suchoff, Benjamin, and Jack Heller. 1971. "Studies Relating to Automatization of Bartók Archives," *Computers and the Humanities* V/5 (May): 309-310.
Suess, John G. 1967. "A Pilot Study on 'Rhythmic Levels'," *Computers and the Humanities* I/5 (May): 226.
Sychra, Antonín. 1964. "Hudba a Kybernetika," *Nové Cestu Hudby* I (1964): 234-267. [Summary in German: "Musik und Kybernetik," pp. 278-279.]

_________. 1965. "Möglichkeiten der Anwendung der Kybernetik und der Informationstheorie in der marxistischen Musikwissenschaft," *Beiträge zur Musikwissenschaft* VII/4: 402-407.

_________. 1970. "Die Anwendung der Kybernetik und der Informations-Theorie in der Marxistischen Ästhetik," *Beiträge zur Musikwissenschaft* XII/2: 83-108.

Teitelbaum, Richard. 1965. "Intervallic Relations in Atonal Music," *Journal of Music Theory* IX/1 (Spring): 72-127.

Wenker, Jerome R. 1964. A Computational Method for the Analysis of Anglo-American Folksongs. M.A. thesis. Bloomington, IN: Indiana University.

_________. 1968. "A Music Compiler for Musicologists and Ethnomusicology," *Computers and the Humanities* II/5 (May): 244.

_________. 1969. "An Analytic Approach to Folk Music," *Computers and the Humanities* IV/2 (November): 138.

_________. 1970. "A Computer Oriented Music Notation Including Ethnomusicological Symbols," *Musicology and the Computer: Three Symposia*, edited by Barry S. Brook. New York: The City University of New York Press. pp. 91-129.

Willis, Thomas Creighton. 1966. Music in Orchestra Hall: A Pilot Study in the Use of Computers and Other Data Processing Equipment for Research in the History of Music Performance. Ph.D. dissertation. Evanston, IL: Northwestern University.

Wilson, Dean C. 1967. An Analytical and Statistical Study of the Harmony in Carl Nielsen's Six Symphonies. Ph.D. dissertation. East Lansing, MI: Michigan State University.

Winckel, Fritz. 1964. "Die informationstheoretische Analyse musikalischer Strukturen," *Die Musikforschung* XVII/1: 1-14.

_________. 1967. "Neue Wege der mathematischen Analyse von Musikstrukturen," *Wiener Akademie Festschrift*. Wien: Lafite. pp. 78-88.

Winograd, Terry. 1968. "Linguistics and the Computer Analysis of Tonal Harmony," *Journal of Music Theory* XII/1 (Spring): 2-49. Reprinted in *Machine Models of Music*, edited by Stephen M. Schwanauer and David A. Levitt. Cambridge, MA: The MIT Press, 1993. pp. 113-153.

Wittlich, Gary E. 1969. "Programming a Computer for Musical Analysis," *Your Musical Cue* V/6 (April): 3-13.

Youngblood, Joseph E. 1958. "Style as Information." *Journal of Music Theory* II/1 (April): 24-35.

_________. 1960. Music and Language: Some Related Analytical Techniques. Ph.D. disseration. Bloomington, IN: Indiana University.

_________. 1967. "Root Progression and Composer Identification," *Computers and the Humanities* II/2 (November): 87.

_________. 1970. "Root Progressions and Composer Identification," *The Computer and Music*, edited by Harry B. Lincoln. Ithaca: Cornell University Press. pp. 172-178.

Zaripov, Rudolf K. 1963. *Kibernetica i Muzyka*. Moscow: Znanie.

_________. 1969. "'Cybernetics and Music,' translated from the Russion by J. G. K. Russel, with commentary by Michael KASSLER," *Perspectives of New Music*, VII/2 (Spring-Summer): 115-154.

_________. 1971. *Kibernetica i Muzyka*. Moscow: Nauka.

Zimmerman, Franklin B. 1966. "Melodic Indexing for General and Specialized Use," *Notes* XXII: 1187-1192.

Computer-Assisted Music Analysis in the 1970s

From its beginning, computer-assisted music analysis was frequently used in folk song research. The statistical methods used to analyze art music did not differ from those that were most commonly applied to the analysis of folk songs. However, folk music is smaller in scope and less complex, often involving only a single voice. These are the main reasons computer-assisted analysis continued to be centered on folk songs up to the end of the 1970s, even though computers became more and more powerful, easily capable of handling the greater complexity of multi-part art music.

Many approaches of computer-assisted analysis, applied to folk songs, followed Bartók's methods of analysis and classification. Bartók's cataloging of East-European melodies not only was based on melody and text incipits, but also on different inner-musical characteristics. Bartók's methods of classification were then further developed by Alica Elschekova (1966, 1975) and Ludwig Bielawski (1973). Hereby, 'classification' means "the division of a great variety [of songs] into sub-groups on the basis of similarity with regard to certain characteristics and the arrangement of the sub-groups"[1] (Jesser 1991, 39).[2] The main focus of computer-assisted analysis of folk music was the search for rules that put melodies into a specific category and the search for procedures that determined melodic variants. This, in turn, led to the development of analytical methods that investigated single or combined characteristics of music.

Dalia Cohen and Ruth Katz (1974, 1977), for instance, analyzed Arabic and Israeli folk songs, attempting to construct a stylistic comparison. Calculations included pitch frequencies and their relation to specific modes (major, Dorian, Mixolydian, and hedjaz), transition frequencies, frequencies of certain tone groupings, and pitch distributions in certain contexts of the songs (opening notes, final notes, phrase endings). Furthermore, the characteristics related to style included tone durations and rhythmic groupings. Finally, the occurrences of certain musical characteristics were matched with each other to find specific correlations. Findings of this research were discriminations of songs in different modes, e.g. with regard to the existence of non-immediate repetition, the loca-

1 ". . . das Einteilen einer Vielfalt in Unterabteilungen aufgrund von Ähnlichkeit in bestimmten Eigenschaften und das Ordnen der so gewonnenen Gruppen".

2 The problem of similarity of musical structures cannot be discussed here, because it goes far beyond the question of using the computer as an analytical tool. Instead, it must be referred to such extensive and specialized publications like Kluge 1974a, Steinbeck 1982, and Jesser 1991. See also the literature cited in these monographs. In Jesser 1991, see also detailed comments and references regarding classification of melodies in general and regarding rules to bring the melodies in a specific order.

tion of the *finalis*, the appearance of upbeats, the existence of exceptional meters, the appearance of specific metric patterns, the maximum number of time values, the maximum proportion between the longest and the shortest note, etc. Cohen's and Katz' approach was successful, or at least has not been falsified up to this point, because of the combination of many musical characteristics and the calculation of correlations between them.

Deborah and Philip Scherrer (1971) developed a measurement of melodic variation by correlating melodic contour with rhythmic movement. The degree of 'alikeness' between two graphs of melodic motion was calculated, whereby a 'lag' could shift the graphs horizontally to avoid calculation errors in case of differences in tone durations between the two melodies. Thus, the computer program[3] was able to calculate correlation coefficients of the contour of two melodies, even if the rhythmic structures of the two melodies were very divergent.

With regard to the computer-assisted analysis of *art music*, one important project of the 1970s was Dorothy Susan Gross' dissertation research and her subsequent investigations. Her dissertation (Gross 1975a) was more or less 'only' a *description* of a new "set of computer programs to aid in music analysis"[4], which had the goal "to duplicate the more routine aspects of analysis" (Ibid., 165). Since Gross' research was not primarily directed at analyzing a great number of compositions, the value of her research should be seen in her methodological ideas and in the potentials as well as the structure of the programs. The latter will be described here in more detail, as they were unique at the time for their complexity and interactivity. The following lists of procedures and "switches"[5] also show the great variety of characteristics analyzed. The software included the following programs:

- Linear Grouping Program (looking for linear patterns formed by up to 12 consecutive events in the same voice),
- Vertical Grouping Program (listing and counting the vertical structures in a piece of music without identifying them),

3 The computer program was written in FORTRAN IV. The computer used was the CDC 6600 computer at the Space Science Laboratory of the University of California.

4 The CAL SNOBOL programs were written for a CDC 6600 computer. The music was encoded with MUSTRAN; besides tone duration and pitch, this alphanumerical code also included all the dynamic and articulation markings as well as descriptive words. The software included programs for translating the input data (i.e., music, encoded in MUSTRAN) into an internal numerical code (on which the calculations were based) and for checking the data for errors. The 'dialog' between user and computer was realized mostly via punched cards. A later version was developed in SPITBOL for an IBM 370/168 computer; see Gross 1975b and 1981 (which are still only *descriptions* of the programs without presenting fundamental analytical, and musicologically useful, results, based on an acceptable amount of compositions).

5 Those "switches" would select one of two sets of instructions.

- Program for Thematic Analysis (searching for themes submitted by the user),
- Program for Harmonic and Set Analysis (labeling the chords [roots and quality][6] and/or sets in a piece, using the list of groups from the Vertical Grouping Program as reference), and
- Program for cumulative counting (accumulating data from two or more pieces).

Each program used switches for specifying and 'individualizing' the analytical process.[7] Switches of the "Linear Grouping Program" comprised

- interval calculations (included; not included; diatonic; measured upwards in semitones),
- rhythmic and metric calculations (disregard rhythmic positions; calculate rhythmic positions; calculate metric positions),
- minimum number of occurrences in order for a pattern to be printed, parameter to be grouped (pitch; rhythm; articulation; dynamics; chords; sets),
- inversion and retrograde (no consideration of both; scan for inversions; scan for inversions, retrogrades, and retrograde inversions),
- setting the minimum number of occurrences lower, for patterns found in the top voice in order to be printed out (or count equally),
- treatment of rests and repeated notes (no elision over rests or repeated notes; ignoring rests and repetitions of a note; ignoring deviations of a certain number of semitones from the previous note),
- largest number of notes in a group,
- punching cards for the cumulative counting program (no cards; punching captions and information; punching information). (Ibid., 77.)

Switches of the "Vertical Grouping Program" comprised

- margins (in beats and/or fractions of beats),
- minimum number of occurrences in order for a pattern to be printed,
- ordering of groups (unordered groups; ordered groups of struck notes; ordered groups of sounding notes),
- parameters to be printed (pitch; rhythms; articulation; dynamics),
- storing results for use in the "Harmonic and Set Analysis Program" (yes; no),

---

6 Incomplete chords, which could not be identified, were labeled "ambiguous". (Gross 1975a, 109.)

7 These user-controlled switches represent a feature, developed mainly in the 1970s for a rather controlled dialog between analyst and computer program. Unfortunately, most descriptions of music analysis programs did not include such details, so that a reconstruction of the history of this methodological feature is not possible.

- octave reduction of pitches (yes; no),
- interval calculation (yes; no),
- punching cards for the "Cumulative Counting Program" (no cards; punch captions and information; punch information). (Ibid., 88.)

The "Thematic Analysis Program" had switches for

- interval calculations (included; not included; diatonic; measured upward in semitones),
- rhythmic and metric calculation (disregard rhythmic positions; calculate rhythmic positions; calculate metric positions),
- parameter to be scanned (pitch),
- treatment of rests and repeated notes (no elision over rests or repeated notes; ignoring rests and repetitions; ignoring deviations of a certain number of semitones from the previous note). (Ibid., 101.)

Switches of the "Harmonic and Set Analysis Program" were

- style of analysis (chords including ninth, eleventh, and thirteenth chords; chords excluding ninth, eleventh, and thirteenth chords; sets in optimal normal order),
- treatment of dissonances (no skipping of non-chords; disregard non-chords if there is a chord nearby; disregard non-chords). (Ibid., 110.)

The accuracy of the set of computer programs was demonstrated by analyzing one piece each by J. S. Bach, J. Haydn, F. Chopin, and L. Dallapiccola. However, Gross' project was important because of the combination of melodic, harmonic, as well as set theoretical analyses within a comprehensive set of programs.

Already in the early 1970s, Ian A. Morton (1974a) modeled a FORTRAN-program[8] for the analysis of tonal music on the level of perception, whereby the program was based on a musical-psychological, 'auditory harmony model'.[9] Program data included key signature, letter names of the notes, as well as their time value and octave. The program supplied every note in a composition with at least one numeric that relates to the key signature, to the tones that sound with it, and to those that precede and follow it. These numerics were "ob-

8 The program was executed on a CDC 6600 computer. – See also Morton 1967 and Morton and Lofstedt 1970.

9 This model was proposed by J. C. R. Licklider and was applied to several features of tonal music by P. C. Boomsliter and W. Creel; see Morton 1974a, 262.

tained solely on the basis of relational context within a stringently defined architecture of musical structures and keys" (Morton 1974a, 265). From the numerics, the following information could be extracted: the melodic relationships between consecutive notes in each voice, the harmonic relationships between consecutive events, summaries of compound events, summaries of ambiguous events, durations of harmonies, and a graphic representation of the harmonic flow of the composition (ibid.). Using this program, Morton analyzed Bach chorales as well as the first two harmonized measures of *Tristan*. In the Bach chorales, an unexpected number of (harmonic) ratios of greater complexity, such as 81/80, 128/105 or 160/147 (besides the classic diatonic ratios 3/2, 5/4, 5/3 etc.), were found, and even such unusual relationships as 1323/1280 and 1701/1600 (ibid.). The analysis of the first two measures of *Tristan* also reflected the complexity of human perception. With this research, Morton developed an early cognitive approach to computer-assisted music analysis, and was, thus, one of the heralds of the cognitive boom in the 1980s and 1990s.

Mario Baroni and Carlo Jacoboni (1973, 1975, 1977, 1978) pursued an analysis project that targeted selected soprano parts of Bach chorales and produced rules by which the melodies, phrases, and cadences can be described. Baroni and Jacoboni developed a generative grammar derived from these rules, which was then used for a computer program to generate new chorale melodies (phrases).

In 1974, Bo Alphonce presented a computer-assisted foundation of set theoretical analyses and provided, with it, a basis for later approaches in this field. He developed a new algorithm for computing prime forms of sets from cardinality 0 to 12 over a binary exponential series and their transformations, based on all (4095) transpositions and inversions of every prime form.[10] Another (SNOBOL3-) computer program produced a complete list of subsets for all prime forms of the twelve-tone-system. Furthermore, Alphonce developed an analytical approach for invariance relations of sets or subsets: the results can be mathematically represented (and visualized) in invariance matrices and used as analytical tools. Different possibilities of interpreting similarity relations were described as a power of his analytical model. Alphonce' two analytical programs[11], using this methodological framework, were for either monophonic or polyphonic/homophonic input (in the latter case, for pieces in which the set cannot be assumed to be mostly linearly). These programs which, as Alphonce points out, require interaction between the analyst and the program, could be used for either calculating characteristics of sets or twelve-tone rows or for ana-

10 Alphonce was interpreting the pc integers as exponents to the base 2 and summing up the corresponding powers of 2. – The program was written in FORTRAN.

11 These programs were written in FORTRAN for an IBM 370 computer. About the history of those programs see Alphonce 1974a, 171.

lyzing – even tonal – pieces of music with regard to their inner structure of subsets.

Later on, the invariance matrices calculated by Alphonce were used as databases for several other analytical programs drawing on set theory. But Alphonce also reached the limits of his computer applications, especially concerning computer-aided segmentation: "In some early runs I came dangerously close to the proverbial truckload of output. Measure 1 of Schoenberg's op. 23 no. 4 generated a pile of output about an inch thick when scanned for all equivalent pitch-class collections. . . . Clearly, some output segments would quickly strike me as analytically convincing, but the price was too high, wading through large numbers of irrelevant and coincidental finds. . . . In general, however, I had to turn to human pre-segmentation."[12]

David Stech (1976, 1981) went a different methodological direction in that he developed a FORTRAN-program for the analysis of small musical models. His goal was to detect different types of rhythmic, melodic or intervalic patterns and their inversion, retrograde and retrograde-inversion in strictly linear music, i.e. in music in which a fixed number of voices is defined. The objects of Stech's analyses were John Dunstable's isorhythmic motet "Veni Sancte Spiritus", Paul Hindemith's "Fuga nona in B-flat" (from *Ludis Tonalis*) and Edgar Varése's "Density 21.5". Stech demonstrated, that the computer can process such analyses very fast and accurately, but he did not take perceivable variations of such patterns into account, i.e. he did not pay attention to the problem of variation and similarity.

Norbert Böker-Heil (1974) developed forms of graphical representation for interpretative analysis. He used different graphs showing the progress

- of sound-density (how many voices participate, in average, in sound events in every measure),
- of the dissonant behavior[13],
- of the melodic activity (tone progressions or sizes of intervals), and
- of tone durations.

Böker-Heil also introduced three-dimensional diagrams, in which different conditions were connected with each other. Based on this, it was possible to determine "style-specific forming constants" ["stilspezifische Formungskonstanten"]

12 Bo Alphonce in a personal communication with Peter Castine, cited after Castine 1994, 17.

13 "Here, every vertical 'chord' is considered to be 'dissonant', which does not belong to the group of perfect consonances (two-voices) of the major or minor triads or of corresponding sixth chords." ["Als dissonant gilt hier jede Tonschichtung, die nicht zur Gruppe der vollkommenen Konsonanzen (zweistimmig), der Dur- bzw. Moll-Dreiklänge oder der entsprechenden Sextakkorde gehört."] (Ibid., 109).

(ibid., 111) of polyphonic music, which could practically not be found in any other way.

At Ohio State University, Ann Kariger Blombach (1976) carried out her dissertation research on developing a conceptual framework for the use of the computer in music analysis. Her extensive methodological study contains a critical review and an evaluation of previous projects in computer-assisted music analysis, observing three major phases in such analytical attempts: (1) data preparation, (2) computer instructions, and (3) utilization of results. Another chapter discusses "the potential role of the computer in its practical application to music analysis problems," including useful capabilities of computers and limitations of using a computer in music analysis (ibid., 7-8). She also discusses practical difficulties and makes suggestions to solve them. Blombach's dissertation is an exemplary research project in that it then defines and develops a music-analytical problem, describing in detail the methodology from preparation to the interpretation of the results.

In the Soviet Union, music theorists also developed unique approaches to mathematical and computer-assisted music analysis. M. I. Rojterstejn (1973), for instance, calculated graphs and matrices of pitch-transition probabilities of compositions by Bach and Shostakovich. Using statistical analysis, Moisej G. Boroda explicated "metric-rhythmic melody units" (Boroda 1977) as well as (purely) rhythmic units (Boroda 1978), which can be found in a variety of musical styles. Boroda (1977) showed that the segmentation of every melody is dependent on the metric-rhythmical structure, specifically their interrelations. Boroda also showed that the average length of a "metric-rhythmic melody unit" can be compared to the length of words in language. Citing compositions from different style periods, Boroda gave examples for the arrangement of melodic fragments as "metric-rhythmic melody units". M. A. Iglickij (1973) developed an algorithm for stepwise modulation between any major and minor key; he suggested using this system for analyzing strategies of modulations and their frequencies. B. M. Gasparov (1974a) developed a structuralist approach to music analysis; as a specific application of his approach, Gasparov analyzed harmonic distributions in early compositions by Beethoven. Finally, T. P. Karlina and V. K. Detlovs (1968) analyzed sequences, and melodic shiftings, in melodies and harmonies; these sequences and shifting were then classified, depending on interval and pitch repertoire. Karlina and Detlovs analyzed works by Bach, Haydn, and Tchaikovsky, and showed that the application of statistical measurements (e.g., mean, standard deviation) made it possible to identify personal characteristics as well as evolutionary tendencies in the use of certain melodic or harmonic sequences.

Fred T. Hofstetter (1974, 1979) developed a different approach to the analysis of tonal music: Referring to earlier investigations by William Paisley, especially referring to procedures for extracting a database in studies of style,

Hofstetter modified Paisley's model for analyzing natural language as shown in Figure 1. This model shows how different norms, i.e. sources of variation, influence a message:

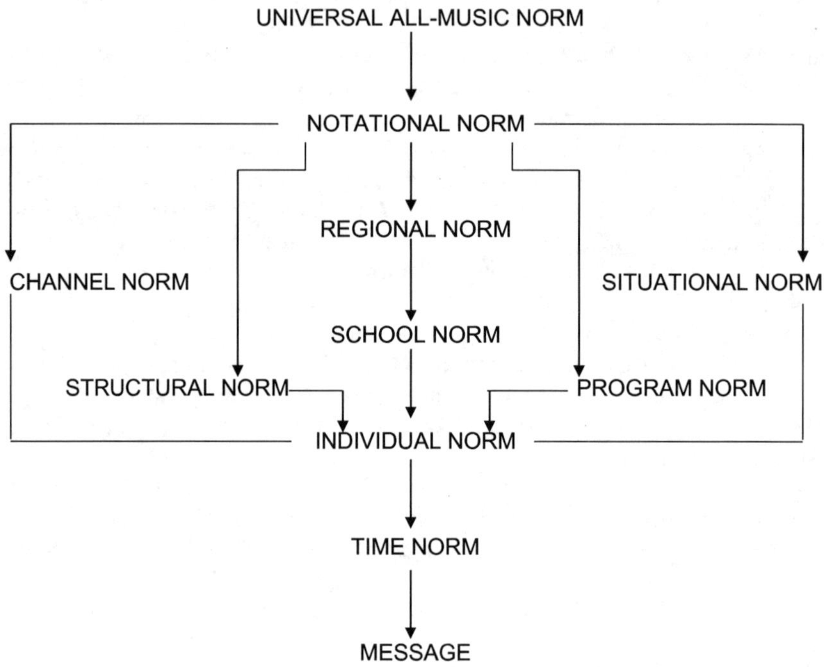

Figure 1: Modified Paisley Model for Selecting a Controlled Database in Studies of Style (Hofstetter 1979, 111)

Hofstetter's methodical procedure was characterized by isolating national influences on 130 'melodies' from 16 string quartets by Czech, French, German and Russian composers of the 19th century. Isolating national influences was accomplished by specifically choosing two string quartets each by Dvorak, Smetana, D'Indy, Saint-Saens, Mendelssohn, Schumann, Borodin and Tschaikowski. Thus, time norm (19th century), notational norm (traditional Western notation), "channel norm" (only string quartets were analyzed), situational norm (all quartets chosen for the study were mature works), and program norm (no extra musical associations) were each controlled. Through quantitative analyses of the interval repertory (using the chi-square-test of independence), it was possible to verify 'qualitative' analyses[14]. Hofstetter could show that, first, national differences between Czech, French, German and Russian chamber music exist, second, French chamber music was influenced by German music, and third, Russian chamber music shows the greatest national influence. With this method, Hofstetter demonstrated, furthermore, similarities between Czech and Russian chamber music. These similarities were probably due to geographical dependencies.

While Hofstetter's study can be criticized with regard to insufficient verification of his method and insufficient musical material analyzed, his study is a great advance compared to most of the studies carried out during the 1960s and early 1970s: different normative levels (see Figure 1) are acknowledged. This seems especially important for the categorization of different genres, but also of different parts (voices); not only different genres have different structural characteristics, but also different parts within a composition are characterized by such structural features.

In the 1970s, the search for a musical grammar was probably the most important development in computer-assisted music analysis. The basis for this search was provided by the insight that specific compositions could be represented in terms of a list of grammatical production rules. One of these forms of representation is the parse tree which graphically represents the syntactic structure of a composition. One of the first attempts of applying Schenker's theory of tonality to computer-assisted analysis of music was made by Michael Kassler (1975a, 1975b, 1977; see also Kassler 1964a). He explicated the middleground of Schenker's theory and programmed[15] the decisions procedures for formalized languages that constitute this explication (see Kassler 1975b, 7). A LISP-based system for the study of Schenkerian analysis was developed by Robert E. Frankel, Stanley J. Rosenschein, and Stephen W. Smoliar (1976, 1978). Since the programmed procedures were essentially a description of Schenker's hearing of the musical works, this approach was one of the first to model musical perception on a digital computer. Schenker's tonal and transformational hierarchies were represented within the context of a symbol-manipulation system in terms of tree transformations. A data structure was implemented that modeled the process by which the hierarchy was (supposedly) created. To demonstrate their computerized modeling, Frankel, Rosenschein, and Smoliar analyzed parts of Beethoven's "Ode to Joy". They summarized their work as follows: "Although we have not yet reached the axiomatisation stage, our LISP-based system may prove of immediate value to the musicologist and the composer. Computer-aided musicological and compositional projects have a long history. We feel our

14 Here, Hofstetter referred to Cobbett 1929.

15 Kassler wrote his programs in the APL programming language and used IBM 360/50 and CDC Cyber 72 computers.

formalism of Schenker's notions of musical structure could significantly effect future developments of both fields. In almost all documented attempts to use the computer as a tool for stylistic analysis, the data structures employed represented musical information in the form of strings of characters. . . . The representations fail to capture any hierarchical structure internal to a composition. . . . We have, in fact, the capabilities for modeling such a growth process in our LISP system as shown above by our analysis. By contrast, those data and control structures which are based entirely on string manipulation are inadequate in this respect. In fact, with a LISP-based model the musicologist may more readily ask questions about 'deep structure' and its transformations which he may use to establish criteria for stylistic analysis." (Frankel, Rosenschein, and Smoliar 1976, 29-30.)

Already in the early 1970s, Otto Laske's search for a grammar of music was an exploration of a "generative theory of music" (Laske 1972, 1973a, 1974a, 1975a). But Laske's grammar concept was based not on notated music, but on a formal model of empirically acquired musical *activity*. Thus, Laske's studies were early studies in musical cognition. He was interested in formal properties of cognitive tasks that process musical input. "Instead of producing a taxonomic analysis of musical structures, Laske has turned to what is essentially a project in cognitive psychology." (Roads 1979, 52) Laske's understanding of 'sonology' expressed "the relationship between the syntactic structure of a music and its physical representation in so far as this relationship is determined by grammatical rules" (Laske 1975a, 31). Laske tried to explicate musical grammars as computer programs in so far as they, more or less, relate to musical activity, such as composing or listening. This provided the basis for a unique analytical approach developed in the early 1980s (Laske 1984; see 2.5.).

The 1970s were a rich decade for computer-assisted music analysis. Existing (statistical and information-theoretical) methods were refined, separate measurements were converted into complex, multi-factor analyses, and, most importantly, the core of computer-assisted, analytical methods was extended by psychological and set theoretical approaches as well as approaches drawing on Schenkerian analysis and generative grammars.

Literature Published in the 1970s and Other Relevant Literature

Adamčiak, Milan. 1975. "Die semiotische Analyse des Musikwerkes," *Methoden der ethnomusikologischen Analyse*, edited by Oskár Elschek. Bratislava: Sekcia hudobnej vedy-etnomuzikológia, Umenovedný ústav, Slovenská akademia vied. p. 12.

Adams, Charles R. 1976. "Melodic Contour Typology," *Ethnomusicology* XX/2 (May): 179-215.

Addison, Don. 1974. "Elements of Style in Performing the Chinese *P'i-p'a*," *Selected Reports in Ethnomusicology* II/1: 118-139.

Allen, John R. Ed. 1976. "Directory of Scholars Active," *Computers and the Humanities* X/1 (January-February): 41-55.

_________. Ed. 1977. "Directory of Scholars Active," *Computers and the Humanities* XI/1 (January-February): 24-46.

Alphonce, Bo H. 1970. "Music Theory at Yale – A Case Study and a Project Report," *Svensk Tidskrift for Musikforskning* LII: 38-46.

_________. 1974a. The Invariance Matrix. Ph.D. dissertation. New Haven, CT: Yale University.

_________. 1974b. "The Invariance Matrix as an Analytical Tool," *International Musicological Society: Report of the Eleventh Congress, Copenhagen 1972*, edited by Henrik Glahn, Søren Sørensen, and Peter Ryom. Copenhagen: Edition W. Hansen. pp. 228-235.

_________. 1980. "Music Analysis by Computer – A Field for Theory Formation," *Computer Music Journal* IV/2 (Summer): 26-35.

Anonymous. 1970a. "Directory of Scholars Active," *Computers and the Humanities* IV/5 (May): 323-357.

Anonymous. 1970b. "Directory of Scholars Active," *Computers and the Humanities* V/2 (November): 84-128.

Anonymous. 1971a. "Directory of Scholars Active," *Computers and the Humanities* V/5 (May): 291-320.

Anonymous. 1971b. "Directory of Scholars Active," *Computers and the Humanities* VI/2 (November): 114-124.

Anonymous. 1972a. "Directory of Scholars Active," *Computers and the Humanities* VI/5 (May): 301-320.

Anonymous. 1972b. "Directory of Scholars Active," *Computers and the Humanities* VII/2 (November): 111-128.

Anonymous. 1973. "Directory of Scholars Active," *Computers and the Humanities* VII/5 (May): 295-318.

Anonymous. 1974a. "Directory of Scholars Active," *Computers and the Humanities* VIII/1 (January): 40-55.

Anonymous. 1974b. "Directory of Scholars Active," *Computers and the Humanities* VIII/4 (July): 250-257.

Anonymous. 1975a. "Directory of Scholars Active," *Computers and the Humanities* IX/1 (January): 30-35.

Anonymous. 1975b. "Directory of Scholars Active," *Computers and the Humanities* IX/4 (July): 187-196.

Anonymous. 1979a. "Directory of Scholars Active," *Computers and the Humanities* XIII/1 (January-March): 43-63.

Anonymous. 1979b. "Directory of Scholars Active," *Computers and the Humanities* XIII/3 (July-September): 247-267.

Anonymous. 1979c. "Annual Bibliography for 1977 and Supplement to Preceding Years," *Computers and the Humanities* XIII/2 (April-June): 172-183.

Aranovskij, Mark G. 1974. "Myslenije, jazyk, semantika," *Problemy muzykalnovo myslenija.* Moskow: Muzyka. 90-128.

_________. *Sintaksiceskaja struktura melodii.* Moskva, Russia: Muzyka.

Arom, Simha. 1970. "Essai d'une notation des monodies à des fins d'analyse," *Revue de Musicologie* 55: 172-216.

_________. 1980. "Structuration du Temps dans les Musiques d'Afrique Centrale: Periodicité, Mètre, Rhythmique et Polyrhythmie," *Revue de Musicologie* 70 (1984): 5-36.

Ashton, Alan Conway. 1971. Electronics, Music and Computer. Ph.D. dissertation. Salt Lake City, UT: University of Utah.

Askenfelt, Anders. 1979. "Automatic Computer Notation of Played Melodies," *Computers and the Humanities* XIII/1 (January-March): 58-59.

Avenary, Hanoch. 1973. "Analysis of Musical Modes on a Quantitative Base," *Computational Musicology Newsletter* I/1: 13.

_________. 1977. "The Northern and Southern Idioms of Early European Music: A New Approach to an Old Problem," *Acta Musicologica* XLIX/1: 27-49.

Baggi, Denis L. 1974. Realization of the Unfigured Bass by Digital Computer. Ph.D. dissertation. Berkeley, CA: University of California.

Bailey, Robert Lee. 1980. Music and Mathematics: An Interface in the Writings of Leonhard Euler. EDD thesis, State University of New York at Buffalo.

Ballo, Igor. 1978. "FIS, metóda triedenia melódií z hlàdiska podobnosti," *Musicologica Slovaca* VI (1978): 175-182.

Ballová, Luba. 1976a. "Methoden der Quantifizierung von Melodieähnlichkeiten," *Hudobná klasifikácia a samocinné pocitace: predbezná zpráva 6. Etnomuzikologického seminára = Musikklassifikation und elektronische Datenverarbeitung: Vorbericht des 6. Ethnomusikologischen Seminars, Kocovce, 6.-10. Október 1975*, edited by Oskár Elschek. Bratislava: Sekcia hudobnej vedy-etnomuzikológia, Umenovedný ústav, Slovenská akademia vied. 2 p.

_________. 1976b. "Štruktúra testovacích súborov pre výskum podobnosti" ["The structure of test sets in the investigation of similarities"], *Lidová píseň a samočinný počítač III: Sborník materiálů ze 3. semináře o využití samočinného počítače při studiu lidové písně (Brno 15.-16.10.1974)*, ed. by Dušan Holý, Karel Pala, and Miloš Štědroň. Praha: Státni pedagogické nakladatelstvi. pp. 211-218.

_________. 1978. "Algoritmizácia Vyhodnocovania Podobnosti Melódií," *Musicologica slovaca* VI: 167-174.

Barbaud, Pierre. 1974. "Methodes d'analyse de textes harmoniques," *Informatique musicale: Journées d'etude 1973. Textes des conférences E.R.A.T.T.O.*, edited by Hélène Charnassé and Henri Ducasse. Paris: Centre de documentation sciences humaines. pp. 165-176.

Barenholtz, Jerry, Z. Wolofsky, I. Ganapathy, Thomas W. Calvert, and P. O'Hara. 1977. "Computer Interpretation of Dance Notation," *Computing in the Humanities: Proceedings of the Third International Conference on Computing in the Humanities*, edited by Serge Lusignan and John S. North. Waterloo, Ontario: The University of Waterloo Press. pp. 235-240.

Baron, John H. 1971. "First Report on the Use of Computer Programming to Study the Secular Solo Songs in France from 1600 to 1660," *Bericht über den internationalen musikwissenschaftlichen Kongress: Bonn 1970*, ed. by Carl Dahlhaus et al. Kassel: Bärenreiter. pp. 333-336.

Baroni, Mario. 1969. "Linguaggio Musicale della Sonata a Quattro Italiana del Secolo XVI,"*Computers and the Humanities* III/5 (May): 312.

Baroni, Mario, and Carlo Jacoboni. 1973. "Four-part Choral Generation," *Computational Musicology Newsletter* I/1: 10.

Baroni, Mario, and Carlo Jacoboni. 1975. "Analysis and Generation of Bach's Choral melodies," *Actes du 1er congress international de semiotique musicale*, edited by Gino Stefani. Pesaro: Centro di iniziativa culturale. pp. 125-134.

Baroni, Mario, and Carlo Jacoboni. 1976. *Verso una grammatica della melodia*. Bologna, Italy: Università Studi di Bologna, 1976.

Baroni, Mario, and Carlo Jacoboni. 1977. "A Grammar of Melody," *Computers and the Humanities* XI/1 (January-February): 42.
Baroni, Mario, and Carlo Jacoboni. 1978. *Proposal for a Grammar of Melody. The Bach Chorales*. Montreal: Les presses de l'Université de Montral.
Baroni, Mario, and Carlo Jacoboni. 1979. "Formal Analogies in Different Phrases of a Monodic Composition," *The Third Colloquium on Musical Informatics*, April 1-2, 1979, Padua University, Italy. See abstract in *Computers in the Humanities* XVI/4 (1982): 264.
Barth-Wehrenalp, Renate. 1974. Studien zu Adan de le Hale. Ph.D. thesis. University of Vienna.
_________. 1982. *Studien zu Adan de le Hale*. Tutzing, Germany: H. Schneider, 1982.
Bartmiński, Jerzy. 1975. "Komputery w badaniach nat pieśnią ludową," *Literatura Ludowa* 19 (January-February): 54-56.
Bartmiński, Jerzy, et al. 1976. "Diskuse," *Lidová píseň a samočinný počítač III: Sborník materiálů ze 3. semináře o využití samočinného počítače při studiu lidové písně (Brno 15.-16.10.1974)*, ed. by Dušan Holý, Karel Pala, and Miloš Štědroň. Praha: Státni pedagogické nakladatelstvi. pp. 357-411.
Battier, Marc, and Jacques Arveiller. 1978. *Musique et informatique: une bibliographie indexée*, réédition augmentée. Paris: Elmeratto.
Bauer, Hans-Joachim. 1976. "Statistik, eine objektive Methode zur Analyse von Kunst?" *International Review of the Aesthetics and Sociology of Music* VII/2 (December): 249-263.
Bauer-Mengelberg, Stefan. 1968. "'The Truth, the Whole Truth, and Nothing but the Truth'," *Computer Studies in the Humanities and Verbal Behavior* I/2 (August): 52-54.
_________. 1970. "The Ford-Columbia Input Language," *Musicology and the Computer: Three Symposia*, edited by Barry S. Brook. New York: The City University of New York Press. 48-52.
_________. 1974. "Digital Alternate Representation of Musical Scores (DARMS)," *Computers and the Humanities* VIII/4 (July): 255.
Bengtsson, Ingmar. 1967a. "On Melody Registration and 'Mona'," *Elektronische Datenverarbeitung in der Musikwissenschaft*, edited by Harald Heckmann. Regensburg: Gustav Bosse. pp. 136-174.
_________. 1967b. "Numericode – A Code System for Thematic Incipits," *Svensk Tidskrift för Musikforskning* 49: 5-40.
_________. 1970. "Studies with the Aid of Computers of 'Music As Performed'," *IMS: Report on the Tenth Congress, Lubljana 1967*, edited by Dragotin Cvetko. Kassel: Bärenreiter. pp. 443-444.
_________. 1971. "Analysis of Rhythmic Performance," *Computers and the Humanities* V/5 (May): 310.
Bengtsson, Ingmar, Alf Gabrielsson, and Barbro Gabrielsson. 1978. "RHYTHM-SYVARD, A Computer Program for Analysis of Rhythmic Performance," *Svensk Tidskrift for Musikforskning* LX/1: 15-24.
Bengtsson, Ingmar, Alf Gabrielsson, and Stig-Magnus Thorsén. 1969. "Empirisk Rytmforskning. En Orientering om Musikvetenskaplig Bakgrund, Utveckling och Några aktuella Projekt," *Svensk Tidskrift för Musikforskning* 51: 49-118.
Bent, Ian D. 1973. "Analysis of Melodic Structure," *Computers and the Humanities* VII/5 (May): 314.
_________. 1977. "Analysis of Melodic Structure," *Computers and the Humanities* XI/1 (January-February): 41.

_________. 1980. "Analysis," *The New Grove Dictionary of Music and Musicians*, edited by Stanley Sadie, vol. 1. London: Macmillan. 340-388.

_________. 1987. *Analysis*, with a glossary by William Drabkin. London: Macmillan.

Bent, Ian, and John Morehen. 1978. "Computers in the Analysis of Music," *Proceedings of the Royal Musical Association* CIV (1977-78): 30-46.

Bernard, Jean J. 1974. "Sciences exactes et musicologie," *Informatique musicale: Journées d'etude 1973. Textes des conférences E.R.A.T.T.O.*, edited by Hélène Charnassé and Henri Ducasse. Paris: Centre de documentation sciences humaines. pp. 115-124.

Berrett, Joshua. 1979. "Alan Lomax: Some Reconsiderations," *Journal of Jazz Studies* VI/1: 54-63.

Bersano, James Richard. 1980. Formalized Aspect Analysis of Sound Texture. PhD thesis, Indiana University.

Bertoni, Alberto, Goffredo Haus, Giancarlo Mauri, and Mauro Torelli. 1978a. "A Mathematical Model for Analyzing and Structuring Musical Texts," *Interface* VII: 31-43.

Bertoni, Alberto, Goffredo Haus, Giancarlo Mauri, and Mauro Torelli. 1978b. "Analysis and Compacting of Musical Texts," *Journal of Cybernetics* 8: 257-272.

Bielawski, Ludwik. 1975. "Ähnlichkeiten und Zusammenhänge – System und Syntagma in der ethnomusikologischen Analyse," *Methoden der ethnomusikologischen Analyse*, edited by Oskár Elschek. Bratislava: Sekcia hudobnej vedy-etnomuzikológia, Umenovedný ústav, Slovenská akademia vied. pp. 32-33.

Blombach, Ann Kariger. 1976. A Conceptual Framework for the Use of the Computer in Music Analysis. Ph.D. dissertation. Columbus, OH: Ohio State University.

_________. 1981. "An Introductory Course in Computer-Assisted Music Analysis: The Computer and the Bach Chorales," *Journal of Computer-Based Instruction* 8 (February): 70-77.

_________. 1982. "Harmony vs. Counterpoint in the Bach Chorales," *Computing in the Humanities*, edited by Richard W. Bailey. Amsterdam: North-Holland Publishing Company. pp. 79-88.

Boggs, Beverly. 1973. "Analysis of Ethnomusicological Transcritions," *Computational Musicology Newsletter* I/1: 14.

Boggs, J. K. 1973. "Music Ancoding," *Computational Musicology Newsletter* I/1: 3.

Böker-Heil, Norbert. 1971a. "Programmierte Musikanalyse," *Computers and the Humanities* V/5 (May): 314.

_________. 1971b. "DODEK - Eine Computerdemonstration," *Zeitschrift für Musiktheorie* II/2: 2-14.

_________. 1972a. "Weiße Mensuralnotation als Computer-Input und -Output," *Acta Musicologica* XLIII/1-2 (January-June): 21-33.

_________. 1972b. "Ein algebraisches Modell des Dur-Moll-Tonalen Systems," *Bericht über den 1. Internationalen Kongress für Musiktheorie Stuttgart 1971*, ed. by Peter Rummenhöller, Friedrich Christoph Reininghaus, and Jürgen Habakuk Traber. Stuttgart, Germany: Ichthys-Verlag. pp. 64-107.

_________. 1973. "Plotting Conventional Music Notation," *Journal of Music Theory* XVI/1-2 (Spring-Winter): 72-101.

_________. 1974a. "Der Zustand polyphoner Strukturen: Ein Beispiel Automatischer Stilbeschreibung," *International Musicological Society: Report of the Eleventh Congress, Copenhagen 1972*, edited by Henrik Glahn, Søren Sørensen, and Peter Ryom. Copenhagen: Edition W. Hansen. pp. 108-120.

_________. 1974b. "Musikalische Stilanalyse und Computer. Einige grundsätzliche Erwägungen," *International Musicological Society: Report of the Eleventh Congress,*

Copenhagen 1972, edited by Henrik Glahn, Søren Sørensen, and Peter Ryom. Copenhagen: Edition W. Hansen. pp. 45-50.

_________. 1976. "Die maschinenverständliche Darstellung musikalischer Sachverhalte," *Hudobná klasifikácia a samocinné pocitace: predbezná zpráva 6. Etnomuzikologického seminára = Musikklassifikation und elektronische Datenverarbeitung: Vorbericht des 6. Ethnomusikologischen Seminars, Kocovce, 6.-10. Október 1975*, edited by Oskár Elschek. Bratislava: Sekcia hudobnej vedy-etnomuzikológia, Umenovedný ústav, Slovenská akademia vied. 2 p.

_________. 1981. "Computer-Simulation eines musikalischen Verstehensprozesses," *International Musicological Society: Report of the Twelfth Congress, Berkeley 1977*, edited by Daniel Heartz and Bonnie C. Wade. Kassel: Bärenreiter. pp. 324-329.

Böker-Heil, Norbert, and Harald Heckmann. 1979. "Elektronische Datenverarbeitung," *Die Musik in Geschichte und Gegenwart*, vol. 16. Kassel: Bärenreiter. pp. 36-51.

Boody, Charles George. 1975. Non-Compositional Applications of the Computer to Music Published in America Through June of 1972. Ph.D. dissertation. Minneapolis, MN: University of Minnesota.

_________. 1978. The Micro-Computer as an Input Device for Music Analysis or Composition by Computer. Ann Arbor, MI: MPublishing, University of Michigan Library.

Boroda, Moisej G. 1973. "K voprosu o metroritmiceski elementarnoj edinice v muzyke," *Bulletin of the Academy of Science of the Georgian SSR* 71/3: 745-748.

_________. 1974. "O castotnoj strukture muzykalnych soobscenij," *Bulletin of the Academy of Science of the Georgian SSR* 76/2 (1974): 178-202.

_________. 1977. "O melodiceskoj elementarnoj edinice," *MAAFAT'75 1 vsesoûznyj seminar po masinnym aspektam algoritmiceskogo formalizovannogo analiza muzykal'nyh tekstov. (Erevan-Dilizan, 27.10.-1.11.1975 g.): materialy*, edited by Vladimir Leonidovic Gosovskij. Erevan: Izdat. Akad. nauk Armânskoj SSR. pp. 112-120.

_________. 1978. "Ob opredelenii informacionnoj melodiceskoj edinicy tipa frazy v muzyke," *Bulletin of the Academy of Science of the Georgian SSR* 89/1: 57-60.

_________. 1979. Principy Organizacii Povtorov na Microurovne Muzykalnovo Teksta. Dissertation. Tiblissi.

_________. 1980. "Häufigkeitsstrukturen musikalischer Texte," *Glottometrika 3*, edited by Wolfhart Matthäus. Bochum: Studienverlag Dr. N. Brockmeyer. pp. 36-96.

Boroda, Moisej G., and Jurij K. Orlov. 1978. "O sravnenii skorostej vosprijatija informacijonnych edinic v muzyke i reci," [*Proceedings of the Conference "The Functioning of Communication Systems"*]. Erevan: Academy of Science. pp. 58-62.

Boroda, Moisej G., I. Sch. Nabareyshvili, Jurij K. Orlov, R. Ja. Tshitashvili. 1977. "O Karaktere raspredelenija informatcionnuych edinic maloj tshastotyu v chudoshestvennych tekstach," *Semiotika i Informatika* IX: 23-35.

Borris, Siegfried. 1971. Review of *Musikalische Stilanalyse auf der Grundlage eines Modelles für Lernprozesse* by Hermann Gerhard Rohrer, *Musik und Bildung* III/11 (November): 567-568.

Boucourechliev, Andre. 1970. "Transmutations," *L'Arc* 40: 49-56.

Bowles, Edmund. 1965. "Computers and Musicology," *Computers for the Humanities: A Record of the Conference Sponsored by Yale University on a Grant from IBM, January 22-23, 1965*. New Haven, CT: Yale University Press. pp. 103-108.

_________. 1970a. "Discussion," *Musicology and the Computer: Three Symposia*, edited by Barry S. Brook. New York: The City University of New York Press. pp. 37-38.

__________. 1970b. "Musicke's Handmaiden: Or Technology in the Service of the Arts," *The Computer and Music*, edited by Harry B. Lincoln. Ithaca: Cornell University Press. pp. 3-20.

__________. 1970c. "Musicology and Computers" [A Review of Harald Heckmann, *Elektronische Datenverarbeitung der Musikwissenschaft*], *Computers and the Humanities* IV/3 (January): 207-219.

Brantley, Daniel Lawrence. 1977. Disputed Authorship of Musical Works: A Quantitative Approach to the Attribution of the Quartets Published as Haydn's Opus 3. Ph.D. dissertation. Iowa City, IA: University of Iowa.

Braun, Hartmut. 1975. "Das Problem der Zeilenbegrenzung," *Methoden der ethnomusikologischen Analyse*, edited by Oskár Elschek. Bratislava: Sekcia hudobnej vedy-etnomuzikológia, Umenovedný ústav, Slovenská akademia vied. pp. 40-41.

Bridgman, Nanie. 1973. "Catalogue par incipit musicaux," *Informatique et Sciences Humaines* 19 (December): 33-38.

Brincker, Jens. 1966a. "Kvantitativ musikanalyse," *Dansk Musiktidsskrift* XLI: 175-178.

__________. 1966b. Review of *Informationstheorie und Computermusik* by Lejaren A. Hiller, *Dansk Musiktidsskrift* XLI: 186.

__________. 1970. "Statistical Analysis of Music: An Application of Information Theory," *Svensk Tidskrift för Musikforsking* 52: 53-57.

Brinkman, Alexander R. 1978. Johann Sebastian Bach's Orgelbüchlein: A Computer-Assisted Analysis of the in Fluence of the Cantus Firmus on the Contrapuntal Voices. Ph.D. dissertation. Rochester, NY: University of Rochester, Eastman School of Music.

__________. 1979. "A Computer-Assisted Analysis of Melodic Borrowing from the Cantus Firmus in the Chorale Preludes in Bach's 'Orgelbüchlein'," *Proceedings of the 1978 International Computer Music Conference*, compiled by Curtis Roads. [Menlo Park, CA]: Computer Music Journal. pp. 732-760.

__________. 1980. "The Melodic Process in Johann Sebastian Bach's *Orgelbüchlein*," *Music Theory Spectrum* II (Spring): 46-73.

Broeckx, Jan L., and Walter Landrieu. 1972. "Comparative Study of Style, Based on Five Liedmelodies," *Interface* I/1 (April): 29-92.

Brook, Barry S. 1965a. "The Simplified 'Plaine and Easy Code System," *Fontes Artis Musicae* XII: 156-160.

__________. 1965b. "Utilization of Data Processing Techniques in Music Documentation," *Fontes Artis Musicae* XII (May): 112-122.

__________. 1967. "Music Bibliography and the Computer," *Papers from the West Virginia University Conference on Computer Applications in Music*, edited by Gerald Lefkoff. Morgantown: West Virginia University Library. pp. 9-27.

__________. 1969. "Style and Content Analysis in Music: The Simplified 'Plaine and Easy Code'," *The Analysis of Communication Content*, edited by George Gerbner et al. New York: John Wiley & Sons. pp. 287-296.

__________. Ed. 1970a. *Musicology and the Computer: Three Symposia*. New York: The City University of New York Press.

__________. 1970b. "Music Documentation of the Future," *Musicology and the Computer: Three Symposia*, edited by Barry S. Brook. New York: The City University of New York Press. pp. 28-36.

__________. 1970c. "The Plaine and Easie Code," *Musicology and the Computer: Three Symposia*, edited by Barry S. Brook. New York: The City University of New York Press. pp. 53-56.

Burns, Betty Beryl Remy. 1972. An Electronic Data Processing System for the Organization and Documentaion of the 16th Century Motet. Ph.D. dissertation. Cincinnati, OH: University of Cincinnati.
Byrd, Donald Alvin. 1970a. "Music Notation by Computer," *Computers and the Humanities* V/2 (November): 111.
_________. 1970b. "Transcription by Plotter," *Random Bits* V/9 (May): 6-8.
_________. 1971. "Humanities Programming for Creative Work," *Random Bits* VI/5 (January): 1, 8-12.
_________. 1974. "A System for Music Printing by Computer," *Computers and the Humanities* VIII/3 (May): 161-172.
_________. 1975. "Music Programs at Indiana University," *Computational Musicology Newsletter* II/1: 2-4.
_________. 1976. "Music Notation by Computer," *Computers and the Humanities* X/1 (January-February): 51-52.
_________. 1977. "An Integrated Computer Music Software System," *Computer Music Journal* I/2 (April): 55-60.
_________. 1984. Music Notation by Computer. Ph.D. dissertation. Bloomington, IN: Indiana University.
Calvert, Thomas W. 1979. "Computer Interpretation of Dance Notation," *Computers and the Humanities* XIII/1 (January-March): 58.
Campbell, Warren Colman. 1970. Computer Analysis of Musical Performance. Ph.D. dissertation. Storrs, CT: University of Connecticut.
Campos, Arthur Nogueira. 1973. "Music Analysis," *Computational Musicology Newsletter* I/1: 14.
Cantor, Don. 1971. "A Computer Program that Accepts Common Musical Notation," *Computers in the Humanities* VI (November): 103-109.
Castine, Peter. 1994. *Set Theory Objects. Abstractions for Computer-Aided Analysis and Composition of Serial and Atonal Music*. Frankfurt/M.: Peter Lang.
Castman, Bernt, and Lars Elve Larsson. 1974. Ett dataprogram (RHYTHMSYVARD) för bearbetning av rytmiska duraionsvärden. Mimeographed. Uppsala, Sweden: Instutionen för Musikvetenskap.
Chalupka, Lubomír. 1975. "Kybernetik und EDV im Dienste der Musikanalyse," *Methoden der ethnomusikologischen Analyse*, edited by Oskár Elschek. Bratislava: Sekcia hudobnej vedy-etnomuzikológia, Umenovedný ústav, Slovenská akademia vied. pp. 7-8.
Chalupka, Lubomír, and Viera Chalupková. 1978. "Spracovianie Suboru L'udovych Piesni na SP MSP 2A," *Musicologica slovaca* (Czechoslovakia) VI: 203-208.
Chalupková, Viera. 1978. "Tonalna Analyza Suboru Piesni a Jej Vyhodnotenie," *Musicologica slovaca* (Czechoslovakia) VI: 209-215.
Chalupková, Viera, and Lubomír Chalupka. 1976. "Die Bearbeitung von Volksliedern aus dem Záhorie auf einer EDV-Anlage," *Hudobná klasifikácia a samocinné pocitace: predbezná zpráva 6. Etnomuzikologického seminára = Musikklassifikation und elektronische Datenverarbeitung: Vorbericht des 6. Ethnomusikologischen Seminars, Kocovce, 6.-10. Október 1975*, edited by Oskár Elschek. Bratislava: Sekcia hudobnej vedy-etnomuzikológia, Umenovedný ústav, Slovenská akademia vied. 2 p.
Charnassé, Hélène. 1973. "Musicologie et Informatique: Les grands axes de recherche," *Informatique et Sciences Humaines* 19 (December): 19-31.
_________. 1974. "Transcrition Automatique de Tablatures," *Informatique musicale: Journées d'etude 1973. Textes des conférences E.R.A.T.T.O.*, edited by Hélène Char-

nassé and Henri Ducasse. Paris: Centre de documentation sciences humaines. pp. 25-47.

_________. 1976. "La transcription automatique des tablatures: le language d'entree," *Proceedings of the Second Annual Music Computation Conference: November 7-9, 1975 at the University of Illinois at Urbana-Champaign*, compiled by James Beauchamp and John Melby. Urbana, IL: Office of Continuing Education and Public Service in Music, University of Illinois. pp. 13-27.

Charnassé, Hélène, and Henri Ducasse. Eds. 1974. *Informatique musicale: Journées d'etude 1973. Textes des conférences E.R.A.T.T.O.* Paris: Centre de documentation sciences humaines.

Charnassé, Hélène, and Henri Ducasse. 1971. "De l'emploi de l'ordinateur pour la transcription des trablatures," *Revue de Musicologie* 57/2: 107-133.

Charnassé, Hélène, and Henri Ducasse. 1975. "Automated Tablature Transcription," *Computational Musicology Newsletter* II/1: 9-10.

Charnassé, Hélène, Raymond Meylon, and Henri Ducasse. 1977. "Transcription automatique de notations musicales en tablatures," *Computers and the Humanities* XI/1 (January-February): 41-42.

Chenoweth, Vida. 1974. *Melodic Perception and Analysis: A Manual on Ethnic Melody.* Ukarumpa: Summer Institute of Linguistics.

Chenoweth, Vida, and Darlene Bee. 1971. "Comparative-Generative Models of a New Guinea Melodic Structure," *American Anthropoligist* 73: 773-782.

Chmurny, Rudolf. 1978. "DIS, metoda Vyhodnocovania Podobnosti Melodii," *Musicologica slovaca* [Czechoslovakia] VI: 183-186.

Ciamaga, Gustav. 1971. "The Training of the Computer in the Use of New technological Means," *Music and Technology*. Paris: La Revue Musicale. pp. 143-150.

Cinková, Irena. 1976. "Využití informačního szstému asti pro analýzu a třídění lidových písní," *Lidová píseň a samočinný počítač III: Sborník materiálů ze 3. semináře o využití samočinného počítače při studiu lidové písně (Brno 15.-16.10.1974)*, ed. by Dušan Holý, Karel Pala, and Miloš Štědroň. Praha: Státni pedagogické nakladatelstvi. pp. 183-195.

Clauß, Günter and Heinz Ebner. 1978. *Grundlagen der Statistik für Psychologen, Pädagogen und Soziologen*, 7th ed. Berlin: Technik Verlag.

Clifton, Thomas. 1973. "Music and the a priori," *Journal of Music Theory* 17/1: 66-85.

Cobbett, Walter Willson. Ed. 1929. *Cobbett's Cyclopedic Survey of Chamber Music*. London: Oxford University Press.

Cohen, Dalia, and Ruth Katz. 1974. "Quantitative Analysis of Monophonic Music: Towards a More Precise Definition of Style," *Orbis Musicae* III-IV: 83-96.

Cohen, Dalia, and Ruth Katz. 1977. *The Israeli Folk Song: A Methodological Example of Computer Analysis of Monophonic Music*. Jerusalem: The Magnes Press.

Colquhoun, Daryl George. 1979. "Computer Piano Concertos," *Computers and the Humanities* XIII/3 (July-September): 261.

Couturier, Marcel. 1974. "L'emploi du langage forcod en collecte et traitement d'inventaires après deces," *Informatique musicale: Journées d'etude 1973. Textes des conférences E.R.A.T.T.O.*, edited by Hélène Charnassé and Henri Ducasse. Paris: Centre de documentation sciences humaines. pp. 104-114.

Crane, Frederick, and Judith Fiehler. 1970. "Numerical Methods of Comparing Musical Styles," *The Computer and Music*, edited by Harry B. Lincoln. Ithaca: Cornell University Press. pp. 209-222.

Cuddy, Lola L., Annabel J. Cohen, and J. Miller. 1979. "Melody Recognition: The Experimental Application of Musical Rules," *Canadian Journal of Psychology* XXXIII/3: 148-157.

Czekanowska-Kulinska, Anna. 1970. "Polish Mathematical Methods in the Classification of Slavic Folk Songs," *IMS: Report on the Tenth Congress, Lubljana 1967*, edited by Dragotin Cvetko. Kassel: Bärenreiter. pp. 440-443.

_________. 1977. "Comparative and quantitative methods in international research projects on folk music," *Ethnologia Slavica* VIII-IX (1976-77): 307-18.

Deihl, Ned C. 1971. Computer-Assisted Instruction and Instrumental Music: Implications for Teaching and Research," *Journal of Research in Music Education* XIX/3 (Fall): 299-306.

Delalande, François. 1972. "L'analyse des musiques electro-acoustiques," *Musique en Jeu*: 50-56.

de la Motte-Haber, Helga. 1970. "Die Abhängigkeit des Sonanzeindrucks von der Intervallstruktur," *Bericht über den Internationalen Musikwissenschaftlichen Kongress Leipzig 1966*, edited by Carl Dahlhaus et al. Kassel: Bärenreiter. pp. 477-482.

Demorgon, Jacques. 1974. Une communication de masse: la chanson a succes. Essai d'une premiere systematisation de son etude en France de 1946 a 1966. Ph.D. dissertation. Paris, France: Department of Sociology. University of Paris V.

Ducasse, Henri. 1973a. "Introduction," *Informatique et Sciences Humaines* 19 (December): 7-15.

_________. 1973b. "Compte-rendu de Journees d'Etudes d'Informatique Musicale," *Informatique et Sciences Humaines* 19 (December): 67-70.

_________. 1974. "Un problem de saisie de l'information," *Informatique musicale: Journées d'etude 1973. Textes des conférences E.R.A.T.T.O.*, edited by Hélène Charnassé and Henri Ducasse. Paris: Centre de documentation sciences humaines. pp. 48-65.

Ducasse, Henri, and Denys Pages. 1976. "Un systeme de constitution et d'exploitation de donnees pour l'identification et l'analyse de textes musicaux," *Revue de Musicologie* [France] LXII/2: 292-293.

Duisberg, Robert Adamy. 1980. A digital representation of musical samples and a calculation thereon of autocorrelation as a function of frequency. D.M.A. dissertation. Seattle, WA: University of Washington.

Dürrenmatt, Hans-Rudolf, Murray Gold, and Jan LaRue. 1970. "Die Notierung Thematischer Incipits auf 'Mark-Sense-Cards'," *Fontes Artes Musicae* XVII/1-2 (January-August): 15-23.

Egeland Hansen, Finn. 1967a. "Det gregorianske repertoire i Codex H 159 Montpellier," *Dansk Arbog for Musikforskning* V (1966-67): 181-182.

_________. 1967b. "Investigation of Tonal Properties of the Gregorian Repertory," *Computers and the Humanities* I/5 (May): 226.

_________. 1970. "Musikalsk analyse ved hjaepl af modeller," *Svensk Tidskrift för Musikforskning* 52: 50-53.

_________. 1974. "Tonality in Gregorian chant based on an investigation of the melodies in Codex H 159, Montpellier," *[IMS] Report of the Eleventh Congress, Copenhagen, 1972*, edited by Henrik Glahn, Søren Sørensen, Peter Ryom. Copenhagen: Edition W. Hansen. pp. 425-431.

Ellis, Mark. 1980. Linear Aspects of the Fugues of J. S. Bach's "The Well-Tempered Clavier": A Quantitative Survey. Ph.D. dissertation. Nottingham, UK: University of Nottingham.

Elschek, Oskár. Ed. 1976a. *Hudobná klasifikácia a samocinné pocitace: predbezná zpráva 6. Etnomuzikologického seminára = Musikklassifikation und elektronische Datenverarbeitung: Vorbericht des 6. Ethnomusikologischen Seminars, Kocovce, 6.-10. Október 1975*. Bratislava: Sekcia hudobnej vedy-etnomuzikológia, Umenovedný ústav, Slovenská akademia vied.
_________. 1976b. "Die Anwendungsbereiche der gegenwärtigen Musikklassifikation," *Hudobná klasifikácia a samocinné pocitace: predbezná zpráva 6. Etnomuzikologického seminára = Musikklassifikation und elektronische Datenverarbeitung: Vorbericht des 6. Ethnomusikologischen Seminars, Kocovce, 6.-10. Október 1975*, edited by Oskár Elschek. Bratislava: Sekcia hudobnej vedy-etnomuzikológia, Umenovedný ústav, Slovenská akademia vied. 2 p.
_________. 1978. "Ludová piesen a samocinny pocítac 2," *Musicologica slovaca* VI: 163-308.
Elschek, Oskár, et al. 1975a. "Protokoll der Schlußsitzung des ethnomusikologischen Seminars," *Methoden der ethnomusikologischen Analyse*, edited by Oskár Elschek. Bratislava: Sekcia hudobnej vedy-etnomuzikológia, Umenovedný ústav, Slovenská akademia vied. pp. 53-57.
Elschek, Oskár, et al. 1975b. "Protokoll der geschlossenen Sitzung der Study Group of Folk Music Systematisation of Folk Music des IFMC (26. September 1974)," *Methoden der ethnomusikologischen Analyse*, edited by Oskár Elschek. Bratislava: Sekcia hudobnej vedy-etnomuzikológia, Umenovedný ústav, Slovenská akademia vied. pp. 59-62.
Elschek, Oskár, et al. 1976. "Protokoll der Schlußsitzung des ethnomusikologischen Seminars," *Hudobná klasifikácia a samocinné pocitace: predbezná zpráva 6. Etnomuzikologického seminára = Musikklassifikation und elektronische Datenverarbeitung: Vorbericht des 6. Ethnomusikologischen Seminars, Kocovce, 6.-10. Október 1975*, edited by Oskár Elschek. Bratislava: Sekcia hudobnej vedy-etnomuzikológia, Umenovedný ústav, Slovenská akademia vied. 6 p.
Elscheková, Alica. 1965. "General Considerations on the Classification of Folk Tunes," *Studia Musicologica Academiae Scientiarum Hungaricae* VII/1-4: 259-262.
_________. 1966. "Methods of Classification of Folk Tunes," *Journal of International Folk Music Council* XVIII: 56-76.
_________. 1969. "Technologie der Datenverarbeitung bei der Klassifizierung von Volksliedern," *Methoden der Klassifikation von Volksliedweisen*, edited by Oskár Elschek. Bratislava: Verlag der Slowakischen Akademie der Wissenschaften. pp. 93-122.
_________. 1972. "Klasifikacie Kratkych Motivickych Usekov Netrofickych i Strofickych Piesni Tradicnymi a Netradicnymi Technikami," *Lidová písen a samostatný pocítac I*, edited by Dušan Holý and Oldrich Sirovátka. Brno: Klub uživatelů MSP. pp. 219-243.
_________. 1975a. "Systematisierung, Klassifikation und Katalogisierung von Volksliedweisen," *Handbuch des Volksliedes*, edited by Rolf Wilhelm Brednich, Lutz Röhrich and Wolfgang Suppan, vol. 2. München: Fink. pp. 549-582.
_________. 1975b. "Die Entwicklung der ethnomusikologischen Analyse," *Methoden der ethnomusikologischen Analyse*, edited by Oskár Elschek. Bratislava: Sekcia hudobnej vedy-etnomuzikológia, Umenovedný ústav, Slovenská akademia vied. pp. 20-21.
_________. 1976a. "Klasifikácia krátkych motivických úsekov nestrofických i strofických piesní tradičnými i netradičnými technikami," *Lidová píseň a samočinný počítač III: Sborník materiálů ze 3. semináře o využití samočinného počítače při studiu lidové písně (Brno 15.-16.10.1974)*, ed. by Dušan Holý, Karel Pala, and Miloš Štědroň. Praha: Státni pedagogické nakladatelstvi. pp. 219-243.

_________. 1976b. “Entwicklung der ethnomusikalischen Klassifikation,” *Hudobná klasifikácia a samocinné pocitace: predbezná zpráva 6. Etnomuzikologického seminára = Musikklassifikation und elektronische Datenverarbeitung: Vorbericht des 6. Ethnomusikologischen Seminars, Kocovce, 6.-10. Október 1975*, edited by Oskár Elschek. Bratislava: Sekcia hudobnej vedy-etnomuzikológia, Umenovedný ústav, Slovenská akademia vied. 3 p.

_________. 1978. “Metoda Vyhidnocivania Melodickych Podobnosti Pomocou Klasifikacnych Tabuliek,” *Musicologica slovaca* [Czechoslovakia] VI: 217-234.

Entwisle, Jeffrey Lynn. 1973. Visual Perception and Analysis of Musical Scores, B.S. thesis. Boston, MA: Massachusetts Institute of Technology, Department of Humanities.

Erickson, Raymond F. 1968a. “Music Analysis and the Computer,” *Journal of Music Theory* XII/2 (Winter): 240-263.

_________. 1968b. “Music Analysis and the Computer: A Report on Some Current Approaches and the Outlook for the Future,” *Computers and the Humanities* III/2 (November): 87-104.

_________. 1969. “A General Purpose System for Computer Aided Musical Studies,” *Journal of Music Theory* XIII/2 (Winter): 276-294.

_________. 1970a. Rhythmic Problems and Melodic Structure in Organum Purum: A Computer-Assisted Study. Ph.D. dissertation. New Haven, CT: Yale University.

_________. 1970b. “A Syntax-Directed, Changeable System for Processing Data for Music Analysis,” *Computers and the Humanities* IV/5 (May): 343.

_________. 1970c. “Music and the Computer in the Sixties,” *AFIPS Conference Proceedings* 36: 281-285.

_________. 1971a. “Rhythmic Problems and Melodic Structure in Organum Purum: A Computer-Assisted Study,” *Computers and the Humanities* V/5 (May): 312-313.

_________. 1971b. “DUPACK (DARMS Utility Package),” *Computers and the Humanities* V/5 (May): 313.

_________. 1971c. The Ford-Columbia Music Representation (DARMS). [New York: IBM Systems Research Institute].

_________. 1972a. “The Computer and Music,” *Journal of the American Musicological Society* XXV/1 (Spring): 102-107.

_________. 1972b. Abstract of *Rhythmic Problems and Melodic Structure in Organum Purum: A Computer-Assisted Study* by R. F. Erickson, *Computers and the Humanities* VI/4 (March): 254.

_________. 1972c. “The Uses of Computers in Music: A State of the Art Report,” *First USA-Japan Computer Conference Proceedings: October 3-5, 1972, Tokyo, Japan*. Montvale, NJ: American Federation of Information Processing Societies. pp. 124-129.

_________. 1975a. “‘The DARMS Project’: A Status Report,” *Computers and the Humanities* IX/6 (November): 291-298.

_________. 1975b. “‘The Darms Project’: A Status Report,” *Computational Musicology Newsletter* II/1: 7-8.

_________. 1976. DARMS: A Reference Manual. New York: Department of Music, Queens College.

_________. 1977. “MUSICOMP 76 and The State of DARMS,” *College Music Symposium* XVII/1 (Spring): 90-101.

Ermedahl, Gunnar. 1975. “Notskrift och inspelning som underlag for musikalisk analys,” *Svensk Tidskrift for Musikforskning* LVII/2: 65-66.

Evarts, John. 1970. “Stockholm,” *World of Music* XII/3: 52-56. [Report on the UNESCO meeting “Music and Technology”]

Feld, Steven. 1974. "Linguistic Models in Ethnomusicology," *Ethnomusicology* XVIII/2 (May): 197-217.

_________. 1990. "Linguistic Models in Ethnomusicology," *Ethnomusicological Theory and Method*, edited by Kaufman Shelemay. New York: Garland. pp. 183-203.

Fink, Michael. 1972. Music Analysis: An Annotated Bibliography. Los Alamitos: Southwest Regional Laboratory for Educational Research and Development. Technical Report Vol. 43.

Fiore, Mary E. 1967. "Harmonic Structure in Variation Movements by Anton von Webern," *Computers and the Humanities* I/5 (May): 225.

_________. 1968. "Harmonic Structure in Variation Movements by Webern," *Computers and the Humanities* II/5 (May): 243.

_________. 1970. "Webern's Use of Motive in the Piano Variations," *The Computer and Music*, edited by Harry B. Lincoln. Ithaca: Cornell University Press. pp. 115-122.

Fornůsek, Jaroslav. 1972. "Aplikace zkusenosti z projektovani uloh na samocinnem pocitaci pro oblast lidove pisne," *Lidová písen a samostatný pocítac I*, edited by Dušan Holý and Oldrich Sirovátka. Brno: Klub uživatelů MSP. pp. 11-18.

_________. 1976. "Vyžití existujících projectů pro spraování dat o lidové písni," *Lidová píseň a samočinný počítač III: Sborník materiálů ze 3. semináře o využití samočinného počítače při studiu lidové písně (Brno 15.-16.10.1974)*, ed. by Dušan Holý, Karel Pala, and Miloš Štědroň. Praha: Státni pedagogické nakladatelstvi. pp. 45-55.

Forte, Allen. 1970. "The Structure of Atonal Music: Practical Aspects of a Computer-Oriented Research Project," *Musicology and the Computer: Three Symposia*, edited by Barry S. Brook. New York: The City University of New York Press. 10-18.

_________. 1973. *The Structure of Atonal Music*. New Haven: Yale University Press.

Frankel, Robert E., Stanley J. Rosenschein, and Stephen W. Smoliar. 1974. The Modeling of Musical Perception on a Digital Computer Via Schenkerian Theory. Music Report No. 4, April 1975. Philadelphia: Moore School of Electrical Engineering, University of Pennsylvania.

Frankel, Robert E., Stanley J. Rosenschein, and Stephen W. Smoliar. 1976a. Schenker's Theory of Tonal Music: Its Explication Through Computational Processes. Music Project Report No. 7. Philadelphia: University of Pennsylvania, Department of Computer and Information Science.

Frankel, Robert E., Stanley J. Rosenschein, and Stephen W. Smoliar. 1976b. "A LISP-Based System for the Study of Schenkerian Analysis," *Computers and the Humanities* X/1 (January-February): 21-32.

Frankel, Robert E., Stanley J. Rosenschein, and Stephen W. Smoliar. 1978. "Schenker's Theory of Tonal Music - its Explication through Computational Processes," *International Journal of Man-Machine Studies* X: 121-138.

Fraser, Robert. 1974. "Computer Implementation of Musical Linguistics," *Computers and the Humanities* VIII/1 (January): 49-50.

Frisbie, Charlotte J. 1971. "Anthropological and Ethnomusicological Implications of a Comparative Analysis of Bushmen and African Pygmy Music," *Ethnology* X/3 (July): 265-290.

Fuller, Ramon Conrad. 1965. An Information Theory Analysis of Anton Webern's 'Symphonie,' opus 21 (with) 'Music for Two Channel Tape and Two Percussionists'. D.M.A. thesis. University of Illinois at Urbana Champaign.

_________. 1970. "Toward a Theory of Webernian Harmony, via Analysis with a Digital Computer," *The Computer and Music*, edited by Harry B. Lincoln. Ithaca: Cornell University Press. pp. 123-131.

Gabura, A. James. 1965. "Computer Analysis of Musical Style," *Proceedings of the 20th National Conference: Cleveland, Ohio, August 24-26, 1965*. New York: Association for Computing Machinery. pp. 303-314.

_________. 1967. Music Style Analysis by Computer. M.Sc. thesis, University of Toronto.

_________. 1970. "Musical Style Analysis by Computer," *The Computer and Music*, edited by Harry B. Lincoln. Ithaca: Cornell University Press. pp. 223-276.

Gadviev, Shamil Allgedar. 1979. "Statistic Analysis of Structure of Azerbaijzan Folk Songs," *Proceedings of the 1978 International Computer Music Conference*, compiled by Curtis Roads. [Menlo Park, CA]: Computer Music Journal. pp. 761-774.

Galko, Ladislav. 1975. "Die musikalische Liedanalyse für einen Inzipienkatalog," *Methoden der ethnomusikologischen Analyse*, edited by Oskár Elschek. Bratislava: Sekcia hudobnej vedy-etnomuzikológia, Umenovedný ústav, Slovenská akademia vied. pp. 38-39.

Gasparov, Boris M. 1972. "Strukturnyj metod v muzykozananii," *Sovetskaya Muzyka* 4: 42-51.

_________. 1974a. "O nekotorych principach strukturnogo analiza muzyki," *Problemy muzykalnogo myshlenija*. Moskow: Muzyka. pp. 129-152.

_________. 1974b. "Nekotorye Deskriptivnye Problemy Muzykal'noj Semantiki," *Acta et Commentationes Universitatis Tartuensis, Trudy po Znakovym Sistemam* 8: 120-137.

Gelnár, Jaromír. 1976. "Die Beziehungen zwischen dem Musikmaterial und dem Klassifikationssystem," *Hudobná klasifikácia a samocinné pocitace: predbezná zpráva 6. Etnomuzikologického seminára = Musikklassifikation und elektronische Datenverarbeitung: Vorbericht des 6. Ethnomusikologischen Seminars, Kocovce, 6.-10. Október 1975*, edited by Oskár Elschek. Bratislava: Sekcia hudobnej vedy-etnomuzikológia, Umenovedný ústav, Slovenská akademia vied. 2 p.

Gelnár, Jaromír, and Lubomír Šváb. 1976. "Analýza Rytmického průběhu ve folklórních nápěvech pmocí matematických metod," *Lidová píseň a samočinný počítač III: Sborník materiálů ze 3. semináře o využití samočinného počítače při studiu lidové písně (Brno 15.-16.10.1974)*, ed. by Dušan Holý, Karel Pala, and Miloš Štědroň. Praha: Státni pedagogické nakladatelstvi. pp. 245-252.

Gilbert, Steven E. 1970. The Trichord: An Analytic Outlook for Twentieth-Century Music. Ph.D. dissertation. New Haven, CT: Yale University.

Goldberg, Robert P. 1970. "Experimental Music Information System," *Computers and the Humanities* IV/5 (May): 345-346.

Goller, Gottfried. 1970. "Zur Bezeichnung der Neumen in der germanischen Choralnotation," *Bericht über den Internationalen Musikwissenschaftlichen Kongress, Leipzig, 1966*, ed. by Carl Dahlhaus, Reiner Kluge, Ernst H. Meyer, and Walter Wiora. Kassel: Bärenreiter. pp. 173-175.

Gomberg, David Aaron. 1975. A Computer-Oriented System for Music Printing. D.Sc. dissertation. Saint Louis, MO: Washington University.

Gould, Murray J., and George W. Logemann. 1970. "ALMA: Alphanumeric Language for Music Analysis," *Musicology and the Computer: Three Symposia*, edited by Barry S. Brook. New York: The City University of New York Press. pp. 57-90.

Greussay, Patrick. 1972. "Un modèle informatique de description de structures musicales," *Recherches linguistiques* 1: 89-128.

_________. 1973a. "Procédures LISP d'analyse de relations harmoniques," *Artinfo-Musinfo* 13: 1-7.

_________. 1973b. Modeles de descriptions symboliques en analyse musicale. Ph.D. dissertation. Paris, France: University of Paris VIII.

_________. 1974. "Structures de controle en description symbolique d'analyses musicales," *Informatique musicale: Journées d'etude 1973. Textes des conférences E.R.A.T.T.O.*, edited by Hélène Charnassé and Henri Ducasse. Paris, France: Centre de documentation sciences humaines. pp. 177-203.

Grey, John M. 1978. "Timbre Discrimination in Musical Patterns," *Journal of the Acoustical Society of America* 64: 467-472.

Grey, John M., and John W. Gordon. 1978. "Perceptual Effects of Spectral Modifications on Musical Timbres," *Journal of the Acoustical Society of America* 63 (May): 1493-1500.

Gross, Dorothy Susan. 1973. "Music Department," *Computational Musicology Newsletter* I/1: 14.

_________. 1975a. A Set of Computer Programs to Aid in Music Analysis, Ph.D. dissertation. Bloomington, IN: Indiana University.

_________. 1975b. "A Computer Package for Music Analysis," *Proceedings of the 2nd Indiana University Computer Network Conference on Instructional Computer Applications*. [s.l.]: Indiana University Computing Network. pp. 6-10.

_________. 1975c. "A Set of Computer Prtograms to Aid in Music Analysis," *Computational Musicology Newsletter* II/1: 16.

_________. 1980. "A Project in Computer-Assisted Harmonic Analysis," *Proceedings of the International Computer Music Conference*, edited by. Hubert S. Howe. San Francisco: Computer Music Association. pp. 525-533.

_________. 1981. "A Computer Project in Music Analysis," *Computing in the Humanities*, edited by Peter C. Patton and Renee A. Holoien. Lexington: Lexington Books. pp. 299-313.

_________. 1984. "Computer Applications to Music Theory: a Retrospective," *Computer Music Journal* VIII/4 (Winter): 35-42.

Gutknecht, Dieter. 1972. *Untersuchungen zur Melodik des Hugenottenpsalters*. Regensburg: Bosse.

Haefer, John Richard. 1971. Selected Cantatas of Alan Hovhaness: A Linear Analysis. M.M. thesis. Tucson, AZ: University of Arizona.

Hall, Thomas B. 1975. "Some computer aids for the preparation of critical editions of Renaissance Music," *Tijdschrift van de Vereniging voor Nederlandse Muziek Geschiedenis* 25/1: 38-53.

Halmos, István. 1973. "Automation of Analysis and Classification of Folk Tunes. Part One: Comparison Note by Note," *Computational Musicology Newsletter* I/1: 15.

_________. 1976. "Experiments in Automation of Analysis, Systematization and Listing of Monodic Folk Tunes," *Hudobná klasifikácia a samocinné pocitace: predbezná zpráva 6. Etnomuzikologického seminára = Musikklassifikation und elektronische Datenverarbeitung: Vorbericht des 6. Ethnomusikologischen Seminars, Kocovce, 6.-10. Október 1975*, edited by Oskár Elschek. Bratislava: Sekcia hudobnej vedy-etnomuzikológia, Umenovedný ústav, Slovenská akademia vied. 2 p.

Halmos, István, Miklós Havass, and György Köszegi. 1975. Experiments in Automation of Analysis, Systematization, and Listing of Monodic Folk Tunes. Budapest, Hungary: Institute of Musicology, Hungarian Academy of Sciences.

Halperin, David. 1978. A Structural Analysis of Troubadour Music. M.A. thesis. Tel Aviv, Israel: Tel Aviv University.

_________. 1980. "Distributional Structure in Troubadour Music," *Orbis Musicae* VII (1979-80): 15-26.

Hanzelin, Fred Lee. 1978. The Software for Computer Assisted Graphical Representation of Single Instrument Melodic Lines and Harmonic Spectra Using DARMS Encoding and Acoustical Data. Ph.D. thesis, University of Illinois at Urbana-Campaign.

Hasty, Christopher F. 1978. A Theory of Segmentation Developed from Late Works of Stefan Wolpe. Ph.D. dissertation. New Haven, CT: Yale University.

Haus, Goffredo. 1979. "Musical Text Transformations by Operators," Paper presented at The Third Colloquium on Musical Informatics, April 1-2, 1979, Padua University, Italy. See abstract in *Computers in the Humanities* XVI/4 (December): 264.

Heckmann, Harald. 1964. "Neue Methoden der Verarbeitung musikalischer Daten," *Die Musikforschung* XVII/4: 381-383.

_________. Ed. 1967a. *Elektronische Datenverarbeitung in der Musikwissenschaft*. Regensburg: Gustav Bosse.

_________. 1967b. "Elektronische Datenverarbeitung in der Musikwissenschaft: Eine Einleitung," *Elektronische Datenverarbeitung in der Musikwissenschaft*, edited by Harald Heckmann. Regensburg: Gustav Bosse. pp. VII-XVII.

_________. 1970. "Elektronische Datenverarbeitung in der Musikwissenschaft," *IMS: Report on the Tenth Congress, Lubljana 1967*, edited by Dragotin Cvetko. Kassel: Bärenreiter. pp. 424-427.

_________. 1971. "Katalog 'Deutsches Tenorlied des 16. Jahrhunderts," *Computers and the Humanities* V/5 (May): 313-314.

_________. 1972. "Informationstheorie und Computer," *Informatik. Vorträge anläßlich der Jahresversammlung vom 14. bis 17. Oktober 1971 zu Halle (Saale)*, edited by Jocahim-Hermann Scharf. Nova Acta Leopoldina vol. 37/1, no. 206. Leipzig: Barth. pp. 619-627.

_________. 1973a. "Musik - Dokumentation, Musik - Information," *Neue Zeitschrift für Musik* 134/8: 479-482.

_________. 1973b. "Musikwissenschaft, Dokumentation, Information," *Musicae Scientae Collectanea. Festschrift Karl Gustav Fellerer zum 70. Geburtstag*, edited by Heinrich Hüschen. Köln. pp. 219-224.

Heller, Jack J., and Warren C. Campbell. 1971. "Music Performance Analysis," *Council for Research in Music Education Bulletin* 24 (Spring): 1-9.

Heller, Jack J., and Warren C. Campbell. 1972. Computer Analysis of the Auditory Characteristics of Musical Performance. Final Report, Project No. 9-0546A, Grant No. OEG-0-9-160546-4439 (010). Washington: U.S. Dept. of Health, Education and Welfare, Office of Education, Bureau of Research.

Helm, Everett. 1971. "UNESCO Report on the Stockholm Meeting," *Music and Technology*. Paris: La Revue Musicale. pp. 193-206.

Henriksen, Jon Petter. 1976. Satsteknisk analyse ved hjelp av datamaskin. En musikologisk vinning? M.A. thesis. University of Oslo.

Henry, Edward O. 1976. "The Variety of Music in a North Indian Village: Reassessing Cantometrics," *Ethnomusicology* XX/1 (January): 49-66.

Herndon, Marcia. 1972. "The computer and music (Review of)," *Ethnomusicology: Journal of the Society for Ethnomusicology* 16/2 (May): 290-292.

Hessert, Norman Dale. 1971. The Use of Information Theory in Musical Analysis. Ph.D. dissertation. Bloomington, IN: Indiana University.

Hill, George R., and Murray Gould. 1970. *A Thematic Locator for Mozart's Works, as Listed in Koechel's Chronologisch-Thematisches Verzeichnis*, 6th edition. Hackensack, NJ: Boonin.

Hinderer, Drew Elliott. 1975. Music Analysis and the Genuine Instance Problem. PhD thesis, The University of Michigan.

Hofstetter, Fred T. 1972. "A Computer System for Musical Description," *Journal of the Graduate Music Students at the Ohio State University* 3: 4-42.

_________. 1973. "Computer Applications to Music at OSU," *Computational Musicology Newsletter* I/1: 2.

_________. 1974. A Quantitative Method for the Study of Musical Style Applied to National Differences and Similarities in the Use of Melodic Intervals During the Mid-Nineteenth to Early Twentieth Centuries. Ph.D. dissertation. Columbus, OH: The Ohio State University.

_________. 1979. "The Nationalistic Fingerprint in Nineteenth-Century Romantic Chamber Music," *Computers and the Humanities* XIII/2 (April-June): 105-119.

Holtzman, Steven R. 1977. "A Program for Key Determination," *Interface* VI/1: 29-56.

Holý, Dušan. 1976a. "Projekt der Dokumentation und Klassifikation des Volksliedes auf der Grundlage des ASTI Informationssystems," *Hudobná klasifikácia a samocinné pocitace: predbezná zpráva 6. Etnomuzikologického seminára = Musikklassifikation und elektronische Datenverarbeitung: Vorbericht des 6. Ethnomusikologischen Seminars, Kocovce, 6.-10. Október 1975*, edited by Oskár Elschek. Bratislava: Sekcia hudobnej vedy-etnomuzikológia, Umenovedný ústav, Slovenská akademia vied. 3 p.

_________. 1976b. "Dosavadní postupy a výsledky studia lidové písně pomocí smočinného počítače na půdě ČSSR," *Lidová píseň a samočinný počítač III: Sborník materiálů ze 3. semináře o využití samočinného počítače při studiu lidové písně (Brno 15.-16.10.1974)*, ed. by Dušan Holý, Karel Pala, and Miloš Štědroň. Praha: Státni pedagogické nakladatelstvi. pp. 25-35.

_________. 1976c. "Glosy k dokumentačnímu záznamu, segmentaci a popisu tematické výstavby lidové písně," *Lidová píseň a samočinný počítač III: Sborník materiálů ze 3. semináře o využití samočinného počítače při studiu lidové písně (Brno 15.-16.10.1974)*, ed. by Dušan Holý, Karel Pala, and Miloš Štědroň. Praha: Státni pedagogické nakladatelstvi. pp. 155-182.

Holý, Dušan, Antonin Bartošik, and Stanislav Zabadal. 1970. "Samočinný počítač-pomocník při analýze a klasifikaci lidových písní," *Opus musicum* [Czechoslovakia] II/5-6: 155-164.

Holý, Dušan, Antonin Bartošik, and Stanislav Zabadal. 1972. "Cíle úkoly postupy perspektivy. Za studium lidovych pisni pomoci samočinneho počítač," *Lidová písen a samostatný pocítac I*, edited by Dušan Holý and Oldrich Sirovátka. Brno: Klub uživatelů MSP. pp. 19-42.

Holý, Dušan, Karel Pala, and Miloš Štědroň. Eds. 1976. *Lidová píseň a samočinný počítač III: Sborník materiálů ze 3. semináře o využití samočinného počítače při studiu lidové písně (Brno 15.-16.10.1974)*. Praha: Státni pedagogické nakladatelstvi.

Holý, Dušan, and Oldrich Sirovátka. Eds. 1972. *Lidová písen a samostatný pocítac I*. Brno: Klub uživatelů MSP. Mimeographed.

Hoshovskyj, Vladimir. 1965. "The Experiment of Systemizing and Cataloguing Folk Tunes following the Principles of Musical Dialectology and Cybernetics," *Studia Musicologica Academiae Scientiarum Hungaricae* VII/1-4: 273-286.

_________. 1975. "Katalogisierungsanalyse – Algorithmus einer umfassenden formalisierten Beschreibung," *Methoden der ethnomusikologischen Analyse*, edited by Oskár Elschek. Bratislava: Sekcia hudobnej vedy-etnomuzikológia, Umenovedný ústav, Slovenská akademia vied. pp. 28-29.

Howe, Hubert S. 1971. "Two Parameters of Melodic Line as Stylistic Discriminants by David Sheldon Lewis; Some Techniques for Computer-Aided Analysis of Musical Scores by Donald Margedo Pederson [Review]," *Perspectives of New Music* 9-10/2-1 (Spring/Summer-Autumn/Winter): 350-355.

Huber, Alfred. 1974. "Informationstheorie und Musikanalyse," *Melos* XLI/4 (July-August): 207-210.

Hudson, Barton. 1970. "Toward a Comprehensive French Chanson Catalog," *The Computer and Music*, edited by Harry B. Lincoln. Ithaca: Cornell University Press. 277-287.

Hughes, Matt. 1965. Tonal Orientation in Skiabin's Preludes: An Analysis on the Basis of Information Theory. M.A. thesis. University of Texas at Austin.

_________. 1977. "A Quantitative Analysis," *Readings in Schenkerian Analysis*, edited by Maury Yeston. New Haven: Yale University Press. 144-164.

Huglo, Michel. 1974. "Le classement par ordinateur des listes de repons liturgiques: les problemes musicologiques," *Informatique musicale: Journées d'etude 1973. Textes des conférences E.R.A.T.T.O.*, edited by Hélène Charnassé and Henri Ducasse. Paris: Centre de documentation sciences humaines. pp. 125-134.

Huglo, Michel, and Knud Ottosen. 1974. "Le classement par ordinateur des listes de repons liturgiques, *Informatique musicale: Journées d'etude 1973. Textes des conférences E.R.A.T.T.O.*, edited by Hélène Charnassé and Henri Ducasse. Paris: Centre de documentation sciences humaines. pp. 125-143.

Hultberg, W. Earle. 1970. "Transcription of Tablature to Standard Notation," *The Computer and Music*, edited by Harry B. Lincoln. Ithaca: Cornell University Press. 289-292.

Iglickij, M. A. 1973. "Rodstvo tonalnostej i zadaca ob otyskanii modulajacionnych planov," *Muzykalnoje Iskusstvo i Nauka* II: 192-205.

Imberty, Michel. 1975. "Sémantique musicale: Approche structural, approche expérimentale," *Actes du 1er congress international de semiotique musicale*, edited by Gino Stefani. Pesaro: Centro di iniziativa culturale. pp. 225-244.

Jackson, Roland. 1966. "Harmonic Analysis," *Computers and the Humanities* I/2 (November): 52.

_________. 1970a. "Harmony before and after 1910: A Computer Comparison," *The Computer and Music*, edited by Harry B. Lincoln. Ithaca: Cornell University Press. pp. 132-146.

_________. 1970b. "The Computer as a 'Student' of Harmony," *IMS: Report on the Tenth Congress, Lubljana 1967*, edited by Dragotin Cvetko. Kassel: Bärenreiter. pp. 435-440.

Jackson, Roland, and Philip Bernzott. 1970. "A Musical Input Language and a Sample Program for Musical Analysis," *Musicology and the Computer: Three Symposia*, edited by Barry S. Brook. New York: The City University of New York Press. 130-150.

Jammers, Ewald; Bielitz, Matthias; Bender, Iring; Ebenhoh, Wolfgang. 1970. "Das Heidelberger Programm für die elektronische Datenverarbeitung in der musikwissenschaftlichen Byzantinistik," *Sitzungsberichte der Heidelberger Akademie der Wissenschaften, naturwissenschaftliche Klasse* II (1969-70): 3-23.

Jansen, Paule. 1974. "Emploi de l'ordinateur pour le depouillement des periodiques litteraires," *Informatique musicale: Journées d'etude 1973. Textes des conférences E.R.A.T.T.O.*, edited by Hélène Charnassé and Henri Ducasse. Paris: Centre de documentation sciences humaines. pp. 93-103.

Jesser, Barbara. 1991. *Interaktive Melodienanalyse. Methodik und Anwendung computergestützter Anaylseverfahren in Musikethnologie und Volksliedforschung: Typologische*

Untersuchung der Balladensammlung des DVA. Studien zur Volksliedforschung 12. Bern: Peter Lang.
John, Robert W. 1970a. "A Pilot Computer Catalog of Early American Shape-Note Hymn Tunes," *Computers and the Humanities* IV/5 (May): 345.
_________. 1970b. "A Pilot Computer Catalog of Early American Sheet Music," *Computers and the Humanities* IV/5 (May): 345.
Kaden, Christian. 1976. "Strukturelle Segmentierung von Musik - Probleme, Schwierigkeiten, Möglichkeiten," *Beiträge zur Musikwissenschaft* 18: 149-162 and 293-334.
_________. 1978. "Ludwig van Beethoven, Sinfonie Nr. 8, zweiter Satz, Allegretto scherzando. Ansätze zu einer statistischen Strukturanalyse." *Bericht über den Internationalen Beethoven Kongreß 20. bis 23. März 1977 in Berlin*, edited by H. Goldschmidt, K.-H. Köhler, and K. Niemann. Leipzig: Deutscher Verlag für Musik. pp. 113-130.
Kaegi, Werner. 1971. "Music and Technology in the Europe of 1970," *Music and Technology*. Paris: La Revue Musicale. pp. 9-31.
Kagan, Alan L., and Charles T. Brown. 1970. "Computerized Analysis and Classification of Asian Musical Style," *Computers and the Humanities* IV/5 (May): 347.
Karkoschka, Erhard. 1972. "Letzter Schreck: der Computer," *Melos* 39/5: 285-288.
_________. 1979. "On the Analysis of Melodic Activity," *Interface* VIII/2 (October): 117-127.
Karlina, T. P., and Vilnis K. Detlovs. 1968. "Statisticeskij analiz sekvencij v melodii," *Latvijskij matematiceskij ezegodnik* 4 (1968): 165-173.
Karp, Theodore. 1970. "A Test for Melodic Borrowings among Notre Dame *Organa Dupla*," *The Computer and Music*, edited by Harry B. Lincoln. Ithaca: Cornell University Press. pp. 293-295.
Kasem-Bek, Jan. 1978. "Informationstheorie und Analyse musikalischer Werke," *Archiv für Musikwissenschaft* 35: 62-75.
Kassler, Michael. 1964a. A Report of Work, Directed Toward Explication of Schenker's Theory of Tonality, Done in Summer 1962 as the First Phase of a Project Concerned with the Applications of High-Speed Automatic Digital Computers to Music ana Musicology. Princeton, NJ: Princeton University Music Department. (Mimeographed.)
_________. 1964b. MIR – A Simple Programming Language For Musical Information Retrieval. Technical Report No. 3, Project 295D, March 1964. Princeton, New Jersey: Princeton University, Department of Music. [University of California at Berkeley: Music Library, calling no. ML 74 .4 M4 K 35 1964 MUSI]
_________. 1966. "Toward Musical Information Retrieval," *Perspectives of New Music* IV/2 (Spring-Summer): 59-67.
_________. 1968. A Trinity of Essays. Ph.D. dissertation. Princeton, NJ: Princeton University.
_________. 1970a. "An Essay Toward Specification of a Music-Reading Machine," *Musicology and the Computer: Three Symposia*, edited by Barry S. Brook. New York: The City University of New York Press. pp. 151-175.
_________. 1970b. "MIR – A Simple Programming Language for Musical Information Retrieval," *The Computer and Music*, edited by Harry B. Lincoln. Ithaca: Cornell University Press. pp. 299-327.
_________. 1972. "Optical Character-Recognition of Printed Music: A Review of Two Dissertations," *Perspectives of New Music* XI/1 (Autumn-Winter): 250-254.
_________. 1975a. "Explication of Theories of Tonality," *Computational Musicology Newsletter* II/1: 17.

_________. 1975b. Proving Musical Theorems I: The Middleground of Heinrich Schenker's Theory of Tonality. Technical Report No. 103. Sydney: The University of Sydney, Basser Department of Computer Science.

_________. 1975c. "Explication of Theories of Tonalities," *Computers and the Humanities* IX/4 (July): 192-193.

_________. 1977. "Explication of the Middleground of Schenker's Theory of Tonality," *Miscellanea Musicologica* IX: 72-81.

_________. 1981. "Transferring a tonality theory to a computer," *International Musicological Society: Report of the Twelfth Congress, Berkeley 1977*, edited by Daniel Heartz and Bonnie C. Wade. Kassel: Bärenreiter. pp. 339-347.

Kassler, Michael, and Hubert S. Howe Jr. 1980. "Computers and Music," *The New Grove Dictionary of Music and Musicians*, edited by Stanley Sadie, vol. 2. London: Macmillan. pp. 603-615.

Kawano, Hiroshi. 1969. "Ongaku-teki komyunikeishon no joho-bunseki," *Ongaku gaku: Journal of the Japanese Musicological Society* XV/3-4: 1-21.

_________. 1975. "The Informational Analysis of Musical Communication," *Computational Musicology Newsletter* II/1: 15.

Kluge, Reiner. 1967. "Faktorenanalytische Typenbestimmung an einstimmigen Volksmelodien," *Computers and the Humanities* II/2 (November): 88-89.

_________. 1970a. "Volksliedanalyse und -systematisierung mit Hilfe eines Rechenautomaten," *Bericht über den Internationalen Musikwissenschaftlichen Kongress Leipzig 1966*, edited by Carl Dahlhause et al. Kassel: Bärenreiter. pp. 158-465.

_________. 1970b. "Zur Automatischen Quantitativen Bestimmung Musikalischer Ähnlichkeit," *IMS: Report on the Tenth Congress, Lubljana 1967*, edited by Dragotin Cvetko. Kassel: Bärenreiter. pp. 450-457.

_________. 1974a. *Faktorenanalytische Typenbestimmung an Volksliedmelodien.* Beiträge zur musikwissenschaftlichen Forschung in der DDR 6. Leipzig: Deutscher Verlag für Musik.

_________. 1974b. "Was kann die Kybernetik der Musikwissenschaft helfen?," *Report of the Eleventh Congress, Copenhagen, 1972*, edited by Henrik Glahn, Søren Sørensen, and Peter Ryom. Copenhagen: Edition W. Hansen. pp. 486-495.

_________. 1976a. "Anmerkungen zur Rolle des Rechenverfahrens im musikwissenschaftlichen Experiment," *International Review of the Aesthetics and Sociology of Music* VII/1: 5-42.

_________. 1976b. "Über typologische Klassifikation von Melodien und elektronische Datenverarbeitung bei der Melodie-Analyse und -Klassifikation," *Hudobná klasifikácia a samocinné pocitace: predbezná zpráva 6. Etnomuzikologického seminára = Musikklassifikation und elektronische Datenverarbeitung: Vorbericht des 6. Ethnomusikologischen Seminars, Kocovce, 6.-10. Október 1975*, edited by Oskár Elschek. Bratislava: Sekcia hudobnej vedy-etnomuzikológia, Umenovedný ústav, Slovenská akademia vied. 3 p.

Knopoff, Leon, and William Hutchinson. 1978. "An Index of Melodic Activity," *Interface* VII/4 (December): 205-229.

Knowlton, Prentise H. 1973. "Capture and Display of Keyboard Music," *Datamation*: 56-60.

Kolata, Gina Bari. 1978. "Singing Styles and Human Cultures: How are They Related?" *Science* CC/4339 (April): 287-288.

Kongas-Maranda, Elli. 1970. "Deep Significance and Surface Significance: Is Cantometrics Possible?" *Semiotica* II/2: 173-184.

Kostka, Stephan M. 1969a. The Hindemith String Quartetts: A Computer-Assisted Study of Selected Aspects of Style. Ph.D. dissertation. Madison, WI: University of Wisconsin.

__________. 1969b. "Statistics in Style Research," *Computers and the Humanities* III/5 (May): 310.

__________. 1971. "Recent Developments in Computer-Assisted Musical Scholarship," *Computers and the Humanities* VI/1 (September): 15-21.

__________. 1974. *A Bibliography of Computer Applications in Music*. Hackensack, NJ: Joseph Boonin.

__________. 1984. "The M-PARC System for Musical Encoding (Mnemonic pitch and rhythm code, version 3). Unpublished Manuscript, The University of Texas at Austin, Department of Music, Austin.

Krumhansl, Carol L., and Roger N. Shepard. 1979. "Quantification of the Hierarchy of Tonal Functions Within a Diatonic Context," *Journal of Experimental Psychology: Human Perception and Performance* V/4: 579-594.

Kupper, Hubert. 1966. "Computer and Musikwissenschaft," *IBM Nachrichten* XVI/180 (December): 297-303.

__________. 1970a. *Statistische Untersuchungen zur Modusstruktur der Gregorianik*. Regensburg: Bosse.

__________. 1970b. *Computer und musikalische Kompositionen*. Braunschweig: Vieweg.

__________. 1972. "GEASCOP - Ein Kompositionsprogramm," *Informatik. Vorträge anläßlich der Jahresversammlung vom 14. bis 17. Oktober 1971 zu Halle (Saale)*, edited by Jocahim-Hermann Scharf. Nova Acta Leopoldina vol. 37/1, no. 206. Leipzig: Barth. 629-655.

Labussiere, Annie. 1974. "Codage des structures rythmo-melodiques a partier de creations vocales," *Informatique musicale: Journées d'etude 1973. Textes des conférences E.R.A.T.T.O.*, edited by Hélène Charnassé and Henri Ducasse. Paris: Centre de documentation sciences humaines. pp. 66-92.

Lande, Tor Sverre. 1978. "Musikkanalyse med Datamskin," *Studia Musicologica Norvegia* IV: 47-60.

LaRue, Jan. 1970a. "New Directions for Style Analysis," *Musicology and the Computer: Three Symposia*, edited by Barry S. Brook. New York: The City University of New York Press. pp. 194-197.

__________. 1970b. "Some Computer Aids to Musicology," *Bericht über den Internationalen Musikwissenschaftlichen Kongress Leipzig 1966*, edited by Carl Dahlhause et al. Kassel: Bärenreiter. pp. 466-469.

__________. 1970c. "Future Technological Directions," *IMS: Report on the Tenth Congress, Lubljana 1967*, edited by Dragotin Cvetko. Kassel: Bärenreiter. pp. 457-460.

Laske, Otto. 1972. "On Musical Strategies With a View to a Generative Grammar for Music," *Interface* I/2: 111-125.

__________. 1973a. "On the Methodology and Implementation of a Procedural Theory of Music," *Computational Musicology Newsletter* I/1: 15-16.

__________. 1973b. "Toward a Musical Intelligence System: OBSERVER," *Numus West* IV: 11-16.

__________. 1974a. "In Search of a Generative Grammar for Music," *Perspectives of New Music* XII/1-2 (Autumn-Summer): 351-378. Reprinted in *Machine Models of Music*, edited by Stephen M. Schwanauer and David A. Levitt. Cambridge, MA: The MIT Press, 1993. pp. 214-240.

__________. 1974b. "Toward a Center for Studies in Musical Intelligence," *Numus West* V: 44-46.

_________. 1974c. "The Information Processing Approach to Musical Cognition," *Interface* III/2 (December): 109-136.

_________. 1974d. "Musical Acoustics (Sonology): A Questionable Science Reconsidered," *Numus-West* 6: 35-40.

_________. 1975a. *Introduction to a Generative Theory of Music*. Sonological Reports. Utrecht: Institute for Sonology.

_________. 1975b. "Musical Semantics: A Procedural Point of View," *Actes du 1er congress international de semiotique musicale*, edited by Gino Stefani. Pesaro: Centro di iniziativa culturale. pp. 214-224.

_________. 1975c. "Sufficiency Analysis of Music-Syntactic Composition," *Computers and the Humanities* IX/1 (January): 33.

_________. 1975d. "Studies in Musical Problem Solving," *Computers and the Humanities* IX/4 (July): 192.

_________. 1977a. *Music, Memory and Thought: Explorations in Cognitive Musicology*. Ann Arbor: University Research Press.

_________. 1977b. "Toward a Process Model of Musical Structures," *Proceedings of the International Workshop on the Cognitive Viewpoint*, edited by Marc T. De Mey, R. Pinxten, M. Poriau, F. Vandamme. Ghent, Belgium: Communication and Cognition. pp. 295-304.

_________. 1984. "KEITH: A Rule-System for Making Music-Analytical Discoveries," *Musical Grammars and Computer Analysis*, edited by Mario Baroni and Laura Callegari. Florence: Leo S. Olschki. pp. 165-199.

Lefkoff, Gerald. Ed. 1970. "Automated Discovery of Similar Segments in the Forty-eight Permutations of a Twelve-Tone Row," *The Computer and Music*, edited by Harry B. Lincoln. Ithaca: Cornell University Press. pp. 147-153.

Leipp, Emile, and Moncef Mlouka. 1974. "Apports de l'acoustique musicale a l'etude digitale des musiques ethniques," *Informatique musicale: Journées d'etude 1973. Textes des conférences E.R.A.T.T.O.*, edited by Hélène Charnassé and Henri Ducasse. Paris: Centre de documentation sciences humaines. pp. 144-164.

Leng, Ladislav. 1972. "O niektorych možnostiach využitia SP pri klasifikácii ozdobovanych ludovych instrumentalnych melodii," *Lidová písen a samostatný pocítac I*, edited by Dušan Holý and Oldrich Sirovátka. Brno: Klub uživatelů MSP. pp. 207-213.

Lerdal, Fred, and Ray Jackendoff. 1977. "Toward a Formal Theory of Tonal Music," *Journal of Music Theory* 21/1 (Spring): 111-171.

Levy, Morten. 1975. "On the Problem of Defining Musical Units," *Actes du 1er congress international de semiotique musicale*, edited by Gino Stefani. Pesaro: Centro di iniziativa culturale. pp. 135-149.

Lidov, David. 1975. *On Musical Phrase*. Montréal: Les Presses de l'Université.

Lidov, David, and Jim Gabura. 1973. "A Melody Writing Algorithm Using a Formal Language Model," *Computer Studies in the Humanities and Verbal Behavior* XIV/3-4: 138-148.

Lieberman, Fredric. 1970. "Computer-Aided Analysis of Javanese Music," *The Computer and Music*, edited by Harry B. Lincoln. Ithaca: Cornell University Press. pp. 181-192.

Lincoln, Harry B. Ed. 1970a. *The Computer and Music*. Ithaca: Cornell University Press.

_________. 1970b. "The Current State of Music Research and the Computer," *Computer and the Humanities* V/1 (September): 29-36.

_________. 1970c. "Thematic Indexing by Computer, Including Development of Necessary Hardware to Permit Printing of Music by Computer," *Computers and the Humanities* V/2 (November): 109-110.

__________. 1970d. A Study of Computer Techniques for Music Research. Final Report, Project No. 9-B-101, Grant No. OEG-2-9-420101-1067. Washington, DC: Office of Education, U.S. Department of Health, Education and Welware, Office of Education, Bureau of Research.

__________. 1970e. "Teaching Computer Applications in Musicology," *IBM Symposium on Introducing the Computer into the Humanities* [DocumentG 320-1044-0]. Poughkeepsie, NY: IBM. pp. 67-71.

__________. 1972a. "Uses of the Computer in Music Composition and Research," *Advances in Computers*, edited by Morris Rubinoff, vol. 12. New York: Academic Press. pp. 73-114.

__________. 1972b. "A Fortran Computer Program for Transcribing Franconian Rhythm," (Review of)," *Bulletin of the Council for Research in Music Education* 29 (Summer): 39-41.

__________. 1974. "Use of the Computer in Music Research: A Short Report on Accomplishments, Limitations, and Future Needs," *Computers and the Humanities* VIII/5-6 (September-November): 285-289.

__________. 1976. "Tablature pour les luths," *Computers and the Humanities* X/6 (November-December): 360-361.

__________. 1977. "Indices of the Italian Madrigal, 1530-1550," *Computers and the Humanities* XI/1 (January-February): 41.

Lindblom, Björn, and Johan Sundberg. 1970. "Towards a Generative Theory of Melody," *Svensk Tidskrift för Musikforskning* 52: 71-88.

Lockwood, Lewis. 1966. "MIR ('Musical Information Retrieval')," *Computers and the Humanities* I/2 (November): 51.

__________. 1970a. "A Stylistic Investigation of the Masses of Josquin Desprez with the Aid of the Computer: a Progress Report," *Musicology and the Computer: Three Symposia*, edited by Barry S. Brook. New York: The City University of New York Press. pp. 19-27.

__________. 1970b. "Computer Assistance in the Investigation of Accidentals in Renaissance Music," *IMS: Report on the Tenth Congress, Lubljana 1967*, edited by Dragotin Cvetko. Kassel: Bärenreiter. pp. 444-449.

Lönn, Anders. 1972. "Trends and Tendencies in Recent Swedish Musicology," *Acta Musicologica* 44/1: 11-25.

Lomax, Alan. 1976. *Cantometrics: An Approach to the Anthropology of Music*. Berkeley, CA: The University of California Press.

Longuet-Higgins, H. Christopher. 1976. "Perception of Melodies," *Nature* 263: 646-653. Reprinted in H. Christopher Longuet-Higgins, *Mental Processes: Studies in Cognitive Science*. Cambridge, MA: MIT Press, 1987. pp. 105-129.

__________. 1978. "The Perception of Music," *Interdisciplinary Science Reviews* 3 (June): 148-156. Reprinted as "Grammars of Music" in H. Christopher Longuet-Higgins, *Mental Processes: Studies in Cognitive Science*. Cambridge, MA: MIT Press, 1987. pp. 130-149.

__________. 1979. "The Perception of Music," *Proceedings of the Royal Society of London* Series B 205: 307-322. Reprinted in H. Christopher Longuet-Higgins, *Mental Processes: Studies in Cognitive Science*. Cambridge, MA: MIT Press, 1987. pp. 169-187.

Longuet-Higgins, H. Christopher, and Mark J. Steedman. 1971. "On Interpreting Bach," *Machine Intelligence 6*, edited by Bernard Meltzer and Donald Michie. Edinburgh: Edinburgh University Press. pp. 221-241.

Lord, Charles Hubbard. 1978. An Explication of Some Recent Mathematical Approaches to Music Analysis. Ph.D. dissertation. Bloomington, IN: Indiana University.
Ludvová, Jitka. 1974. "The Application of Analytical Methods of Information Theory to Tonal Music," *De musica disputationes Pragenses* II/4: 72-85.
Marillier, Cecil Glyn. 1971. Tonal Structure in the Symphonies of F. J. Haydn. M.A. thesis. North Dunedin, New Zealand: University of Otago.
Maser, Siegfried. 1971. *Numerische Ästhetik. Neue mathematische Verfahren zur quantitativen Beschreibung und Bewertung ästhetischer Zustände*, 3rd edition. Stuttgart: Krämer.
Mathews, Max V. 1972. Review of *The Computer and Music* by Harry B. Lincoln, *Computer Studies in the Humanities and Verbal Behavior* III/4 (November): 224-225.
Maultsby, Portia Katrenia. 1972. "Afro-American Music, 1619-1861: An Analytical Study," *Computers and the Humanities* VII/2 (November): 125.
_________. 1974. Afro-American Religious Music: 1619-1861. Historical Development and Computer Analysis of one Hundred Sprituals. Ph.D. dissertation. Madison, WI: The University of Wisconsin.
McMullen, Patrick T. 1974. "Influence of Number of Different Pitches and Melodic Redundancy on Preference Responses," *Journal of Research in Music Education* XXII: 198-204.
Meehan, James R. 1979. "An Artifical Intelligence Approach to Tonal Music Theory," *Proceedings of the ACM*. New York: Association for Computing Machinery. pp. 116-120.
Melkus, Ilja. 1976. "Některé Příklady Vyžití Samočinného počíytače v zahraniční muzikologii," *Lidová píseň a samočinný počítač III: Sborník materiálů ze 3. semináře o využití samočinného počítače při studiu lidové písně (Brno 15.-16.10.1974)*, ed. by Dušan Holý, Karel Pala, and Miloš Štědroň. Praha: Státni pedagogické nakladatelstvi. pp. 333-338.
Mendel, Arthur. 1969. "Some Preliminary Attempts at Computer-Assisted Style Analysis in Music," *Computers and the Humanities* IV/1 (September): 41-52.
_________. 1976a. "Towards Objective Criteria for Establishing Chronology and Authenticity: What Help Can the Computer Give?" *Josquin des Prez. Proceedings of the international Josquin festival-conference held at The Juilliard School at Lincoln Center in New York City, 21-25 June 1971*, edited by Edward E. Lowinsky. London: Oxford University Press. pp. 297-308.
_________. 1976b. "Critical Editions of Josquin Desprez," *Computers and the Humanities* X/1 (January-February): 52.
_________. 1979. "Recension of the Sources of the Works of Josquin Dezpres," *Computers and the Humanities* XIII/3 (July-September): 260.
Mendel, Arthur, and Thomas Hall. 1973. "Princeton Computer Tools for Musical Research," *Informatique et Sciences Humaines* 19 (December): 39-59. French translation: "Usage de l'ordinateur dans la recherche musicale à Princeton," pp. 61-65.
Mermet, Jean, and Denis Jaeger. 1974. "Un peripherique d'ordinateur a l'usage des musiciens," *Informatique musicale: Journées d'etude 1973. Textes des conférences E.R.A.T.T.O.*, edited by Hélène Charnassé and Henri Ducasse. Paris: Centre de documentation sciences humaines. pp. 204-218.
Meylan, Raymond. 1970. "Teorie de la Centonisation," *IMS: Report on the Tenth Congress, Lubljana 1967*, edited by Dragotin Cvetko. Kassel: Bärenreiter. pp. 427-430.
_________. 1974. "Limites de l'objectivite dans les ecritures instrumentales de la Renaissance," *Informatique musicale: Journées d'etude 1973. Textes des conférences*

E.R.A.T.T.O., edited by Hélène Charnassé and Henri Ducasse. Paris: Centre de documentation sciences humaines. pp. 1-9.

Miller, Alyce Sands, et al. 1972. "Annual Bibliography for 1971," *Computers and the Humanities* VI/4 (March): 235-251.

Moles, Abraham A. 1973. *Kunst & Computer*. Köln: M. DuMont Schauberg.

Moomaw, Charles J. 1973. A PL-1 Program for the Harmonic Analysis of Music by the Theories of Paul Hindemith and Howard Hanson. M.M. thesis. Cincinnati, OH: University of Cincinnati.

Moore, F. 1971. "Musica ed elaboratori elettronici," *Scienza & Tecnica: Annuario della EST, Enciclopedia della Scienza e della Tecnica*: 490-498.

Moorer, James Anderson. 1973. "Segmentation and Analysis of Continuous Musical Sound," *Computational Musicology Newsletter* I/1: 3-4.

__________. 1975. On the Segmentation and Analysis of Continuous Musical Sound by Digital Computer. Ph.D. dissertation. Stanford, CA: Stanford University.

Morehen, John, and Ian Bent. 1978. "Computers in the Analysis of Music," *Proceedings of the Royal Musical Association* CIV (1977/78): 30-46.

Morehen, John, and Ian Bent. 1979. "Computer Applications in Musicology," *The Musical Times* 120/7 (July): 563-566.

Morse, Margaret Beverly. 1974. A Quantitative Stylistic Analysis of the Agnus Dei Mass Movements of Guillaume Dufay Supporting the Doubtful Authenticity of the Missa Caput. M.M. thesis. West Hartford, CT: Hartt College of Music.

Morton, Ian A. 1973. "Analysis of Tonal Music at the Level of Perception," *Computational Musicology Newsletter* I/1: 16.

__________. 1974a. "Analysis of Tonal Music at the Level of Perception," *Computers in the Humanities*, edited by J. L. Mitchel. Minneapolis: University of Minnesota Press. pp. 261-266.

__________. 1974b. "Judgmental Factors in the Perception of Tonal Music," *Computers and the Humanities* VIII/1 (January): 51.

Morton, Ian, and John Lofstedt. 1970. "FORTRAN Music Programs Involving Numerically Related Tones," *The Computer and Music*, edited by Harry B. Lincoln. Ithaca: Cornell University Press. pp. 154-162.

Móži, Alexander. 1976. "Pokus o harmonickú analýzu inštrumentálnej hudby pomocou numerického kódového systému," *Lidová píseň a samočinný počítač III: Sborník materiálů ze 3. semináře o využití samočinného počítače při studiu lidové písně (Brno 15.-16.10.1974)*, ed. by Dušan Holý, Karel Pala, and Miloš Štědroň. Praha: Státni pedagogické nakladatelstvi. pp. 287-309.

Nakamura, Yasuaki, and Seiji Inokuchi. 1979. "Music Information Processing System and Its Applications to Comparative Musicology," *Proceedings of the Sixth International Joint Conference on Artificial Intelligence, Tokyo, August 20-23, 1979* [*IJCAI-79*]. [s.l.]: IJCAI, 1979. pp. 633-635.

Nake, Frieder. 1974. *Ästhetik als Informationsverarbeitung. Grundlagen und Anwendungen der Informatik im Bereich ästhetischer Produktion und Kritik*. Wien: Springer.

Narmour, Eugene. 1977. *Beyond Schenkerianism: The Need for Alternatives in Music Analysis*. Chicago: University of Chicago Press.

Nattiez, Jean-Jacques. 1972. "Is a Descriptive Seomiotics of Music Possible?" *Language Sciences* 23: 1-7.

__________. 1973a. "Musical Semiotics," *Computational Musicology Newsletter* I/1: 17.

__________. 1973b. "Linguistics: A New Approach for Musical Analysis?" *International Review of the Aesthetics and Sociology of Music* IV/1 (June): 51-69.

_________. 1975. “From Taxonomic Analysis to Stylistic Characterization: Debussy’s Syrinx,” *Actes du 1er congress international de semiotique musicale*, edited by Gino Stefani. Pesaro: Centro di iniziativa culturale. pp. 83-110.

Nelson, Gary Lee. 1973. “COMPOSE: A Program for Musical Composition,” *Computational Musicology Newsletter* I/1: 11.

_________. 1974a. Anton Webern’s ‘Five Canons’ op. 16: A Test Case for Computer-Aided Analysis and Synthesis of Musical Style. Ph.D. dissertation. St Louis, MO: Washington University.

_________. 1974b. “Pattern Recognition in Musical Score,” *Computers and the Humanities* VIII/1 (January): 50-51.

Pala, Karel. 1976. “Poznámy k popisu tematické stavby lidové písně,” *Lidová píseň a samočinný počítač III: Sborník materiálů ze 3. semináře o využití samočinného počítače při studiu lidové písně (Brno 15.-16.10.1974)*, ed. by Dušan Holý, Karel Pala, and Miloš Štědroň. Praha: Státni pedagogické nakladatelstvi. pp. 197-210.

Paszkowska, Elzbieta. 1977. “Struktura napiecia w klasyoznej formie sonatowej,” *Muzyka* [Poland] XXII/4: 14-37.

Patrick, Philip Howard. 1973. A Computer Study of a Suspension Formation in the Masses of Josquin Desprez. Ph.D. dissertation. Princeton, NJ: Princeton University.

Patrick, P. Howard. 1974. “A Computer Study of a Suspension Formation in the Masses of Josquin Desprez,” *Computer and the Humanities* VIII/5-6 (September-November): 321-331.

Patrick, P. Howard, and Karen Strickler. 1978. “A Computer-Assisted Study of Dissonance in the Masses of Josquin Desprez,” *Computers and the Humanities* 12/4: 341-364.

Patrick, Robert Lee. 1971. A Computer-Based Thematic Index to the Works of Heinrich Schütz. D.M.A. dissertation. Lexington, KY: University of Kentucky.

Pawlak, Aleksander. 1975. “Die Analyse und Klassifikation der Melodien aus der Region Kujawa,” *Methoden der ethnomusikologischen Analyse*, edited by Oskár Elschek. Bratislava: Sekcia hudobnej vedy-etnomuzikológia, Umenovedný ústav, Slovenská akademia vied. pp. 36-37.

Peterson, Don Laurel. 1975. Tonal Characteristics in the Kyrie and Sanctus Sections of Twelve L’homme arme Masses: A Computer-Assisted Study. Ph.D. dissertation. Madison, WI: University of Wisconsin.

Philippot, Michel P. 1970. “Muss es sein,” *L’Arc* [France] 40: 82-95.

Piotrowski, Zbigniew. 1974. “O zastosowaniu komputerow w muzyce mowi Lejaren Hiller,” *Ruch Muzyczny* [Poland] IV (February): 3-4.

Piszczalski, Martin B., and Bernard A. Galler. 1979. “Computer Analysis and Transcription of Performed Music: a Project Report,” *Computers and the Humanities* 13/3 (July-September): 195-206.

Pletka, Vaclav. 1974. “Methodologische Probleme der Arbeiterliedforschung,” *Arbeiterklasse und Musik: theoretische Positionen in der deutschen Arbeiterklasse zur Musikkultur vor 1945: Eine Dokumentation des Arbeiterliederarchivs*, edited by Charlotte Albrecht, Inge Lammel, Ilse Schütt, and Marlene Weller. Berlin: Akademie der Künste der Deutschen Demokratischen Republik. pp. 32-35.

Polansky, Larry. 1979. “A Hierarchical Gestalt Analysis of Ruggles’ Portals,” *Proceedings of the 1978 International Computer Music Conference*, vol. 2, edited by Curtis Roads. Evanston: Northwestern University. pp. 790-852.

Prerau, David S. 1970a. “Computer Pattern Recognition of Standard Engraved Music Notation,” *Computers and the Humanities* IV/5 (May): 344.

_________. 1970b. Computer Pattern Recognition of Standard Engraved Music Notation. PhD dissertation. Boston, MA: Massachussetts Institute of Technology.

_________. 1971. "Computer Pattern Recognition of Printed Music," *AFIPS Conference Proceedings* 39: 153-162.

_________. 1975. "DO-RE-MI: A Program that Recognizes Music Notation," *Computers and the Humanities* IX/1 (January): 25-29.

Rabson, Carolyn. 1979. "National Tune Index," *Computers and the Humanities* XIII/3 (July-September): 261.

Rader, Gary M. 1974. "A Method for Composing Simple Traditional Music by Computer," *Communications of the ACM* November 1974: 631-638. Reprinted in *Machine Models of Music*, edited by Stephen M. Schwanauer and David A. Levitt. Cambridge, MA: The MIT Press, 1993. pp. 242-260.

_________. 1975. "A Method for Composing Simple Traditional Music by Computer," *Computational Musicology Newsletter* II/1: 14.

Raskin, Jeffrey F. 1973. "On Keyboard Input of Music to the Computer," *Computational Musicology Newsletter* I/1: 4.

Ratner, Leonard G. 1970. "Ars Combinatoria: Chance and Choice in Eighteenth-Century Music," *Studies in Eighteenth Century Music: A Tribute to Karl Geiringer on his Seventieth Birthday*, edited by H. C. Robbins Landon. New York, NY: Oxford University Press. pp. 343-363.

Ravnikar, Bruno. 1972. "Nekaj rezultatov proucevanja glasbene folklore z metodami matematicne statistike," *Rad XVII Kongresa Saveza udruzenja folklorista Jugoslavije, Porec, 1970*, edited by Vinko Zganec. Zagreb, Jugoslavia: Savez udruzenja folklorista Jugoslavije, Drustvo folklorista Hrvatske. pp. 271-286.

Reckziegel, Walter. 1970. "Ein Subjektives Tempomaß," *Bericht über den Internationalen Musikwissenschaftlichen Kongress Leipzig 1966*, edited by Carl Dahlhause et al. Kassel: Bärenreiter. pp. 457-458.

Reier, Ellen Jane, and Warren Reier. 1976. "The Introit Trope Repertory at Nevers," *Nordiskt Kollokvium III. I Latinsk Liturgiforskning*, edited by Knud Ottosen. HelsinkiL Helsingfors University. pp. 97-110.

Reinecke, Hans-Peter. 1970. "Anwendung Informationstheoretischer und Korrelationsstatistischer Verfahren für die Analyse Musikalischer Strukturen," *IMS: Report on the Tenth Congress, Lubljana 1967*, edited by Dragotin Cvetko. Kassel: Bärenreiter. pp. 430-434.

Remmel, M. Ed. 1976. *Towards a Monographical Analysis of Some Folk-Song Arrangements*. Tallin: Academy of the Sciences of the Estonian S.S.R., Department of Social Sciences.

Remmel, Mart N. Ed. 1977. *Problemy taksonomii estonskich runiceskich melodij*. Tallin: Academy of Science.

Riedel, Johannes. 1970. "A Computer-Assisted Study of Ecuadorian Urban Music," *Computers and the Humanities* V/2 (November): 111.

Riotte, Andre. 1974. "Informatique musicale: jonction nouvelle entre art et science," *Euro-Spectra* XIII/1 (March): 2-15.

Roads, Curtis. 1979. "Grammars as Representations for Music," *Computer Music Journal* III/1 (March): 48-55.

Rohrer, Hermann G. 1971. *Musikalische Stilanalyse auf der Grundlage eines Modelles für Lernprozesse*. Berlin: Siemens AG.

Rojterstejn, Mihail I. 1973. "Graf i matrica kak instrumenty ladovogo analiza," *Muzykalnoje Iskusstvo i Nauka*. Moskva: Muzyka. pp. 175-189.

_________. 1974. "'Muzykalnye' structury v poezii Bloka," *O Muzyke. Problemy analiza: k semidesiatiletiiu so dnia rozhdeniia i piatidesiatiletiiu nauchno-pedagogicheskoi deiatel'nosti zasluzhennogo deiatelia iskusstv RSFSR, doktora iskusstvovedeniia professora Viktora Abramovicha Tsukkermana*, edited by V. P. Bobrovskii and G. L. Golovinskii. Moskow: Sovetskij Kompozitor. pp. 323-343.

Rothgeb, John. 1971a. "Musical Research by Computer: Some Current Limitations [Review of Harry B. Lincoln, ed., *The Computer and Music*]," *Computers and the Humanities* V/3 (January): 178-182.

_________. 1971b. "Some Early Efforts in Computational Musicology," *Computers and the Humanities* VI/1 (September): 56-58.

_________. 1971c. Harmonizing the unfigured bass: a computational study. Ph.D. dissertation. New Haven, CT: Yale University.

_________. 1979. "Simulating Musical Skills by Digital Computer," *ACM/CSC-ER: ACM Annual Conference / Annual Meeting* (January): 121-125. Revised in *Computer Music Journal* 4/2 (Summer 1980): 36-40. Reprinted in *The Music Machine*, edited by Curtis Roads. Cambridge, MA: MIT Press, 1989. pp. 657-662.

Ryžov, L. 1972. *Točnyje metody i muzykalnoje iskusstvo*. Rostov na Donu: Rostov University Press.

Sands, Alyce E., et al. 1970. "Annual Bibliography for 1969," *Computers and the Humanities* IV/5 (May): 319-322.

Sands, Alyce E., et al. 1971. "Annual Bibliography for 1970," *Computers and the Humanities* V/4 (March): 215-238.

Scharf, Joachim-Hermann. 1972. "Einführung in 'Computer und Musikwissenschaft'," *Informatik. Vorträge anläßlich der Jahresversammlung vom 14. bis 17. Oktober 1971 zu Halle (Saale)*, edited by Jocahim-Hermann Scharf. Leipzig: Barth. pp. 563-572.

Scherrer, Deborah K. 1973. "Computer-Aided Music Analysis," *Computational Musicology Newsletter* I/1: 17.

Scherrer, Deborah K., and Philip H. Scherrer. 1971. "An Experiment in the Computer Measurement of Melodic Variation in Folksong," *Journal of American Folklore* 84/332 (April-June): 230-241.

Schiødt, Nanna. 1965. "Data Processing Applied to Byzantine Chant," *Fontes Artis Musicae* XII/2-3: 122-123.

_________. 1971. "A Computer-Aided Analysis of Thirty-Five Byzantine Hymns," *Studies in Eastern Chant II*, edited by Miloš Velimirović. London: Oxford University Press. pp. 129-154.

Sellek, John. 1968. "Music Information Retrieval," *Computers and the Humanities* III/2 (November): 112.

_________. 1969. "Music Information Retrieval," *Computers and the Humanities* III/5 (May): 310.

_________. 1970. "Musical Information Retrieval (MIR)," *Computers and the Humanities* V/2 (November): 110.

Sentieri, Alfred Richard. 1978. A Method for the Specification of Style Change in Music: A Computer-Aided Study of Selected Venetian Sacred Compositions from the Time of Gabrieli to the Time of Vivaldi. Ph.D. thesis. Ohio State University.

Ševčíková, Marie. 1976. "Tematická Výstavba lidové písně," *Lidová píseň a samočinný počítač III: Sborník materiálů ze 3. semináře o využití samočinného počítače při studiu lidové písně (Brno 15.-16.10.1974)*, ed. by Dušan Holý, Karel Pala, and Miloš Štědroň. Praha: Státni pedagogické nakladatelstvi. pp. 145-153.

Shamos, Michael Ian. 1971. "Computer Investigation of Highland Bagpipe Music," *Computers and the Humanities* V/5 (May): 311-312.

Shatzkin, Merton. 1970. "Chords and Chord Progression in J. S. Bach's 371 Chorales," *Computers and the Humanities* IV/5 (May): 347.

_________. 1973. "Bach Chorales," *Computational Musicology Newsletter* I/1: 17.

Silverman, Faye-Ellen. 1974. "Report from New York City: Computer Conference, June 1973," *Current Musicology* 17 (January): 77-80.

Sirovátka, Oldřich. 1976. "Členění písňového textu," *Lidová píseň a samočinný počítač III: Sborník materiálů ze 3. semináře o využití samočinného počítače při studiu lidové písně (Brno 15.-16.10.1974)*, ed. by Dušan Holý, Karel Pala, and Miloš Štědroň. Praha: Státni pedagogické nakladatelstvi. pp. 107-119.

Smoliar, Stephen William. 1971a. A Parallel-Processing Model of Musical Structures. Ph.D. dissertation. Boston, MA: Massachussetts Institute of Technology.

_________. 1971b. *A Parallel-Processing Model of Musical Structures*. Cambridge, MA: Project Mac, Massachusetts Institute of Technology.

_________. 1972a. "Music Theory – A Programming Linguistic Approach," *Proceedings of the ACM 25th Annual Conference*. New York: Association for Computing Machinery. pp. 100-114.

_________. 1972b. Music Theory – A Programming Linguistic Approach. Technical Report # 15. Haifa, Israel: Israel Institute of Technology.

_________. 1973. Systemic Aspects of Musical Activity. Technical Report # 28. Haifa, Israel: Israel Institute of Technology.

_________. 1974a. "Process Structuring and Music Theory," *Journal of Music Theory* XVIII/2 (Autumn): 308-336. Reprinted in *Machine Models of Music*, edited by Stephen M. Schwanauer and David A. Levitt. Cambridge, MA: The MIT Press, 1993. pp. 188-212.

_________. 1974b. "An Interactive Computer Music Facility," *Computers and the Humanities* VIII/4 (July): 254-255.

_________. 1975a. "Proposal for an Interactive Computer-Music Facility," *Computational Musicology Newsletter* II/1: 5-6.

_________. 1975b. "Process Structuring and Music Theory," *Computational Musicology Newsletter* II/1: 17.

_________. 1976a. "Music Programs: An Approach to Music Theory Through Computational Linguistics," *Journal of Music Theory* XX/1 (Spring): 105-131.

_________. 1976b. Schenker: A Computer Aid for Analysing Tonal Music. Music Project Report No. 6. [Philadelphia]: Department of Computer and Information Science, University of Pennsylvania.

_________. 1977. "SCHENKER: A Computer Aid for Analyzing Tonal Music," *SIGLASH Newsletter* X/1-2: 30-61.

Smoliar, Stephen W., and M. Joseph Willson. 1974. "Proposal for an Interactive Computer-Music Facility," *Numus-West* V: 39-43.

Snell, James Loftin. 1979. Design for a Formal System for Deriving Tonal Music. Master's thesis. Binghamton, NY: State University of New York at Binghamton.

Solomon, Larry. 1976. *Music Analysis System*. Software 1976, 1982, 1984.

Sørensen, Av Olve. 1978. "Metoder og Metodeproblemer ved Harmonisk Analyse med EDB," *Studia Musicologica Norvegica* IV: 201-216.

Sørensen, Olve. 1980. "Musikkanalyse med datamaskin II," *Nordisk musik och musikvetenskap under 1970-talet: en rapport från 8:e Nordiska musikforskar-kongressen, Ljung-*

skile folkhögskola 25-30 juni 1979, edited by Anders Carlsson and Jan Ling. Göteborg: Musikvetenskapliga institutionen, Göteborgs universitet. pp. 177-192.
Srinivasan, R. 1978. "Studies on Indian Musical Scales. Part I: Computer Analysis of Venkatamakhi's Melakarta Scheme," *Journal of the Sangeet Natak Academy* [India] 49 (July-September): 33-42.
_________. 1980. "Studies on Indian Musical Scales. Part II: On the Degree of Relatedness of Ragas and Application to 72 Melas," *Journal of the Sangeet Natak Academy* [India] 58 (October-December): 27-38.
Starr, Daniel, and Robert Morris. 1977. "A General Theory of Combinatoriality and the Aggregate (Part 1)," *Perspectives of New Music* XVI/1 (Autumn-Winter): 3-35.
Starr, Daniel, and Robert Morris. 1978. "A General Theory of Combinatoriality and the Aggregate (Part 2)," *Perspectives of New Music* XVI/2 (Spring-Summer): 50-84.
Stech, David. 1976. A Computer-Assisted Approach to Micro-Analysis of Melodic Lines. Ph.D. dissertation. East Lansing, MI: Michigan State University.
________. 1981. "A Computer-Assisted Approach to Micro-Analysis of Melodic Lines," *Computers and the Humanities* XV/4 (December): 211-221.
Štědroň, Miloš. 1971. "Možnosti intervalové a melodické analýzy," *Opus Musicum* [Czechoslovakia] III/7 (July): 202-208.
_________. 1975. "K analýze vokální melodiky Janáčkovy opery Věc Makropulos s využitím samočinného počítače," *Hudebni Veda* [Czechoslovakia] XII/1: 46-64.
_________. 1976. "K intervalovým charakteristikám jednotlivých rolí v Janáčkově opeře Věc Makropulos: Úvahy nad výsledky počítačové analýzy vokální melodiky," *Lidová píseň a samočinný počítač III: Sborník materiálů ze 3. semináře o využití samočinného počítače při studiu lidové písně (Brno 15.-16.10.1974)*, ed. by Dušan Holý, Karel Pala, and Miloš Štědroň. Praha: Státni pedagogické nakladatelstvi. pp. 263-285.
_________. 1978. "Zjistovani Typicnosti Nekterych Melodickych Struktur ve Vokalni Melodice Janackovy Opery Věc Makropulos Zapomoci SP," *Musicologica slovaca* [Czechoslovakia] VI: 187-198.
Štědroň, Miloš, et al. 1976. "Kriticky o možnostech hudební analýzy," *Lidová píseň a samočinný počítač III: Sborník materiálů ze 3. semináře o využití samočinného počítače při studiu lidové písně (Brno 15.-16.10.1974)*, ed. by Dušan Holý, Karel Pala, and Miloš Štědroň. Praha: Státni pedagogické nakladatelstvi. pp. 339-356.
Steedman, Mark J. 1977. "The Perception of Musical Rhythm and Metre," *Perception* VI: 555-569.
Steinbeck, Wolfram. 1976a. "The Use of the Computer in the Analysis of German Folksongs," *Computers and the Humanities* X/5 (September/October): 287-296.
_________. 1976b. "Die Liederbank Kiel," *Jahrbuch des Staatlichen Instituts for Musikforschung* 1976: 94-108.
_________. 1976c. Review of *Faktorenanalytische Typenbestimmung an Volksliedmelodien* by Reiner Kluge, *Jahrbuch für Volksliedforschung* 21: 217-218.
_________. 1978. "Zur Methodik der Analyse deutscher volkstümlicher Lieder mit Hilfe elektronischer Rechenanlagen," *Beiträge zur Musikgeschichte Nordeuropas. Kurt Gudewill zum 65. Geburtstag*, edited by Uwe Haensel. Wolfenbüttel: Möseler. pp. 323-341.
_________. 1979. "Die Liederbank Kiel," *Computers and the Humanities* XIII/3 (July-September): 263.
_________. 1980. "ANTOC. Ein neues Verfahren zur Aufzeichnung von Melodien durch den Computer," *Bericht über den Internationalen musikwissenschaftlichen Kongress*

Berlin 1974, edited by Hellmut Kühn and Peter Nitsche. Kassel: Bärenreiter. pp. 546-553.

_________. 1982. *Struktur und Ähnlichkeit. Methoden automatisierter Melodienanalyse.* Kieler Schriften zur Musikwissenschaft 25. Kassel: Bärenreiter.

Stephan, Claudio. 1971. "Harmonic and Phraseologic Computer Aided Music Analysis," *Computers and the Humanities* VI/2 (November): 123.

_________. 1977. "Computer Aided Music Analysis," *Computers and the Humanities* XI/1 (January-February): 42.

Stoffer, Thomas H. 1979. *Aspekte einer generativen Syntax zur Beschreibung musikalischer Strukturen für eine kognitive Musikpsychologie.* Berichte des Psychologischen Instituts der Ruhr-Universität Bochum, Arbeitseinheit Kognitionspsychologie, Nr. 11, 1979.

Stroh, Wolfgang Martin. 1972. "Über Schwierigkeiten bei der mathematischen Darstellung musikalischer Sachverhalte," *Neue Zeitschrift für Musik* X: 567-572.

Suchoff, Benjamin. 1967a. "Computer Applications to Bartók's Serbo-Croatian Material," *Tempo* 80 (Spring): 15-19.

_________. 1967b. "Computer Applications to Béla Bartók's Serbo-Croatian Material," *Computers and the Humanities* II/2 (November): 88.

_________. 1968a. "Bartók, Ethnomusicology, and the Computer," *Institute for Computer Research in the Humanities Newsletter* IV/4 (December): 3-6.

_________. 1968b. "Computerized Folk Song Research and the Problem of Variants," *Computers and the Humanities* II/4 (March): 155-158.

_________. 1969a. "Some Problems in Computer-Oriented Bartokian Ethnomusicology," *Ethnomusicology* XIII/3 (September): 489-497.

_________. 1969b. "A Computerized Data Bank of Musical and Textual Information on Bartok's Six String Quartets," *Computers and the Humanities* III/5 (May): 311.

_________. 1970a. "Computer-Oriented Comparative Musicology," *The Computer and Music*, edited by Harry B. Lincoln. Ithaca: Cornell University Press. pp. 193-206.

_________. 1970b. "Aplicarea calculatorelor elektronice la etnomuzicologia Bartokiana," *Musica* XI (November): 10-14.

_________. 1970c. "A Bartoki nepzenekutatas es az elektronikus szamitogepeg," *Muzsika* XIII (July): 6-8; (August): 4-6.

_________. 1971. "The Computer and Bartók Research in America," *Journal of Research in Music Education* XIX/1 (Spring): 3-16.

_________. 1972a. "A National Science Computer Network: A Report on the First Working Seminar," *Computers and the Humanities* VII/2 (November): 96-97.

_________. 1972b. "Recent Developments in Computer-Assisted Musical Scholarship [Review of]," *Computing Review* 13/2 (February): 68-69.

_________. 1973a. "An Application of GRIPHOS to Bartók's Turkish Folk Music Materials," *Computational Musicology Newsletter* I/1: 18.

_________. 1973b. "Toward a Computer Typography for Music Research: A Progress Report (Review of)," *Computing Review* 14/5 (May): 224-225.

_________. 1973c. "The Computer and Bartók Research in America," *Magyar zenetörténeti Tanulmányok: Mosonyi Mihály és Bartók Béla émlékére* [Studies on the History of Hungarian Music in Memory of Mihály Mosonyi and Bela Bartók], edited by Ferenc Bonis. Budapest: Zenemükiadó. pp. 313-327.

_________. 1979. "The COMMPUTE Program," *Computers and the Humanities* XIII/3 (July-September): 262.

Suchoff, Benjamin, and Jack Heller. 1970. "Studies Relating to Automation of Bartók Archives," *Computers and the Humanities* V/2 (November): 110.
Suchoff, Benjamin, and Jack Heller. 1971. "Studies Relating to Automatization of Bartók Archives," *Computers and the Humanities* V/5 (May): 309-310.
Suchoff, Benjamin, and Jack Heller. 1977. "Computer Oriented Music Materials Permuted for User Transformation or Exchange (COMMPUTE)," *Computers and the Humanities* XI/1 (January-February): 42.
Sundberg, Johan, and Björn Lindblom. 1975. "A Generative Theory of Swedish Nursery Tunes," *Actes du 1er congress international de semiotique musicale*, edited by Gino Stefani. Pesaro: Centro di iniziativa culturale. pp. 111-124.
Sundberg, Johan, and Björn Lindblom. 1976. "Generative Theories in Language and Music Descriptions," *Cognition* IV: 99-122. Reprinted in *Machine Models of Music*, edited by Stephen M. Schwanauer and David A. Levitt. Cambridge, MA: The MIT Press, 1993. pp. 262-286.
Sward, Rosalie La Grow. 1979. "The Computer Assists in Attempting to Solve a Problem of Twentieth Century Music," *Proceedings of the 1978 International Computer Music Conference*, vol. 2, edited by Curtis Roads. Evanston, IL: Northwestern University. 853-872.
Sychra, Antonín. 1964. "Hudba a Kybernetika," *Nové Cestu Hudby* I (1964): 234-267. [Summary in German: "Musik und Kybernetik," pp. 278-279.]
_________. 1965. "Möglichkeiten der Anwendung der Kybernetik und der Informationstheorie in der marxistischen Musikwissenschaft," *Beiträge zur Musikwissenschaft* VII/4: 402-407.
_________. 1970. "Die Anwendung der Kybernetik und der Informations-Theorie in der Marxistischen Ästhetik," *Beiträge zur Musikwissenschaft* XII/2: 83-108.
Tadeusiewicz, Ryszard, and Aleksander Sodo. 1979. "Kompozycje muzyczne z komputera," *Problemy* (Poland) XII (December): 25-30.
Tänzer, Peter. 1973. "Musik und Kybernetik," *Neue Zeitschrift für Musik* 134/8 (1973): 483-492.
Tenney, James C., and Larry Polansky. 1978. Hierarchical Gestalt Perception in Music: A 'Metric Space' Model. Mimeographed. Toronto: York University Music Department.
Tesař, Stanislav. 1976. "K možnostem využití SP v hymnologii," *Lidová píseň a samočinný počítač III: Sborník materiálů ze 3. semináře o využití samočinného počítače při studiu lidové písně (Brno 15.-16.10.1974)*, ed. by Dušan Holý, Karel Pala, and Miloš Štědroň. Praha: Státni pedagogické nakladatelstvi. pp. 253-261.
Tischler, Hans. 1970. "A Complete Edition of the *Magnus Liber Organi*," *Computers and the Humanities* V/2 (November): 111.
_________. 1973. "Parisian Two-Part Organa," *Computational Musicology Newsletter* I/1: 18.
Tokumaru, Yoshihiko. 1970. "Joho-riron to ongaku-kodo," *Arima daigoro sensei koki kinen ronbunshu* [*Daigoro Festschrift*], edited by Kunitachi Ongaku Daigaku. Tokyo: Kunitachi Music College. pp. 195-212.
Toncrová, Marta. 1976. "Zur Frage der individuellen und normalisierten Fassung des Volksliedes vom Gesichtspunkt der Klassifikation," *Hudobná klasifikácia a samocinné pocitace: predbezná zpráva 6. Etnomuzikologického seminára = Musikklassifikation und elektronische Datenverarbeitung: Vorbericht des 6. Ethnomusikologischen Seminars, Kocovce, 6.-10. Október 1975*, edited by Oskár Elschek. Bratislava: Sekcia hudobnej vedy-etnomuzikológia, Umenovedný ústav, Slovenská akademia vied. 1 p.

Trowbridge, Lynn Mason. 1970. "The Burgundian Chanson: An Index and Analysis of Incipits," *Computers and the Humanities* IV/5 (May): 343-344.

__________. 1971. "An Analytical and Indexing System for Incipits of Renaissance Polyphonic Compositions," *Computers and the Humanities* V/5 (May): 310.

Ulrich, John Wade. 1977. "The Analysis and Synthesis of Jazz by Computer," *Proceedings of the 5th International Joint Conference on Artificial Intelligence 1977 (IJCAI-77)*, vol. 2. Pittsburgh, PA: Carnegie-Mellon University. pp. 865-872.

Urup, Henning. 1972. Danske Folkedanse. En beskrivelse og undersogelse af det danske folkelige melodistof med hertil horende dansebeskrivelser. M.A. thesis. Kobenhavn, Denmark: University of Kobenhavn.

Vercoe, Barry L. 1971. Reviews of *The computer and music*, edited Hary B. Lincoln; *Musicology and the computer*, edited Barry S. Brook. *Perspectives of New Music* IX/X (Spring/Summer-Autumn/Winter): 323-330.

__________. 1974. "Music computation conference: a report and summary," *Perspectives of New Music* XIII/1 (Fall): 234-238.

Victor, Michele. 1975. "L'Informatique musicale," *Musique En jeu* (France) XVIII (April): 45-62.

Vikis-Freibergs, Vaira, and Imants Freibergs. 1978. "Formulaic Analysis of the Computer-Accessible Corpus of Latvian Sun-Songs," *Computers and the Humanities* XII/4: 329-339.

Völz, Horst. 1975. "Beitrag zur formalen Musikanalyse und -synthese," *Beiträge zur Musikwissenschaft* XVII/2-3: 127-154.

Vos, Piet G. 1976. Identification of Metre in Music. Bericht Nr. 76 ON 06. Nijmegen, Netherlands: University of Nijmegen.

Wagner, Christoph, Ernst Piontek, and Ludwig Teckhaus. 1973. "Piano Learning and Programmed Instruction," *Journal of Research in Music Education* XXI/2 (Summer): 106-22.

Wagner, Günther. 1976. "Exaktwissenschaftliche Musikanalyse und Informationsästhetik." *International Review of Aesthetics and Sociology of Music* VII/1 (June): 63-76.

Waite, Stephen V. F., et al. 1973. "Annual Bibliography for 1972 and Supplement to Preceding Years," *Computers and the Humanities* VII/4 (March): 229-252.

Waite, Stephen V. F., et al. 1974. "Annual Bibliography for 1973 and Supplement to Preceding Years," *Computers and the Humanities* VIII/2 (March): 99-113.

Waite, Stephen V. F., et al. 1975. "Annual Bibliography for 1974 and Supplement to Preceding Years," *Computers and the Humanities* IX/3 (May): 127-144.

Waite, Stephen V. F., et al. 1976. "Annual Bibliography for 1975 and Supplement to Preceding Years," *Computers and the Humanities* X/2 (March-April): 101-121.

Waite, Stephen V. F., et al. 1977. "Annual Bibliography for 1976 and Supplement to Preceding Years," *Computers and the Humanities* XI/2 (March-April): 100-118.

Walker, Thomas. 1970. "The computer and music (Review of)," *Notes: Quarterly Journal of the Music Library Association* 27/2 (December): 178-183.

Warburton, Thomas. 1971. Review of *The Opening Sonata-Allegro Movements in a Randomly Selected Sample of Solo Keyboard Sonatas Published in the Years 1742-1774* by Roger Jaques Kamien, *Current Musicology* XI: 118-121.

Wenker, Jerome R. 1964. A Computational Method for the Analysis of Anglo-American Folksongs. M.A. thesis. Bloomington, IN: Indiana University.

__________. 1968. "A Music Compiler for Musicologists and Ethnomusicology," *Computers and the Humanities* II/5 (May): 244.

_________. 1969. "An Analytic Approach to Folk Music," *Computers and the Humanities* IV/2 (November): 138.
_________. 1970. "A Computer Oriented Music Notation Including Ethnomusicological Symbols," *Musicology and the Computer: Three Symposia*, edited by Barry S. Brook. New York: The City University of New York Press. pp. 91-129.
_________. 1972a. "A Music Compiler for Musicologists and Ethnomusicologists," *Computers and the Humanities* VII/2 (November): 124.
_________. 1972b. "An Analytic Approach to Folk Music," *Computers and the Humanities* VII/2 (November): 124-125.
_________. 1972c. "MUSTRAN II - An Extended *MUS*ic *TRAN*slator," *Computers and the Humanities* VII/2 (November): 125.
_________. 1973a. "Music Encoding - Keypunch," *Computational Musicology Newsletter* I/1: 6-7.
_________. 1973b. "Editorial Forword," *Computational Musicology Newsletter* I/1: 1-2.
_________. 1974. "MUSTRAN II: A Foundation for Computational Musicology," *Computers in the Humanities*, edited by J. L. Mitchell. Edinburgh: Edinburgh University Press. pp. 267-280.
_________. 1976. "On the Indexing of Melodies," *Hudobná klasifikácia a samocinné pocitace: predbezná zpráva 6. Etnomuzikologického seminára = Musikklassifikation und elektronische Datenverarbeitung: Vorbericht des 6. Ethnomusikologischen Seminars, Kocovce, 6.-10. Október 1975*, edited by Oskár Elschek. Bratislava: Sekcia hudobnej vedy-etnomuzikológia, Umenovedný ústav, Slovenská akademia vied. 1 p.
_________. 1978. A Computer-Aided Analysis of Anglo-Canadian Folktunes. Ph.D. dissertation. Bloomington, IN: Indiana University.
Whitney, Thomas G. 1977. "Music analysis: SLAM simplified or how the computer compares 16th century Bourgeois with eighteenth century Bach," *Creative Computing* III/2: 88-89.
Winckel, Fritz. 1964. "Die informationstheoretische Analyse musikalischer Strukturen," *Die Musikforschung* XVII/1: 1-14.
_________. 1967. "Neue Wege der mathematischen Analyse von Musikstrukturen," *Wiener Akademie Festschrift*. Wien: Lafite. pp. 78-88.
_________. 1975. "Das Wirkgefuge von Musikstrukturen in der Analyse durch Computer und Kybernetik," *Festschrift Kurt Blaukopf*, edited by Irmgard Bontinck and Otto Brusatti. Wien: Universal Edition. pp. 156-163.
Wittlich, Gary E. 1969. "Programming a Computer for Musical Analysis," *Your Musical Cue* V/6 (April): 3-13.
_________. 1971. "Music as Information," *Your Musical Cue* VII/3 (December-January): 3-9.
_________. 1973a. "Project Score," *Computational Musicology Newsletter* I/1: 6.
_________. 1973b. "Pattern Structure Studies," *Computational Musicology Newsletter* I/1: 19.
_________. 1973c. "Scale Index," *Computational Musicology Newsletter* I/1: 19.
Wittlich, Gary, Donald Byrd, and Rosalee Nerheim. 1978. "A System for Interactive Encoding of Music Scores Under Computer Control," *Computers and the Humanities* XII/4: 309-319.
Wolff, Anthony B. 1972. "Development of a DARMS-to-Canonical DARMS Translator," *Computers and the Humanities* VI/5 (May): 316.
_________. 1977. "Problems of Representation in Musical Computing," *Computers and the Humanities* XI/1 (January-February): 3-12.

Xenakis, Iannis. 1971. *Formalized Music. Thought and Mathematics in Composition*. Bloomington: Indiana University Press.

Youngblood, Joseph E. 1967. "Root Progression and Composer Identification," *Computers and the Humanities* II/2 (November): 87.

_________. 1970. "Root Progressions and Composer Identification," *The Computer and Music*, edited by Harry B. Lincoln. Ithaca: Cornell University Press. pp. 172-178.

Zaripov, Rudolf K. 1963. *Kibernetica i Muzyka*. Moscow: Znanie.

_________. 1969. "'Cybernetics and Music,' translated from the Russion by J. G. K. Russel, with commentary by Michael KASSLER," *Perspectives of New Music*, VII/2 (Spring-Summer): 115-154.

_________. 1971. *Kibernetica i Muzyka*. Moscow: Nauka.

Zimmerly, John David. 1978. A Computer-Assisted Study of Selected Kyries from the Parody Masses of Clemens non Papa. M.A. thesis. East Lansing, MI: Michigan State University.

Zoch, Josef. 1972. "Vztah mezi vokaly a melodii v lidove pisni," *Lidová písen a samostatný pocítac I*, edited by Dušan Holý and Oldrich Sirovátka. Brno: Klub uživatelů MSP. pp. 215-219.

Zwink, Eberhard. 1974. *Paul Hindemiths "Unterweisung im Tonsatz" als Konsequenz der Entwicklung seiner Kompositionstechnik. Graphische und Statistische Musikanalyse*. Göppingen: Alfred Kümmerle.

Alphabetical Bibliography (Through the 1970s)

Abraham, Gerald. 1967. "Musical Scholarship in the 20th Century," *Studies in Music* I: 1-10.

Adamčiak, Milan. 1975. "Die semiotische Analyse des Musikwerkes," *Methoden der ethnomusikologischen Analyse*, edited by Oskár Elschek. Bratislava: Sekcia hudobnej vedy-etnomuzikológia, Umenovedný ústav, Slovenská akademia vied. p. 12.

Adams, Charles R. 1976. "Melodic Contour Typology," *Ethnomusicology* XX/2 (May): 179-215.

Addison, Don. 1974. "Elements of Style in Performing the Chinese *P'i-p'a*," *Selected Reports in Ethnomusicology* II/1: 118-139.

Allen, John R. Ed. 1976. "Directory of Scholars Active," *Computers and the Humanities* X/1 (January-February): 41-55.

_________. Ed. 1977. "Directory of Scholars Active," *Computers and the Humanities* XI/1 (January-February): 24-46.

Alphonce, Bo H. 1970. "Music Theory at Yale – A Case Study and a Project Report," *Svensk Tidskrift for Musikforskning* LII: 38-46.

_________. 1974a. The Invariance Matrix. Ph.D. dissertation. New Haven, CT: Yale University.

_________. 1974b. "The Invariance Matrix as an Analytical Tool," *International Musicological Society: Report of the Eleventh Congress, Copenhagen 1972*, edited by Henrik Glahn, Søren Sørensen, and Peter Ryom. Copenhagen: Edition W. Hansen. pp. 228-235.

_________. 1980. "Music Analysis by Computer – A Field for Theory Formation," *Computer Music Journal* IV/2 (Summer): 26-35.

_________. 1989a. "Computer Applications: Analysis and Modeling," *Music Theory Spectrum* XI/1 (Spring): 49-59.

_________. 1989b. "Computer Applications in Music Research: A Retrospective," *Computers in Music Research* I (Fall): 1-74.

_________. 1989c. "[Review of] Deta S. Davis, Computer Applications in Music: A Bibliography," *Computers in Music Research* I (Fall): 133-159.

Andrus, Donald George. 1968. An Analysis of the Acoustics of Tamtam Sounds. D.M.A. dissertation. Urbana, IL: University of Illinois.

Anonymous. 1966. "Computer Programs Designed to Solve Humanistic Problems," *Computers and the Humanities* I/2 (November): 39-55.

Anonymous. 1967a. "Directory of Scholars Active," *Computers and the Humanities* I/5 (May): 178-241.

Anonymous. 1967b. "Directory of Scholars Active," *Computers and the Humanities* II/2 (November): 71-93.

Anonymous. 1968a. "Directory of Scholars Active," *Computers and the Humanities* II/5 (May): 223-250.

Anonymous. 1968b. "Directory of Scholars Active," *Computers and the Humanities* III/2 (November): 105-118.

Anonymous. 1969a. "Directory of Scholars Active," *Computers and the Humanities* III/5 (May): 280-320.

Anonymous. 1969b. "Directory of Scholars Active," *Computers and the Humanities* IV/2 (November): 125-141.

Anonymous. 1970a. "Directory of Scholars Active," *Computers and the Humanities* IV/5 (May): 323-357.
Anonymous. 1970b. "Directory of Scholars Active," *Computers and the Humanities* V/2 (November): 84-128.
Anonymous. 1971a. "Directory of Scholars Active," *Computers and the Humanities* V/5 (May): 291-320.
Anonymous. 1971b. "Directory of Scholars Active," *Computers and the Humanities* VI/2 (November): 114-124.
Anonymous. 1972a. "Directory of Scholars Active," *Computers and the Humanities* VI/5 (May): 301-320.
Anonymous. 1972b. "Directory of Scholars Active," *Computers and the Humanities* VII/2 (November): 111-128.
Anonymous. 1973. "Directory of Scholars Active," *Computers and the Humanities* VII/5 (May): 295-318.
Anonymous. 1974a. "Directory of Scholars Active," *Computers and the Humanities* VIII/1 (January): 40-55.
Anonymous. 1974b. "Directory of Scholars Active," *Computers and the Humanities* VIII/4 (July): 250-257.
Anonymous. 1975a. "Directory of Scholars Active," *Computers and the Humanities* IX/1 (January): 30-35.
Anonymous. 1975b. "Directory of Scholars Active," *Computers and the Humanities* IX/4 (July): 187-196.
Anonymous. 1979a. "Directory of Scholars Active," *Computers and the Humanities* XIII/1 (January-March): 43-63.
Anonymous. 1979b. "Directory of Scholars Active," *Computers and the Humanities* XIII/3 (July-September): 247-267.
Anonymous. 1979c. "Annual Bibliography for 1977 and Supplement to Preceding Years," *Computers and the Humanities* XIII/2 (April-June): 172-183.
Aranovskij, Mark G. 1974. "Myslenije, jazyk, semantika," *Problemy muzykalnovo myslenija.* Moskow: Muzyka. pp. 90-128.
_________. 1991. *Sintaksiceskaja struktura melodii: issledovanie.* Moskva, Russia: Muzyka.
Arom, Simha. 1970. "Essai d'une notation des monodies à des fins d'analyse," *Revue de Musicologie* 55: 172-216.
_________. 1980. "Structuration du Temps dans les Musiques d'Afrique Centrale: Periodicité, Mètre, Rhythmique et Polyrhythmie," *Revue de Musicologie* 70 (1984): 5-36.
Ashford, Theodore H. A. 1967. "Analysis of Musical Relationships in Contemporary Music," *Computers and the Humanities* I/5 (May): 224.
Ashton, Alan Conway. 1971. Electronics, Music and Computer. Ph.D. dissertation. Salt Lake City, UT: University of Utah.
Askenfelt, Anders. 1979. "Automatic Computer Notation of Played Melodies," *Computers and the Humanities* XIII/1 (January-March): 58-59.
Avenary, Hanoch. 1973. "Analysis of Musical Modes on a Quantitative Base," *Computational Musicology Newsletter* I/1: 13.
_________. 1977. "The Northern and Southern Idioms of Early European Music: A New Approach to an Old Problem," *Acta Musicologica* XLIX/1: 27-49.
Babbitt, Milton. 1955. "Some Aspects of Twelve-Tone Composition," *The Score and I.M.A. Magazine* 12: 53-61.

_________. 1960. "Twelve-Tone Invariants as Compositional Determinatns," *The Music Quaterly* 46: 246-259.

_________. 1961. "Set-Structure as a Compositional Determinant," *Journal of Music Theory* V/1 (Spring): 72-94.

_________. 1965. "The Use of Computers in Musicological Research," *Perspectives of New Music* III/2 (Spring-Summer): 74-83.

Baggi, Denis L. 1974. Realization of the Unfigured Bass by Digital Computer. Ph.D. dissertation. Berkeley, CA: University of California.

Bailey, Robert Lee. 1980. Music and Mathematics: An Interface in the Writings of Leonhard Euler. EDD thesis, State University of New York at Buffalo.

Baker, Robert Allen. 1963. A Statistical Analysis of the Harmonic Practice of the 18th and Early 19th Centuries. Ph.D. thesis. Champaign, IL: University of Illinois.

Ballo, Igor. 1978. "FIS, metóda triedenia melódií z hlàdiska podobnosti," *Musicologica Slovaca* VI (1978): 175-182.

Ballová, Luba. 1976a. "Methoden der Quantifizierung von Melodieähnlichkeiten," *Hudobná klasifikácia a samocinné pocitace: predbezná zpráva 6. Etnomuzikologického seminára = Musikklassifikation und elektronische Datenverarbeitung: Vorbericht des 6. Ethnomusikologischen Seminars, Kocovce, 6.-10. Október 1975*, edited by Oskár Elschek. Bratislava: Sekcia hudobnej vedy-etnomuzikológia, Umenovedný ústav, Slovenská akademia vied. 2 p.

_________. 1976b. "Štruktúra testovacích súborov pre výskum podobnosti" ["The structure of test sets in the investigation of similarities"], *Lidová píseň a samočinný počítač III: Sborník materiálů ze 3. semináře o využití samočinného počítače při studiu lidové písně (Brno 15.-16.10.1974)*, ed. by Dušan Holý, Karel Pala, and Miloš Štědroň. Praha: Státni pedagogické nakladatelstvi. pp. 211-218.

_________. 1978. "Algoritmizácia Vyhodnocovania Podobnosti Melódií," *Musicologica Slovaca* VI: 167-174.

Barbaud, Pierre. 1974. "Methodes d'analyse de textes harmoniques," *Informatique musicale: Journées d'etude 1973. Textes des conférences E.R.A.T.T.O.*, edited by Hélène Charnassé and Henri Ducasse. Paris: Centre de documentation sciences humaines. pp. 165-176.

Barenholtz, Jerry, Z. Wolofsky, I. Ganapathy, Thomas W. Calvert, and P. O'Hara. 1977. "Computer Interpretation of Dance Notation," *Computing in the Humanities: Proceedings of the Third International Conference on Computing in the Humanities*, edited by Serge Lusignan and John S. North. Waterloo, Ontario: The University of Waterloo Press. pp. 235-240.

Baron, John H. 1971. "First Report on the Use of Computer Programming to Study the Secular Solo Songs in France from 1600 to 1660," *Bericht über den internationalen musikwissenschaftlichen Kongress: Bonn 1970*, ed. by Carl Dahlhaus et al. Kassel: Bärenreiter. pp. 333-336.

Baroni, Mario. 1969. "Linguaggio Musicale della Sonata a Quattro Italiana del Secolo XVI,"*Computers and the Humanities* III/5 (May): 312.

Baroni, Mario, and Carlo Jacoboni. 1973. "Four-part Choral Generation," *Computational Musicology Newsletter* I/1: 10.

Baroni, Mario, and Carlo Jacoboni. 1975. "Analysis and Generation of Bach's Choral melodies," *Actes du 1er congress international de semiotique musicale*, edited by Gino Stefani. Pesaro: Centro di iniziativa culturale. pp. 125-134.

Baroni, Mario, and Carlo Jacoboni. 1976. *Verso una grammatica della melodia*. Bologna, Italy: Università Studi di Bologna, 1976.

Baroni, Mario, and Carlo Jacoboni. 1977. "A Grammar of Melody," *Computers and the Humanities* XI/1 (January-February): 42.
Baroni, Mario, and Carlo Jacoboni. 1978. *Proposal for a Grammar of Melody. The Bach Chorales*. Montreal: Les presses de l'Université de Montral.
Baroni, Mario, and Carlo Jacoboni. 1979. "Formal Analogies in Different Phrases of a Monodic Composition," *The Third Colloquium on Musical Informatics*, April 1-2, 1979, Padua University, Italy. See abstract in *Computers in the Humanities* XVI/4 (1982): 264.
Barth-Wehrenalp, Renate. 1974. Studien zu Adan de le Hale. Ph.D. thesis. University of Vienna.
_________. 1982. *Studien zu Adan de le Hale*. Tutzing, Germany: H. Schneider, 1982.
Bartmiński, Jerzy. 1975. "Komputery w badaniach nat pieśnią ludową," *Literatura Ludowa* 19 (January-February): 54-56.
Bartmiński, Jerzy, et al. 1976. "Diskuse," *Lidová píseň a samočinný počítač III: Sborník materiálů ze 3. semináře o využití samočinného počítače při studiu lidové písně (Brno 15.-16.10.1974)*, ed. by Dušan Holý, Karel Pala, and Miloš Štědroň. Praha: Státni pedagogické nakladatelstvi. pp. 357-411.
Battier, Marc, and Jacques Arveiller. 1978. *Musique et informatique: une bibliographie indexée*, réédition augmentée. Paris: Elmeratto.
Bauer, Hans-Joachim. 1976. "Statistik, eine objektive Methode zur Analyse von Kunst?" *International Review of the Aesthetics and Sociology of Music* VII/2 (December): 249-263.
Bauer-Mengelberg, Stefan. 1968. "'The Truth, the Whole Truth, and Nothing but the Truth'," *Computer Studies in the Humanities and Verbal Behavior* I/2 (August): 52-54.
_________. 1970. "The Ford-Columbia Input Language," *Musicology and the Computer: Three Symposia*, edited by Barry S. Brook. New York: The City University of New York Press. 48-52.
_________. 1974. "Digital Alternate Representation of Musical Scores (DARMS)," *Computers and the Humanities* VIII/4 (July): 255.
Bauer-Mengelberg, Stefan, and Melvin Ferentz. 1965. "On Eleven-Interval Twelve-Tone Rows," *Perspectives of New Music* III/2 (Spring-Summer): 93-103.
Bean, Calvert. 1961. Information Theory Applied to the Analysis of a Particular Formal Process in Tonal Music. Ph.D. dissertation. Champaign, IL: University of Illinois.
Beauchamp, James W. 1967. A Computer System for Time-Variant Harmonic Analysis and Synthesis of Musical Tones. Technical Report No. 15, Electrical Engineering Publication No. 992. Urbana, IL: University of Illinois School of Music Experimental Music Studio.
Bebbington, Brian. 1968. "Folkmusic and Computers," *African Music* IV/2: 56-58.
Bengtsson, Ingmar. 1967a. "On Melody Registration and 'Mona'," *Elektronische Datenverarbeitung in der Musikwissenschaft*, edited by Harald Heckmann. Regensburg: Gustav Bosse. pp. 136-174.
_________. 1967b. "Numericode – A Code System for Thematic Incipits," *Svensk Tidskrift för Musikforskning* 49: 5-40.
_________. 1970. "Studies with the Aid of Computers of 'Music As Performed'," *IMS: Report on the Tenth Congress, Lubljana 1967*, edited by Dragotin Cvetko. Kassel: Bärenreiter. pp. 443-444.
_________. 1971. "Analysis of Rhythmic Performance," *Computers and the Humanities* V/5 (May): 310.

Bengtsson, Ingmar, Alf Gabrielsson, and Barbro Gabrielsson. 1978. "RHYTHM-SYVARD, A Computer Program for Analysis of Rhythmic Performance," *Svensk Tidskrift for Musikforskning* LX/1: 15-24.
Bengtsson, Ingmar, Alf Gabrielsson, and Stig-Magnus Thorsén. 1969. "Empirisk Rytmforskning. En Orientering om Musikvetenskaplig Bakgrund, Utveckling och Några aktuella Projekt," *Svensk Tidskrift för Musikforskning* 51: 49-118.
Bense, Max. 1954. *Aesthetica.* Stuttgart: Deutsche Verlags-Anstalt.
_________. 1966a. "Ästhetik und Programmierung." *IBM-Nachrichten* 16: 294-296.
_________. 1966b. "Projekter til en generativ aestetik," *Dansk Musiktidsskrift* XLI: 179-82.
_________. 1969. *Einführung in die informationstheoretische Ästhetik.* Reinbek bei Hamburg: Rowohlt.
Bent, Ian D. 1973. "Analysis of Melodic Structure," *Computers and the Humanities* VII/5 (May): 314.
_________. 1977. "Analysis of Melodic Structure," *Computers and the Humanities* XI/1 (January-February): 41.
_________. 1980. "Analysis," *The New Grove Dictionary of Music and Musicians*, edited by Stanley Sadie, vol. 1. London: Macmillan. 340-388.
_________. 1987. *Analysis*, with a glossary by William Drabkin. London: Macmillan.
Bent, Ian, and John Morehen. 1978. "Computers in the Analysis of Music," *Proceedings of the Royal Musical Association* CIV (1977-78): 30-46.
Berger, Arthur. 1964. "New Linguistic Modes and the New Theory," *Perspectives of New Music* III/1 (Autumn-Winter): 1-9.
Berlind, Gary. 1966. "Writings on the Use of Computers in Music," *College Music Symposium* 6 (1966): 143-152.
_________. 1967. "GRIPHOS: An Interim Report," *Current Musicology* V: 149-152.
_________. [n.d.]. Writings on the Use of Computers in Music. Compiled by Gary Berlind in collaboration with Barry S. Brook, Lejaren A. Hiller Jr., Jan P. LaRue, and George W. Logemann. New York: New York University, Institute for Computer Research in the Humanities. Mimeographed.
Berlind, Gary, Barry S. Brook, Charles M. Dollar, Dee F. Green, Kenneth Janda, Richard Jensen, Louis T. Milic, and Robert Zemsky. 1967. "Annual Bibliography for 1966," *Computers and the Humanities* I/4 (March): 143-156.
Berlind, Gary, and George W. Logeman. 1969. "An Algorithm for Musical Transposition," *Computer Studies in the Humanities and Verbal Behavior* II (August): 102-108.
Bernard, Jean J. 1974. "Sciences exactes et musicologie," *Informatique musicale: Journées d'etude 1973. Textes des conférences E.R.A.T.T.O.*, edited by Hélène Charnassé and Henri Ducasse. Paris: Centre de documentation sciences humaines. pp. 115-124.
Bernstein, Lawrence F. 1964. "Data Processing and the Thematic Index," *Fontes Artis Musicae* XI/1 (January-April): 159-165.
_________. 1967. "University of Chicago Chanson Project," *Computers and the Humanities* I/5 (May): 221.
Bernstein, Lawrence F. and Joseph P. Olive. 1969. "Computers and the 16th-century Chanson: A Pilot Project at the University of Chicago," *Computers and the Humanities* III/3 (January): 153-160.
Bernzott, Philip. 1968. Musical Analysis with Computer: Some Programs and Descriptions. M.M. thesis. Chicago Musical College.
Berrett, Joshua. 1979. "Alan Lomax: Some Reconsiderations," *Journal of Jazz Studies* VI/1 (Fall-Winter): 54-63.

Bersano, James Richard. 1980. Formalized Aspect Analysis of Sound Texture. PhD thesis, Indiana University.

Bertoni, Alberto, Goffredo Haus, Giancarlo Mauri, and Mauro Torelli. 1978a. "A Mathematical Model for Analyzing and Structuring Musical Texts," *Interface* VII: 31-43.

Bertoni, Alberto, Goffredo Haus, Giancarlo Mauri, and Mauro Torelli. 1978b. "Analysis and Compacting of Musical Texts," *Journal of Cybernetics* 8: 257-272.

Bielawski, Ludwik. 1975. "Ähnlichkeiten und Zusammenhänge – System und Syntagma in der ethnomusikologischen Analyse," *Methoden der ethnomusikologischen Analyse*, edited by Oskár Elschek. Bratislava: Sekcia hudobnej vedy-etnomuzikológia, Umenovedný ústav, Slovenská akademia vied. pp. 32-33.

Binkley, Thomas E. 1967. "Electronic Processing of Musical Materials," *Elektronische Datenverarbeitung in der Musikwissenschaft*, edited by Harald Heckmann. Regensburg: Gustav Bosse. pp. 1-20.

Birkhoff, George David. 1931. "A Mathematical Approach to Aesthetics," *Scientia* (September): 133-146.

_________. 1950. *Collected Mathematical Papers*, vol. 3. New York: American Mathematical Society.

Blombach, Ann Kariger. 1976. A Conceptual Framework for the Use of the Computer in Music Analysis. Ph.D. dissertation. Columbus, OH: Ohio State University.

_________. 1981. "An Introductory Course in Computer-Assisted Music Analysis: The Computer and the Bach Chorales," *Journal of Computer-Based Instruction* 8 (February): 70-77.

_________. 1982. "Harmony vs. Counterpoint in the Bach Chorales," *Computing in the Humanities*, edited by Richard W. Bailey. Amsterdam: North-Holland Publishing Company. pp. 79-88.

Boggs, Beverly. 1973. "Analysis of Ethnomusicological Transcritions," *Computational Musicology Newsletter* I/1: 14.

Boggs, J. K. 1973. "Music Ancoding," *Computational Musicology Newsletter* I/1: 3.

Böker-Heil, Norbert. 1971a. "Programmierte Musikanalyse," *Computers and the Humanities* V/5 (May): 314.

_________. 1971b. "DODEK - Eine Computerdemonstration," *Zeitschrift für Musiktheorie* II/2: 2-14.

_________. 1972a. "Weiße Mensuralnotation als Computer-Input und -Output," *Acta Musicologica* XLIII/1-2 (January-June): 21-33.

_________. 1972b. "Ein algebraisches Modell des Dur-Moll-Tonalen Systems," *Bericht über den 1. Internationalen Kongress für Musiktheorie Stuttgart 1971*, ed. by Peter Rummenhöller, Friedrich Christoph Reininghaus, and Jürgen Habakuk Traber. Stuttgart, Germany: Ichthys-Verlag. pp. 64-107.

_________. 1973. "Plotting Conventional Music Notation," *Journal of Music Theory* XVI/1-2 (Spring-Winter): 72-101.

_________. 1974a. "Der Zustand polyphoner Strukturen: Ein Beispiel Automatischer Stilbeschreibung," *International Musicological Society: Report of the Eleventh Congress, Copenhagen 1972*, edited by Henrik Glahn, Søren Sørensen, and Peter Ryom. Copenhagen: Edition W. Hansen. pp. 108-120.

_________. 1974b. "Musikalische Stilanalyse und Computer. Einige grundsätzliche Erwägungen," *International Musicological Society: Report of the Eleventh Congress, Copenhagen 1972*, edited by Henrik Glahn, Søren Sørensen, and Peter Ryom. Copenhagen: Edition W. Hansen. pp. 45-50.

_________. 1976. "Die maschinenverständliche Darstellung musikalischer Sachverhalte," *Hudobná klasifikácia a samocinné pocitace: predbezná zpráva 6. Etnomuzikologického seminára = Musikklassifikation und elektronische Datenverarbeitung: Vorbericht des 6. Ethnomusikologischen Seminars, Kocovce, 6.-10. Október 1975*, edited by Oskár Elschek. Bratislava: Sekcia hudobnej vedy-etnomuzikológia, Umenovedný ústav, Slovenská akademia vied. 2 p.

_________. 1981. "Computer-Simulation eines musikalischen Verstehensprozesses," *International Musicological Society: Report of the Twelfth Congress, Berkeley 1977*, edited by Daniel Heartz and Bonnie C. Wade. Kassel: Bärenreiter. pp. 324-329.

Böker-Heil, Norbert, and Harald Heckmann. 1979. "Elektronische Datenverarbeitung," *Die Musik in Geschichte und Gegenwart*, vol. 16. Kassel: Bärenreiter. pp. 36-51.

Boody, Charles George. 1975. Non-Compositional Applications of the Computer to Music Published in America Through June of 1972. Ph.D. dissertation. Minneapolis, MN: University of Minnesota.

_________. 1978. The Micro-Computer as an Input Device for Music Analysis or Composition by Computer. Ann Arbor, MI: MPublishing, University of Michigan Library.

_________. 1989. Review of Fred T. Hofstetter's *Computer Literacy for Musicians*, *Computers and Music Research* I: 123-131.

Boroda, Moisej G. 1973. "K voprosu o metroritmiceski elementarnoj edinice v muzyke," *Bulletin of the Academy of Science of the Georgian SSR* 71/3: 745-748.

_________. 1974. "O castotnoj strukture muzykalnych soobscenij," *Bulletin of the Academy of Science of the Georgian SSR* 76/2: 178-202.

_________. 1977. "O melodiceskoj elementarnoj edinice," *MAAFAT'75 1 vsesoûznyj seminar po masinnym aspektam algoritmiceskogo formalizovannogo analiza muzykal'nyh tekstov. (Erevan-Dilizan, 27.10.-1.11.1975 g.): materialy*, edited by Vladimir Leonidovic Gosovskij. Erevan: Izdat. Akad. nauk Armânskoj SSR. pp. 112-120.

_________. 1978. "Ob opredelenii informacionnoj melodiceskoj edinicy tipa frazy v muzyke," *Bulletin of the Academy of Science of the Georgian SSR* 89/1: 57-60.

_________. 1979. Principy Organizacii Povtorov na Microurovne Muzykalnovo Teksta. Dissertation. Tiblissi.

_________. 1980. "Häufigkeitsstrukturen musikalischer Texte," *Glottometrika 3*, edited by Wolfhart Matthäus. Bochum: Studienverlag Dr. N. Brockmeyer. pp. 36-96.

Boroda, Moisej G., and Jurij K. Orlov. 1978. "O sravnenii skorostej vosprijatija informacijonnych edinic v muzyke i reci," [*Proceedings of the Conference "The Functioning of Communication Systems"*]. Erevan: Academy of Science. pp. 58-62.

Boroda, Moisej G., I. Sch. Nabareyshvili, Jurij K. Orlov, R. Ja. Tshitashvili. 1977. "O Karaktere raspredelenija informatcionnuych edinic maloj tshastotyu v chudoshestvennych tekstach," *Semiotika i Informatika* IX: 23-35.

Borris, Siegfried. 1971. Review of *Musikalische Stilanalyse auf der Grundlage eines Modelles für Lernprozesse* by Hermann Gerhard Rohrer, *Musik und Bildung* III/11 (November): 567-568.

Boucourechliev, Andre. 1970. "Transmutations," *L'Arc* 40: 49-56.

Bowles, Edmund. 1965. "Computers and Musicology," *Computers for the Humanities: A Record of the Conference Sponsored by Yale University on a Grant from IBM, January 22-23, 1965*. New Haven, CT: Yale University Press. pp. 103-108.

_________. 1970a. "Discussion," *Musicology and the Computer: Three Symposia*, edited by Barry S. Brook. New York: The City University of New York Press. pp. 37-38.

__________. 1970b. "Musicke's Handmaiden: Or Technology in the Service of the Arts," *The Computer and Music*, edited by Harry B. Lincoln. Ithaca: Cornell University Press. pp. 3-20.

__________. 1970c. "Musicology and Computers" [A Review of Harald Heckmann, *Elektronische Datenverarbeitung der Musikwissenschaft*], *Computers and the Humanities* IV/3 (January): 207-219.

Brantley, Daniel Lawrence. 1977. Disputed Authorship of Musical Works: A Quantitative Approach to the Attribution of the Quartets Published as Haydn's Opus 3. Ph.D. dissertation. Iowa City, IA: University of Iowa.

Braun, Hartmut. 1975. "Das Problem der Zeilenbegrenzung," *Methoden der ethnomusikologischen Analyse*, edited by Oskár Elschek. Bratislava: Sekcia hudobnej vedy-etnomuzikológia, Umenovedný ústav, Slovenská akademia vied. pp. 40-41.

Braun, P. 1964. "On a Human Movement Analyzer," *Computational Linguistics* 3: 189-204.

Brawley, John Gray. 1959. An Application of Information Theory to Musical Rhythm. M.M. thesis. Bloomington, IN: Indiana University.

Brender, Maurita P., and Ronald F. Brender. 1967. "Computer Transcription and Analysis of Mid-Thirteenth Century Musical Notation," *Journal of Music Theory* XI/2 (Winter): 198-221.

Bridgman, Nanie. 1973. "Catalogue par incipit musicaux," *Informatique et Sciences Humaines* 19 (December): 33-38.

Brincker, Jens. 1966a. "Kvantitativ musikanalyse," *Dansk Musiktidsskrift* XLI: 175-178.

__________. 1966b. Review of *Informationstheorie und Computermusik* by Lejaren A. Hiller, *Dansk Musiktidsskrift* XLI: 186.

__________. 1970. "Statistical Analysis of Music: An Application of Information Theory," *Svensk Tidskrift för Musikforsking* 52: 53-57.

Brinkman, Alexander R. 1978. Johann Sebastian Bach's Orgelbüchlein: A Computer-Assisted Analysis of the in Fluence of the Cantus Firmus on the Contrapuntal Voices. Ph.D. dissertation. Rochester, NY: University of Rochester, Eastman School of Music.

__________. 1979. "A Computer-Assisted Analysis of Melodic Borrowing from the Cantus Firmus in the Chorale Preludes in Bach's 'Orgelbüchlein'," *Proceedings of the 1978 International Computer Music Conference*, compiled by Curtis Roads. [Menlo Park, CA]: Computer Music Journal. pp. 732-760.

__________. 1980. "The Melodic Process in Johann Sebastian Bach's *Orgelbüchlein*," *Music Theory Spectrum* II (Spring): 46-73.

Broeckx, Jan L., and Walter Landrieu. 1972. "Comparative Study of Style, Based on Five Liedmelodies," *Interface* I/1 (April): 29-92.

Bronson, Bertrand H. 1949. "Mechanical Help in the Study of Folk Song." *Journal of American Folklore* LII/244 (April-June): 81-86.

__________. 1959. "Toward the Comparative Analysis of British-American Folk Tunes." *Journal of American Folklore* LXXII: 165-191.

Brook, Barry S. 1965a. "The Simplified 'Plaine and Easy Code System," *Fontes Artis Musicae* XII: 156-160.

__________. 1965b. "Utilization of Data Processing Techniques in Music Documentation," *Fontes Artis Musicae* XII (May): 112-122.

__________. 1967. "Music Bibliography and the Computer," *Papers from the West Virginia University Conference on Computer Applications in Music*, edited by Gerald Lefkoff. Morgantown: West Virginia University Library. pp. 9-27.

__________. 1969. “Style and Content Analysis in Music: The Simplified ‘Plaine and Easy Code’,” *The Analysis of Communication Content*, edited by George Gerbner et al. New York: John Wiley & Sons. pp. 287-296.

__________. Ed. 1970a. *Musicology and the Computer: Three Symposia*. New York: The City University of New York Press.

__________. 1970b. “Music Documentation of the Future,” *Musicology and the Computer: Three Symposia*, edited by Barry S. Brook. New York: The City University of New York Press. pp. 28-36.

__________. 1970c. “The Plaine and Easie Code,” *Musicology and the Computer: Three Symposia*, edited by Barry S. Brook. New York: The City University of New York Press. pp. 53-56.

Brook, Barry S., and Murray Gould. 1964. “Notating Music with Ordinary Typewriter Characters,” *Fontes Artis Musicae* XI/1 (January-April): 142-159.

Brooks, Frederick P., A. L. Hopkins, P. G. Neumann, and W. V. Wright. 1957. “An Experiment in Musical Composition.” *IRE Transactions on Electronic Computers* VI (September): 175-182. (An errata see in vol. 7 (1958): 60.) Reprinted in *Machine Models of Music*, edited by Stephen M. Schwanauer and David A. Levitt. Cambridge, MA: The MIT Press, 1993. pp. 23-40.

Brown, Charles T. 1968. “To Determine the Melodic Contour of a Melody,” *Student Musicologists at Minnesota* III : 87-92.

Brown, Charles T., and Robert D. Oudal. 1969. “The 1968 Introductory Seminar in the Use of Computers in Musical Projects,” *Student Musicologists at Minnesota* 3 (1968-1969): 87-92.

Bukharov, R. G., and M. S. Rytvinsskaya. 1962. “Simulating a Probabalistic Process Connected with a Melody,” *Kazan Universitet Uchenyia Zapiski* 122: 82.

Burns, Betty Beryl Remy. 1972. An Electronic Data Processing System for the Organization and Documentaion of the 16th Century Motet. Ph.D. dissertation. Cincinnati, OH: University of Cincinnati.

Byrd, Donald Alvin. 1970a. “Music Notation by Computer,” *Computers and the Humanities* V/2 (November): 111.

__________. 1970b. “Transcription by Plotter,” *Random Bits* V/9 (May): 6-8.

__________. 1971. “Humanities Programming for Creative Work,” *Random Bits* VI/5 (January): 1, 8-12.

__________. 1974. “A System for Music Printing by Computer,” *Computers and the Humanities* VIII/3 (May): 161-172.

__________. 1975. “Music Programs at Indiana University,” *Computational Musicology Newsletter* II/1: 2-4.

__________. 1976. “Music Notation by Computer,” *Computers and the Humanities* X/1 (January-February): 51-52.

__________. 1977. “An Integrated Computer Music Software System,” *Computer Music Journal* I/2 (April): 55-60.

__________. 1984. Music Notation by Computer. Ph.D. dissertation. Bloomington, IN: Indiana University.

Calvert, Thomas W. 1979. “Computer Interpretation of Dance Notation,” *Computers and the Humanities* XIII/1 (January-March): 58.

Campbell, Warren Colman. 1970. Computer Analysis of Musical Performance. Ph.D. dissertation. Storrs, CT: University of Connecticut.

Campos, Arthur Nogueira. 1973. “Music Analysis,” *Computational Musicology Newsletter* I/1: 14.

Cantor, Don. 1971. "A Computer Program that Accepts Common Musical Notation," *Computers in the Humanities* VI (November): 103-109.

Castman, Bernt, and Lars Elve Larsson. 1974. Ett dataprogram (RHYTHMSYVARD) för bearbetning av rytmiska duraionsvärden. Mimeographed. Uppsala, Sweden: Instutionen för Musikvetenskap.

Chalupka, Lubomír. 1975. "Kybernetik und EDV im Dienste der Musikanalyse," *Methoden der ethnomusikologischen Analyse*, edited by Oskár Elschek. Bratislava: Sekcia hudobnej vedy-etnomuzikológia, Umenovedný ústav, Slovenská akademia vied. pp. 7-8.

Chalupka, Lubomír, and Viera Chalupková. 1978. "Spracovianie Suboru L'udovych Piesni na SP MSP 2A," *Musicologica slovaca* (Czechoslovakia) VI: 203-208.

Chalupková, Viera. 1978. "Tonalna Analyza Suboru Piesni a Jej Vyhodnotenie," *Musicologica slovaca* (Czechoslovakia) VI: 209-215.

Chalupková, Viera, and Lubomír Chalupka. 1976. "Die Bearbeitung von Volksliedern aus dem Záhorie auf einer EDV-Anlage," *Hudobná klasifikácia a samocinné pocitace: predbezná zpráva 6. Etnomuzikologického seminára = Musikklassifikation und elektronische Datenverarbeitung: Vorbericht des 6. Ethnomusikologischen Seminars, Kocovce, 6.-10. Október 1975*, edited by Oskár Elschek. Bratislava: Sekcia hudobnej vedy-etnomuzikológia, Umenovedný ústav, Slovenská akademia vied. 2 p.

Charnassé, Hélène. 1973. "Musicologie et Informatique: Les grands axes de recherche," *Informatique et Sciences Humaines* 19 (December): 19-31.

_________. 1974. "Transcrition Automatique de Tablatures," *Informatique musicale: Journées d'etude 1973. Textes des conférences E.R.A.T.T.O.*, edited by Hélène Charnassé and Henri Ducasse. Paris: Centre de documentation sciences humaines. pp. 25-47.

_________. 1976. "La transcription automatique des tablatures: le language d'entree," *Proceedings of the Second Annual Music Computation Conference: November 7-9, 1975 at the University of Illinois at Urbana-Champaign*, compiled by James Beauchamp and John Melby. Urbana, IL: Office of Continuing Education and Public Service in Music, University of Illinois. pp. 13-27.

Charnassé, Hélène, and Henri Ducasse. Eds. 1974. *Informatique musicale: Journées d'etude 1973. Textes des conférences E.R.A.T.T.O.* Paris: Centre de documentation sciences humaines.

Charnassé, Hélène, and Henri Ducasse. 1971. "De l'emploi de l'ordinateur pour la transcription des trablatures," *Revue de Musicologie* 57/2: 107-133.

Charnassé, Hélène, and Henri Ducasse. 1975. "Automated Tablature Transcription," *Computational Musicology Newsletter* II/1: 9-10.

Charnassé, Hélène, Raymond Meylon, and Henri Ducasse. 1977. "Transcription automatique de notations musicales en tablatures," *Computers and the Humanities* XI/1 (January-February): 41-42.

Chenoweth, Vida. 1974. *Melodic Perception and Analysis: A Manual on Ethnic Melody.* Ukarumpa: Summer Institute of Linguistics.

Chenoweth, Vida, and Darlene Bee. 1971. "Comparative-Generative Models of a New Guinea Melodic Structure," *American Anthropoligist* 73: 773-782.

Chmurny, Rudolf. 1978. "DIS, metoda Vyhodnocovania Podobnosti Melodii," *Musicologica slovaca* [Czechoslovakia] VI: 183-186.

Ciamaga, Gustav. 1971. "The Training of the Computer in the Use of New technological Means," *Music and Technology*. Paris: La Revue Musicale. pp. 143-150.

Cinková, Irena. 1976. "Využití informačního szstému asti pro analýzu a třídění lidových písní," *Lidová píseň a samočinný počítač III: Sborník materiálů ze 3. semináře o vyu-*

žití samočinného počítače při studiu lidové písně (Brno 15.-16.10.1974), ed. by Dušan Holý, Karel Pala, and Miloš Štědroň. Praha: Státni pedagogické nakladatelstvi. pp. 183-195.
Citron, Jack. 1966. "MUSPEC," *Computers and the Humanities* I/2 (November): 52.
Clauß, Günter and Heinz Ebner. 1978. *Grundlagen der Statistik für Psychologen, Pädagogen und Soziologen*, 7th ed. Berlin: Technik Verlag.
Clifton, Thomas. 1973. "Music and the a priori," *Journal of Music Theory* 17/1: 66-85.
Cobin, Marian W. 1967. "Musicology and the Computer in New Orleans," *Computers and the Humanities* I/4 (March): 131-133.
Cohen, Dalia, and Ruth Katz. 1974. "Quantitative Analysis of Monophonic Music: Towards a More Precise Definition of Style," *Orbis Musicae* III-IV: 83-96.
Cohen, Dalia, and Ruth Katz. 1977. *The Israeli Folk Song: A Methodological Example of Computer Analysis of Monophonic Music*. Jerusalem: The Magnes Press.
Cohen, Joel E. 1961. "Some Relationships Between Music and Mathematics," *Music Education Journal* 48/1 (September): 104-109.
_________. 1962. "Information Theory and Music," *Behavioral Science* VII/2 (April): 137-163.
_________. 1964. "Teorie informací a hudba," *Nové Cesty Hudby: Sborník studií o novodobých skladebných smerech a vedeckých názorech na hudbu*, edited by Eduard Herzog. Praha: Státní hudební vydavatelství. pp. 180-215.
Collins, Walter S. 1965. "A New Tool for Musicology," *Music & Letters* XLVI/2 (April): 122-125.
Colquhoun, Daryl George. 1979. "Computer Piano Concertos," *Computers and the Humanities* XIII/3 (July-September): 261.
Coons, Edgar, and David Kraehenbuehl. 1958. "Information as a Measure of Structure in Music," *Journal of Music Theory* II/2 (November): 127-161.
Cope, David. 1991. *Computers and Musical Style*. Madison, Wisconsin: A-R Editions.
_________. 1996. *Experiments in Musical Intelligence*. Wisconsin: A-R Editions.
_________. 2008. *Hidden Structure: Music Analysis Using Computers*. Wisconsin: A-R Editions.
Couturier, Marcel. 1974. "L'emploi du langage forcod en collecte et traitement d'inventaires après deces," *Informatique musicale: Journées d'etude 1973. Textes des conférences E.R.A.T.T.O.*, edited by Hélène Charnassé and Henri Ducasse. Paris: Centre de documentation sciences humaines. pp. 104-114.
Crane, Frederick. 1968. "Statistical Comparison of Musical Styles," *Computers and the Humanities* II/5 (May): 244.
Crane, Frederick, and Judith Fiehler. 1970. "Numerical Methods of Comparing Musical Styles," *The Computer and Music*, edited by Harry B. Lincoln. Ithaca: Cornell University Press. pp. 209-222.
Csébfalvy, Károly, and Miklós Havass. 1965. "A Direct Computer Processing of Folk Tunes," *Computational Linguistics* 4: 125-129.
Csébfalvy, Károly, Miklós Havass, Pál Járdányi, and Lajos Vargyas. 1965. "Systematization of Tunes by Computers," *Studia Musicologica Academiae Scientiarum Hungaricae* VII/1-4: 253-257.
Cuddy, Lola L., Annabel J. Cohen, and J. Miller. 1979. "Melody Recognition: The Experimental Application of Musical Rules," *Canadian Journal of Psychology* XXXIII/3: 148-157.
Curry, Jerry L. 1969. A Computer-Aided Analytical Study of Kyries in Selected Masses of Johannes Ockeghem. Ph.D. dissertation. Iowa City, IA: University of Iowa.

Czekanowska, Anna. 1969. "Zastosowanie polskicg metod statystycznych do klasyfikacji melodii ludowych," *Muzyka* [Poland] XIV/1: 3-18.

Czekanowska-Kulinska, Anna. 1970. "Polish Mathematical Methods in the Classification of Slavic Folk Songs," *IMS: Report on the Tenth Congress, Lubljana 1967*, edited by Dragotin Cvetko. Kassel: Bärenreiter. pp. 440-443.

_________. 1977. "Comparative and quantitative methods in international research projects on folk music," *Ethnologia Slavica* VIII-IX (1976-77): 307-18.

Deihl, Ned C. 1971. Computer-Assisted Instruction and Instrumental Music: Implications for Teaching and Research," *Journal of Research in Music Education* XIX/3 (Fall): 299-306.

Delalande, François. 1972. "L'analyse des musiques electro-acoustiques," *Musique en Jeu*: 50-56.

de la Motte, Diether. 1987. *Musikalische Analyse*. Kassel: Bärenreiter.

de la Motte-Haber, Helga. 1970. "Die Abhängigkeit des Sonanzeindrucks von der Intervallstruktur," *Bericht über den Internationalen Musikwissenschaftlichen Kongress Leipzig 1966*, edited by Carl Dahlhaus et al. Kassel: Bärenreiter. pp. 477-482.

Demorgon, Jacques. 1974. Une communication de masse: la chanson a succes. Essai d'une premiere systematisation de son etude en France de 1946 a 1966. Ph.D. dissertation. Paris, France: Department of Sociology. University of Paris V.

Detlovs, Vilnis K. 1968. "O statisticeskom analize muzyki," *Latvijskij matematiceskij ezegodnik* [Riga] 3: 101-120.

Draeger, Hans Heinz. 1964. "Analysis and Synthesis of Musical Structures on the Basis of Information Theory," *Bericht über den neunten internationalen Kongress Salzburg 1964*, edited by Franz Giegling, vol. 1. Kassel: Bärenreiter. pp. 261-268.

_________. 1967. "A Quantitative Analysis of Music as Exemplified by Beethoven's Sketches for his Opus 131," *Festschrift für Walter Wiora zum 30. Dezember 1966*, edited by Ludwig Finscher and Christoph-Hellmut Mahling. Hamburg: Bärenreiter. pp. 79-85.

Ducasse, Henri. 1973a. "Introduction," *Informatique et Sciences Humaines* 19 (December): 7-15.

_________. 1973b. "Compte-rendu de Journees d'Etudes d'Informatique Musicale," *Informatique et Sciences Humaines* 19 (December): 67-70.

_________. 1974. "Un problem de saisie de l'information," *Informatique musicale: Journées d'etude 1973. Textes des conférences E.R.A.T.T.O.*, edited by Hélène Charnassé and Henri Ducasse. Paris: Centre de documentation sciences humaines. pp. 48-65.

Ducasse, Henri, and Denys Pages. 1976. "Un systeme de constitution et d'exploitation de donnees pour l'identification et l'analyse de textes musicaux," *Revue de Musicologie* [France] LXII/2: 292-293.

Duisberg, Robert Adamy. 1980. A digital representation of musical samples and a calculation thereon of autocorrelation as a function of frequency. D.M.A. dissertation. Seattle, WA: University of Washington.

Dunsby, Johnathan, and Arnold Whittall. 1988. *Music Analysis in Theory and Practice*. London: Faber Music.

Dürrenmatt, Hans-Rudolf, Murray Gold, and Jan LaRue. 1970. "Die Notierung Thematischer Incipits auf 'Mark-Sense-Cards'," *Fontes Artes Musicae* XVII/1-2 (January-August): 15-23.

Egeland Hansen, Finn. 1967a. "Det gregorianske repertoire i Codex H 159 Montpellier," *Dansk Arbog for Musikforskning* V (1966-67): 181-182.

_________. 1967b. "Investigation of Tonal Properties of the Gregorian Repertory," *Computers and the Humanities* I/5 (May): 226.

_________. 1970. "Musikalsk analyse ved hjaepl af modeller," *Svensk Tidskrift för Musikforskning* 52: 50-53.

_________. 1974. "Tonality in Gregorian Chant Based on an Investigation of the Melodies in Codex H 159, Montpellier," *[IMS] Report of the Eleventh Congress, Copenhagen, 1972*, edited by Henrik Glahn, Søren Sørensen, Peter Ryom. Copenhagen: Edition W. Hansen. pp. 425-431.

Ellis, Mark. 1980. Linear Aspects of the Fugues of J. S. Bach's "The Well-Tempered Clavier": A Quantitative Survey. Ph.D. dissertation. Nottingham, UK: University of Nottingham.

Elschek, Oskár. Ed. 1976a. *Hudobná klasifikácia a samocinné pocitace: predbezná zpráva 6. Etnomuzikologického seminára = Musikklassifikation und elektronische Datenverarbeitung: Vorbericht des 6. Ethnomusikologischen Seminars, Kocovce, 6.-10. Október 1975*. Bratislava: Sekcia hudobnej vedy-etnomuzikológia, Umenovedný ústav, Slovenská akademia vied.

_________. 1976b. "Die Anwendungsbereiche der gegenwärtigen Musikklassifikation," *Hudobná klasifikácia a samocinné pocitace: predbezná zpráva 6. Etnomuzikologického seminára = Musikklassifikation und elektronische Datenverarbeitung: Vorbericht des 6. Ethnomusikologischen Seminars, Kocovce, 6.-10. Október 1975*, edited by Oskár Elschek. Bratislava: Sekcia hudobnej vedy-etnomuzikológia, Umenovedný ústav, Slovenská akademia vied. 2 p.

_________. 1978. "Ludová piesen a samocinny pocítac 2," *Musicologica slovaca* VI: 163-308.

Elschek, Oskár, et al. 1975a. "Protokoll der Schlußsitzung des ethnomusikologischen Seminars," *Methoden der ethnomusikologischen Analyse*, edited by Oskár Elschek. Bratislava: Sekcia hudobnej vedy-etnomuzikológia, Umenovedný ústav, Slovenská akademia vied. pp. 53-57.

Elschek, Oskár, et al. 1975b. "Protokoll der geschlossenen Sitzung der Study Group of Folk Music Systematisation of Folk Music des IFMC (26. September 1974)," *Methoden der ethnomusikologischen Analyse*, edited by Oskár Elschek. Bratislava: Sekcia hudobnej vedy-etnomuzikológia, Umenovedný ústav, Slovenská akademia vied. pp. 59-62.

Elschek, Oskár, et al. 1976. "Protokoll der Schlußsitzung des ethnomusikologischen Seminars," *Hudobná klasifikácia a samocinné pocitace: predbezná zpráva 6. Etnomuzikologického seminára = Musikklassifikation und elektronische Datenverarbeitung: Vorbericht des 6. Ethnomusikologischen Seminars, Kocovce, 6.-10. Október 1975*, edited by Oskár Elschek. Bratislava: Sekcia hudobnej vedy-etnomuzikológia, Umenovedný ústav, Slovenská akademia vied. 6 p.

Elscheková, Alica. 1965. "General Considerations on the Classification of Folk Tunes," *Studia Musicologica Academiae Scientiarum Hungaricae* VII/1-4: 259-262.

_________. 1966. "Methods of Classification of Folk Tunes," *Journal of International Folk Music Council* XVIII: 56-76.

_________. 1969. "Technologie der Datenverarbeitung bei der Klassifizierung von Volksliedern," *Methoden der Klassifikation von Volksliedweisen*, edited by Oskár Elschek. Bratislava: Verlag der Slowakischen Akademie der Wissenschaften. pp. 93-122.

_________. 1972. "Klasifikacie Kratkych Motivickych Usekov Netrofickych i Strofickych Piesni Tradicnymi a Netradicnymi Technikami," *Lidová písen a samostatný pocítac I*, edited by Dušan Holý and Oldrich Sirovátka. Brno: Klub uživatelů MSP. pp. 219-243.

_________. 1975a. "Systematisierung, Klassifikation und Katalogisierung von Volksliedweisen," *Handbuch des Volksliedes*, edited by Rolf Wilhelm Brednich, Lutz Röhrich and Wolfgang Suppan, vol. 2. München: Fink. pp. 549-582.

_________. 1975b. "Die Entwicklung der ethnomusikologischen Analyse," *Methoden der ethnomusikologischen Analyse*, edited by Oskár Elschek. Bratislava: Sekcia hudobnej vedy-etnomuzikológia, Umenovedný ústav, Slovenská akademia vied. pp. 20-21.

_________. 1976a. "Klasifikácia krátkych motivických úsekov nestrofických i strofických piesní tradičnými i netradičnými technikami," *Lidová píseň a samočinný počítač III: Sborník materiálů ze 3. semináře o využití samočinného počítače při studiu lidové písně (Brno 15.-16.10.1974)*, ed. by Dušan Holý, Karel Pala, and Miloš Štědroň. Praha: Státni pedagogické nakladatelstvi. pp. 219-243.

_________. 1976b. "Entwicklung der ethnomusikalischen Klassifikation," *Hudobná klasifikácia a samocinné pocitace: predbezná zpráva 6. Etnomuzikologického seminára = Musikklassifikation und elektronische Datenverarbeitung: Vorbericht des 6. Ethnomusikologischen Seminars, Kocovce, 6.-10. Október 1975*, edited by Oskár Elschek. Bratislava: Sekcia hudobnej vedy-etnomuzikológia, Umenovedný ústav, Slovenská akademia vied. 3 p.

_________. 1978. "Metoda Vyhidnocivania Melodickych Podobnosti Pomocou Klasifikacnych Tabuliek," *Musicologica slovaca* [Czechoslovakia] VI: 217-234.

Entwisle, Jeffrey Lynn. 1973. Visual Perception and Analysis of Musical Scores, B.S. thesis. Boston, MA: Massachusetts Institute of Technology, Department of Humanities.

Erickson, Raymond F. 1968a. "Music Analysis and the Computer," *Journal of Music Theory* XII/2 (Winter): 240-263.

_________. 1968b. "Music Analysis and the Computer: A Report on Some Current Approaches and the Outlook for the Future," *Computers and the Humanities* III/2 (November): 87-104.

_________. 1969. "A General Purpose System for Computer Aided Musical Studies," *Journal of Music Theory* XIII/2 (Winter): 276-294.

_________. 1970a. Rhythmic Problems and Melodic Structure in Organum Purum: A Computer-Assisted Study. Ph.D. dissertation. New Haven, CT: Yale University.

_________. 1970b. "A Syntax-Directed, Changeable System for Processing Data for Music Analysis," *Computers and the Humanities* IV/5 (May): 343.

_________. 1970c. "Music and the Computer in the Sixties," *AFIPS Conference Proceedings* 36: 281-285.

_________. 1971a. "Rhythmic Problems and Melodic Structure in Organum Purum: A Computer-Assisted Study," *Computers and the Humanities* V/5 (May): 312-313.

_________. 1971b. "DUPACK (DARMS Utility Package)," *Computers and the Humanities* V/5 (May): 313.

_________. 1971c. The Ford-Columbia Music Representation. [New York : IBM Systems Research Institute].

_________. 1972a. "The Computer and Music," *Journal of the American Musicological Society* XXV/1 (Spring): 102-107.

_________. 1972b. Abstract of *Rhythmic Problems and Melodic Structure in Organum Purum: A Computer-Assisted Study* by R. F. Erickson, *Computers and the Humanities* VI/4 (March): 254.

_________. 1972c. "The Uses of Computers in Music: A State of the Art Report," *First USA-Japan Computer Conference Proceedings: October 3-5, 1972, Tokyo, Japan*. Montvale, NJ: American Federation of Information Processing Societies. pp. 124-129.

________. 1975a. "'The DARMS Project': A Status Report," *Computers and the Humanities* IX/6 (November): 291-298.

________. 1975b. "'The Darms Project': A Status Report," *Computational Musicology Newsletter* II/1: 7-8.

________. 1976. DARMS: A Reference Manual. New York: Department of Music, Queens College.

________. 1977. "MUSICOMP 76 and The State of DARMS," *College Music Symposium* XVII/1 (Spring): 90-101.

Ermedahl, Gunnar. 1975. "Notskrift och inspelning som underlag for musikalisk analys," *Svensk Tidskrift for Musikforskning* LVII/2: 65-66.

Evarts, John. 1970. "Stockholm," *World of Music* XII/3: 52-56. [Report on the UNESCO meeting "Music and Technology".]

Feld, Steven. 1974. "Linguistic Models in Ethnomusicology," *Ethnomusicology* XVIII/2 (May): 197-217.

________. 1990. "Linguistic Models in Ethnomusicology," *Ethnomusicological Theory and Method*, edited by Kaufman Shelemay. New York: Garland. pp. 183-203.

Fennelly, Brian. 1967. "A Descriptive Language for the Analysis of Electronic Music," *Perspectives of New Music* VI/1 (Autumn-Winter): 79-95.

Ferentzy, Eors N. 1965. "On Formal Music Analysis-Synthesis: Its Application in Music Education," *Computational Linguistics* 4: 107.

__________. 1966. Progress Report on the Project Analysis of Musical Styles by an Electronic Computer, Sponsored by Washington State University. Unpublished Report. Pullman, WA: Washington State University Pullman.

________. 1967. "A Syntax-Directed Compiler to Analyze Musical Compositions and Text," *Computers and the Humanities* I/5 (May): 225.

Ferentzy, Eors N., and Miklós Havass. 1964. "Human Movement Analysis by Computer: Electronic Choreography and Composition," *Computational Linguistics* 3: 129-188.

Filip, Miroslav. 1964. "Zákonitosti vyvoja harmónie vo svetle základnych myslienok teórie informácie," *Nové Cesty Hudby* (1964): 216-233. [Summary in German: "Entwicklungsgesetzed er Harmonie im Lichte der Grundgedankend er Informationstheorie," pp. 276-277.]

Fink, Michael. 1972. Music Analysis: An Annotated Bibliography. Los Alamitos: Southwest Regional Laboratory for Educational Research and Development. Technical Report Vol. 43.

Fiore, Mary E. 1967. "Harmonic Structure in Variation Movements by Anton von Webern," *Computers and the Humanities* I/5 (May): 225.

________. 1968. "Harmonic Structure in Variation Movements by Webern," *Computers and the Humanities* II/5 (May): 243.

________. 1970. "Webern's Use of Motive in the Piano Variations," *The Computer and Music*, edited by Harry B. Lincoln. Ithaca: Cornell University Press. pp. 115-122.

Fornůsek, Jaroslav. 1972. "Aplikace zkusenosti z projektovani uloh na samocinnem pocitaci pro oblast lidove pisne," *Lidová písen a samostatný pocítac I*, edited by Dušan Holý and Oldrich Sirovátka. Brno: Klub uživatelů MSP. pp. 11-18.

________. 1976. "Vyžití existujících projectů pro spraování dat o lidové písni," *Lidová píseň a samočinný počítač III: Sborník materiálů ze 3. semináře o využití samočinného počítače při studiu lidové písně (Brno 15.-16.10.1974)*, ed. by Dušan Holý, Karel Pala, and Miloš Štědroň. Praha: Státni pedagogické nakladatelstvi. pp. 45-55.

Forte, Allen. 1964. "A Theory of Set-Complexes for Music," *Journal of Music Theory* VIII/2 (Winter): 136-183.

_________. 1965. "The Domain and Relations of Set-Complex Theory," *Journal of Music Theory* IX/1 (Spring): 173-180.

_________. 1966. "A Program for the Analytic Reading of Scores," *Journal of Music Theory* X/2 (Winter): 330-364. Reprinted in *Machine Models of Music*, edited by Stephen M. Schwanauer and David A. Levitt. Cambridge, MA: The MIT Press, 1993. pp. 55-81.

_________. 1967a. "Computer-Implemented Analysis of Musical Structure," *Papers from the West Virginia University Conference on Computer Applications in Music*, edited by Gerald Lefkoff. Morgantown: West Virginia University Library. pp. 29-42.

_________. 1967b. "Music and Computing: The Present Situation," *Computers and the Humanities* II/1 (September): 32-35.

_________. 1967c. "Structure of Atonal Music," *Computers and the Humanities* II/2 (November): 86.

_________. 1967d. *Analytic Reading of Musical Scores*. Cambridge: Massachusetts Institute of Technology, April 1967.

_________. 1967e. "The Programming Language SNOBOL3: An Introduction," *Computers and the Humanities* I/5 (May): 157-163.

_________. 1967f. "Structure of Atonal Music," *Computers and the Humanities* I/5 (May): 224-225.

_________. 1970. "The Structure of Atonal Music: Practical Aspects of a Computer-Oriented Research Project," *Musicology and the Computer: Three Symposia*, edited by Barry S. Brook. New York: The City University of New York Press. pp. 10-18.

_________. 1973. *The Structure of Atonal Music*. New Haven: Yale University Press.

Frank, Helmar. 1964. *Kybernetische Analysen subjektiver Sachverhalte*. Quickborn bei Hamburg: Schnelle.

_________. 1968. *Informationsästhetik: Grundlagenprobleme und erste Anwendungen auf die mime pure*, 2nd ed. Quickborn bei Hamburg: Schnelle.

Frankel, Robert E., Stanley J. Rosenschein, and Stephen W. Smoliar. 1974. The Modeling of Musical Perception on a Digital Computer Via Schenkerian Theory. Music Report No. 4, April 1975. Philadelphia: Moore School of Electrical Engineering, University of Pennsylvania.

Frankel, Robert E., Stanley J. Rosenschein, and Stephen W. Smoliar. 1976a. Schenker's Theory of Tonal Music: Its Explication Through Computational Processes. Music Project Report No. 7. Philadelphia: University of Pennsylvania, Department of Computer and Information Science.

Frankel, Robert E., Stanley J. Rosenschein, and Stephen W. Smoliar. 1976b. "A LISP-Based System for the Study of Schenkerian Analysis," *Computers and the Humanities* X/1 (January-February): 21-32.

Frankel, Robert E., Stanley J. Rosenschein, and Stephen W. Smoliar. 1978. "Schenker's Theory of Tonal Music - its Explication through Computational Processes," *International Journal of Man-Machine Studies* X: 121-138.

Fraser, Robert. 1974. "Computer Implementation of Musical Linguistics," *Computers and the Humanities* VIII/1 (January): 49-50.

Freedman, M. David. 1967. "Analysis of Musical Instrument Tones," *Journal of the Acoustical Society of America* XLI (April): 793-806.

Freeman, Linton C., and Alan P. Merriam. 1956. "Statistical Classification in Anthropology: An Application to Ethnomusicology," *American Anthropologist* 58/3 (June): 464-472.

Frisbie, Charlotte J. 1971. "Anthropological and Ethnomusicological Implications of a Comparative Analysis of Bushmen and African Pygmy Music," *Ethnology* X/3 (July): 265-290.

Fucks, Wilhelm. 1955. *Mathematische Analyse von Sprachelementen, Sprachstil und Sprache*. Köln: Westdeutscher Verlag.

_________. 1956. "Mathematical Theory of Word Formation." *Information Theory: Papers Read at a Symposium on Information Theory Held at the Royal Institution, London, September 12th to 16th, 1955*, edited by Colin Cherry. London: Butterworths Scientific Publications. pp. 154-170.

_________. 1957. "Gibt es mathematische Gesetze in Sprache und Musik?" *Umschau in Wissenschaft und Technik* 1957/2: 33-37.

_________. 1958. *Mathematische Analyse der Formalstruktur von Musik*. Köln: Westdeutscher Verlag.

_________. 1962. "Mathematische Musikanalyse und Randomfolgen. Zufall und Musik." *Gravesaner Blätter* VI: 132-145.

_________. 1963. *Mathematische Analyse von Formalstrukturen von Werken der Musik*. Köln: Westdeutscher Verlag.

_________. 1964. "Gibt es mathematische Gesetze in Sprache und Musik?" *Kybernetik*, edited by Helmar Frank, 4th ed. Frankfurt am Main: Umschau Verlag. pp. 175-187.

_________. 1968. *Nach allen Regeln der Kunst. Diagnosen über Literatur, Musik, bildende Kunst - die Werke, ihre Autoren und Schöpfer*. Stuttgart: Deutsche Verlags-Anstalt.

Fucks, Wilhelm, and Josef Lauter. 1965. *Exaktwissenschaftliche Musikanalyse*. Köln: Westdeutscher Verlag.

Fuller, Ramon Conrad. 1965. An Information Theory Analysis of Anton Webern's 'Symphonie,' opus 21 (with) 'Music for Two Channel Tape and Two Percussionists'. D.M.A. thesis. University of Illinois at Urbana Champaign.

_________. 1970. "Toward a Theory of Webernian Harmony, via Analysis with a Digital Computer," *The Computer and Music*, edited by Harry B. Lincoln. Ithaca: Cornell University Press. pp. 123-131.

Gabura, A. James. 1965. "Computer Analysis of Musical Style," *Proceedings of the 20th National Conference: Cleveland, Ohio, August 24-26, 1965*. New York: Association for Computing Machinery. pp. 303-314.

_________. 1967. Music Style Analysis by Computer. M.Sc. thesis, University of Toronto.

_________. 1970. "Musical Style Analysis by Computer," *The Computer and Music*, edited by Harry B. Lincoln. Ithaca: Cornell University Press. pp. 223-276.

Gadviev, Shamil Allgedar. 1979. "Statistic Analysis of Structure of Azerbaijzan Folk Songs," *Proceedings of the 1978 International Computer Music Conference*, compiled by Curtis Roads. [Menlo Park, CA]: Computer Music Journal. pp. 761-774.

Galko, Ladislav. 1975. "Die musikalische Liedanalyse für einen Inzipienkatalog," *Methoden der ethnomusikologischen Analyse*, edited by Oskár Elschek. Bratislava: Sekcia hudobnej vedy-etnomuzikológia, Umenovedný ústav, Slovenská akademia vied. pp. 38-39.

Gasparov, Boris M. 1972. "Strukturnyj metod v muzykozananii," *Sovetskaya Muzyka* 4: 42-51.

_________. 1974a. "O nekotorych principach strukturnogo analiza muzyki," *Problemy muzykalnogo myshlenija*. Moskow: Muzyka. 129-152.

_________. 1974b. "Nekotorye Deskriptivnye Problemy Muzykal'noj Semantiki," *Acta et Commentationes Universitatis Tartuensis, Trudy po Znakovym Sistemam* 8: 120-137.

Gelnár, Jaromír. 1976. "Die Beziehungen zwischen dem Musikmaterial und dem Klassifikationssystem," *Hudobná klasifikácia a samocinné pocitace: predbezná zpráva 6. Etnomuzikologického seminára = Musikklassifikation und elektronische Datenverarbeitung: Vorbericht des 6. Ethnomusikologischen Seminars, Kocovce, 6.-10. Október 1975*, edited by Oskár Elschek. Bratislava: Sekcia hudobnej vedy-etnomuzikológia, Umenovedný ústav, Slovenská akademia vied. 2 p.

Gelnár, Jaromír, and Lubomír Šváb. 1976. "Analýza Rytmického průběhu ve folklórních nápěvech pmocí matematických metod," *Lidová píseň a samočinný počítač III: Sborník materiálů ze 3. semináře o využití samočinného počítače při studiu lidové písně (Brno 15.-16.10.1974)*, ed. by Dušan Holý, Karel Pala, and Miloš Štědroň. Praha: Státni pedagogické nakladatelstvi. pp. 245-252.

Gilbert, Steven E. 1970. The Trichord: An Analytic Outlook for Twentieth-Century Music. Ph.D. dissertation. New Haven, CT: Yale University.

Goldberg, Robert P. 1970. "Experimental Music Information System," *Computers and the Humanities* IV/5 (May): 345-346.

Goldman, Stanford. 1953. *Information Theory*. New York: Dover.

Goller, Gottfried. 1969. "Zur Bezeichnung der Neumen in der germanischen Choralnotation des 12. bis 14. Jahrhunderts," *Kirchenmusikalisches Jahrbuch* [Germany] LIII: 99-100.

_________. 1970. "Zur Bezeichnung der Neumen in der germanischen Choralnotation," *Bericht über den Internationalen Musikwissenschaftlichen Kongress, Leipzig, 1966*, ed. by Carl Dahlhaus, Reiner Kluge, Ernst H. Meyer, and Walter Wiora. Kassel: Bärenreiter. pp. 173-175.

Gomberg, David Aaron. 1975. A Computer-Oriented System for Music Printing. D.Sc. dissertation. Saint Louis, MO: Washington University.

Gould, Murray. 1967. "A Keypunchable Notation for the Liber Usualis," *Elektronische Datenverarbeitung in der Musikwissenschaft*, edited by Harald Heckmann. Regensburg: Gustav Bosse. pp. 25-40.

_________. 1968. "An Introduction to Computing in Music" [Review of *Papers from the West Virginia University Conference on Computer Applications in Music* by Gerald Lefkoff (Ed.)], *Computers and the Humanities* II/5 (May): 262-263.

Gould, Murray, and George W. Logemann. 1966. ALMA: An Alphanumeric Language for Music Analysis. New York University: Institute for Computer Research in the Humanities. [Los Angeles: University of California Library / Music Library, calling no. ML 432 G 734a]

Gould, Murray J., and George W. Logemann. 1970. "ALMA: Alphanumeric Language for Music Analysis," *Musicology and the Computer: Three Symposia*, edited by Barry S. Brook. New York: The City University of New York Press. pp. 57-90.

Grauer, Viktor A . 1965. "Some Song-Style Clusters – A Preliminary Study," *Ethnomusicology* IX/3 (September): 265-271.

Greussay, Patrick. 1972. "Un modèle informatique de description de structures musicales," *Recherches linguistiques* 1: 89-128.

_________. 1973a. "Procédures LISP d'analyse de relations harmoniques," *Artinfo-Musinfo* 13: 1-7.

_________. 1973b. Modèles de descriptions symboliques en analyse musicale. Ph.D. dissertation. Paris, France: University of Paris VIII.

_________. 1974. "Structures de controle en description symbolique d'analyses musicales," *Informatique musicale: Journées d'etude 1973. Textes des conférences E.R.A.T.T.O.*,

edited by Hélène Charnassé and Henri Ducasse. Paris, France: Centre de documentation sciences humaines. pp. 177-203.
Grey, John M. 1978. "Timbre Discrimination in Musical Patterns," *Journal of the Acoustical Society of America* 64: 467-472.
Grey, John M., and John W. Gordon. 1978. "Perceptual Effects of Spectral Modifications on Musical Timbres," *Journal of the Acoustical Society of America* 63 (May): 1493-1500.
Gross, Dorothy Susan. 1973. "Music Department," *Computational Musicology Newsletter* I/1: 14.
_________. 1975a. A Set of Computer Programs to Aid in Music Analysis, Ph.D. dissertation. Bloomington, IN: Indiana University.
_________. 1975b. "A Computer Package for Music Analysis," *Proceedings of the 2nd Indiana University Computer Network Conference on Instructional Computer Applications*. [s.l.]: Indiana University Computing Network. pp. 6-10.
_________. 1975c. "A Set of Computer Prtograms to Aid in Music Analysis," *Computational Musicology Newsletter* II/1: 16.
_________. 1980. "A Project in Computer-Assisted Harmonic Analysis," *Proceedings of the International Computer Music Conference*, edited by. Hubert S. Howe. San Francisco: Computer Music Association. pp. 525-533.
_________. 1981. "A Computer Project in Music Analysis," *Computing in the Humanities*, edited by Peter C. Patton and Renee A. Holoien. Lexington: Lexington Books. pp. 299-313.
_________. 1984. "Computer Applications to Music Theory: a Retrospective," *Computer Music Journal* VIII/4 (Winter): 35-42.
Guntzenhäuser, Rul. 1962. *Ästhetisches Maß und ästhetische Information. Einführung in die Theorie G. D. Birkhoffs und die Redundanztheorie ästhetischer Prozesse*. Quickborn bei Hamburg: Schnelle.
Gutknecht, Dieter. 1972. *Untersuchungen zur Melodik des Hugenottenpsalters*. Regensburg: Bosse.
Haefer, John Richard. 1971. Selected Cantatas of Alan Hovhaness: A Linear Analysis. M.M. thesis. Tucson, AZ: University of Arizona.
Hall, Thomas B. 1975. "Some computer aids for the preparation of critical editions of Renaissance Music," *Tijdschrift van de Vereniging voor Nederlandse Muziek Geschiedenis* 25/1: 38-53.
Halmos, István. 1973. "Automation of Analysis and Classification of Folk Tunes. Part One: Comparison Note by Note," *Computational Musicology Newsletter* I/1: 15.
_________. 1976. "Experiments in Automation of Analysis, Systematization and Listing of Monodic Folk Tunes," *Hudobná klasifikácia a samocinné pocitace: predbezná zpráva 6. Etnomuzikologického seminára = Musikklassifikation und elektronische Datenverarbeitung: Vorbericht des 6. Ethnomusikologischen Seminars, Kocovce, 6.-10. Október 1975*, edited by Oskár Elschek. Bratislava: Sekcia hudobnej vedy-etnomuzikológia, Umenovedný ústav, Slovenská akademia vied. 2 p.
Halmos, István, Miklós Havass, and György Köszegi. 1975. Experiments in Automation of Analysis, Systematization, and Listing of Monodic Folk Tunes. Budapest, Hungary: Institute of Musicology, Hungarian Academy of Sciences.
Halperin, David. 1978. A Structural Analysis of Troubadour Music. M.A. thesis. Tel Aviv, Israel: Tel Aviv University.
_________. 1980. "Distributional Structure in Troubadour Music," *Orbis Musicae* VII (1979-80): 15-26.

Hanson, Jens L. 1969. An Operational Approach to Theory of Rhythm. Ph.D. dissertation. New Haven, CT: Yale University.

Hanzelin, Fred Lee. 1978. The Software for Computer Assisted Graphical Representation of Single Instrument Melodic Lines and Harmonic Spectra Using DARMS Encoding and Acoustical Data. Ph.D. thesis, University of Illinois at Urbana-Campaign.

Hartmann, Karl L. 1962. Versuch einer mathematischen Musiklehre. Wien: Karl L. Hartmann.

Hasty, Christopher F. 1978. A Theory of Segmentation Developed from Late Works of Stefan Wolpe. Ph.D. dissertation. New Haven, CT: Yale University.

Hatano, Giyoo. 1968. "Ongaku eno johoron-teki sekkin," *Ongaku Gaku. Journal of the Japanese Musicological Society* XIV: 54-64.

Haus, Goffredo. 1979. "Musical Text Transformations by Operators," Paper presented at The Third Colloquium on Musical Informatics, April 1-2, 1979, Padua University, Italy. See abstract in *Computers in the Humanities* XVI/4 (December): 264.

Havass, Miklós. 1964. "A Simulation of Music Composition. Synthetically Composed Folkmusic," *Computational Linguistics* 3: 107-128.

Heckmann, Harald. 1964. "Neue Methoden der Verarbeitung musikalischer Daten," *Die Musikforschung* XVII/4: 381-383.

_________. Ed. 1967a. *Elektronische Datenverarbeitung in der Musikwissenschaft.* Regensburg: Gustav Bosse.

_________. 1967b. "Elektronische Datenverarbeitung in der Musikwissenschaft: Eine Einleitung," *Elektronische Datenverarbeitung in der Musikwissenschaft*, edited by Harald Heckmann. Regensburg: Gustav Bosse. pp. VII-XVII.

_________. 1970. "Elektronische Datenverarbeitung in der Musikwissenschaft," *IMS: Report on the Tenth Congress, Lubljana 1967*, edited by Dragotin Cvetko. Kassel: Bärenreiter. pp. 424-427.

_________. 1971. "Katalog 'Deutsches Tenorlied des 16. Jahrhunderts," *Computers and the Humanities* V/5 (May): 313-314.

_________. 1972. "Informationstheorie und Computer," *Informatik. Vorträge anläßlich der Jahresversammlung vom 14. bis 17. Oktober 1971 zu Halle (Saale)*, edited by Jocahim-Hermann Scharf. Nova Acta Leopoldina vol. 37/1, no. 206. Leipzig: Barth. pp. 619-627.

_________. 1973a. "Musik - Dokumentation, Musik - Information," *Neue Zeitschrift für Musik* 134/8: 479-482.

_________. 1973b. "Musikwissenschaft, Dokumentation, Information," *Musicae Scientae Collectanea. Festschrift Karl Gustav Fellerer zum 70. Geburtstag*, edited by Heinrich Hüschen. Köln. pp. 219-224.

Heike, Georg. 1961. "Informationstheorie und musikalische Komposition," *Melos* XXVIII/9: 269-272.

Heller, Jack J., and Warren C. Campbell. 1971. "Music Performance Analysis," *Council for Research in Music Education Bulletin* 24 (Spring): 1-9.

Heller, Jack J., and Warren C. Campbell. 1972. Computer Analysis of the Auditory Characteristics of Musical Performance. Final Report, Project No. 9-0546A, Grant No. OEG-0-9-160546-4439 (010). Washington: U.S. Dept. of Health, Education and Welfare, Office of Education, Bureau of Research.

Helm, Everett. 1971. "UNESCO Report on the Stockholm Meeting," *Music and Technology*. Paris: La Revue Musicale. pp. 193-206.

Henriksen, Jon Petter. 1976. Satsteknisk analyse ved hjelp av datamaskin. En musikologisk vinning? M.A. thesis. University of Oslo.

Henry, Edward O. 1976. “The Variety of Music in a North Indian Village: Reassessing Cantometrics,” *Ethnomusicology* XX/1 (January): 49-66.
Herndon, Marcia. 1972. “The computer and music (Review of),” *Ethnomusicology: Journal of the Society for Ethnomusicology* 16/2 (May): 290-292.
Hessert, Norman Dale. 1971. The Use of Information Theory in Musical Analysis. Ph.D. dissertation. Bloomington, IN: Indiana University.
Hill, George R., and Murray Gould. 1970. *A Thematic Locator for Mozart's Works, as Listed in Koechel's Chronologisch-Thematisches Verzeichnis*, 6th edition. Hackensack, NJ: Boonin.
Hill, George R., Murray Gould, David Noon, Hans-Rudolf Diirrenmatt, and Jan LaRue. 1969. “*A Thematic Locator for Mozart's Works as Listed in Köchel's Chronologischthematisches Verzeichnis*,” *Computers and the Humanities* III/5 (May): 311-312.
Hiller, Lejaren A., Jr. 1962. Information Theory and Musical Analysis. Mimeographed. Urbana: University of Illinois, Experimental Music Studio. Technical Report No. 5, July 1962. 40 p. (University of Cincinnati Library, MUS ML 3817 .I4 no. 5)
__________. 1964. *Informationstheorie und Computermusik: Zwei Vorträge, gehalten auf den “Internationalen Ferienkursen für Neue Musik” Darmstadt 1963*. Darmstädter Beiträge zur Neuen Musik 8. Mainz: B. Schott's Söhne.
__________. 1967. Analysis and Synthesis of Musical Sounds by Analog and Digital Techniques. An Interim Progress Report to The National Science Foundation (Contract US-NSF-GK-594).
__________. 1968. Music Composed with Computer – An Historical Survey. Technical Report No. 18. Urbana, IL: University of Illinois, Experimental Music Studio.
Hiller, Lejaren A., and Calvert Bean. 1966. “Information Theory Analyses of Four Sonata Expositions,” *Journal of Music Theory* X/1 (Spring): 96-137.
Hiller, Lejaren A., and James W. Beauchamp. 1965. “Research in Music with Electronics,” *Science* CL: 161-169.
Hiller, Lejaren A., and James W. Beauchamp. 1968. Review of Completed and Proposed Research on Analysis and Synthesis of Musical Sounds by Analog and Digital Techniques. Technical Report No. 19. Urbana, IL: University of Illinois, Experimental Music Studio.
Hiller, Lejaren A., and Ramon Fuller. 1967. “Structure and Information in Webern's Symphonie, Op. 21,” *Journal of Music Theory* XI/1 (Spring): 60-115.
Hiller, Lejaren A., and Leonard M. Isaacson. 1959. *Experimental Music. Composition with an Electronic Computer*. New York: McGraw-Hill.
Hinderer, Drew Elliott. 1975. Music Analysis and the Genuine Instance Problem. PhD thesis, The University of Michigan.
Hofstetter, Fred T. 1972. “A Computer System for Musical Description,” *Journal of the Graduate Music Students at the Ohio State University* 3: 4-42.
__________. 1973. “Computer Applications to Music at OSU,” *Computational Musicology Newsletter* I/1: 2.
__________. 1974. A Quantitative Method for the Study of Musical Style Applied to National Differences and Similarities in the Use of Melodic Intervals During the Mid-Nineteenth to Early Twentieth Centuries. Ph.D. dissertation. Columbus, OH: The Ohio State University.
__________. 1979. “The Nationalistic Fingerprint in Nineteenth-Century Romantic Chamber Music,” *Computers and the Humanities* XIII/2 (April-June): 105-119.
Holtzman, Steven R. 1977. “A Program for Key Determination,” *Interface* VI/1: 29-56.

Holý, Dušan. 1976a. "Projekt der Dokumentation und Klassifikation des Volksliedes auf der Grundlage des ASTI Informationssystems," *Hudobná klasifikácia a samocinné pocitace: predbezná zpráva 6. Etnomuzikologického seminára = Musikklassifikation und elektronische Datenverarbeitung: Vorbericht des 6. Ethnomusikologischen Seminars, Kocovce, 6.-10. Október 1975*, edited by Oskár Elschek. Bratislava: Sekcia hudobnej vedy-etnomuzikológia, Umenovedný ústav, Slovenská akademia vied. 3 p.

_________. 1976b. "Dosavadní postupy a výsledky studia lidové písně pomocí smočinného počítače na půdě ČSSR," *Lidová píseň a samočinný počítač III: Sborník materiálů ze 3. semináře o využití samočinného počítače při studiu lidové písně (Brno 15.-16.10.1974)*, ed. by Dušan Holý, Karel Pala, and Miloš Štědroň. Praha: Státni pedagogické nakladatelstvi. pp. 25-35.

_________. 1976c. "Glosy k dokumentačnímu záznamu, segmentaci a popisu tematické výstavby lidové písně," *Lidová píseň a samočinný počítač III: Sborník materiálů ze 3. semináře o využití samočinného počítače při studiu lidové písně (Brno 15.-16.10.1974)*, ed. by Dušan Holý, Karel Pala, and Miloš Štědroň. Praha: Státni pedagogické nakladatelstvi. pp. 155-182.

Holý, Dušan, Antonin Bartošik, and Stanislav Zabadal. 1970. "Samočinný počítač-pomocník při analýze a klasifikaci lidových písní," *Opus musicum* [Czechoslovakia] II/5-6: 155-164.

Holý, Dušan, Antonin Bartošik, and Stanislav Zabadal. 1972. "Cíle úkoly postupy perspektivy. Za studium lidovych pisni pomoci samočinneho počítač," *Lidová písen a samostatný pocítac I*, edited by Dušan Holý and Oldrich Sirovátka. Brno: Klub uživatelů MSP. pp. 19-42.

Holý, Dušan, Karel Pala, and Miloš Štědroň. Eds. 1976. *Lidová píseň a samočinný počítač III: Sborník materiálů ze 3. semináře o využití samočinného počítače při studiu lidové písně (Brno 15.-16.10.1974)*. Praha: Státni pedagogické nakladatelstvi.

Holý, Dušan, and Oldrich Sirovátka. Eds. 1972. *Lidová písen a samostatný pocítac I*. Brno: Klub uživatelů MSP. Mimeographed.

Hood, Mantle. 1967. "Improvisation and Music Theory of the Javanese Gamelan," *Computers and the Humanities* II/2 (September): 88.

Hoshovskyj, Vladimir. 1965. "The Experiment of Systemizing and Cataloguing Folk Tunes following the Principles of Musical Dialectology and Cybernetics," *Studia Musicologica Academiae Scientiarum Hungaricae* VII/1-4: 273-286.

_________. 1975. "Katalogisierungsanalyse – Algorithmus einer umfassenden formalisierten Beschreibung," *Methoden der ethnomusikologischen Analyse*, edited by Oskár Elschek. Bratislava: Sekcia hudobnej vedy-etnomuzikológia, Umenovedný ústav, Slovenská akademia vied. pp. 28-29.

Howe, Hubert S. 1965. "Some Combinatorial Properties of Pitch Structures," *Perspectives of New Music* IV/1 (Fall-Winter): 45-61.

_________. 1966. "Music and Electronics: A Report," *Perspectives of New Music* IV: 68-75.

_________. 1971. "Two Parameters of Melodic Line as Stylistic Discriminants by David Sheldon Lewis; Some Techniques for Computer-Aided Analysis of Musical Scores by Donald Margedo Pederson [Review]," *Perspectives of New Music* 9-10/2-1 (Spring/Summer-Autumn/Winter): 350-355.

Huber, Alfred. 1974. "Informationstheorie und Musikanalyse," *Melos* XLI/4 (July-August): 207-210.

Hudson, Barton. 1970. "Toward a Comprehensive French Chanson Catalog," *The Computer and Music*, edited by Harry B. Lincoln. Ithaca: Cornell University Press. pp. 277-287.

Hughes, Matt. 1965. Tonal Orientation in Skiabin's Preludes: An Analysis on the Basis of Information Theory. M.A. thesis. University of Texas at Austin.
_________. 1977. "A Quantitative Analysis," *Readings in Schenkerian Analysis*, edited by Maury Yeston. New Haven: Yale University Press. 144-164.
Huglo, Michel. 1974. "Le classement par ordinateur des listes de repons liturgiques: les problemes musicologiques," *Informatique musicale: Journées d'etude 1973. Textes des conférences E.R.A.T.T.O.*, edited by Hélène Charnassé and Henri Ducasse. Paris: Centre de documentation sciences humaines. pp. 125-134.
Huglo, Michel, and Knud Ottosen. 1974. "Le classement par ordinateur des listes de repons liturgiques, *Informatique musicale: Journées d'etude 1973. Textes des conférences E.R.A.T.T.O.*, edited by Hélène Charnassé and Henri Ducasse. Paris: Centre de documentation sciences humaines. pp. 125-143.
Hultberg, W. Earle. 1970. "Transcription of Tablature to Standard Notation," *The Computer and Music*, edited by Harry B. Lincoln. Ithaca: Cornell University Press. pp. 289-292.
Iglickij, M. A. 1973. "Rodstvo tonalnostej i zadaca ob otyskanii modulajacionnych planov," *Muzykalnoje Iskusstvo i Nauka* II: 192-205.
Imberty, Michel. 1975. "Sémantique musicale: Approche structural, approche expérimentale," *Actes du 1er congress international de semiotique musicale*, edited by Gino Stefani. Pesaro: Centro di iniziativa culturale. pp. 225-244.
Jackson, Roland. 1966. "Harmonic Analysis," *Computers and the Humanities* I/2 (November): 52.
_________. 1970a. "Harmony before and after 1910: A Computer Comparison," *The Computer and Music*, edited by Harry B. Lincoln. Ithaca: Cornell University Press. pp. 132-146.
_________. 1970b. "The Computer as a 'Student' of Harmony," *IMS: Report on the Tenth Congress, Lubljana 1967*, edited by Dragotin Cvetko. Kassel: Bärenreiter. pp. 435-440.
Jackson, Roland, and Philip Bernzott. 1966. "Harmonic Analysis with Computer – A Progress Report," *ICRH Newsletter* I/9 (May): 3-4.
Jackson, Roland, and Philip Bernzott. 1970. "A Musical Input Language and a Sample Program for Musical Analysis," *Musicology and the Computer: Three Symposia*, edited by Barry S. Brook. New York: The City University of New York Press. pp. 130-150.
Jammers, Ewald; Bielitz, Matthias; Bender, Iring; Ebenhoh, Wolfgang. 1970. "Das Heidelberger Programm für die elektronische Datenverarbeitung in der musikwissenschaftlichen Byzantinistik," *Sitzungsberichte der Heidelberger Akademie der Wissenschaften, naturwissenschaftliche Klasse* II (1969-70): 3-23.
Jansen, Paule. 1974. "Emploi de l'ordinateur pour le depouillement des periodiques litteraires," *Informatique musicale: Journées d'etude 1973. Textes des conférences E.R.A.T.T.O.*, edited by Hélène Charnassé and Henri Ducasse. Paris: Centre de documentation sciences humaines. pp. 93-103.
Jesser, Barbara. 1988. "Rechnergestützte Melodieanalyse - Sackgasse oder Inspiration für die Volksliedforschung" *Musikpädagogische Forschung* IX: 213-228.
_________. 1991. *Interaktive Melodienanalyse. Methodik und Anwendung computergestützter Anaylseverfahren in Musikethnologie und Volksliedforschung: typologische Untersuchung der Balladensammlung des DVA.* Studien zur Volksliedforschung 12. Bern: Peter Lang.
John, Robert W. 1970a. "A Pilot Computer Catalog of Early American Shape-Note Hymn Tunes," *Computers and the Humanities* IV/5 (May): 345.

_________. 1970b. "A Pilot Computer Catalog of Early American Sheet Music," *Computers and the Humanities* IV/5 (May): 345.
Joiner, Richard E. 1969. "Gregorian Chant," *Computer Studies in the Humanities and Verbal Behavior* II/4 (December): 213-219.
Kaden, Christian. 1976. "Strukturelle Segmentierung von Musik - Probleme, Schwierigkeiten, Möglichkeiten," *Beiträge zur Musikwissenschaft* 18: 149-162 and 293-334.
_________. 1978. "Ludwig van Beethoven, Sinfonie Nr. 8, zweiter Satz, Allegretto scherzando. Ansätze zu einer statistischen Strukturanalyse." *Bericht über den Internationalen Beethoven Kongreß 20. bis 23. März 1977 in Berlin*, edited by H. Goldschmidt, K.-H. Köhler, and K. Niemann. Leipzig: Deutscher Verlag für Musik. pp. 113-130.
Kaegi, Werner. 1971. "Music and Technology in the Europe of 1970," *Music and Technology*. Paris: La Revue Musicale. pp. 9-31.
Kagan, Alan L., and Charles T. Brown. 1970. "Computerized Analysis and Classification of Asian Musical Style," *Computers and the Humanities* IV/5 (May): 347.
Kamien, Roger Jaques. 1964. The Opening Sonata-Allegro Movements in a Randomly Selected Sample of Solo Keyboard Sonatas Published in the Years 1742-1774. Ph.D. dissertation. Princeton, NJ: Princeton University.
Karkoschka, Erhard. 1972. "Letzter Schreck: der Computer," *Melos* 39/5: 285-288.
_________. 1979. "On the Analysis of Melodic Activity," *Interface* VIII/2 (October): 117-127.
Karlina, T. P., and Vilnis K. Detlovs. 1968. "Statisticeskij analiz sekvencij v melodii," *Latvijskij matematiceskij ezegodnik* 4: 165-173.
Karp, Theodore. 1970. "A Test for Melodic Borrowings among Notre Dame *Organa Dupla*," *The Computer and Music*, edited by Harry B. Lincoln. Ithaca: Cornell University Press. pp. 293-295.
Kasem-Bek, Jan. 1978. "Informationstheorie und Analyse musikalischer Werke," *Archiv für Musikwissenschaft* 35: 62-75.
Kassler, Michael. 1964a. A Report of Work, Directed Toward Explication of Schenker's Theory of Tonality, Done in Summer 1962 as the First Phase of a Project Concerned with the Applications of High-Speed Automatic Digital Computers to Music ana Musicology. Princeton, NJ: Princeton University Music Department. (Mimeographed.)
_________. 1964b. MIR – A Simple Programming Language For Musical Information Retrieval. Technical Report No. 3, Project 295D, March 1964. Princeton, New Jersey: Princeton University, Department of Music. [University of California at Berkeley: Music Library, calling no. ML 74 .4 M4 K 35 1964 MUSI]
_________. 1966. "Toward Musical Information Retrieval," *Perspectives of New Music* IV/2 (Spring-Summer): 59-67.
_________. 1968. A Trinity of Essays. Ph.D. dissertation. Princeton, NJ: Princeton University.
_________. 1970a. "An Essay Toward Specification of a Music-Reading Machine," *Musicology and the Computer: Three Symposia*, edited by Barry S. Brook. New York: The City University of New York Press. pp. 151-175.
_________. 1970b. "MIR – A Simple Programming Language for Musical Information Retrieval," *The Computer and Music*, edited by Harry B. Lincoln. Ithaca: Cornell University Press. pp. 299-327.
_________. 1972. "Optical Character-Recognition of Printed Music: A Review of Two Dissertations," *Perspectives of New Music* XI/1 (Autumn-Winter): 250-254.
_________. 1975a. "Explication of Theories of Tonality," *Computational Musicology Newsletter* II/1: 17.

_________. 1975b. Proving Musical Theorems I: The Middleground of Heinrich Schenker's Theory of Tonality. Technical Report No. 103. Sydney: The University of Sydney, Basser Department of Computer Science.
_________. 1975c. "Explication of Theories of Tonalities," *Computers and the Humanities* IX/4 (July): 192-193.
_________. 1977. "Explication of the Middleground of Schenker's Theory of Tonality," *Miscellanea Musicologica* IX: 72-81.
_________. 1981. "Transferring a tonality theory to a computer," *International Musicological Society: Report of the Twelfth Congress, Berkeley 1977*, edited by Daniel Heartz and Bonnie C. Wade. Kassel: Bärenreiter. pp. 339-347.
Kassler, Michael, and Hubert S. Howe Jr. 1980. "Computers and Music," *The New Grove Dictionary of Music and Musicians*, edited by Stanley Sadie, vol. 2. London: Macmillan. pp. 603-615.
Kawano, Hiroshi. 1969. "Ongaku-teki komyunikeishon no joho-bunseki," *Ongaku gaku: Journal of the Japanese Musicological Society* XV/3-4: 1-21.
_________. 1975. "The Informational Analysis of Musical Communication," *Computational Musicology Newsletter* II/1: 15.
Kiefer, Thomas M. 1969. "Continuous Geographical Distributions of Musical Patterns: A Test Case from the Northwest Coast," *American Anthropologist* 71/4 (August): 701-705.
Kirschenbaum, Howard. 1967. "Music Analysis by Computer," *Music Educators Journal* 53 (February): 94-97.
Kluge, Reiner. 1967. "Faktorenanalytische Typenbestimmung an einstimmigen Volksmelodien," *Computers and the Humanities* II/2 (November): 88-89.
_________. 1970a. "Volksliedanalyse und -systematisierung mit Hilfe eines Rechenautomaten," *Bericht über den Internationalen Musikwissenschaftlichen Kongress Leipzig 1966*, edited by Carl Dahlhause et al. Kassel: Bärenreiter. pp. 158-465.
_________. 1970b. "Zur Automatischen Quantitativen Bestimmung Musikalischer Ähnlichkeit," *IMS: Report on the Tenth Congress, Lubljana 1967*, edited by Dragotin Cvetko. Kassel: Bärenreiter. pp. 450-457.
_________. 1974a. *Faktorenanalytische Typenbestimmung an Volksliedmelodien*. Beiträge zur musikwissenschaftlichen Forschung in der DDR 6. Leipzig: Deutscher Verlag für Musik.
_________. 1974b. "Was kann die Kybernetik der Musikwissenschaft helfen?," *Report of the Eleventh Congress, Copenhagen, 1972*, edited by Henrik Glahn, Søren Sørensen, and Peter Ryom. Copenhagen: Edition W. Hansen. pp. 486-495.
_________. 1976a. "Anmerkungen zur Rolle des Rechenverfahrens im musikwissenschaftlichen Experiment," *International Review of the Aesthetics and Sociology of Music* VII/1: 5-42.
_________. 1976b. "Über typologische Klassifikation von Melodien und elektronische Datenverarbeitung bei der Melodie-Analyse und -Klassifikation," *Hudobná klasifikácia a samocinné pocitace: predbezná zpráva 6. Etnomuzikologického seminára = Musikklassifikation und elektronische Datenverarbeitung: Vorbericht des 6. Ethnomusikologischen Seminars, Kocovce, 6.-10. Októher 1975*, edited by Oskár Elschek. Bratislava: Sekcia hudobnej vedy-etnomuzikológia, Umenovedný ústav, Slovenská akademia vied. 3 p.
Knopoff, Leon. 1965. " Some Technological Advances in Musical Analysis," *Studia Musicologica Academiae Scientiarum Hungaricae* VII/1-4: 301-307.

__________. 1966. “A Progress Report on an Experiment in Musical Synthesis,” *Selected Reports* I/1: 49-60 [Los Angeles: University of California, Institute of Ethnomusicology].
Knopoff, Leon, and William Hutchinson. 1978. “An Index of Melodic Activity,” *Interface* VII/4 (December): 205-229.
Knowlton, Prentise H. 1973. “Capture and Display of Keyboard Music,” *Datamation*: 56-60.
Kobrin, Edward G., and Theodore H. A. Ashford. 1968. “A Solution to the Problems of Vertical Serialization,” *Perspectives of New Music* VI/2 (Spring-Summer): 119-124.
Kolata, Gina Bari. 1978. “Singing Styles and Human Cultures: How are They Related?” *Science* CC/4339 (April): 287-288.
Kolinski, Mieczyslaw. 1965a. “The General Dierction of Melodic Movement,” *Ethnomusicology* IX/3 (September): 240-264.
__________. 1965b. “The Structure of Melodic Movement - A New Method of Analysis (revised version),” *Studies in Ethnomusicology* 2: 96-120.
Kongas-Maranda, Elli. 1970. “Deep Significance and Surface Significance: Is Cantometrics Possible?” *Semiotica* II/2: 173-184.
Kostka, Stephan M. 1969a. The Hindemith String Quartetts: A Computer-Assisted Study of Selected Aspects of Style. Ph.D. dissertation. Madison, WI: University of Wisconsin.
__________. 1969b. “Statistics in Style Research,” *Computers and the Humanities* III/5 (May): 310.
__________. 1971. “Recent Developments in Computer-Assisted Musical Scholarship,” *Computers and the Humanities* VI/1 (September): 15-21.
__________. 1974. *A Bibliography of Computer Applications in Music*. Hackensack, NJ: Joseph Boonin.
__________. 1984. The M-PARC System for Musical Encoding (Mnemonic Pitch and Rhythm Code, Version 3). Unpublished Manuscript. Austin, TX: The University of Texas at Austin, Department of Music.
Kraehenbuehl, David, and Edgar Coons. 1959. “Information as a Measure of the Experience of Music,” *Journal of Aesthetics & Art Criticism* XVII/4 (June): 510-522.
Krumhansl, Carol L., and Roger N. Shepard. 1979. “Quantification of the Hierarchy of Tonal Functions Within a Diatonic Context,” *Journal of Experimental Psychology: Human Perception and Performance* V/4: 579-594.
Kupper, Hubert. 1966. “Computer and Musikwissenschaft,” *IBM Nachrichten* XVI/180 (December): 297-303.
__________. 1970a. *Statistische Untersuchungen zur Modusstruktur der Gregorianik*. Regensburg: Bosse.
__________. 1970b. *Computer und musikalische Kompositionen*. Braunschweig: Vieweg.
__________. 1972. “GEASCOP - Ein Kompositionsprogramm,” *Informatik. Vorträge anläßlich der Jahresversammlung vom 14. bis 17. Oktober 1971 zu Halle (Saale)*, edited by Jocahim-Hermann Scharf. Nova Acta Leopoldina vol. 37/1, no. 206. Leipzig: Barth. 629-655.
Labussiere, Annie. 1974. “Codage des structures rythmo-melodiques a partier de creations vocales,” *Informatique musicale: Journées d'etude 1973. Textes des conférences E.R.A.T.T.O.*, edited by Hélène Charnassé and Henri Ducasse. Paris: Centre de documentation sciences humaines. pp. 66-92.
Lachartre, Nicole. 1969. “Les musiques artificielles,” *Diagrammes du Monde* 146 (April): 1-96.
Ladner, Robert, Jr. 1968. “Computer Analysis of Music Forms,” *Music Journal* 26 (October): 33, 58.

Lande, Tor Sverre. 1978. "Musikkanalyse med Datamskin," *Studia Musicologica Norvegia* IV: 47-60.
LaRue, Jan. 1966. "The Computer Seminar at Binghamton: A Report," *Notes* XXIII: 236-240.
_________. 1967. "Two Problems in Music Analysis: The Computer Lends a Hand," *Computers in Humanistic Research*, edited by Edmund A. Bowles. Englewood Cliffs: Prentice Hall. pp. 194-203.
_________. 1968. "Two Options for Input of Thematic Incipits," *Institute for Computer Research in the Humanities Newsletter* IV/3 (November): 3-6.
_________. 1970a. "New Directions for Style Analysis," *Musicology and the Computer: Three Symposia*, edited by Barry S. Brook. New York: The City University of New York Press. pp. 194-197.
_________. 1970b. "Some Computer Aids to Musicology," *Bericht über den Internationalen Musikwissenschaftlichen Kongress Leipzig 1966*, edited by Carl Dahlhause et al. Kassel: Bärenreiter. pp. 466-469.
_________. 1970c. "Future Technological Directions," *IMS: Report on the Tenth Congress, Lubljana 1967*, edited by Dragotin Cvetko. Kassel: Bärenreiter. pp. 457-460.
LaRue, Jan, and Marian W. Cobin. 1967. "The Ruge-Seignelay Catalogue: An Exercise in Automated Entries," *Elektronische Datenverarbeitung in der Musikwissenschaft*, edited by Harald Heckmann. Regensburg: Gustav Bosse. pp. 41-56.
LaRue, Jan, and Murray Gould. 1969. "Correlational Analysis to Establish Authenticity of 18th-Century Symphonies," *Computers and the Humanities* III/5 (May): 311.
LaRue, Jan, and George W. Logemann. 1966. "EDP for Thematic Catalogues," *Notes* XXII: 1179-1186.
Laske, Otto. 1972. "On Musical Strategies With a View to a Generative Grammar for Music," *Interface* I/2: 111-125.
_________. 1973a. "On the Methodology and Implementation of a Procedural Theory of Music," *Computational Musicology Newsletter* I/1: 15-16.
_________. 1973b. "Toward a Musical Intelligence System: OBSERVER," *Numus West* IV: 11-16.
_________. 1974a. "In Search of a Generative Grammar for Music," *Perspectives of New Music* XII/1-2 (Autumn-Summer): 351-378. Reprinted in *Machine Models of Music*, edited by Stephen M. Schwanauer and David A. Levitt. Cambridge, MA: The MIT Press, 1993. pp. 214-240.
_________. 1974b. "Toward a Center for Studies in Musical Intelligence," *Numus West* V: 44-46.
_________. 1974c. "The Information Processing Approach to Musical Cognition," *Interface* III/2 (December): 109-136.
_________. 1974d. "Musical Acoustics (Sonology): A Questionable Science Reconsidered," *Numus-West* 6: 35-40.
_________. 1975a. *Introduction to a Generative Theory of Music*. Sonological Reports. Utrecht: Institute for Sonology.
_________. 1975b. "Musical Semantics: A Procedural Point of View," *Actes du 1er congress international de semiotique musicale*, edited by Gino Stefani. Pesaro: Centro di iniziativa culturale. pp. 214-224.
_________. 1975c. "Sufficiency Analysis of Music-Syntactic Composition," *Computers and the Humanities* IX/1 (January): 33.
_________. 1975d. "Studies in Musical Problem Solving," *Computers and the Humanities* IX/4 (July): 192.

_________. 1977a. *Music, Memory and Thought: Explorations in Cognitive Musicology*. Ann Arbor: University Research Press.

_________. 1977b. "Toward a Process Model of Musical Structures," *Proceedings of the International Workshop on the Cognitive Viewpoint*, edited by Marc T. De Mey, R. Pinxten, M. Poriau, F. Vandamme. Ghent, Belgium: Communication and Cognition. pp. 295-304.

Lauter, Josef, and Roland Mix. 1967. "The Information Content of Music," *Nachrichtentechnische Zeitschrift* XX/2: 86-89.

Lefkoff, Gerald. Ed. 1967a. *Papers from the West Virginia University Conference on Computer Applications in Music*. Morgantown: West Virginia University Library.

_________. 1967b. "Computers and the Study of Musical Style," *Papers from the West Virginia University Conference on Computer Applications in Music*, edited by Gerald Lefkoff. Morgantown: West Virginia University Library. pp. 43-61.

_________. 1970. "Automated Discovery of Similar Segments in the Forty-eight Permutations of a Twelve-Tone Row," *The Computer and Music*, edited by Harry B. Lincoln. Ithaca: Cornell University Press. pp. 147-153.

Lehr, Mangham D. 1968. "Canon One," *Computers and the Humanities* II/5 (May): 244.

Leipp, Emile, and Moncef Mlouka. 1974. "Apports de l'acoustique musicale a l'etude digitale des musiques ethniques," *Informatique musicale: Journées d'etude 1973. Textes des conférences E.R.A.T.T.O.*, edited by Hélène Charnassé and Henri Ducasse. Paris: Centre de documentation sciences humaines. pp. 144-164.

Leng, Ladislav. 1972. "O niektorych možnostiach využitia SP pri klasifikácii ozdobovanych ludovych instrumentalnych melodii," *Lidová písen a samostatný pocítac I*, edited by Dušan Holý and Oldrich Sirovátka. Brno: Klub uživatelů MSP. pp. 207-213.

Lerdal, Fred, and Ray Jackendoff. 1977. "Toward a Formal Theory of Tonal Music," *Journal of Music Theory* 21/1 (Spring): 111-171.

Levy, Morten. 1975. "On the Problem of Defining Musical Units," *Actes du 1er congress international de semiotique musicale*, edited by Gino Stefani. Pesaro: Centro di iniziativa culturale. pp. 135-149.

Lewin, David. 1968. "Some Applications of Communication Theory to the Study of Twelve-Tone Music," *Journal of Music Theory* 12/1 (Spring): 50-84.

Lewis, David Sheldon. 1968. Two Parameters of Melodic Line as Stylistic Discriminants. Ph.D. dissertation. Morgantown, WV: West Virginia University.

Lidov, David. 1975. *On Musical Phrase*. Montréal: Les Presses de l'Université.

Lidov, David, and Jim Gabura. 1973. "A Melody Writing Algorithm Using a Formal Language Model," *Computer Studies in the Humanities and Verbal Behavior* XIV/3-4: 138-148.

Lieberman, Fredric. 1970. "Computer-Aided Analysis of Javanese Music," *The Computer and Music*, edited by Harry B. Lincoln. Ithaca: Cornell University Press. pp. 181-192.

Lincoln, Harry B. 1966. "Incipit Interval Sequence Program," *Computers and the Humanities* I/2 (November): 52.

_________. 1967a. "Musicology and the Computer: The Thematic Index," *Computers in Humanistic Research*, edited by Edmund A. Bowles. Englewood Cliffs: PrenticeHall. pp. 184-193.

_________. 1967b. "Some Criteria and Techniques for Developing Computerized Thematic Indices," *Elektronische Datenverarbeitung in der Musikwissenschaft*, edited by Harald Heckmann. Regensburg: Gustav Bosse. pp. 57-62.

_________. 1967c. "Thematic Index of Sixteenth-Century Italian Music," *Computers and the Humanities* II/2 (November): 86.

__________. 1968a. "The Thematic Index: A Computer Application to Musicology," *Computers and the Humanities* II/5 (May): 215-220.
__________. 1968b. Development of Computerized Techniques in Music Research with Emphasis on the Thematic Index. Final Report, Project No. 7-8276, Grant No. OEG 1-7-078272-3898. Washington, DC: Office of Education, U.S. Department of Health, Education, and Welware.
__________. 1968c. "Thematic Index of Sixteenth-Century Italian Music," *Computers and the Humanities* II/5 (May): 243.
__________. 1969a. "A Computer Application in Musicology: The Thematic Index," *Information Processing 68. Proceedings of the IFIP Congress 1968*, edited by A. J. H. Morrel. Amsterdam: North Holland. pp. 957-961.
__________. 1969b. Development of Computerized Techniques in Music Research with Emphasis on the Thematic Index. Washington: Office of Education, U.S. Department of Health, Education, and Welware.
__________. 1969c. "The computer and music research: Prospects and problems," *Bulletin of the Council for Research in Music Education* 18 (Fall): 1-9.
__________. 1969d. "A Computer Application in Musicology: The Thematic Index," *Information Processing* 68: 957-961.
__________. Ed. 1970a. *The Computer and Music*. Ithaca: Cornell University Press.
__________. 1970b. "The Current State of Music Research and the Computer," *Computer and the Humanities* V/1 (September): 29-36.
__________. 1970c. "Thematic Indexing by Computer, Including Development of Necessary Hardware to Permit Printing of Music by Computer," *Computers and the Humanities* V/2 (November): 109-110.
__________. 1970d. A Study of Computer Techniques for Music Research. Final Report, Project No. 9-B-101, Grant No. OEG-2-9-420101-1067. Washington, DC: Office of Education, U.S. Department of Health, Education and Welware, Office of Education, Bureau of Research.
__________. 1970e. "Teaching Computer Applications in Musicology," *IBM Symposium on Introducing the Computer into the Humanities* [Document G 320-1044-0]. Poughkeepsie, NY: IBM. 1969. pp. 67-71.
__________. 1972a. "Uses of the Computer in Music Composition and Research," *Advances in Computers*, edited by Morris Rubinoff, vol. 12. New York: Academic Press. pp. 73-114.
__________. 1972b. "A Fortran Computer Program for Transcribing Franconian Rhythm," (Review of)," *Bulletin of the Council for Research in Music Education* 29 (Summer): 39-41.
__________. 1974. "Use of the Computer in Music Research: A Short Report on Accomplishments, Limitations, and Future Needs," *Computers and the Humanities* VIII/5-6 (September-November): 285-289.
__________. 1976. "Tablature pour les luths," *Computers and the Humanities* X/6 (November-December): 360-361.
__________. 1977. "Indices of the Italian Madrigal, 1530-1550," *Computers and the Humanities* XI/1 (January-February): 41.
Lindblom, Björn, and Johan Sundberg. 1970. "Towards a Generative Theory of Melody," *Svensk Tidskrift för Musikforskning* 52: 71-88.
Locke, David. 1981. "Cantometrics: An Approach to the Anthropology of Music by Alan Lomax [Book Review]," *Ethnomusicology* XXV/3 (September): 527-529.

Lockwood, Lewis. 1966. "MIR ('Musical Information Retrieval')," *Computers and the Humanities* I/2 (November): 51.

__________. 1970a. "A Stylistic Investigation of the Masses of Josquin Desprez with the Aid of the Computer: a Progress Report," *Musicology and the Computer: Three Symposia*, edited by Barry S. Brook. New York: The City University of New York Press. pp. 19-27.

__________. 1970b. "Computer Assistance in the Investigation of Accidentals in Renaissance Music," *IMS: Report on the Tenth Congress, Lubljana 1967*, edited by Dragotin Cvetko. Kassel: Bärenreiter. pp. 444-449.

Lönn, Anders. 1972. "Trends and Tendencies in Recent Swedish Musicology," *Acta Musicologica* 44/1: 11-25.

Logemann, George W. 1966a. "Prepare Music Input Data," *Computers and the Humanities* I/2 (November): 51.

__________. 1966b. "Harmonic and Time-line Input and Statistics," *Computers and the Humanities* I/2 (November): 51-52.

__________. 1967a. "The Canons in the Musical Offering of J. S. Bach: An Example of Computational Musicology," *Elektronische Datenverarbeitung in der Musikwissenschaft*, edited by Harald Heckmann. Regensburg: Gustav Bosse. pp. 63-87.

__________. 1967b. "MUSE: A Syntax-Directed System for Music Analysis," *Computers and the Humanities* I/5 (May): 224.

Lomax, Alan. 1962. "Song Structure and Social Structure." *Ethnology* I/4 (October): 425-451.

__________. 1968. *Folk Song Style and Culture*. Washington, DC: American Association for the Advancement of Science.

__________. 1976. *Cantometrics: An Approach to the Anthropology of Music*. Berkeley, CA: The University of California Press.

Lombardi, Carlo. 1967. "Investigation of Style of Keyboard Composition of Ruttini and Haydn," *Computers and the Humanities* I/5 (May): 226-227.

Longuet-Higgins, H. Christopher. 1976. "Perception of Melodies," *Nature* 263: 646-653. Reprinted in H. Christopher Longuet-Higgins, *Mental Processes: Studies in Cognitive Science*. Cambridge, MA: MIT Press, 1987. pp. 105-129.

__________. 1978. "The Perception of Music," *Interdisciplinary Science Reviews* 3 (June): 148-156. Reprinted as "Grammars of Music" in H. Christopher Longuet-Higgins, *Mental Processes: Studies in Cognitive Science*. Cambridge, MA: MIT Press, 1987. pp. 130-149.

__________. 1979. "The Perception of Music," *Proceedings of the Royal Society of London* Series B 205: 307-322. Reprinted in H. Christopher Longuet-Higgins, *Mental Processes: Studies in Cognitive Science*. Cambridge, MA: MIT Press, 1987. pp. 169-187.

Longuet-Higgins, H. Christopher, and Mark J. Steedman. 1971. "On Interpreting Bach," *Machine Intelligence 6*, edited by Bernard Meltzer and Donald Michie. Edinburgh: Edinburgh University Press. pp. 221-241.

Lord, Charles Hubbard. 1978. An Explication of Some Recent Mathematical Approaches to Music Analysis. Ph.D. dissertation. Bloomington, IN: Indiana University.

Lott, William Loyd. 1968. Arabic 1620: An Analysis and Procedure for Composing Computer Music. M.M. thesis. Denton, TX: North Texas State University.

Ludvová, Jitka. 1974. "The Application of Analytical Methods of Information Theory to Tonal Music," *De musica disputationes Pragenses* II/4: 72-85.

Mala, Hana. 1967. "Statistická srovnávací analyza sboru Leose Janácka a moravskych lidovych písní," *Hudebni Veda* IV/4: 602-627.

Mandelbrot, B. 1957. "[Review of] W. Fucks, Mathematische Analyse von Sprachelementen, Sprachstil und Sprache," *Word: Journal of the Linguistic Circle of New York* 13: 159-160.

Marillier, Cecil Glyn. 1971. Tonal Structure in the Symphonies of F. J. Haydn. M.A. thesis. North Dunedin, New Zealand: University of Otago.

Maser, Siegfried. 1971. *Numerische Ästhetik. Neue mathematische Verfahren zur quantitativen Beschreibung und Bewertung ästhetischer Zustände*, 3rd edition. Stuttgart: Krämer.

Mason, Robert M. 1969a. "An Encoding Algorithm and Tables for the Digital Analysis of Harmony I," *Journal of Research in Music Education* 17/3 (Autumn): 286-300.

_________. 1969b. "An Encoding Algorithm and Tables for the Digital Analysis of Harmony II," *Journal of Research in Music Education* 17/4 (Winter): 369-387.

Mathews, Max V. 1969. *The Technology of Computer Music*. Cambridge, MA: The M.I.T. Press.

_________. 1972. Review of *The Computer and Music* by Harry B. Lincoln, *Computer Studies in the Humanities and Verbal Behavior* III/4 (November): 224-225.

Maultsby, Portia Katrenia. 1972. "Afro-American Music, 1619-1861: An Analytical Study," *Computers and the Humanities* VII/2 (November): 125.

_________. 1974. Afro-American Religious Music: 1619-1861. Historical Development and Computer Analysis of one Hundred Sprituals. Ph.D. dissertation. Madison, WI: The University of Wisconsin.

McHose, Allen I. 1950. "Musical Research in the Definition of Bach's Contrapuntal Harmonic Style," *Proceedings of the Music Teachers National Association* 42: 126-150.

McMullen, Patrick T. 1974. "Influence of Number of Different Pitches and Melodic Redundancy on Preference Responses," *Journal of Research in Music Education* XXII: 198-204.

Meehan, James R. 1979. "An Artifical Intelligence Approach to Tonal Music Theory," *Proceedings of the ACM*. New York: Association for Computing Machinery. pp. 116-120.

Melkus, Ilja. 1976. "Některé Příklady Vyžití Samočinného počíytače v zahraniční muzikologii," *Lidová píseň a samočinný počítač III: Sborník materiálů ze 3. semináře o využití samočinného počítače při studiu lidové písně (Brno 15.-16.10.1974)*, ed. by Dušan Holý, Karel Pala, and Miloš Štědroň. Praha: Státni pedagogické nakladatelstvi. pp. 333-338.

Mendel, Arthur. 1969. "Some Preliminary Attempts at Computer-Assisted Style Analysis in Music," *Computers and the Humanities* IV/1 (September): 41-52.

_________. 1976a. "Towards Objective Criteria for Establishing Chronology and Authenticity: What Help Can the Computer Give?" *Josquin des Prez. Proceedings of the international Josquin festival-conference held at The Juilliard School at Lincoln Center in New York City, 21-25 June 1971*, edited by Edward E. Lowinsky. London: Oxford University Press. pp. 297-308.

_________. 1976b. "Critical Editions of Josquin Desprez," *Computers and the Humanities* X/1 (January-February): 52.

_________. 1979. "Recension of the Sources of the Works of Josquin Dezpres," *Computers and the Humanities* XIII/3 (July-September): 260.

Mendel, Arthur, and Thomas Hall. 1973. "Princeton Computer Tools for Musical Research," *Informatique et Sciences Humaines* 19 (December): 39-59. French translation: "Usage de l'ordinateur dans la recherche musicale à Princeton," pp. 61-65.

Mendel, Arthur, and Lewis Lockwood. 1967. "Music Information Retrieval," *Computers and the Humanities* I/5 (May): 226.

Mermet, Jean, and Denis Jaeger. 1974. "Un peripherique d'ordinateur a l'usage des musiciens," *Informatique musicale: Journées d'etude 1973. Textes des conférences E.R.A.T.T.O.*, edited by Hélène Charnassé and Henri Ducasse. Paris: Centre de documentation sciences humaines. pp. 204-218.

Meyer, Leonard B. 1957. "Meaning in Music and Information Theory." *Journal of Aesthetics & Art Criticism* XV/4 (June): 412-424.

Meylan, Raymond. 1965. "Utilization des Calculatrices Electroniques pour la comparaison Interne du Repertoire des Basses Danses de Quinzi," *Fontes Artis Musicae* 12 (May): 128-134.

_________. 1966. "Recherche de Parents parmi les Basses Danses du Quinzi," *Acta Musicologica* 38 (January): 46-66.

_________. 1967. "Symbolisierung einer Melodie auf Lochkarten," *Elektronische Datenverarbeitung in der Musikwissenschaft*, edited by Harald Heckmann. Regensburg: Gustav Bosse. pp. 21-24.

_________. 1968. *L'enigme de la musique des basses danses du quinzième siècle*. Publications de la Societe Suisse de Musicologie. Bern: Haupt.

_________. 1970. "Teorie de la Centonisation," *IMS: Report on the Tenth Congress, Lubljana 1967*, edited by Dragotin Cvetko. Kassel: Bärenreiter. pp. 427-430.

_________. 1974. "Limites de l'objectivite dans les ecritures instrumentales de la Renaissance," *Informatique musicale: Journées d'etude 1973. Textes des conférences E.R.A.T.T.O.*, edited by Hélène Charnassé and Henri Ducasse. Paris: Centre de documentation sciences humaines. pp. 1-9.

Miller, Alyce Sands, et al. 1972. "Annual Bibliography for 1971," *Computers and the Humanities* VI/4 (March): 235-251.

Mix, Roland. 1967. "Die Entropieabnahme bei Abhängigkeit zwischen mehreren simultanen Informationsquellen und bei Übergang zu Markoff-Ketten höherer Ordnung, untersucht an musikalischen Beispielen," *Theorien zur Formalanalyse mehrstimmiger Musik*, by Walter Reckziegel. Köln: Westdeutscher Verlag. pp. 39-80.

Moles, Abraham A. 1956a. "Informationstheorie der Musik." *Nachrichtentechnische Fachberichte* 3: 47-55.

_________. 1956b. "Informationstheorie und ästhetische Empfindung." *Gravesaner Blätter* VI (December): 3-9.

_________. 1958. *Théorie de l'information et perception esthétique*. Paris: Flammarion & Cie. American edition: *Information Theory and Esthetic Perception*, translated by Joel E. Cohen. Urbana: University of Illinois Press, 1966.

_________. 1962. "Das neue Verhältnis zwischen Musik und Mathematik," *Gravesaner Blätter* VI: 98-103.

_________. 1964. "Uvedení do soucasného stavu hudby," *Nové Cesty Hudby*: 36-53.

_________. 1966. *Information Theory and Esthetic Perception*, translated by Joel E. Cohen. Urbana: University of Illinois Press.

_________. 1973. *Kunst & Computer*. Köln: M. DuMont Schauberg.

_________. 1986. "Approche informationnelle de la perception et de la creation Musicale," *International Review of the Aesthetics and Sociology of Music* (Croatia) XVII/2 (December): 273-297.

Moomaw, Charles J. 1973. A PL-1 Program for the Harmonic Analysis of Music by the Theories of Paul Hindemith and Howard Hanson. M.M. thesis. Cincinnati, OH: University of Cincinnati.

Moore, F. 1971. "Musica ed elaboratori elettronici," *Scienza & Tecnica: Annuario della EST, Enciclopedia della Scienza e della Tecnica*: 490-498.

Moorer, James Anderson. 1973. "Segmentation and Analysis of Continuous Musical Sound," *Computational Musicology Newsletter* I/1: 3-4.

__________. 1975. On the Segmentation and Analysis of Continuous Musical Sound by Digital Computer. Ph.D. dissertation. Stanford, CA: Stanford University.

Morehen, John, and Ian Bent. 1978. "Computers in the Analysis of Music," *Proceedings of the Royal Musical Association* CIV (1977/78): 30-46.

Morehen, John, and Ian Bent. 1979. "Computer Applications in Musicology," *The Musical Times* 120/7 (July): 563-566.

Morse, Margaret Beverly. 1974. A Quantitative Stylistic Analysis of the Agnus Dei Mass Movements of Guillaume Dufay Supporting the Doubtful Authenticity of the Missa Caput. M.M. thesis. West Hartford, CT: Hartt College of Music.

Morton, Ian A. 1967. "FORTRAN Music Programs Involving Numerically Related Tones," *Computers and the Humanities* II/2 (November): 87-88.

__________. 1973. "Analysis of Tonal Music at the Level of Perception," *Computational Musicology Newsletter* I/1: 16.

__________. 1974a. "Analysis of Tonal Music at the Level of Perception," *Computers in the Humanities*, edited by J. L. Mitchel. Minneapolis: University of Minnesota Press. pp. 261-266.

__________. 1974b. "Judgmental Factors in the Perception of Tonal Music," *Computers and the Humanities* VIII/1 (January): 51.

Morton, Ian, and John Lofstedt. 1970. "FORTRAN Music Programs Involving Numerically Related Tones," *The Computer and Music*, edited by Harry B. Lincoln. Ithaca: Cornell University Press. pp. 154-162.

Móži, Alexander. 1976. "Pokus o harmonickú analýzu inštrumentálnej hudby pomocou numerického kódového systému," *Lidová píseň a samočinný počítač III: Sborník materiálů ze 3. semináře o využití samočinného počítače při studiu lidové písně (Brno 15.-16.10.1974)*, ed. by Dušan Holý, Karel Pala, and Miloš Štědroň. Praha: Státni pedagogické nakladatelstvi. pp. 287-309.

Nakamura, Yasuaki, and Seiji Inokuchi. 1979. "Music Information Processing System and Its Applications to Comparative Musicology," *Proceedings of the Sixth International Joint Conference on Artificial Intelligence, Tokyo, August 20-23, 1979* [*IJCAI-79*]. [s.l.]: IJCAI, 1979. pp. 633-635.

Nake, Frieder. 1974. *Ästhetik als Informationsverarbeitung. Grundlagen und Anwendungen der Informatik im Bereich ästhetischer Produktion und Kritik.* Wien: Springer.

Narmour, Eugene. 1977. *Beyond Schenkerianism: The Need for Alternatives in Music Analysis.* Chicago: University of Chicago Press.

Nash, Stephen G. Ed. 1990. *A History of Scientific Computing.* New York: ACM Press.

Nathan, Hans. 1958. "The Twelve-Tone Compositions of Luigi Dallapiccola," The *Musical Quarterly* 44 (July): 289-310.

Nattiez, Jean-Jacques. 1972. "Is a Descriptive Seomiotics of Music Possible?" *Language Sciences* 23: 1-7.

__________. 1973a. "Musical Semiotics," *Computational Musicology Newsletter* I/1: 17.

__________. 1973b. "Linguistics: A New Approach for Musical Analysis?" *International Review of the Aesthetics and Sociology of Music* IV/1 (June): 51-69.

__________. 1975. "From Taxonomic Analysis to Stylistic Characterization: Debussy's Syrinx," *Actes du 1er congress international de semiotique musicale*, edited by Gino Stefani. Pesaro: Centro di iniziativa culturale. pp. 83-110.

Nelson, Gary Lee. 1973. "COMPOSE: A Program for Musical Composition," *Computational Musicology Newsletter* I/1: 11.

_________. 1974a. Anton Webern's 'Five Canons' op. 16: A Test Case for Computer-Aided Analysis and Synthesis of Musical Style. Ph.D. dissertation. St Louis, MO: Washington University.

_________. 1974b. "Pattern Recognition in Musical Score," *Computers and the Humanities* VIII/1 (January): 50-51.

Nettl, Bruno. 1958. "Some Linguistic Approaches to Musical Analysis," *Journal of the International Folk Music Council* X: 37-41.

Neumann, P. G., and H. Schappert. 1959. "Komponieren mit elektronischen Rechenautomaten," *Nachrichtentechnische Zeitschrift* VIII: 403-407.

Norman, Philip B. 1945. *A Quantitative Study of Harmonic Similarities in Certain Specified Works of Bach, Beethoven and Wagner*. New York, NY: Carl Fischer.

Ortmann, Otto. 1937. "Interval Frequency as a Determinant of Melodic Style," *Beabody Bulletin* (December): 3-10.

Oudal, Robert D. 1969. "The 1968 Introductory Seminar in the Use of Computers in Musical Projects: A Summary Report of Reactions, Frustrations, and Achievements," *Student Musicologists at Minnesota* III (1968-69): 66-109.

Owen, Jonathan. 1979. "Computer Implementation of Harmonic Analysis of Music," *IUCC Bulletin* I/3 (Winter): 119-121.

Paisley, William J. 1964. "Identifying the Unknown Communicator in Painting, Literature and Music: the Significance of Minor Encoding Habits," *Journal of Communication* XIV/4 (December): 219-237.

_________. 1969. "Studying 'Style' as Deviation from Encoding Norms," *The Analysis of Communication Content. Developments in Scientific Theories and Computer Techniques*, edited by George Gerbner, Ole R. Holsti, Klaus Krippendorff, William J. Paisley and Philip J. Stone. New York: Wiley & Sons. pp. 133-146.

Pala, Karel. 1976. "Poznámy k popisu tematické stavby lidové písně," *Lidová píseň a samočinný počítač III: Sborník materiálů ze 3. semináře o využití samočinného počítače při studiu lidové písně (Brno 15.-16.10.1974)*, ed. by Dušan Holý, Karel Pala, and Miloš Štědroň. Praha: Státni pedagogické nakladatelstvi. pp. 197-210.

Pape, U. 1969. "Ein Verfahren zur Verschlüsselung und Symbolisierung von Kompositionen in Hinblick auf eine Musikanalyse mit EDV-Anlagen," *Elektronische Datenverarbeitung* XI (July): 342-345.

Paszkowska, Elzbieta. 1977. "Struktura napiecia w klasyoznej formie sonatowej," *Muzyka* [Poland] XXII/4: 14-37.

Patrick, Philip Howard. 1973. A Computer Study of a Suspension Formation in the Masses of Josquin Desprez. Ph.D. dissertation. Princeton, NJ: Princeton University.

Patrick, P. Howard. 1974. "A Computer Study of a Suspension Formation in the Masses of Josquin Desprez," *Computer and the Humanities* VIII/5-6 (September-November): 321-331.

Patrick, P. Howard, and Karen Strickler. 1978. "A Computer-Assisted Study of Dissonance in the Masses of Josquin Desprez," *Computers and the Humanities* 12/4: 341-364.

Patrick, Robert Lee. 1971. A Computer-Based Thematic Index to the Works of Heinrich Schütz. D.M.A. dissertation. Lexington, KY: University of Kentucky.

Pawlak, Aleksander. 1975. "Die Analyse und Klassifikation der Melodien aus der Region Kujawa," *Methoden der ethnomusikologischen Analyse*, edited by Oskár Elschek. Bratislava: Sekcia hudobnej vedy-etnomuzikológia, Umenovedný ústav, Slovenská akademia vied. pp. 36-37.

Pederson, Donald Margedo. 1968. Some Technique for Computer-Aided Analysis of Musical Scores. Ph.D. dissertation. Iowa City, IA: The University of Iowa.

Peterson, Don Laurel. 1975. Tonal Characteristics in the Kyrie and Sanctus Sections of Twelve L'homme arme Masses: A Computer-Assisted Study. Ph.D. dissertation. Madison, WI: University of Wisconsin.
Philippot, Michel P. 1970. "Muss es sein," *L'Arc* [France] 40: 82-95.
Pikler, Andrew G. 1960. "Automatische Bewertung von Musikaufführungen," *Gravesaner Blätter* V: 137-139.
Pinkerton, Richard C. 1956. "Information Theory and Melody." *Scientific America* 194/2 (February): 77-86.
Piotrowska, Maria. 1968. Wybrane aspekty problematyki Jeux venitiens jako wstep do badan strukturalnych nad tworczoscia Witolda Lutoslawskiego. M.A. thesis. Warszawa, Poland: University of Warszawa.
Piotrowski, Zbigniew. 1974. "O zastosowaniu komputerow w muzyce mowi Lejaren Hiller," *Ruch Muzyczny* [Poland] IV (February): 3-4.
Piszczalski, Martin B., and Bernard A. Galler. 1979. "Computer Analysis and Transcription of Performed Music: a Project Report," *Computers and the Humanities* 13/3 (July-September): 195-206.
Pletka, Vaclav. 1974. "Methodologische Probleme der Arbeiterliedforschung," *Arbeiterklasse und Musik: theoretische Positionen in der deutschen Arbeiterklasse zur Musikkultur vor 1945: Eine Dokumentation des Arbeiterliederarchivs*, edited by Charlotte Albrecht, Inge Lammel, Ilse Schütt, and Marlene Weller. Berlin: Akademie der Künste der Deutschen Demokratischen Republik. pp. 32-35.
Polansky, Larry. 1979. "A Hierarchical Gestalt Analysis of Ruggles' Portals," *Proceedings of the 1978 International Computer Music Conference*, vol. 2, edited by Curtis Roads. Evanston: Northwestern University. pp. 790-852.
Prerau, David S. 1970a. "Computer Pattern Recognition of Standard Engraved Music Notation," *Computers and the Humanities* IV/5 (May): 344.
__________. 1970b. Computer Pattern Recognition of Standard Engraved Music Notation. PhD dissertation. Boston, MA: Massachussetts Institute of Technology.
__________. 1971. "Computer Pattern Recognition of Printed Music," *AFIPS Conference Proceedings* 39: 153-162.
__________. 1975. "DO-RE-MI: A Program that Recognizes Music Notation," *Computers and the Humanities* IX/1 (January): 25-29.
Pruett, James W. 1966. "The Harpur College Music-Computer Seminar: A Report," *Computers and the Humanities* I/2 (November): 34-38.
__________. 1968. Review of *Papers of the West Virginia University Conference on Computer Applications in Music* by Gerald Lefkoff (Ed.), *Computer Studies in the Humanities and Verbal Behavior* I/3 (October): 155.
Pruslin, Dennis Howard. 1966. Automatic Recognition of Sheet Music. Sc.D. dissertation. Boston, MA: Massachusetts Institute of Technology.
Pulkert, Oldrich. 1967. "Hudba, samocinne pocitace a jine novinky" ["Music, Computers, and Other Novelties"], *Hudebni veda* 3: 479-484.
Quastler, H. 1956. Discussion, following Mathematical Theory of Word Formation, by W. Fucks, *Information Theory: Papers Read at a Symposium on Information Theory Held at the Royal Institution, London, September 12th to 16th, 1955*, edited by Colin Cherry. London: Butterworths Scientific Publications. pp. 168-169.
Rabson, Carolyn. 1979. "National Tune Index," *Computers and the Humanities* XIII/3 (July-September): 261.
Rader, Gary M. 1974. "A Method for Composing Simple Traditional Music by Computer," *Communications of the ACM* November 1974: 631-638. Reprinted in *Machine Models*

of Music, edited by Stephen M. Schwanauer and David A. Levitt. Cambridge, MA: The MIT Press, 1993. pp. 242-260.

_________. 1975. "A Method for Composing Simple Traditional Music by Computer," *Computational Musicology Newsletter* II/1: 14.

Randall, J. K. 1964. "A Report from Princeton," *Perspectives of New Music* III (Spring): 84-92.

_________. 1967. "Three Lectures to Scientists," *Perspectives of New Music* V/2 (Spring-Summer): 124-140.

Raskin, Jeffrey F. 1967. A Hardware Independent Computer Drawing System Using List Structured Modeling: The Quick-Draw Graphics Systems. M.S. thesis. State College, PA: Pennsylvania State University.

_________. 1973. "On Keyboard Input of Music to the Computer," *Computational Musicology Newsletter* I/1: 4.

Ratner, Leonard G. 1970. "Ars Combinatoria: Chance and Choice in Eighteenth-Century Music," *Studies in Eighteenth Century Music: A Tribute to Karl Geiringer on his Seventieth Birthday*, edited by H. C. Robbins Landon. New York, NY: Oxford University Press. pp. 343-363.

Ravnikar, Bruno. 1972. "Nekaj rezultatov proucevanja glasbene folklore z metodami matematicne statistike," *Rad XVII Kongresa Saveza udruzenja folklorista Jugoslavije, Porec, 1970*, edited by Vinko Zganec. Zagreb, Jugoslavia: Savez udruzenja folklorista Jugoslavije, Drustvo folklorista Hrvatske. pp. 271-286.

Reckziegel, Walter. 1967a. *Theorien zur Formalanalyse mehrstimmiger Musik*. Köln: Westdeutscher Verlag.

_________. 1967b. "Musikanalyse - eine exakte Wissenschaft?" *Elektronische Datenverarbeitung in der Musikwissenschaft*, edited by Harald Heckmann. Regensburg: Bosse, pp. 203-224.

_________. 1967c. "Musikanalyse und Wissenschaft." *Studia Musicologica Academiae Scientiarum Hungaricae* IX/1-2: 163-186.

_________. 1967d. "Die Notenschrift im Computer dargestellt," *Studia Musicologica Academiae Scientiarum Hungaricae* IX/3-4: 395-406.

_________. 1968. "Musik im Datenspeicher," *Die Musikforschung* XXI/4 (October-December): 427-438.

_________. 1970. "Ein Subjektives Tempomaß," *Bericht über den Internationalen Musikwissenschaftlichen Kongress Leipzig 1966*, edited by Carl Dahlhause et al. Kassel: Bärenreiter. pp. 457-458.

Regener, Eric. 1967a. "A Multiple-Pass Transcription and a System for Music Analysis by Computer," *Elektronische Datenverarbeitung in der Musikwissenschaft*, edited by Harald Heckmann. Regensburg: Gustav Bosse. pp. 89-102.

_________. 1967b. "Layered Music-Theoretic Systems," *Perspectives of New Music* VI/1 (Autumn-Winter): 52-62.

Reier, Ellen Jane, and Warren Reier. 1976. "The Introit Trope Repertory at Nevers," *Nordiskt Kollokvium III. I Latinsk Liturgiforskning*, edited by Knud Ottosen. HelsinkiL Helsingfors University. pp. 97-110.

Reinecke, Hans-Peter. 1970. "Anwendung Informationstheoretischer und Korrelationsstatistischer Verfahren für die Analyse Musikalischer Strukturen," *IMS: Report on the Tenth Congress, Lubljana 1967*, edited by Dragotin Cvetko. Kassel: Bärenreiter. pp. 430-434.

Remmel, M. Ed. 1976. *Towards a Monographical Analysis of Some Folk-Song Arrangements*. Tallin: Academy of the Sciences of the Estonian S.S.R., Department of Social Sciences.
Remmel, Mart N. Ed. 1977. *Problemy taksonomii estonskich runiceskich melodij*. Tallin: Academy of Science.
Rhodes, Willard. 1965. "The Use of Computer in the Classification of Folk Tunes," *Studia Musicologica Academiae Scientiarum Hungaricae* VII: 339-343.
Riedel, Johannes. 1970. "A Computer-Assisted Study of Ecuadorian Urban Music," *Computers and the Humanities* V/2 (November): 111.
Riotte, Andre. 1974. "Informatique musicale: jonction nouvelle entre art et science," *Euro-Spectra* XIII/1 (March): 2-15.
Roads, Curtis. 1979. "Grammars as Representations for Music," *Computer Music Journal* III/1 (March): 48-55.
Robison, Tobias D. [n.d.]. A Short Description of the MIR Compiler. Princeton: Princeton University Music Department.
__________. 1967. "IML-MIR: A Data-Processing System for the Analysis of Music," *Elektronische Datenverarbeitung in der Musikwissenschaft*, edited by Harald Heckmann. Regensburg: Bosse. pp. 103-135.
Rohrer, Hermann G. 1971. *Musikalische Stilanalyse auf der Grundlage eines Modelles für Lernprozesse*. Berlin: Siemens AG.
Rojterstejn, Mihail I. 1973. "Graf i matrica kak instrumenty ladovogo analiza," *Muzykalnoje Iskusstvo i Nauka*. Moskva: Muzyka. pp. 175-189.
__________. 1974. "'Muzykalnye' structury v poezii Bloka," *O Muzyke. Problemy analiza: k semidesiatiletiiu so dnia rozhdeniia i piatidesiatiletiiu nauchno-pedagogicheskoi deiatel'nosti zasluzhennogo deiatelia iskusstv RSFSR, doktora iskusstvovedeniia professora Viktora Abramovicha Tsukkermana*, edited by V. P. Bobrovskii and G. L. Golovinskii. Moskow: Sovetskij Kompozitor. pp. 323-343.
Roller, Gilbert H. 1964. The Development of the Methods for Analysis of Musical Composition and for the Formation of a Symmetrical Twelve-tone Row Using the Electronic Digital Computer. Ph.D. dissertation. East Lansing, MI: Michigan State University.
__________. 1965. "Development of a Method for Analysis of Musical Compositions Using an Electronic Digital Computer," *Journal of Research in Music Education* XIII/4 (Winter): 249-252.
Robison, Tobias D. 1967. "IML-MIR: A Data-Processing System for the Analysis of Music," *Elektronische Datenverarbeitung in der Musikwissenschaft*, edited by Harald Heckmann. Regensburg: Gustav Bosse. pp. 103-135.
Rothgeb, John. 1966. "Some Uses of Mathematical Concepts in Theories of Music," *Journal of Music Theory* X/2 (Winter): 200-215.
__________. 1967. "Theories of Tonal Bass Harmonization," *Computers and the Humanities* II/2 (November): 87.
__________. 1968a. "Theories of Tonal Bass Harmonization," *Computers and the Humanities* II/5 (May): 243.
__________. 1968b. Harmonizing the Unfigured Bass: A Computational Study. Ph.D. dissertation. New Haven, CT: Yale University.
__________. 1969. "Simulating Musical Skills by Digital Computer," IEEE Transactions on Computers. Reprinted in *Machine Models of Music*, edited by Stephen M. Schwanauer and David A. Levitt. Cambridge, MA: The MIT Press, 1993. pp. 156-164.

_________. 1971a. "Musical Research by Computer: Some Current Limitations [Review of Harry B. Lincoln, ed., *The Computer and Music*]," *Computers and the Humanities* V/3 (January): 178-182.

_________. 1971b. "Some Early Efforts in Computational Musicology," *Computers and the Humanities* VI/1 (September): 56-58.

_________. 1971c. Harmonizing the unfigured bass: a computational study. Ph.D. dissertation. New Haven, CT: Yale University.

_________. 1979. "Simulating Musical Skills by Digital Computer," *ACM/CSC-ER: ACM Annual Conference / Annual Meeting* (January): 121-125. Revised in *Computer Music Journal* 4/2 (Summer 1980): 36-40. Reprinted in *The Music Machine*, edited by Curtis Roads. Cambridge, MA: MIT Press, 1989. pp. 657-662.

Rubenstein, Nancy Ordelheide. 1969. A Fortran Computer Program for Transcribing Franconian Rhythm. Ph.D. dissertation. St Louis, MO: Washington University.

Ryžov, L. 1972. *Točnyje metody i muzykalnoje iskusstvo*. Rostov na Donu: Rostov University Press.

Sands, Alyce E., et al. 1968. "Annual Bibliography for 1967," *Computers and the Humanities* II/4 (March): 159-176.

Sands, Alyce E., et al. 1969. "Annual Bibliography for 1968," *Computers and the Humanities* III/4 (March): 211-224.

Sands, Alyce E., et al. 1970. "Annual Bibliography for 1969," *Computers and the Humanities* IV/5 (May): 319-322.

Sands, Alyce E., et al. 1971. "Annual Bibliography for 1970," *Computers and the Humanities* V/4 (March): 215-238.

Scharf, Joachim-Hermann. 1972. "Einführung in 'Computer und Musikwissenschaft'," *Informatik. Vorträge anläßlich der Jahresversammlung vom 14. bis 17. Oktober 1971 zu Halle (Saale)*, edited by Jocahim-Hermann Scharf. Leipzig: Barth. pp. 563-572.

Scherrer, Deborah K. 1973. "Computer-Aided Music Analysis," *Computational Musicology Newsletter* I/1: 17.

Scherrer, Deborah K., and Philip H. Scherrer. 1971. "An Experiment in the Computer Measurement of Melodic Variation in Folksong," *Journal of American Folklore* 84/332 (April-June): 230-241.

Schillinger, Joseph. 1948. *The Mathematical Basis of the Arts*. New York: Philosophical Library.

Schiødt, Nanna. 1965. "Data Processing Applied to Byzantine Chant," *Fontes Artis Musicae* XII/2-3: 122-123.

_________. 1971. "A Computer-Aided Analysis of Thirty-Five Byzantine Hymns," *Studies in Eastern Chant II*, edited by Miloš Velimirović. London: Oxford University Press. pp. 129-154.

Schiødt, Nanna, and Bjarner Svejgaard. 1967. "Application of Computer Technique to the Analysis of Byzantine Sticherarion Melodies," *Elektronische Datenverarbeitung in der Musikwissenschaft*, edited by Harald Heckmann. Regensburg: Gustav Bosse. pp. 187-201.

Schot, Joanna Wood. 1962. "Review of *Experimental Music Composition with an Electronic Computer*, by Lejaren Hiller, Jr., and Leonard M. Isaacson," *Mathematics of Computation* 16/80 (October): 507-508.

Sellek, John. 1968. "Music Information Retrieval," *Computers and the Humanities* III/2 (November): 112.

_________. 1969. "Music Information Retrieval," *Computers and the Humanities* III/5 (May): 310.

__________. 1970. "Musical Information Retrieval (MIR)," *Computers and the Humanities* V/2 (November): 110.

Sellek, John, and Roger Bakeman. 1965. "Procedures for the Analysis of Form: Two Computer Applications," *Journal of Music Theory* IX/2 (Winter): 281-293.

Sentieri, Alfred Richard. 1978. A Method for the Specification of Style Change in Music: A Computer-Aided Study of Selected Venetian Sacred Compositions from the Time of Gabrieli to the Time of Vivaldi. Ph.D. thesis. Ohio State University.

Ševčíková, Marie. 1976. "Tematická Výstavba lidové písně," *Lidová píseň a samočinný počítač III: Sborník materiálů ze 3. semináře o využití samočinného počítače při studiu lidové písně (Brno 15.-16.10.1974)*, ed. by Dušan Holý, Karel Pala, and Miloš Štědroň. Praha: Státni pedagogické nakladatelstvi. pp. 145-153.

Shamos, Michael Ian. 1971. "Computer Investigation of Highland Bagpipe Music," *Computers and the Humanities* V/5 (May): 311-312.

Shannon, Claude E., and W. Weaver. 1949. *The Mathematical Theory of Communication*. Urbana: University of Illinois Press.

Shatzkin, Merton. 1970. "Chords and Chord Progression in J. S. Bach's 371 Chorales," *Computers and the Humanities* IV/5 (May): 347.

__________. 1973. "Bach Chorales," *Computational Musicology Newsletter* I/1: 17.

Silverman, Faye-Ellen. 1974. "Report from New York City: Computer Conference, June 1973," *Current Musicology* 17 (January): 77-80.

Simon, Herbert A., and Richard K. Summer. 1968. "Pattern in Music," *Formal Representation of Human Judgement*, edited by B. Kleinmuntz. New York: Wiley. pp. 219-251. Reprinted in *Machine Models of Music*, edited by Stephen M. Schwanauer and David A. Levitt. Cambridge, MA: The MIT Press, 1993. pp. 83-110.

Sirovátka, Oldřich. 1976. "Členění písňového textu," *Lidová píseň a samočinný počítač III: Sborník materiálů ze 3. semináře o využití samočinného počítače při studiu lidové písně (Brno 15.-16.10.1974)*, ed. by Dušan Holý, Karel Pala, and Miloš Štědroň. Praha: Státni pedagogické nakladatelstvi. pp. 107-119.

Smoliar, Stephen William. 1971a. A Parallel-Processing Model of Musical Structures. Ph.D. dissertation. Boston, MA: Massachussetts Institute of Technology.

__________. 1971b. *A Parallel-Processing Model of Musical Structures*. Cambridge, MA: Project Mac, Massachusetts Institute of Technology.

__________. 1972a. "Music Theory – A Programming Linguistic Approach," *Proceedings of the ACM 25th Annual Conference*. New York: Association for Computing Machinery. pp. 100-114.

__________. 1972b. Music Theory – A Programming Linguistic Approach. Technical Report # 15. Haifa, Israel: Israel Institute of Technology.

__________. 1973. Systemic Aspects of Musical Activity. Technical Report # 28. Haifa, Israel: Israel Institute of Technology.

__________. 1974a. "Process Structuring and Music Theory," *Journal of Music Theory* XVIII/2 (Autumn): 308-336. Reprinted in *Machine Models of Music*, edited by Stephen M. Schwanauer and David A. Levitt. Cambridge, MA: The MIT Press, 1993. pp. 188-212.

__________. 1974b. "An Interactive Computer Music Facility," *Computers and the Humanities* VIII/4 (July): 254-255.

__________. 1975a. "Proposal for an Interactive Computer-Music Facility," *Computational Musicology Newsletter* II/1: 5-6.

__________. 1975b. "Process Structuring and Music Theory," *Computational Musicology Newsletter* II/1: 17.

_________. 1976a. "Music Programs: An Approach to Music Theory Through Computational Linguistics," *Journal of Music Theory* XX/1 (Spring): 105-131.

_________. 1976b. Schenker: A Computer Aid for Analysing Tonal Music. Music Project Report No. 6. [Philadelphia]: Department of Computer and Information Science, University of Pennsylvania.

_________. 1977. "SCHENKER: A Computer Aid for Analyzing Tonal Music," *SIGLASH Newsletter* X/1-2: 30-61.

Smoliar, Stephen W., and M. Joseph Willson. 1974. "Proposal for an Interactive Computer-Music Facility," *Numus-West* V: 39-43.

Snell, James Loftin. 1979. Design for a Formal System for Deriving Tonal Music. Master's thesis. Binghamton, NY: State University of New York at Binghamton.

Solomon, Larry. *Music Analysis System*. Software 1976, 1982, 1984.

Sørensen, Av Olve. 1978. "Metoder og Metodeproblemer ved Harmonisk Analyse med EDB," *Studia Musicologica Norvegica* IV: 201-216.

Sørensen, Olve. 1980. "Musikkanalyse med datamaskin II," *Nordisk musik och musikvetenskap under 1970-talet: en rapport från 8:e Nordiska musikforskar-kongressen, Ljungskile folkhögskola 25-30 juni 1979*, edited by Anders Carlsson and Jan Ling. Göteborg: Musikvetenskapliga institutionen, Göteborgs universitet. pp. 177-192.

Springer, G. P. 1956. "Language and Music: Parallels and Divergencies," *For Roman Jakobson*, edited by M. Halle, H. G. Lunt, H. McLean, and C. H. Van Schooneveld. Den Haag: Mouton. pp. 504-513.

Srinivasan, R. 1978. "Studies on Indian Musical Scales. Part I: Computer Analysis of Venkatamakhi's Melakarta Scheme," *Journal of the Sangeet Natak Academy* [India] 49 (July-September): 33-42.

_________. 1980. "Studies on Indian Musical Scales. Part II: On the Degree of Relatedness of Ragas and Application to 72 Melas," *Journal of the Sangeet Natak Academy* [India] 58 (October-December): 27-38.

Stacy, William B. 1969. Style and Register as Correlated Factors in the Horn Parts of Selected Symphonies by Joseph Haydn. M.A. thesis. Chapel Hill, NC: University of North Carolina.

Stahl, V. 1964. Informationswissenschaft und Musikanalyse," *Grundlagenstudien aus Kybernetik und Geisteswissenschaft* 5: 51-58.

Starr, Daniel, and Robert Morris. 1977. "A General Theory of Combinatoriality and the Aggregate (Part 1)," *Perspectives of New Music* XVI/1 (Autumn-Winter): 3-35.

Starr, Daniel, and Robert Morris. 1978. "A General Theory of Combinatoriality and the Aggregate (Part 2)," *Perspectives of New Music* XVI/2 (Spring-Summer): 50-84.

Stech, David. 1976. A Computer-Assisted Approach to Micro-Analysis of Melodic Lines. Ph.D. dissertation. East Lansing, MI: Michigan State University.

________. 1981. "A Computer-Assisted Approach to Micro-Analysis of Melodic Lines," *Computers and the Humanities* XV/4 (December): 211-221.

Štědroň, Miloš. 1971. "Možnosti intervalové a melodické analýzy," *Opus Musicum* [Czechoslovakia] III/7 (July): 202-208.

_________. 1975. "K analýze vokální melodiky Janáčkovy opery Věc Makropulos s využitím samočinného počítače," *Hudebni Veda* [Czechoslovakia] XII/1: 46-64.

_________. 1976. "K intervalovým charakteristikám jednotlivých rolí v Janáčkově opeře Věc Makropulos," *Lidová píseň a samočinný počítač III: Sborník materiálů ze 3. semináře o využití samočinného počítače při studiu lidové písně (Brno 15.-16.10.1974)*, ed. by Dušan Holý, Karel Pala, and Miloš Štědroň. Praha: Státni pedagogické nakladatelstvi. pp. 263-285.

_________. 1978. "Zjistovani Typicnosti Nekterych Melodickych Struktur ve Vokalni Melodice Janackovy Opery Věc Makropulos Zapomoci SP," *Musicologica slovaca* [Czechoslovakia] VI: 187-198.

Štědroň, Miloš, et al. 1976. "Kriticky o možnostech hudební analýzy," *Lidová píseň a samočinný počítač III: Sborník materiálů ze 3. semináře o využití samočinného počítače při studiu lidové písně (Brno 15.-16.10.1974)*, ed. by Dušan Holý, Karel Pala, and Miloš Štědroň. Praha: Státni pedagogické nakladatelstvi. pp. 339-356.

Steedman, Mark J. 1977. "The Perception of Musical Rhythm and Metre," *Perception* VI: 555-569.

Steinbeck, Wolfram. 1976a. "The Use of the Computer in the Analysis of German Folksongs," *Computers and the Humanities* X/5 (September/October): 287-296.

_________. 1976b. "Die Liederbank Kiel," *Jahrbuch des Staatlichen Instituts for Musikforschung* 1976: 94-108.

_________. 1976c. Review of *Faktorenanalytische Typenbestimmung an Volksliedmelodien* by Reiner Kluge, *Jahrbuch für Volksliedforschung* 21: 217-218.

_________. 1978. "Zur Methodik der Analyse deutscher volkstümlicher Lieder mit Hilfe elektronischer Rechenanlagen," *Beiträge zur Musikgeschichte Nordeuropas. Kurt Gudewill zum 65. Geburtstag*, edited by Uwe Haensel. Wolfenbüttel: Möseler. pp. 323-341.

_________. 1979. "Die Liederbank Kiel," *Computers and the Humanities* XIII/3 (July-September): 263.

_________. 1980. "ANTOC. Ein neues Verfahren zur Aufzeichnung von Melodien durch den Computer," *Bericht über den Internationalen musikwissenschaftlichen Kongress Berlin 1974*, edited by Hellmut Kühn and Peter Nitsche. Kassel: Bärenreiter. pp. 546-553.

_________. 1982. *Struktur und Ähnlichkeit. Methoden automatisierter Melodienanalyse.* Kieler Schriften zur Musikwissenschaft 25. Kassel: Bärenreiter.

Stephan, Claudio. 1971. "Harmonic and Phraseologic Computer Aided Music Analysis," *Computers and the Humanities* VI/2 (November): 123.

_________. 1977. "Computer Aided Music Analysis," *Computers and the Humanities* XI/1 (January-February): 42.

Stockmann, Doris. 1969a. "Elektronische Datenverarbeitung in der Ethnologie und den ihr nahestehenden Wissenschaften," *Deutsches Jahrbuch für Volkskunde* XV: 134-158.

_________. 1969b. "Zur Arbeit der Study Group of Folk Music Systematization des IFMC," *Analyse und Klassifikation von Volksmelodien : Bericht über die 3. Arbeitstagung der Study Group of Folk Music Systematization beim International Folk Music Council vom 24. bis 28. Oktober 1967 in Radziejowice*, edited by Doris Stockmann and Jan Steszewski. Krakow : Polskie Wydawnictwo Muzyczne. pp. 9-30.

Stoffer, Thomas H. 1979. *Aspekte einer generativen Syntax zur Beschreibung musikalischer Strukturen für eine kognitive Musikpsychologie.* Berichte des Psychologischen Instituts der Ruhr-Universität Bochum, Arbeitseinheit Kognitionspsychologie, Nr. 11, 1979.

Strang, Gerald. 1966. "Computer Music: Analysis, Synthesis, and Composition," *Journal of the Acoustical Society of America* XXXIX: 1245.

Stroh, Wolfgang Martin. 1972. "Über Schwierigkeiten bei der mathematischen Darstellung musikalischer Sachverhalte," *Neue Zeitschrift für Musik* X: 567-572.

Suchoff, Benjamin. 1967a. "Computer Applications to Bartók's Serbo-Croatian Material," *Tempo* 80 (Spring): 15-19.

_________. 1967b. "Computer Applications to Béla Bartók's Serbo-Croatian Material," *Computers and the Humanities* II/2 (November): 88.

_________. 1968a. "Bartók, Ethnomusicology, and the Computer," *Institute for Computer Research in the Humanities Newsletter* IV/4 (December): 3-6.

_________. 1968b. "Computerized Folk Song Research and the Problem of Variants," *Computers and the Humanities* II/4 (March): 155-158.

_________. 1969a. "Some Problems in Computer-Oriented Bartokian Ethnomusicology," *Ethnomusicology* XIII/3 (September): 489-497.

_________. 1969b. "A Computerized Data Bank of Musical and Textual Information on Bartok's Six String Quartets," *Computers and the Humanities* III/5 (May): 311.

_________. 1970a. "Computer-Oriented Comparative Musicology," *The Computer and Music*, edited by Harry B. Lincoln. Ithaca: Cornell University Press. pp. 193-206.

_________. 1970b. "Aplicarea calculatorelor elektronice la etnomuzicologia Bartokiana," *Musica* XI (November): 10-14.

_________. 1970c. "A Bartoki nepzenekutatas es az elektronikus szamitogepeg," *Muzsika* XIII (July): 6-8; (August): 4-6.

_________. 1971. "The Computer and Bartók Research in America," *Journal of Research in Music Education* XIX/1 (Spring): 3-16.

_________. 1972a. "A National Science Computer Network: A Report on the First Working Seminar," *Computers and the Humanities* VII/2 (November): 96-97.

_________. 1972b. "Recent Developments in Computer-Assisted Musical Scholarship [Review of]," *Computing Review* 13/2 (February): 68-69.

_________. 1973a. "An Application of GRIPHOS to Bartók's Turkish Folk Music Materials," *Computational Musicology Newsletter* I/1: 18.

_________. 1973b. "Toward a Computer Typography for Music Research: A Progress Report (Review of)," *Computing Review* 14/5 (May): 224-225.

_________. 1973c. "The Computer and Bartók Research in America," *Magyar zenetörténeti Tanulmányok: Mosonyi Mihály és Bartók Béla émlékére* [Studies on the History of Hungarian Music in Memory of Mihály Mosonyi and Bela Bartók], edited by Ferenc Bonis. Budapest: Zenemükiadó. pp. 313-327.

_________. 1979. "The COMMPUTE Program," *Computers and the Humanities* XIII/3 (July-September): 262.

Suchoff, Benjamin, and Jack Heller. 1970. "Studies Relating to Automation of Bartók Archives," *Computers and the Humanities* V/2 (November): 110.

Suchoff, Benjamin, and Jack Heller. 1971. "Studies Relating to Automatization of Bartók Archives," *Computers and the Humanities* V/5 (May): 309-310.

Suchoff, Benjamin, and Jack Heller. 1977. "Computer Oriented Music Materials Permuted for User Transformation or Exchange (COMMPUTE)," *Computers and the Humanities* XI/1 (January-February): 42.

Suess, John G. 1967. "A Pilot Study on 'Rhythmic Levels'," *Computers and the Humanities* I/5 (May): 226.

Sundberg, Johan, and Björn Lindblom. 1975. "A Generative Theory of Swedish Nursery Tunes," *Actes du 1er congress international de semiotique musicale*, edited by Gino Stefani. Pesaro: Centro di iniziativa culturale. pp. 111-124.

Sundberg, Johan, and Björn Lindblom. 1976. "Generative Theories in Language and Music Descriptions," *Cognition* IV: 99-122. Reprinted in *Machine Models of Music*, edited by Stephen M. Schwanauer and David A. Levitt. Cambridge, MA: The MIT Press, 1993. pp. 262-286.

Sward, Rosalie La Grow. 1979. "The Computer Assists in Attempting to Solve a Problem of Twentieth Century Music," *Proceedings of the 1978 International Computer Music Conference*, vol. 2, edited by Curtis Roads. Evanston, IL: Northwestern University. 853-872.

Sychra, Antonín. 1964. "Hudba a Kybernetika," *Nové Cestu Hudby* I (1964): 234-267. [Summary in German: "Musik und Kybernetik," pp. 278-279.]

_________. 1965. "Möglichkeiten der Anwendung der Kybernetik und der Informationstheorie in der marxistischen Musikwissenschaft," *Beiträge zur Musikwissenschaft* VII/4: 402-407.

_________. 1970. "Die Anwendung der Kybernetik und der Informations-Theorie in der Marxistischen Ästhetik," *Beiträge zur Musikwissenschaft* XII/2: 83-108.

Tadeusiewicz, Ryszard, and Aleksander Sodo. 1979. "Kompozycje muzyczne z komputera," *Problemy* (Poland) XII (December): 25-30.

Tänzer, Peter. 1973. "Musik und Kybernetik," *Neue Zeitschrift für Musik* 134/8 (1973): 483-492.

Teitelbaum, Richard. 1965. "Intervallic Relations in Atonal Music," *Journal of Music Theory* IX/1 (Spring): 72-127.

Tenney, James C., and Larry Polansky. 1978. Hierarchical Gestalt Perception in Music: A 'Metric Space' Model. Mimeographed. Toronto: York University Music Department.

Tesař, Stanislav. 1976. "K možnostem využití SP v hymnologii," *Lidová píseň a samočinný počítač III: Sborník materiálů ze 3. semináře o využití samočinného počítače při studiu lidové písně (Brno 15.-16.10.1974)*, ed. by Dušan Holý, Karel Pala, and Miloš Štědroň. Praha: Státni pedagogické nakladatelstvi. pp. 253-261.

Tischler, Hans. 1970. "A Complete Edition of the *Magnus Liber Organi*," *Computers and the Humanities* V/2 (November): 111.

_________. 1973. "Parisian Two-Part Organa," *Computational Musicology Newsletter* I/1: 18.

Tokumaru, Yoshihiko. 1970. "Joho-riron to ongaku-kodo," *Arima daigoro sensei koki kinen ronbunshu [Daigoro Festschrift]*, edited by Kunitachi Ongaku Daigaku. Tokyo: Kunitachi Music College. pp. 195-212.

Toncrová, Marta. 1976. "Zur Frage der individuellen und normalisierten Fassung des Volksliedes vom Gesichtspunkt der Klassifikation," *Hudobná klasifikácia a samocinné pocitace: predbezná zpráva 6. Etnomuzikologického seminára = Musikklassifikation und elektronische Datenverarbeitung: Vorbericht des 6. Ethnomusikologischen Seminars, Kocovce, 6.-10. Október 1975*, edited by Oskár Elschek. Bratislava: Sekcia hudobnej vedy-etnomuzikológia, Umenovedný ústav, Slovenská akademia vied. 1 p.

Trowbridge, Lynn Mason. 1970. "The Burgundian Chanson: An Index and Analysis of Incipits," *Computers and the Humanities* IV/5 (May): 343-344.

_________. 1971. "An Analytical and Indexing System for Incipits of Renaissance Polyphonic Compositions," *Computers and the Humanities* V/5 (May): 310.

Ulrich, John Wade. 1977. "The Analysis and Synthesis of Jazz by Computer," *Proceedings of the 5th International Joint Conference on Artificial Intelligence 1977 (IJCAI-77)*, vol. 2. Pittsburgh, PA: Carnegie-Mellon University. pp. 865-872.

Urup, Henning. 1972. Danske Folkedanse. En beskrivelse og undersogelse af det danske folkelige melodistof med hertil horende dansebeskrivelser. M.A. thesis. Kobenhavn, Denmark: University of Kobenhavn.

Vercoe, Barry L. 1971. Reviews of *The computer and music*, edited Hary B. Lincoln; *Musicology and the computer*, edited Barry S. Brook. *Perspectives of New Music* IX/X (Spring/Summer-Autumn/Winter): 323-330.

_________. 1974. "Music computation conference: a report and summary," *Perspectives of New Music* XIII/1 (Fall): 234-238.

Victor, Michele. 1975. "L'Informatique musicale," *Musique En jeu* (France) XVIII (April): 45-62.

Vikis-Freibergs, Vaira, and Imants Freibergs. 1978. "Formulaic Analysis of the Computer-Accessible Corpus of Latvian Sun-Songs," *Computers and the Humanities* XII/4: 329-339.

Völz, Horst. 1975. "Beitrag zur formalen Musikanalyse und -synthese," *Beiträge zur Musikwissenschaft* XVII/2-3: 127-154.

Vos, Piet G. 1976. Identification of Metre in Music. Bericht Nr. 76 ON 06. Nijmegen, Netherlands: University of Nijmegen.

Wagner, Christoph, Ernst Piontek, and Ludwig Teckhaus. 1973. "Piano Learning and Programmed Instruction," *Journal of Research in Music Education* XXI/2 (Summer): 106-22.

Wagner, Günther. 1976. "Exaktwissenschaftliche Musikanalyse und Informationsästhetik." *International Review of Aesthetics and Sociology of Music* VII/1 (June): 63-76.

Waite, Stephen V. F., et al. 1973. "Annual Bibliography for 1972 and Supplement to Preceding Years," *Computers and the Humanities* VII/4 (March): 229-252.

Waite, Stephen V. F., et al. 1974. "Annual Bibliography for 1973 and Supplement to Preceding Years," *Computers and the Humanities* VIII/2 (March): 99-113.

Waite, Stephen V. F., et al. 1975. "Annual Bibliography for 1974 and Supplement to Preceding Years," *Computers and the Humanities* IX/3 (May): 127-144.

Waite, Stephen V. F., et al. 1976. "Annual Bibliography for 1975 and Supplement to Preceding Years," *Computers and the Humanities* X/2 (March-April): 101-121.

Waite, Stephen V. F., et al. 1977. "Annual Bibliography for 1976 and Supplement to Preceding Years," *Computers and the Humanities* XI/2 (March-April): 100-118.

Walker, Thomas. 1970. "The computer and music (Review of)," *Notes: Quarterly Journal of the Music Library Association* 27/2 (December): 178-183.

Warburton, Thomas. 1971. Review of *The Opening Sonata-Allegro Movements in a Randomly Selected Sample of Solo Keyboard Sonatas Published in the Years 1742-1774* by Roger Jaques Kamien, *Current Musicology* XI: 118-121.

Wenker, Jerome R. 1964. A Computational Method for the Analysis of Anglo-American Folksongs. M.A. thesis. Bloomington, IN: Indiana University.

_________. 1968. "A Music Compiler for Musicologists and Ethnomusicology," *Computers and the Humanities* II/5 (May): 244.

_________. 1969. "An Analytic Approach to Folk Music," *Computers and the Humanities* IV/2 (November): 138.

_________. 1970. "A Computer Oriented Music Notation Including Ethnomusicological Symbols," *Musicology and the Computer: Three Symposia*, edited by Barry S. Brook. New York: The City University of New York Press. pp. 91-129.

_________. 1972a. "A Music Compiler for Musicologists and Ethnomusicologists," *Computers and the Humanities* VII/2 (November): 124.

_________. 1972b. "An Analytic Approach to Folk Music," *Computers and the Humanities* VII/2 (November): 124-125.

_________. 1972c. "MUSTRAN II - An Extended *MUS*ic *TRAN*slator," *Computers and the Humanities* VII/2 (November): 125.

_________. 1973a. "Music Encoding - Keypunch," *Computational Musicology Newsletter* I/1: 6-7.

_________. 1973b. "Editorial Forword," *Computational Musicology Newsletter* I/1: 1-2.

_________. 1974. "MUSTRAN II: A Foundation for Computational Musicology," *Computers in the Humanities*, edited by J. L. Mitchell. Edinburgh: Edinburgh University Press. pp. 267-280.

_________. 1976. "On the Indexing of Melodies," *Hudobná klasifikácia a samocinné pocitace: predbezná zpráva 6. Etnomuzikologického seminára = Musikklassifikation und elektronische Datenverarbeitung: Vorbericht des 6. Ethnomusikologischen Seminars, Kocovce, 6.-10. Október 1975*, edited by Oskár Elschek. Bratislava: Sekcia hudobnej vedy-etnomuzikológia, Umenovedný ústav, Slovenská akademia vied. 1 p.

_________. 1978. A Computer-Aided Analysis of Anglo-Canadian Folktunes. Ph.D. dissertation. Bloomington, IN: Indiana University.

Whitney, Thomas G. 1977. "Music analysis: SLAM simplified or how the computer compares 16th century Bourgeois with eighteenth century Bach," *Creative Computing* III/2: 88-89.

Willis, Thomas Creighton. 1966. Music in Orchestra Hall: A Pilot Study in the Use of Computers and Other Data Processing Equipment for Research in the History of Music Performance. Ph.D. dissertation. Evanston, IL: Northwestern University.

Wilson, Dean C. 1967. An Analytical and Statistical Study of the Harmony in Carl Nielsen's Six Symphonies. Ph.D. dissertation. East Lansing, MI: Michigan State University.

Winckel, Fritz. 1964. "Die informationstheoretische Analyse musikalischer Strukturen," *Die Musikforschung* XVII/1: 1-14.

_________. 1967. "Neue Wege der mathematischen Analyse von Musikstrukturen," *Wiener Akademie Festschrift*. Wien: Lafite. pp. 78-88.

_________. 1975. "Das Wirkgefuge von Musikstrukturen in der Analyse durch Computer und Kybernetik," *Festschrift Kurt Blaukopf*, edited by Irmgard Bontinck and Otto Brusatti. Wien: Universal Edition. pp. 156-163.

Winograd, Terry. 1968. "Linguistics and the Computer Analysis of Tonal Harmony," *Journal of Music Theory* XII/1 (Spring): 2-49. Reprinted in *Machine Models of Music*, edited by Stephen M. Schwanauer and David A. Levitt. Cambridge, MA: The MIT Press, 1993. pp. 113-153.

Wittlich, Gary E. 1969. "Programming a Computer for Musical Analysis," *Your Musical Cue* V/6 (April): 3-13.

_________. 1971. "Music as Information," *Your Musical Cue* VII/3 (December-January): 3-9.

_________. 1973a. "Project Score," *Computational Musicology Newsletter* I/1: 6.

_________. 1973b. "Pattern Structure Studies," *Computational Musicology Newsletter* I/1: 19.

_________. 1973c. "Scale Index," *Computational Musicology Newsletter* I/1: 19.

Wittlich, Gary, Donald Byrd, and Rosalee Nerheim. 1978. "A System for Interactive Encoding of Music Scores Under Computer Control," *Computers and the Humanities* XII/4: 309-319.

Wolff, Anthony B. 1972. "Development of a DARMS-to-Canonical DARMS Translator," *Computers and the Humanities* VI/5 (May): 316.

_________. 1977. "Problems of Representation in Musical Computing," *Computers and the Humanities* XI/1 (January-February): 3-12.

Xenakis, Iannis. 1971. *Formalized Music. Thought and Mathematics in Composition*. Bloomington: Indiana University Press.

Youngblood, Joseph E. 1958. "Style as Information." *Journal of Music Theory* II/1 (April): 24-35.

_________. 1960. Music and Language: Some Related Analytical Techniques. Ph.D. disseration. Bloomington, IN: Indiana University.

_________. 1967. "Root Progression and Composer Identification," *Computers and the Humanities* II/2 (November): 87.

_________. 1970. "Root Progressions and Composer Identification," *The Computer and Music*, edited by Harry B. Lincoln. Ithaca: Cornell University Press. pp. 172-178.

Zaripov, Rudolf K. 1963. *Kibernetica i Muzyka*. Moscow: Znanie.

_________. 1969. "'Cybernetics and Music,' translated from the Russion by J. G. K. Russel, with commentary by Michael KASSLER," *Perspectives of New Music*, VII/2 (Spring-Summer): 115-154.

_________. 1971. *Kibernetica i Muzyka*. Moscow: Nauka.

Zimmerly, John David. 1978. A Computer-Assisted Study of Selected Kyries from the Parody Masses of Clemens non Papa. M.A. thesis. East Lansing, MI: Michigan State University.

Zimmerman, Franklin B. 1966. "Melodic Indexing for General and Specialized Use," *Notes* XXII: 1187-1192.

Zoch, Josef. 1972. "Vztah mezi vokaly a melodii v lidove pisni," *Lidová písen a samostatný pocítac I*, edited by Dušan Holý and Oldrich Sirovátka. Brno: Klub uživatelů MSP. pp. 215-219.

Zwink, Eberhard. 1974. *Paul Hindemiths "Unterweisung im Tonsatz" als Konsequenz der Entwicklung seiner Kompositionstechnik. Graphische und Statistische Musikanalyse.* Göppingen: Alfred Kümmerle.

Chronological Bibliography (By Year)

No Date

Berlind, Gary. [n.d.]. Writings on the Use of Computers in Music. Compiled by Gary Berlind in collaboration with Barry S. Brook, Lejaren A. Hiller Jr., Jan P. LaRue, and George W. Logemann. New York: New York University, Institute for Computer Research in the Humanities. Mimeographed.

Robison, Tobias D. [n.d.]. A Short Description of the MIR Compiler. Princeton: Princeton University Music Department.

1931

Birkhoff, George David. 1931. "A Mathematical Approach to Aesthetics," *Scientia* (September): 133-146.

1937

Ortmann, Otto. 1937. "Interval Frequency as a Determinant of Melodic Style," *Beabody Bulletin* (December): 3-10.

1945

Norman, Philip B. 1945. *A Quantitative Study of Harmonic Similarities in Certain Specified Works of Bach, Beethoven and Wagner*. New York, NY: Carl Fischer.

1948

Schillinger, Joseph. 1948. *The Mathematical Basis of the Arts*. New York: Philosophical Library.

1949

Bronson, Bertrand H. 1949. "Mechanical Help in the Study of Folk Song." *Journal of American Folklore* LII/244 (April-June): 81-86.

Shannon, Claude E., and W. Weaver. 1949. *The Mathematical Theory of Communication*. Urbana: University of Illinois Press.

1950

Birkhoff, George David. 1950. *Collected Mathematical Papers*, vol. 3. New York: American Mathematical Society.

McHose, Allen I. 1950. "Musical Research in the Definition of Bach's Contrapuntal Harmonic Style," *Proceedings of the Music Teachers National Association* 42: 126-150.

1953

Goldman, Stanford. 1953. *Information Theory*. New York: Dover.

1954

Bense, Max. 1954. *Aesthetica*. Stuttgart: Deutsche Verlags-Anstalt.

1955

Babbitt, Milton. 1955. "Some Aspects of Twelve-Tone Composition," *The Score and I.M.A. Magazine* 12: 53-61.

Fucks, Wilhelm. 1955. *Mathematische Analyse von Sprachelementen, Sprachstil und Sprache*. Köln: Westdeutscher Verlag.

1956

Freeman, Linton C., and Alan P. Merriam. 1956. "Statistical Classification in Anthropology: An Application to Ethnomusicology," *American Anthropologist* 58/3 (June): 464-472.

Fucks, Wilhelm. 1956. "Mathematical Theory of Word Formation." *Information Theory: Papers Read at a Symposium on Information Theory Held at the Royal Institution, London, September 12th to 16th, 1955*, edited by Colin Cherry. London: Butterworths Scientific Publications. pp. 154-170.

Moles, Abraham A. 1956a. "Informationstheorie der Musik." *Nachrichtentechnische Fachberichte* 3: 47-55.

__________. 1956b. "Informationstheorie und ästhetische Empfindung." *Gravesaner Blätter* VI (December): 3-9.

Pinkerton, Richard C. 1956. "Information Theory and Melody." *Scientific America* 194/2 (February): 77-86.

Quastler, H. 1956. Discussion, following Mathematical Theory of Word Formation, by W. Fucks, *Information Theory: Papers Read at a Symposium on Information Theory Held at the Royal Institution, London, September 12th to 16th, 1955*, edited by Colin Cherry. London: Butterworths Scientific Publications. pp. 168-169.

Springer, G. P. 1956. "Language and Music: Parallels and Divergencies," *For Roman Jakobson*, edited by M. Halle, H. G. Lunt, H. McLean, and C. H. Van Schooneveld. Den Haag: Mouton. pp. 504-513.

1957

Brooks, Frederick P., A. L. Hopkins, P. G. Neumann, and W. V. Wright. 1957. "An Experiment in Musical Composition." *IRE Transactions on Electronic Computers* VI (September): 175-182. (An errata see in vol. 7 (1958): 60.) Reprinted in *Machine Models of Music*, edited by Stephen M. Schwanauer and David A. Levitt. Cambridge, MA: The MIT Press, 1993. pp. 23-40.

Fucks, Wilhelm. 1957. "Gibt es mathematische Gesetze in Sprache und Musik?" *Umschau in Wissenschaft und Technik* 1957/2: 33-37.

Mandelbrot, B. 1957. "[Review of] W. Fucks, Mathematische Analyse von Sprachelementen, Sprachstil und Sprache," *Word: Journal of the Linguistic Circle of New York* 13: 159-160.

Meyer, Leonard B. 1957. "Meaning in Music and Information Theory." *Journal of Aesthetics & Art Criticism* XV/4 (June): 412-424.

1958

Coons, Edgar, and David Kraehenbuehl. 1958. "Information as a Measure of Structure in Music," *Journal of Music Theory* II/2 (November): 127-161.

Fucks, Wilhelm. 1958. *Mathematische Analyse der Formalstruktur von Musik*. Köln: Westdeutscher Verlag.

Moles, Abraham A. 1958. *Théorie de l'information et perception esthétique*. Paris: Flammarion & Cie. American edition: *Information Theory and Esthetic Perception*, translated by Joel E. Cohen. Urbana: University of Illinois Press, 1966.

Nathan, Hans. 1958. "The Twelve-Tone Compositions of Luigi Dallapiccola," The *Musical Quarterly* 44 (July): 289-310.
Nettl, Bruno. 1958. "Some Linguistic Approaches to Musical Analysis," *Journal of the International Folk Music Council* X: 37-41.
Youngblood, Joseph E. 1958. "Style as Information." *Journal of Music Theory* II/1 (April): 24-35.

1959
Brawley, John Gray. 1959. An Application of Information Theory to Musical Rhythm. M.M. thesis. Bloomington, IN: Indiana University.
Bronson, Bertrand H. 1959. "Toward the Comparative Analysis of British-American Folk Tunes." *Journal of American Folklore* LXXII: 165-191.
Hiller, Lejaren A., and Leonard M. Isaacson. 1959. *Experimental Music. Composition with an Electronic Computer*. New York: McGraw-Hill.
Kraehenbuehl, David, and Edgar Coons. 1959. "Information as a Measure of the Experience of Music," *Journal of Aesthetics & Art Criticism* XVII/4 (June): 510-522.
Neumann, P. G., and H. Schappert. 1959. "Komponieren mit elektronischen Rechenautomaten," *Nachrichtentechnische Zeitschrift* VIII: 403-407.

1960
Babbitt, Milton. 1960. "Twelve-Tone Invariants as Compositional Determinatns," *The Music Quaterly* 46: 246-259.
Pikler, Andrew G. 1960. "Automatische Bewertung von Musikaufführungen," *Gravesaner Blätter* V: 137-139.
Youngblood, Joseph E. 1960. Music and Language: Some Related Analytical Techniques. Ph.D. disseration. Bloomington, IN: Indiana University.

1961
Babbitt, Milton. 1961. "Set-Structure as a Compositional Determinant," *Journal of Music Theory* V/1 (Spring): 72-94.
Bean, Calvert. 1961. Information Theory Applied to the Analysis of a Particular Formal Process in Tonal Music. Ph.D. dissertation. Champaign, IL: University of Illinois.
Cohen, Joel E. 1961. "Some Relationships Between Music and Mathematics," *Music Education Journal* 48/1 (September): 104-109.
Heike, Georg. 1961. "Informationstheorie und musikalische Komposition," *Melos* XXVIII/9: 269-272.

1962
Bukharov, R. G., and M. S. Rytvinsskaya. 1962. "Simulating a Probabalistic Process Connected with a Melody," *Kazan Universitet Uchenyia Zapiski* 122: 82.
Cohen, Joel E. 1962. "Information Theory and Music," *Behavioral Science* VII/2 (April): 137-163.
Fucks, Wilhelm. 1962. "Mathematische Musikanalyse und Randomfolgen. Zufall und Musik." *Gravesaner Blätter* VI: 132-145.
Guntzenhäuser, Rul. 1962. *Ästhetisches Maß und ästhetische Information. Einführung in die Theorie G. D. Birkhoffs und die Redundanztheorie ästhetischer Prozesse*. Quickborn bei Hamburg: Schnelle.
Hartmann, Karl L. 1962. Versuch einer mathematischen Musiklehre. Wien: Karl L. Hartmann.

Hiller, Lejaren A., Jr. 1962. Information Theory and Musical Analysis. Mimeographed. Urbana: University of Illinois, Experimental Music Studio. Technical Report No. 5, July 1962. 40 p. (University of Cincinnati Library, MUS ML 3817 .I4 no. 5)

Lomax, Alan. 1962. "Song Structure and Social Structure." *Ethnology* I/4 (October): 425-451.

Moles, Abraham A. 1962. "Das neue Verhältnis zwischen Musik und Mathematik," *Gravesaner Blätter* VI: 98-103.

Schot, Joanna Wood. 1962. "Review of *Experimental Music Composition with an Electronic Computer*, by Lejaren Hiller, Jr., and Leonard M. Isaacson," *Mathematics of Computation* 16/80 (October): 507-508.

1963

Baker, Robert Allen. 1963. A Statistical Analysis of the Harmonic Practice of the 18th and Early 19th Centuries. Ph.D. thesis. Champaign, IL: University of Illinois.

Fucks, Wilhelm. 1963. *Mathematische Analyse von Formalstrukturen von Werken der Musik.* Köln: Westdeutscher Verlag.

Zaripov, Rudolf K. 1963. *Kibernetica i Muzyka.* Moscow: Znanie.

1964

Berger, Arthur. 1964. "New Linguistic Modes and the New Theory," *Perspectives of New Music* III/1 (Autumn-Winter): 1-9.

Bernstein, Lawrence F. 1964. "Data Processing and the Thematic Index," *Fontes Artis Musicae* XI/1 (January-April): 159-165.

Braun, P. 1964. "On a Human Movement Analyzer," *Computational Linguistics* 3: 189-204.

Brook, Barry S., and Murray Gould. 1964. "Notating Music with Ordinary Typewriter Characters," *Fontes Artis Musicae* XI/1 (January-April): 142-159.

Cohen, Joel E. 1964. "Teorie informací a hudba," *Nové Cesty Hudby: Sborník studií o novodobých skladebných smerech a vedeckých názorech na hudbu*, edited by Eduard Herzog. Praha: Státní hudební vydavatelství. pp. 180-215.

Draeger, Hans Heinz. 1964. "Analysis and Synthesis of Musical Structures on the Basis of Information Theory," *Bericht über den neunten internationalen Kongress Salzburg 1964*, edited by Franz Giegling, vol. 1. Kassel: Bärenreiter. pp. 261-268.

Ferentzy, Eors N., and Miklós Havass. 1964. "Human Movement Analysis by Computer: Electronic Choreography and Composition," *Computational Linguistics* 3: 129-188.

Filip, Miroslav. 1964. "Zákonitosti vyvoja harmónie vo svetle základnych myslienok teórie informácie," *Nové Cesty Hudby* (1964): 216-233. [Summary in German: "Entwicklungsgesetzed er Harmonie im Lichte der Grundgedankend er Informationstheorie," pp. 276-277.]

Forte, Allen. 1964. "A Theory of Set-Complexes for Music," *Journal of Music Theory* VIII/2 (Winter): 136-183.

Frank, Helmar. 1964. *Kybernetische Analysen subjektiver Sachverhalte*. Quickborn bei Hamburg: Schnelle.

Fucks, Wilhelm. 1964. "Gibt es mathematische Gesetze in Sprache und Musik?" *Kybernetik*, edited by Helmar Frank, 4th ed. Frankfurt am Main: Umschau Verlag. pp. 175-187.

Havass, Miklós. 1964. "A Simulation of Music Composition. Synthetically Composed Folkmusic," *Computational Linguistics* 3: 107-128.

Heckmann, Harald. 1964. "Neue Methoden der Verarbeitung musikalischer Daten," *Die Musikforschung* XVII/4: 381-383.

Hiller, Lejaren A., Jr. 1964. *Informationstheorie und Computermusik: Zwei Vorträge, gehalten auf den "Internationalen Ferienkursen für Neue Musik" Darmstadt 1963.* Darmstädter Beiträge zur Neuen Musik 8. Mainz: B. Schott's Söhne.
Kamien, Roger Jaques. 1964. The Opening Sonata-Allegro Movements in a Randomly Selected Sample of Solo Keyboard Sonatas Published in the Years 1742-1774. Ph.D. dissertation. Princeton, NJ: Princeton University.
Kassler, Michael. 1964a. A Report of Work, Directed Toward Explication of Schenker's Theory of Tonality, Done in Summer 1962 as the First Phase of a Project Concerned with the Applications of High-Speed Automatic Digital Computers to Music ana Musicology. Princeton, NJ: Princeton University Music Department. (Mimeographed.)
__________. 1964b. MIR – A Simple Programming Language For Musical Information Retrieval. Technical Report No. 3, Project 295D, March 1964. Princeton, New Jersey: Princeton University, Department of Music. [University of California at Berkeley: Music Library, calling no. ML 74 .4 M4 K 35 1964 MUSI]
Moles, Abraham A. 1964. "Uvedení do soucasného stavu hudby," *Nové Cesty Hudby*: 36-53.
Paisley, William J. 1964. "Identifying the Unknown Communicator in Painting, Literature and Music: the Significance of Minor Encoding Habits," *Journal of Communication* XIV/4 (December): 219-237.
Randall, J. K. 1964. "A Report from Princeton," *Perspectives of New Music* III (Spring): 84-92.
Roller, Gilbert H. 1964. The Development of the Methods for Analysis of Musical Composition and for the Formation of a Symmetrical Twelve-tone Row Using the Electronic Digital Computer. Ph.D. dissertation. East Lansing, MI: Michigan State University.
Stahl, V. 1964. Informationswissenschaft und Musikanalyse," *Grundlagenstudien aus Kybernetik und Geisteswissenschaft* 5: 51-58.
Sychra, Antonín. 1964. "Hudba a Kybernetika," *Nové Cestu Hudby* I (1964): 234-267. [Summary in German: "Musik und Kybernetik," pp. 278-279.]
Wenker, Jerome R. 1964. A Computational Method for the Analysis of Anglo-American Folksongs. M.A. thesis. Bloomington, IN: Indiana University.
Winckel, Fritz. 1964. "Die informationstheoretische Analyse musikalischer Strukturen," *Die Musikforschung* XVII/1: 1-14.

1965

Bauer-Mengelberg, Stefan, and Melvin Ferentz. 1965. "On Eleven-Interval Twelve-Tone Rows," *Perspectives of New Music* III/2 (Spring-Summer): 93-103.
Bowles, Edmund. 1965. "Computers and Musicology," *Computers for the Humanities: A Record of the Conference Sponsored by Yale University on a Grant from IBM, January 22-23, 1965.* New Haven, CT: Yale University Press. pp. 103-108.
Brook, Barry S. 1965a. "The Simplified 'Plaine and Easy Code System," *Fontes Artis Musicae* XII: 156-160.
__________. 1965b. "Utilization of Data Processing Techniques in Music Documentation," *Fontes Artis Musicae* XII (May): 112-122.
Collins, Walter S. 1965. "A New Tool for Musicology," *Music & Letters* XLVI/2 (April): 122-125.
Csébfalvy, Károly, and Miklós Havass. 1965. "A Direct Computer Processing of Folk Tunes," *Computational Linguistics* 4: 125-129.
Csébfalvy, Károly, Miklós Havass, Pál Járdányi, and Lajos Vargyas. 1965. "Systematization of Tunes by Computers," *Studia Musicologica Academiae Scientiarum Hungaricae* VII/1-4: 253-257.

Elscheková, Alica. 1965. "General Considerations on the Classification of Folk Tunes," *Studia Musicologica Academiae Scientiarum Hungaricae* VII/1-4: 259-262.
Ferentzy, Eors N. 1965. "On Formal Music Analysis-Synthesis: Its Application in Music Education," *Computational Linguistics* 4: 107.
Forte, Allen. 1965. "The Domain and Relations of Set-Complex Theory," *Journal of Music Theory* IX/1 (Spring): 173-180.
Fucks, Wilhelm, and Josef Lauter. 1965. *Exaktwissenschaftliche Musikanalyse*. Köln: Westdeutscher Verlag.
Fuller, Ramon Conrad. 1965. An Information Theory Analysis of Anton Webern's 'Symphonie,' opus 21 (with) 'Music for Two Channel Tape and Two Percussionists'. D.M.A. thesis. University of Illinois at Urbana Champaign.
Gabura, A. James. 1965. "Computer Analysis of Musical Style," *Proceedings of the 20th National Conference: Cleveland, Ohio, August 24-26, 1965*. New York: Association for Computing Machinery. pp. 303-314.
Grauer, Viktor A . 1965. "Some Song-Style Clusters – A Preliminary Study," *Ethnomusicology* IX/3 (September): 265-271.
Hiller, Lejaren A., and James W. Beauchamp. 1965. "Research in Music with Electronics," *Science* CL: 161-169.
Hoshovskyj, Vladimir. 1965. "The Experiment of Systemizing and Cataloguing Folk Tunes following the Principles of Musical Dialectology and Cybernetics," *Studia Musicologica Academiae Scientiarum Hungaricae* VII/1-4: 273-286.
Howe, Hubert S. 1965. "Some Combinatorial Properties of Pitch Structures," *Perspectives of New Music* IV/1 (Fall-Winter): 45-61.
Hughes, Matt. 1965. Tonal Orientation in Skiabin's Preludes: An Analysis on the Basis of Information Theory. M.A. thesis. University of Texas at Austin.
Knopoff, Leon. 1965. " Some Technological Advances in Musical Analysis," *Studia Musicologica Academiae Scientiarum Hungaricae* VII/1-4: 301-307.
Kolinski, Mieczyslaw. 1965a. "The General Dierction of Melodic Movement," *Ethnomusicology* IX/3 (September): 240-264.
__________. 1965b. "The Structure of Melodic Movement - A New Method of Analysis (revised version)," *Studies in Ethnomusicology* 2: 96-120.
Meylan, Raymond. 1965. "Utilization des Calculatrices Electroniques pour la comparaison Interne du Repertoire des Basses Danses de Quinzi," *Fontes Artis Musicae* 12 (May): 128-134.
Rhodes, Willard. 1965. "The Use of Computer in the Classification of Folk Tunes," *Studia Musicologica Academiae Scientiarum Hungaricae* VII: 339-343.
Roller, Gilbert H. 1965. "Development of a Method for Analysis of Musical Compositions Using an Electronic Digital Computer," *Journal of Research in Music Education* XIII/4 (Winter): 249-252.
Schiødt, Nanna. 1965. "Data Processing Applied to Byzantine Chant," *Fontes Artis Musicae* XII/2-3: 122-123.
Sellek, John, and Roger Bakeman. 1965. "Procedures for the Analysis of Form: Two Computer Applications," *Journal of Music Theory* IX/2 (Winter): 281-293.
Sychra, Antonín. 1965. "Möglichkeiten der Anwendung der Kybernetik und der Informationstheorie in der marxistischen Musikwissenschaft," *Beiträge zur Musikwissenschaft* VII/4: 402-407.
Teitelbaum, Richard. 1965. "Intervallic Relations in Atonal Music," *Journal of Music Theory* IX/1 (Spring): 72-127.

Babbitt, Milton. 1965. "The Use of Computers in Musicological Research," *Perspectives of New Music* III/2 (Spring-Summer): 74-83.

1966

Anonymous. 1966. "Computer Programs Designed to Solve Humanistic Problems," *Computers and the Humanities* I/2 (November): 39-55.
Bense, Max. 1966a. "Ästhetik und Programmierung." *IBM-Nachrichten* 16: 294-296.
__________. 1966b. "Projekter til en generativ aestetik," *Dansk Musiktidsskrift* XLI: 179-82.
Berlind, Gary. 1966. "Writings on the Use of Computers in Music," *College Music Symposium* 6 (1966): 143-152.
Brincker, Jens. 1966a. "Kvantitativ musikanalyse," *Dansk Musiktidsskrift* XLI: 175-178.
__________. 1966b. Review of *Informationstheorie und Computermusik* by Lejaren A. Hiller, *Dansk Musiktidsskrift* XLI: 186.
Citron, Jack. 1966. "MUSPEC," *Computers and the Humanities* I/2 (November): 52.
Elscheková, Alica. 1966. "Methods of Classification of Folk Tunes," *Journal of International Folk Music Council* XVIII: 56-76.
Ferentzy, Eors N. 1966. Progress Report on the Project Analysis of Musical Styles by an Electronic Computer, Sponsored by Washington State University. Unpublished Report. Pullman, WA: Washington State University Pullman.
Forte, Allen. 1966. "A Program for the Analytic Reading of Scores," *Journal of Music Theory* X/2 (Winter): 330-364. Reprinted in *Machine Models of Music*, edited by Stephen M. Schwanauer and David A. Levitt. Cambridge, MA: The MIT Press, 1993. pp. 55-81.
Gould, Murray, and George W. Logemann. 1966. ALMA: An Alphanumeric Language for Music Analysis. New York University: Institute for Computer Research in the Humanities. [Los Angeles: University of California Library / Music Library, calling no. ML 432 G 734a]
Hiller, Lejaren A., and Calvert Bean. 1966. "Information Theory Analyses of Four Sonata Expositions," *Journal of Music Theory* X/1 (Spring): 96-137.
Howe, Hubert S. 1966. "Music and Electronics: A Report," *Perspectives of New Music* IV: 68-75.
Jackson, Roland. 1966. "Harmonic Analysis," *Computers and the Humanities* I/2 (November): 52.
Jackson, Roland, and Philip Bernzott. 1966. "Harmonic Analysis with Computer – A Progress Report," *ICRH Newsletter* I/9 (May): 3-4.
Kassler, Michael. 1966. "Toward Musical Information Retrieval," *Perspectives of New Music* IV/2 (Spring-Summer): 59-67.
Knopoff, Leon. 1966. "A Progress Report on an Experiment in Musical Synthesis," *Selected Reports* I/1: 49-60 [Los Angeles: University of California, Institute of Ethnomusicology].
Kupper, Hubert. 1966. "Computer and Musikwissenschaft," *IBM Nachrichten* XVI/180 (December): 297-303.
LaRue, Jan. 1966. "The Computer Seminar at Binghamton: A Report," *Notes* XXIII: 236-240.
LaRue, Jan, and George W. Logemann. 1966. "EDP for Thematic Catalogues," *Notes* XXII: 1179-1186.
Lincoln, Harry B. 1966. "Incipit Interval Sequence Program," *Computers and the Humanities* I/2 (November): 52.
Lockwood, Lewis. 1966. "MIR ('Musical Information Retrieval')," *Computers and the Humanities* I/2 (November): 51.

Logemann, George W. 1966a. “Prepare Music Input Data,” *Computers and the Humanities* I/2 (November): 51.
__________. 1966b. “Harmonic and Time-line Input and Statistics,” *Computers and the Humanities* I/2 (November): 51-52.
Meylan, Raymond. 1966. “Recherche de Parents parmi les Basses Danses du Quinzi,” *Acta Musicologica* 38 (January): 46-66.
Moles, Abraham A. 1966. *Information Theory and Esthetic Perception*, translated by Joel E. Cohen. Urbana: University of Illinois Press.
Pruett, James W. 1966. “The Harpur College Music-Computer Seminar: A Report,” *Computers and the Humanities* I/2 (November): 34-38.
Pruslin, Dennis Howard. 1966. Automatic Recognition of Sheet Music. Sc.D. dissertation. Boston, MA: Massachusetts Institute of Technology.
Rothgeb, John. 1966. “Some Uses of Mathematical Concepts in Theories of Music,” *Journal of Music Theory* X/2 (Winter): 200-215.
Strang, Gerald. 1966. “Computer Music: Analysis, Synthesis, and Composition,” *Journal of the Acoustical Society of America* XXXIX: 1245.
Willis, Thomas Creighton. 1966. Music in Orchestra Hall: A Pilot Study in the Use of Computers and Other Data Processing Equipment for Research in the History of Music Performance. Ph.D. dissertation. Evanston, IL: Northwestern University.
Zimmerman, Franklin B. 1966. “Melodic Indexing for General and Specialized Use,” *Notes* XXII: 1187-1192.

1967

Abraham, Gerald. 1967. “Musical Scholarship in the 20th Century,” *Studies in Music* I: 1-10.
Anonymous. 1967a. “Directory of Scholars Active,” *Computers and the Humanities* I/5 (May): 178-241.
Anonymous. 1967b. “Directory of Scholars Active,” *Computers and the Humanities* II/2 (November): 71-93.
Ashford, Theodore H. A. 1967. “Analysis of Musical Relationships in Contemporary Music,” *Computers and the Humanities* I/5 (May): 224.
Beauchamp, James W. 1967. A Computer System for Time-Variant Harmonic Analysis and Synthesis of Musical Tones. Technical Report No. 15, Electrical Engineering Publication No. 992. Urbana, IL: University of Illinois School of Music Experimental Music Studio.
Bengtsson, Ingmar. 1967a. “On Melody Registration and ‘Mona’,” *Elektronische Datenverarbeitung in der Musikwissenschaft*, edited by Harald Heckmann. Regensburg: Gustav Bosse. pp. 136-174.
__________. 1967b. “Numericode – A Code System for Thematic Incipits,” *Svensk Tidskrift för Musikforskning* 49: 5-40.
Berlind, Gary. 1967. “GRIPHOS: An Interim Report,” *Current Musicology* V: 149-152.
Berlind, Gary, Barry S. Brook, Charles M. Dollar, Dee F. Green, Kenneth Janda, Richard Jensen, Louis T. Milic, and Robert Zemsky. 1967. “Annual Bibliography for 1966,” *Computers and the Humanities* I/4 (March): 143-156.
Bernstein, Lawrence F. 1967. “University of Chicago Chanson Project,” *Computers and the Humanities* I/5 (May): 221.
Binkley, Thomas E. 1967. “Electronic Processing of Musical Materials,” *Elektronische Datenverarbeitung in der Musikwissenschaft*, edited by Harald Heckmann. Regensburg: Gustav Bosse. pp. 1-20.

Brender, Maurita P., and Ronald F. Brender. 1967. "Computer Transcription and Analysis of Mid-Thirteenth Century Musical Notation," *Journal of Music Theory* XI/2 (Winter): 198-221.
Brook, Barry S. 1967. "Music Bibliography and the Computer," *Papers from the West Virginia University Conference on Computer Applications in Music*, edited by Gerald Lefkoff. Morgantown: West Virginia University Library. pp. 9-27.
Cobin, Marian W. 1967. "Musicology and the Computer in New Orleans," *Computers and the Humanities* I/4 (March): 131-133.
Draeger, Hans Heinz. 1967. "A Quantitative Analysis of Music as Exemplified by Beethoven's Sketches for his Opus 131," *Festschrift für Walter Wiora zum 30. Dezember 1966*, edited by Ludwig Finscher and Christoph-Hellmut Mahling. Hamburg: Bärenreiter. pp. 79-85.
Egeland Hansen, Finn. 1967a. "Det gregorianske repertoire i Codex H 159 Montpellier," *Dansk Arbog for Musikforskning* V (1966-67): 181-182.
_________. 1967b. "Investigation of Tonal Properties of the Gregorian Repertory," *Computers and the Humanities* I/5 (May): 226.
Fennelly, Brian. 1967. "A Descriptive Language for the Analysis of Electronic Music," *Perspectives of New Music* VI/1 (Autumn-Winter): 79-95.
Ferentzy, Eors N. 1967. "A Syntax-Directed Compiler to Analyze Musical Compositions and Text," *Computers and the Humanities* I/5 (May): 225.
Fiore, Mary E. 1967. "Harmonic Structure in Variation Movements by Anton von Webern," *Computers and the Humanities* I/5 (May): 225.
Forte, Allen. 1967a. "Computer-Implemented Analysis of Musical Structure," *Papers from the West Virginia University Conference on Computer Applications in Music*, edited by Gerald Lefkoff. Morgantown: West Virginia University Library. pp. 29-42.
_________. 1967b. "Music and Computing: The Present Situation," *Computers and the Humanities* II/1 (September): 32-35.
_________. 1967c. "Structure of Atonal Music," *Computers and the Humanities* II/2 (November): 86.
_________. 1967d. *Analytic Reading of Musical Scores*. Cambridge: Massachusetts Institute of Technology, April 1967.
_________. 1967e. "The Programming Language SNOBOL3: An Introduction," *Computers and the Humanities* I/5 (May): 157-163.
_________. 1967f. "Structure of Atonal Music," *Computers and the Humanities* I/5 (May): 224-225.
Freedman, M. David. 1967. "Analysis of Musical Instrument Tones," *Journal of the Acoustical Society of America* XLI (April): 793-806.
Gabura, A. James. 1967. Music Style Analysis by Computer. M.Sc. thesis, University of Toronto.
Gould, Murray. 1967. "A Keypunchable Notation for the Liber Usualis," *Elektronische Datenverarbeitung in der Musikwissenschaft*, edited by Harald Heckmann. Regensburg: Gustav Bosse. pp. 25-40.
Heckmann, Harald. Ed. 1967a. *Elektronische Datenverarbeitung in der Musikwissenschaft*. Regensburg: Gustav Bosse.
_________. 1967b. "Elektronische Datenverarbeitung in der Musikwissenschaft: Eine Einleitung," *Elektronische Datenverarbeitung in der Musikwissenschaft*, edited by Harald Heckmann. Regensburg: Gustav Bosse. pp. VII-XVII.

Heckmann, Harald. 1970. "Elektronische Datenverarbeitung in der Musikwissenschaft," *IMS: Report on the Tenth Congress, Lubljana 1967*, edited by Dragotin Cvetko. Kassel: Bärenreiter. pp. 424-427.

Hiller, Lejaren A., Jr. 1967. Analysis and Synthesis of Musical Sounds by Analog and Digital Techniques. An Interim Progress Report to The National Science Foundation (Contract US-NSF-GK-594).

Hiller, Lejaren A., and Ramon Fuller. 1967. "Structure and Information in Webern's Symphonie, Op. 21," *Journal of Music Theory* XI/1 (Spring): 60-115.

Hood, Mantle. 1967. "Improvisation and Music Theory of the Javanese Gamelan," *Computers and the Humanities* II/2 (September): 88.

Kirschenbaum, Howard. 1967. "Music Analysis by Computer," *Music Educators Journal* 53 (February): 94-97.

Kluge, Reiner. 1967. "Faktorenanalytische Typenbestimmung an einstimmigen Volksmelodien," *Computers and the Humanities* II/2 (November): 88-89.

LaRue, Jan. 1967. "Two Problems in Music Analysis: The Computer Lends a Hand," *Computers in Humanistic Research*, edited by Edmund A. Bowles. Englewood Cliffs: Prentice Hall. pp. 194-203.

LaRue, Jan, and Marian W. Cobin. 1967. "The Ruge-Seignelay Catalogue: An Exercise in Automated Entries," *Elektronische Datenverarbeitung in der Musikwissenschaft*, edited by Harald Heckmann. Regensburg: Gustav Bosse. pp. 41-56.

Lauter, Josef, and Roland Mix. 1967. "The Information Content of Music," *Nachrichtentechnische Zeitschrift* XX/2: 86-89.

Lefkoff, Gerald. Ed. 1967a. *Papers from the West Virginia University Conference on Computer Applications in Music*. Morgantown: West Virginia University Library.

_________. 1967b. "Computers and the Study of Musical Style," *Papers from the West Virginia University Conference on Computer Applications in Music*, edited by Gerald Lefkoff. Morgantown: West Virginia University Library. pp. 43-61.

Lincoln, Harry B. 1967a. "Musicology and the Computer: The Thematic Index," *Computers in Humanistic Research*, edited by Edmund A. Bowles. Englewood Cliffs: Prentice-Hall. pp. 184-193.

_________. 1967b. "Some Criteria and Techniques for Developing Computerized Thematic Indices," *Elektronische Datenverarbeitung in der Musikwissenschaft*, edited by Harald Heckmann. Regensburg: Gustav Bosse. pp. 57-62.

_________. 1967c. "Thematic Index of Sixteenth-Century Italian Music," *Computers and the Humanities* II/2 (November): 86.

Logemann, George W. 1967a. "The Canons in the Musical Offering of J. S. Bach: An Example of Computational Musicology," *Elektronische Datenverarbeitung in der Musikwissenschaft*, edited by Harald Heckmann. Regensburg: Gustav Bosse. pp. 63-87.

_________. 1967b. "MUSE: A Syntax-Directed System for Music Analysis," *Computers and the Humanities* I/5 (May): 224.

Lombardi, Carlo. 1967. "Investigation of Style of Keyboard Composition of Ruttini and Haydn," *Computers and the Humanities* I/5 (May): 226-227.

Mala, Hana. 1967. "Statistická srovnávací analyza sboru Leose Janácka a moravskych lidovych písní," *Hudebni Veda* IV/4: 602-627.

Mendel, Arthur, and Lewis Lockwood. 1967. "Music Information Retrieval," *Computers and the Humanities* I/5 (May): 226.

Meylan, Raymond. 1967. "Symbolisierung einer Melodie auf Lochkarten," *Elektronische Datenverarbeitung in der Musikwissenschaft*, edited by Harald Heckmann. Regensburg: Gustav Bosse. pp. 21-24.

Mix, Roland. 1967. "Die Entropieabnahme bei Abhängigkeit zwischen mehreren simultanen Informationsquellen und bei Übergang zu Markoff-Ketten höherer Ordnung, untersucht an musikalischen Beispielen," *Theorien zur Formalanalyse mehrstimmiger Musik*, by Walter Reckziegel. Köln: Westdeutscher Verlag. pp. 39-80.

Morton, Ian A. 1967. "FORTRAN Music Programs Involving Numerically Related Tones," *Computers and the Humanities* II/2 (November): 87-88.

Pulkert, Oldrich. 1967. "Hudba, samocinne pocitace a jine novinky" ["Music, Computers, and Other Novelties"], *Hudebni veda* 3: 479-484.

Randall, J. K. 1967. "Three Lectures to Scientists," *Perspectives of New Music* V/2 (Spring-Summer): 124-140.

Raskin, Jeffrey F. 1967. A Hardware Independent Computer Drawing System Using List Structured Modeling: The Quick-Draw Graphics Systems. M.S. thesis. State College, PA: Pennsylvania State University.

Reckziegel, Walter. 1967a. *Theorien zur Formalanalyse mehrstimmiger Musik*. Köln: Westdeutscher Verlag.

_________. 1967b. "Musikanalyse - eine exakte Wissenschaft?" *Elektronische Datenverarbeitung in der Musikwissenschaft*, edited by Harald Heckmann. Regensburg: Bosse, pp. 203-224.

_________. 1967c. "Musikanalyse und Wissenschaft." *Studia Musicologica Academiae Scientiarum Hungaricae* IX/1-2: 163-186.

_________. 1967d. "Die Notenschrift im Computer dargestellt," *Studia Musicologica Academiae Scientiarum Hungaricae* IX/3-4: 395-406.

Regener, Eric. 1967a. "A Multiple-Pass Transcription and a System for Music Analysis by Computer," *Elektronische Datenverarbeitung in der Musikwissenschaft*, edited by Harald Heckmann. Regensburg: Gustav Bosse. pp. 89-102.

_________. 1967b. "Layered Music-Theoretic Systems," *Perspectives of New Music* VI/1 (Autumn-Winter): 52-62.

Robison, Tobias D. 1967. "IML-MIR: A Data-Processing System for the Analysis of Music," *Elektronische Datenverarbeitung in der Musikwissenschaft*, edited by Harald Heckmann. Regensburg: Bosse. pp. 103-135.

Robison, Tobias D. 1967. "IML-MIR: A Data-Processing System for the Analysis of Music," *Elektronische Datenverarbeitung in der Musikwissenschaft*, edited by Harald Heckmann. Regensburg: Gustav Bosse. pp. 103-135.

Rothgeb, John. 1967. "Theories of Tonal Bass Harmonization," *Computers and the Humanities* II/2 (November): 87.

Schiødt, Nanna, and Bjarner Svejgaard. 1967. "Application of Computer Technique to the Analysis of Byzantine Sticherarion Melodies," *Elektronische Datenverarbeitung in der Musikwissenschaft*, edited by Harald Heckmann. Regensburg: Gustav Bosse. pp. 187-201.

Suchoff, Benjamin. 1967a. "Computer Applications to Bartók's Serbo-Croatian Material," *Tempo* 80 (Spring): 15-19.

_________. 1967b. "Computer Applications to Béla Bartók's Serbo-Croatian Material," *Computers and the Humanities* II/2 (November): 88.

Suess, John G. 1967. "A Pilot Study on 'Rhythmic Levels'," *Computers and the Humanities* I/5 (May): 226.

Wilson, Dean C. 1967. An Analytical and Statistical Study of the Harmony in Carl Nielsen's Six Symphonies. Ph.D. dissertation. East Lansing, MI: Michigan State University.

Winckel, Fritz. 1967. "Neue Wege der mathematischen Analyse von Musikstrukturen," *Wiener Akademie Festschrift*. Wien: Lafite. pp. 78-88.

Youngblood, Joseph E. 1967. "Root Progression and Composer Identification," *Computers and the Humanities* II/2 (November): 87.

1968

Andrus, Donald George. 1968. An Analysis of the Acoustics of Tamtam Sounds. D.M.A. dissertation. Urbana, IL: University of Illinois.

Anonymous. 1968a. "Directory of Scholars Active," *Computers and the Humanities* II/5 (May): 223-250.

Anonymous. 1968b. "Directory of Scholars Active," *Computers and the Humanities* III/2 (November): 105-118.

Bauer-Mengelberg, Stefan. 1968. "'The Truth, the Whole Truth, and Nothing but the Truth'," *Computer Studies in the Humanities and Verbal Behavior* I/2 (August): 52-54.

Bebbington, Brian. 1968. "Folkmusic and Computers," *African Music* IV/2: 56-58.

Bernzott, Philip. 1968. Musical Analysis with Computer: Some Programs and Descriptions. M.M. thesis. Chicago Musical College.

Brown, Charles T. 1968. "To Determine the Melodic Contour of a Melody," *Student Musicologists at Minnesota* III : 87-92.

Crane, Frederick. 1968. "Statistical Comparison of Musical Styles," *Computers and the Humanities* II/5 (May): 244.

Detlovs, Vilnis K. 1968. "O statisticeskom analize muzyki," *Latvijskij matematiceskij ezegodnik* [Riga] 3: 101-120.

Erickson, Raymond F. 1968a. "Music Analysis and the Computer," *Journal of Music Theory* XII/2 (Winter): 240-263.

__________. 1968b. "Music Analysis and the Computer: A Report on Some Current Approaches and the Outlook for the Future," *Computers and the Humanities* III/2 (November): 87-104.

Fiore, Mary E. 1968. "Harmonic Structure in Variation Movements by Webern," *Computers and the Humanities* II/5 (May): 243.

Frank, Helmar. 1968. *Informationsästhetik: Grundlagenprobleme und erste Anwendungen auf die mime pure*, 2nd ed. Quickborn bei Hamburg: Schnelle.

Fucks, Wilhelm. 1968. *Nach allen Regeln der Kunst. Diagnosen über Literatur, Musik, bildende Kunst - die Werke, ihre Autoren und Schöpfer*. Stuttgart: Deutsche Verlags-Anstalt.

Gould, Murray. 1968. "An Introduction to Computing in Music" [Review of *Papers from the West Virginia University Conference on Computer Applications in Music* by Gerald Lefkoff (Ed.)], *Computers and the Humanities* II/5 (May): 262-263.

Hatano, Giyoo. 1968. "Ongaku eno johoron-teki sekkin," *Ongaku Gaku. Journal of the Japanese Musicological Society* XIV: 54-64.

Hiller, Lejaren A., Jr. 1968. Music Composed with Computer – An Historical Survey. Technical Report No. 18. Urbana, IL: University of Illinois, Experimental Music Studio.

Hiller, Lejaren A., and James W. Beauchamp. 1968. Review of Completed and Proposed Research on Analysis and Synthesis of Musical Sounds by Analog and Digital Techniques. Technical Report No. 19. Urbana, IL: University of Illinois, Experimental Music Studio.

Karlina, T. P., and Vilnis K. Detlovs. 1968. "Statisticeskij analiz sekvencij v melodii," *Latvijskij matematiceskij ezegodnik* 4: 165-173.

Kassler, Michael. 1968. A Trinity of Essays. Ph.D. dissertation. Princeton, NJ: Princeton University.

Kobrin, Edward G., and Theodore H. A. Ashford. 1968. "A Solution to the Problems of Vertical Serialization," *Perspectives of New Music* VI/2 (Spring-Summer): 119-124.

Ladner, Robert, Jr. 1968. "Computer Analysis of Music Forms," *Music Journal* 26 (October): 33, 58.

LaRue, Jan. 1968. "Two Options for Input of Thematic Incipits," *Institute for Computer Research in the Humanities Newsletter* IV/3 (November): 3-6.

Lehr, Mangham D. 1968. "Canon One," *Computers and the Humanities* II/5 (May): 244.

Lewin, David. 1968. "Some Applications of Communication Theory to the Study of Twelve-Tone Music," *Journal of Music Theory* 12/1 (Spring): 50-84.

Lewis, David Sheldon. 1968. Two Parameters of Melodic Line as Stylistic Discriminants. Ph.D. dissertation. Morgantown, WV: West Virginia University.

Lincoln, Harry B. 1968a. "The Thematic Index: A Computer Application to Musicology," *Computers and the Humanities* II/5 (May): 215-220.

_________. 1968b. Development of Computerized Techniques in Music Research with Emphasis on the Thematic Index. Final Report, Project No. 7-8276, Grant No. OEG 1-7-078272-3898. Washington, DC: Office of Education, U.S. Department of Health, Education, and Welware.

_________. 1968c. "Thematic Index of Sixteenth-Century Italian Music," *Computers and the Humanities* II/5 (May): 243.

Lomax, Alan. 1968. *Folk Song Style and Culture*. Washington, DC: American Association for the Advancement of Science.

Lott, William Loyd. 1968. Arabic 1620: An Analysis and Procedure for Composing Computer Music. M.M. thesis. Denton, TX: North Texas State University.

Meylan, Raymond. 1968. *L'enigme de la musique des basses danses du quinzième siècle*. Publications de la Societe Suisse de Musicologie. Bern: Haupt.

Pederson, Donald Margedo. 1968. Some Technique for Computer-Aided Analysis of Musical Scores. Ph.D. dissertation. Iowa City, IA: The University of Iowa.

Piotrowska, Maria. 1968. Wybrane aspekty problematyki Jeux venitiens jako wstep do badan strukturalnych nad tworczoscia Witolda Lutoslawskiego. M.A. thesis. Warszawa, Poland: University of Warszawa.

Pruett, James W. 1968. Review of *Papers of the West Virginia University Conference on Computer Applications in Music* by Gerald Lefkoff (Ed.), *Computer Studies in the Humanities and Verbal Behavior* I/3 (October): 155.

Reckziegel, Walter. 1968. "Musik im Datenspeicher," *Die Musikforschung* XXI/4 (October-December): 427-438.

Rothgeb, John. 1968a. "Theories of Tonal Bass Harmonization," *Computers and the Humanities* II/5 (May): 243.

_________. 1968b. Harmonizing the Unfigured Bass: A Computational Study. Ph.D. dissertation. New Haven, CT: Yale University.

Sands, Alyce E., et al. 1968. "Annual Bibliography for 1967," *Computers and the Humanities* II/4 (March): 159-176.

Sellek, John. 1968. "Music Information Retrieval," *Computers and the Humanities* III/2 (November): 112.

Simon, Herbert A., and Richard K. Summer. 1968. "Pattern in Music," *Formal Representation of Human Judgement*, edited by B. Kleinmuntz. New York: Wiley. pp. 219-251. Reprinted in *Machine Models of Music*, edited by Stephen M. Schwanauer and David A. Levitt. Cambridge, MA: The MIT Press, 1993. pp. 83-110.

Suchoff, Benjamin. 1968a. "Bartók, Ethnomusicology, and the Computer," *Institute for Computer Research in the Humanities Newsletter* IV/4 (December): 3-6.

__________. 1968b. "Computerized Folk Song Research and the Problem of Variants," *Computers and the Humanities* II/4 (March): 155-158.
Wenker, Jerome R. 1968. "A Music Compiler for Musicologists and Ethnomusicology," *Computers and the Humanities* II/5 (May): 244.
Winograd, Terry. 1968. "Linguistics and the Computer Analysis of Tonal Harmony," *Journal of Music Theory* XII/1 (Spring): 2-49. Reprinted in *Machine Models of Music*, edited by Stephen M. Schwanauer and David A. Levitt. Cambridge, MA: The MIT Press, 1993. pp. 113-153.

1969

Anonymous. 1969a. "Directory of Scholars Active," *Computers and the Humanities* III/5 (May): 280-320.
Anonymous. 1969b. "Directory of Scholars Active," *Computers and the Humanities* IV/2 (November): 125-141.
Baroni, Mario. 1969. "Linguaggio Musicale della Sonata a Quattro Italiana del Secolo XVI,"*Computers and the Humanities* III/5 (May): 312.
Bengtsson, Ingmar, Alf Gabrielsson, and Stig-Magnus Thorsén. 1969. "Empirisk Rytmforskning. En Orientering om Musikvetenskaplig Bakgrund, Utveckling och Några aktuella Projekt," *Svensk Tidskrift för Musikforskning* 51: 49-118.
Bense, Max. 1969. *Einführung in die informationstheoretische Ästhetik*. Reinbek bei Hamburg: Rowohlt.
Berlind, Gary, and George W. Logeman. 1969. "An Algorithm for Musical Transposition," *Computer Studies in the Humanities and Verbal Behavior* II (August): 102-108.
Bernstein, Lawrence F. and Joseph P. Olive. 1969. "Computers and the 16th-century Chanson: A Pilot Project at the University of Chicago," *Computers and the Humanities* III/3 (January): 153-160.
Brook, Barry S. 1969. "Style and Content Analysis in Music: The Simplified 'Plaine and Easy Code'," *The Analysis of Communication Content*, edited by George Gerbner et al. New York: John Wiley & Sons. pp. 287-296.
Brown, Charles T., and Robert D. Oudal. 1969. "The 1968 Introductory Seminar in the Use of Computers in Musical Projects," *Student Musicologists at Minnesota* 3 (1968-1969): 87-92.
Curry, Jerry L. 1969. A Computer-Aided Analytical Study of Kyries in Selected Masses of Johannes Ockeghem. Ph.D. dissertation. Iowa City, IA: University of Iowa.
Czekanowska, Anna. 1969. "Zastosowanie polskicg metod statystycznych do klasyfikacji melodii ludowych," *Muzyka* [Poland] XIV/1: 3-18.
Elscheková, Alica. 1969. "Technologie der Datenverarbeitung bei der Klassifizierung von Volksliedern," *Methoden der Klassifikation von Volksliedweisen*, edited by Oskár Elschek. Bratislava: Verlag der Slowakischen Akademie der Wissenschaften. pp. 93-122.
Erickson, Raymond F. 1969. "A General Purpose System for Computer Aided Musical Studies," *Journal of Music Theory* XIII/2 (Winter): 276-294.
Goller, Gottfried. 1969. "Zur Bezeichnung der Neumen in der germanischen Choralnotation des 12. bis 14. Jahrhunderts," *Kirchenmusikalisches Jahrbuch* [Germany] LIII: 99-100.
Hanson, Jens L. 1969. An Operational Approach to Theory of Rhythm. Ph.D. dissertation. New Haven, CT: Yale University.

Hill, George R., Murray Gould, David Noon, Hans-Rudolf Diirrenmatt, and Jan LaRue. 1969. "*A Thematic Locator for Mozart's Works as Listed in Köchel's Chronologischthematisches Verzeichnis*," *Computers and the Humanities* III/5 (May): 311-312.
Joiner, Richard E. 1969. "Gregorian Chant," *Computer Studies in the Humanities and Verbal Behavior* II/4 (December): 213-219.
Kawano, Hiroshi. 1969. "Ongaku-teki komyunikeishon no joho-bunseki," *Ongaku gaku: Journal of the Japanese Musicological Society* XV/3-4: 1-21.
Kiefer, Thomas M. 1969. "Continuous Geographical Distributions of Musical Patterns: A Test Case from the Northwest Coast," *American Anthropologist* 71/4 (August): 701-705.
Kostka, Stephan M. 1969a. The Hindemith String Quartetts: A Computer-Assisted Study of Selected Aspects of Style. Ph.D. dissertation. Madison, WI: University of Wisconsin.
__________. 1969b. "Statistics in Style Research," *Computers and the Humanities* III/5 (May): 310.
Lachartre, Nicole. 1969. "Les musiques artificielles," *Diagrammes du Monde* 146 (April): 1-96.
LaRue, Jan, and Murray Gould. 1969. "Correlational Analysis to Establish Authenticity of 18th-Century Symphonies," *Computers and the Humanities* III/5 (May): 311.
Lincoln, Harry B. 1969a. "A Computer Application in Musicology: The Thematic Index," *Information Processing 68. Proceedings of the IFIP Congress 1968*, edited by A. J. H. Morrel. Amsterdam: North Holland. pp. 957-961.
__________. 1969b. Development of Computerized Techniques in Music Research with Emphasis on the Thematic Index. Washington: Office of Education, U.S. Department of Health, Education, and Welware.
__________. 1969c. "The computer and music research: Prospects and problems," *Bulletin of the Council for Research in Music Education* 18 (Fall): 1-9.
__________. 1969d. "A Computer Application in Musicology: The Thematic Index," *Information Processing* 68: 957-961.
Mason, Robert M. 1969a. "An Encoding Algorithm and Tables for the Digital Analysis of Harmony I," *Journal of Research in Music Education* 17/3 (Autumn): 286-300.
__________. 1969b. "An Encoding Algorithm and Tables for the Digital Analysis of Harmony II," *Journal of Research in Music Education* 17/4 (Winter): 369-387.
Mathews, Max V. 1969. *The Technology of Computer Music*. Cambridge, MA: The M.I.T. Press.
Mendel, Arthur. 1969. "Some Preliminary Attempts at Computer-Assisted Style Analysis in Music," *Computers and the Humanities* IV/1 (September): 41-52.
Oudal, Robert D. 1969. "The 1968 Introductory Seminar in the Use of Computers in Musical Projects: A Summary Report of Reactions, Frustrations, and Achievements," *Student Musicologists at Minnesota* III (1968-69): 66-109.
Pape, U. 1969. "Ein Verfahren zur Verschlüsselung und Symbolisierung von Kompositionen in Hinblick auf eine Musikanalyse mit EDV-Anlagen," *Elektronische Datenverarbeitung* XI (July): 342-345.
Paisley, William J. 1969. "Studying 'Style' as Deviation from Encoding Norms," *The Analysis of Communication Content. Developments in Scientific Theories and Computer Techniques*, edited by George Gerbner, Ole R. Holsti, Klaus Krippendorff, William J. Paisley and Philip J. Stone. New York: Wiley & Sons. pp. 133-146.
Rothgeb, John. 1969. "Simulating Musical Skills by Digital Computer," IEEE Transactions on Computers. Reprinted in *Machine Models of Music*, edited by Stephen M. Schwanauer and David A. Levitt. Cambridge, MA: The MIT Press, 1993. pp. 156-164.

Rubenstein, Nancy Ordelheide. 1969. A Fortran Computer Program for Transcribing Franconian Rhythm. Ph.D. dissertation. St Louis, MO: Washington University.

Sands, Alyce E., et al. 1969. "Annual Bibliography for 1968," *Computers and the Humanities* III/4 (March): 211-224.

Sellek, John. 1969. "Music Information Retrieval," *Computers and the Humanities* III/5 (May): 310.

Stacy, William B. 1969. Style and Register as Correlated Factors in the Horn Parts of Selected Symphonies by Joseph Haydn. M.A. thesis. Chapel Hill, NC: University of North Carolina.

Stockmann, Doris. 1969a. "Elektronische Datenverarbeitung in der Ethnologie und den ihr nahestehenden Wissenschaften," *Deutsches Jahrbuch für Volkskunde* XV: 134-158.

__________. 1969b. "Zur Arbeit der Study Group of Folk Music Systematization des IFMC," *Analyse und Klassifikation von Volksmelodien : Bericht über die 3. Arbeitstagung der Study Group of Folk Music Systematization beim International Folk Music Council vom 24. bis 28. Oktober 1967 in Radziejowice*, edited by Doris Stockmann and Jan Steszewski. Krakow : Polskie Wydawnictwo Muzyczne. pp. 9-30.

Suchoff, Benjamin. 1969a. "Some Problems in Computer-Oriented Bartokian Ethnomusicology," *Ethnomusicology* XIII/3 (September): 489-497.

__________. 1969b. "A Computerized Data Bank of Musical and Textual Information on Bartok's Six String Quartets," *Computers and the Humanities* III/5 (May): 311.

Wenker, Jerome R. 1969. "An Analytic Approach to Folk Music," *Computers and the Humanities* IV/2 (November): 138.

Wittlich, Gary E. 1969. "Programming a Computer for Musical Analysis," *Your Musical Cue* V/6 (April): 3-13.

Zaripov, Rudolf K. 1969. "'Cybernetics and Music,' translated from the Russion by J. G. K. Russel, with commentary by Michael KASSLER," *Perspectives of New Music*, VII/2 (Spring-Summer): 115-154.

1970

Alphonce, Bo H. 1970. "Music Theory at Yale – A Case Study and a Project Report," *Svensk Tidskrift for Musikforskning* LII: 38-46.

Anonymous. 1970a. "Directory of Scholars Active," *Computers and the Humanities* IV/5 (May): 323-357.

Anonymous. 1970b. "Directory of Scholars Active," *Computers and the Humanities* V/2 (November): 84-128.

Arom, Simha. 1970. "Essai d'une notation des monodies à des fins d'analyse," *Revue de Musicologie* 55: 172-216.

Bauer-Mengelberg, Stefan. 1970. "The Ford-Columbia Input Language," *Musicology and the Computer: Three Symposia*, edited by Barry S. Brook. New York: The City University of New York Press. 48-52.

Bengtsson, Ingmar. 1970. "Studies with the Aid of Computers of 'Music As Performed'," *IMS: Report on the Tenth Congress, Lubljana 1967*, edited by Dragotin Cvetko. Kassel: Bärenreiter. pp. 443-444.

Boucourechliev, Andre. 1970. "Transmutations," *L'Arc* 40: 49-56.

Bowles, Edmund. 1970a. "Discussion," *Musicology and the Computer: Three Symposia*, edited by Barry S. Brook. New York: The City University of New York Press. pp. 37-38.

__________. 1970b. "Musicke's Handmaiden: Or Technology in the Service of the Arts," *The Computer and Music*, edited by Harry B. Lincoln. Ithaca: Cornell University Press. pp. 3-20.

_________. 1970c. "Musicology and Computers" [A Review of Harald Heckmann, *Elektronische Datenverarbeitung der Musikwissenschaft*], *Computers and the Humanities* IV/3 (January): 207-219.

Brincker, Jens. 1970. "Statistical Analysis of Music: An Application of Information Theory," *Svensk Tidskrift för Musikforsking* 52: 53-57.

Brook, Barry S. Ed. 1970a. *Musicology and the Computer: Three Symposia*. New York: The City University of New York Press.

_________. 1970b. "Music Documentation of the Future," *Musicology and the Computer: Three Symposia*, edited by Barry S. Brook. New York: The City University of New York Press. pp. 28-36.

_________. 1970c. "The Plaine and Easie Code," *Musicology and the Computer: Three Symposia*, edited by Barry S. Brook. New York: The City University of New York Press. pp. 53-56.

Byrd, Donald Alvin. 1970a. "Music Notation by Computer," *Computers and the Humanities* V/2 (November): 111.

_________. 1970b. "Transcription by Plotter," *Random Bits* V/9 (May): 6-8.

Campbell, Warren Colman. 1970. Computer Analysis of Musical Performance. Ph.D. dissertation. Storrs, CT: University of Connecticut.

Crane, Frederick, and Judith Fiehler. 1970. "Numerical Methods of Comparing Musical Styles," *The Computer and Music*, edited by Harry B. Lincoln. Ithaca: Cornell University Press. pp. 209-222.

Czekanowska-Kulinska, Anna. 1970. "Polish Mathematical Methods in the Classification of Slavic Folk Songs," *IMS: Report on the Tenth Congress, Lubljana 1967*, edited by Dragotin Cvetko. Kassel: Bärenreiter. pp. 440-443.

de la Motte-Haber, Helga. 1970. "Die Abhängigkeit des Sonanzeindrucks von der Intervallstruktur," *Bericht über den Internationalen Musikwissenschaftlichen Kongress Leipzig 1966*, edited by Carl Dahlhaus et al. Kassel: Bärenreiter. pp. 477-482.

Dürrenmatt, Hans-Rudolf, Murray Gold, and Jan LaRue. 1970. "Die Notierung Thematischer Incipits auf 'Mark-Sense-Cards'," *Fontes Artes Musicae* XVII/1-2 (January-August): 15-23.

Egeland Hansen, Finn. 1970. "Musikalsk analyse ved hjaepl af modeller," *Svensk Tidskrift för Musikforskning* 52: 50-53.

Erickson, Raymond F. 1970a. Rhythmic Problems and Melodic Structure in Organum Purum: A Computer-Assisted Study. Ph.D. dissertation. New Haven, CT: Yale University.

_________. 1970b. "A Syntax-Directed, Changeable System for Processing Data for Music Analysis," *Computers and the Humanities* IV/5 (May): 343.

_________. 1970c. "Music and the Computer in the Sixties," *AFIPS Conference Proceedings* 36: 281-285.

Evarts, John. 1970. "Stockholm," *World of Music* XII/3: 52-56. [Report on the UNESCO meeting "Music and Technology".]

Fiore, Mary E. 1970. "Webern's Use of Motive in the Piano Variations," *The Computer and Music*, edited by Harry B. Lincoln. Ithaca: Cornell University Press. pp. 115-122.

Forte, Allen. 1970. "The Structure of Atonal Music: Practical Aspects of a Computer-Oriented Research Project," *Musicology and the Computer: Three Symposia*, edited by Barry S. Brook. New York: The City University of New York Press. pp. 10-18.

Fuller, Ramon Conrad. 1970. "Toward a Theory of Webernian Harmony, via Analysis with a Digital Computer," *The Computer and Music*, edited by Harry B. Lincoln. Ithaca: Cornell University Press. pp. 123-131.

Gabura, A. James. 1970. "Musical Style Analysis by Computer," *The Computer and Music*, edited by Harry B. Lincoln. Ithaca: Cornell University Press. pp. 223-276.

Gilbert, Steven E. 1970. The Trichord: An Analytic Outlook for Twentieth-Century Music. Ph.D. dissertation. New Haven, CT: Yale University.

Goldberg, Robert P. 1970. "Experimental Music Information System," *Computers and the Humanities* IV/5 (May): 345-346.

Goller, Gottfried. 1970. "Zur Bezeichnung der Neumen in der germanischen Choralnotation," *Bericht über den Internationalen Musikwissenschaftlichen Kongress, Leipzig, 1966*, ed. by Carl Dahlhaus, Reiner Kluge, Ernst H. Meyer, and Walter Wiora. Kassel: Bärenreiter. pp. 173-175.

Gould, Murray J., and George W. Logemann. 1970. "ALMA: Alphanumeric Language for Music Analysis," *Musicology and the Computer: Three Symposia*, edited by Barry S. Brook. New York: The City University of New York Press. pp. 57-90.

Hill, George R., and Murray Gould. 1970. *A Thematic Locator for Mozart's Works, as Listed in Koechel's Chronologisch-Thematisches Verzeichnis*, 6th edition. Hackensack, NJ: Boonin.

Holý, Dušan, Antonin Bartošik, and Stanislav Zabadal. 1970. "Samočinný počítač-pomocník při analýze a klasifikaci lidových písní," *Opus musicum* [Czechoslovakia] II/5-6: 155-164.

Hudson, Barton. 1970. "Toward a Comprehensive French Chanson Catalog," *The Computer and Music*, edited by Harry B. Lincoln. Ithaca: Cornell University Press. pp. 277-287.

Hultberg, W. Earle. 1970. "Transcription of Tablature to Standard Notation," *The Computer and Music*, edited by Harry B. Lincoln. Ithaca: Cornell University Press. pp. 289-292.

Jackson, Roland. 1970a. "Harmony before and after 1910: A Computer Comparison," *The Computer and Music*, edited by Harry B. Lincoln. Ithaca: Cornell University Press. pp. 132-146.

__________. 1970b. "The Computer as a 'Student' of Harmony," *IMS: Report on the Tenth Congress, Lubljana 1967*, edited by Dragotin Cvetko. Kassel: Bärenreiter. pp. 435-440.

Jackson, Roland, and Philip Bernzott. 1970. "A Musical Input Language and a Sample Program for Musical Analysis," *Musicology and the Computer: Three Symposia*, edited by Barry S. Brook. New York: The City University of New York Press. pp. 130-150.

Jammers, Ewald; Bielitz, Matthias; Bender, Iring; Ebenhoh, Wolfgang. 1970. "Das Heidelberger Programm für die elektronische Datenverarbeitung in der musikwissenschaftlichen Byzantinistik," *Sitzungsberichte der Heidelberger Akademie der Wissenschaften, naturwissenschaftliche Klasse* II (1969-70): 3-23.

John, Robert W. 1970a. "A Pilot Computer Catalog of Early American Shape-Note Hymn Tunes," *Computers and the Humanities* IV/5 (May): 345.

__________. 1970b. "A Pilot Computer Catalog of Early American Sheet Music," *Computers and the Humanities* IV/5 (May): 345.

Kagan, Alan L., and Charles T. Brown. 1970. "Computerized Analysis and Classification of Asian Musical Style," *Computers and the Humanities* IV/5 (May): 347.

Karp, Theodore. 1970. "A Test for Melodic Borrowings among Notre Dame *Organa Dupla*," *The Computer and Music*, edited by Harry B. Lincoln. Ithaca: Cornell University Press. pp. 293-295.

Kassler, Michael. 1970a. "An Essay Toward Specification of a Music-Reading Machine," *Musicology and the Computer: Three Symposia*, edited by Barry S. Brook. New York: The City University of New York Press. pp. 151-175.

_________. 1970b. "MIR – A Simple Programming Language for Musical Information Retrieval," *The Computer and Music*, edited by Harry B. Lincoln. Ithaca: Cornell University Press. pp. 299-327.

Kluge, Reiner. 1970a. "Volksliedanalyse und -systematisierung mit Hilfe eines Rechenautomaten," *Bericht über den Internationalen Musikwissenschaftlichen Kongress Leipzig 1966*, edited by Carl Dahlhause et al. Kassel: Bärenreiter. pp. 158-465.

_________. 1970b. "Zur Automatischen Quantitativen Bestimmung Musikalischer Ähnlichkeit," *IMS: Report on the Tenth Congress, Lubljana 1967*, edited by Dragotin Cvetko. Kassel: Bärenreiter. pp. 450-457.

Kongas-Maranda, Elli. 1970. "Deep Significance and Surface Significance: Is Cantometrics Possible?" *Semiotica* II/2: 173-184.

Kupper, Hubert. 1970a. *Statistische Untersuchungen zur Modusstruktur der Gregorianik*. Regensburg: Bosse.

_________. 1970b. *Computer und musikalische Kompositionen*. Braunschweig: Vieweg.

LaRue, Jan. 1970a. "New Directions for Style Analysis," *Musicology and the Computer: Three Symposia*, edited by Barry S. Brook. New York: The City University of New York Press. pp. 194-197.

_________. 1970b. "Some Computer Aids to Musicology," *Bericht über den Internationalen Musikwissenschaftlichen Kongress Leipzig 1966*, edited by Carl Dahlhause et al. Kassel: Bärenreiter. pp. 466-469.

_________. 1970c. "Future Technological Directions," *IMS: Report on the Tenth Congress, Lubljana 1967*, edited by Dragotin Cvetko. Kassel: Bärenreiter. pp. 457-460.

Lefkoff, Gerald. 1970. "Automated Discovery of Similar Segments in the Forty-eight Permutations of a Twelve-Tone Row," *The Computer and Music*, edited by Harry B. Lincoln. Ithaca: Cornell University Press. pp. 147-153.

Lieberman, Fredric. 1970. "Computer-Aided Analysis of Javanese Music," *The Computer and Music*, edited by Harry B. Lincoln. Ithaca: Cornell University Press. pp. 181-192.

Lincoln, Harry B. Ed. 1970a. *The Computer and Music*. Ithaca: Cornell University Press.

_________. 1970b. "The Current State of Music Research and the Computer," *Computer and the Humanities* V/1 (September): 29-36.

_________. 1970c. "Thematic Indexing by Computer, Including Development of Necessary Hardware to Permit Printing of Music by Computer," *Computers and the Humanities* V/2 (November): 109-110.

_________. 1970d. A Study of Computer Techniques for Music Research. Final Report, Project No. 9-B-101, Grant No. OEG-2-9-420101-1067. Washington, DC: Office of Education, U.S. Department of Health, Education and Welware, Office of Education, Bureau of Research.

_________. 1970e. "Teaching Computer Applications in Musicology," *IBM Symposium on Introducing the Computer into the Humanities* [Document G 320-1044-0]. Poughkeepsie, NY: IBM. pp. 67-71.

Lindblom, Björn, and Johan Sundberg. 1970. "Towards a Generative Theory of Melody," *Svensk Tidskrift för Musikforskning* 52: 71-88.

Lockwood, Lewis. 1970a. "A Stylistic Investigation of the Masses of Josquin Desprez with the Aid of the Computer: a Progress Report," *Musicology and the Computer: Three Symposia*, edited by Barry S. Brook. New York: The City University of New York Press. pp. 19-27.

_________. 1970b. "Computer Assistance in the Investigation of Accidentals in Renaissance Music," *IMS: Report on the Tenth Congress, Lubljana 1967*, edited by Dragotin Cvetko. Kassel: Bärenreiter. pp. 444-449.

Meylan, Raymond. 1970. "Teorie de la Centonisation," *IMS: Report on the Tenth Congress, Lubljana 1967*, edited by Dragotin Cvetko. Kassel: Bärenreiter. pp. 427-430.

Morton, Ian, and John Lofstedt. 1970. "FORTRAN Music Programs Involving Numerically Related Tones," *The Computer and Music*, edited by Harry B. Lincoln. Ithaca: Cornell University Press. pp. 154-162.

Philippot, Michel P. 1970. "Muss es sein," *L'Arc* [France] 40: 82-95.

Prerau, David S. 1970a. "Computer Pattern Recognition of Standard Engraved Music Notation," *Computers and the Humanities* IV/5 (May): 344.

_________. 1970b. Computer Pattern Recognition of Standard Engraved Music Notation. PhD dissertation. Boston, MA: Massachussetts Institute of Technology.

Ratner, Leonard G. 1970. "Ars Combinatoria: Chance and Choice in Eighteenth-Century Music," *Studies in Eighteenth Century Music: A Tribute to Karl Geiringer on his Seventieth Birthday*, edited by H. C. Robbins Landon. New York, NY: Oxford University Press. pp. 343-363.

Reckziegel, Walter. 1970. "Ein Subjektives Tempomaß," *Bericht über den Internationalen Musikwissenschaftlichen Kongress Leipzig 1966*, edited by Carl Dahlhause et al. Kassel: Bärenreiter. pp. 457-458.

Reinecke, Hans-Peter. 1970. "Anwendung Informationstheoretischer und Korrelationsstatistischer Verfahren für die Analyse Musikalischer Strukturen," *IMS: Report on the Tenth Congress, Lubljana 1967*, edited by Dragotin Cvetko. Kassel: Bärenreiter. pp. 430-434.

Riedel, Johannes. 1970. "A Computer-Assisted Study of Ecuadorian Urban Music," *Computers and the Humanities* V/2 (November): 111.

Sands, Alyce E., et al. 1970. "Annual Bibliography for 1969," *Computers and the Humanities* IV/5 (May): 319-322.

Sellek, John. 1970. "Musical Information Retrieval (MIR)," *Computers and the Humanities* V/2 (November): 110.

Shatzkin, Merton. 1970. "Chords and Chord Progression in J. S. Bach's 371 Chorales," *Computers and the Humanities* IV/5 (May): 347.

Suchoff, Benjamin. 1970a. "Computer-Oriented Comparative Musicology," *The Computer and Music*, edited by Harry B. Lincoln. Ithaca: Cornell University Press. pp. 193-206.

_________. 1970b. "Aplicarea calculatorelor elektronice la etnomuzicologia Bartokiana," *Musica* XI (November): 10-14.

_________. 1970c. "A Bartoki nepzenekutatas es az elektronikus szamitogepeg," *Muzsika* XIII (July): 6-8; (August): 4-6.

Suchoff, Benjamin, and Jack Heller. 1970. "Studies Relating to Automation of Bartók Archives," *Computers and the Humanities* V/2 (November): 110.

Sychra, Antonín. 1970. "Die Anwendung der Kybernetik und der Informations-Theorie in der Marxistischen Ästhetik," *Beiträge zur Musikwissenschaft* XII/2: 83-108.

Tischler, Hans. 1970. "A Complete Edition of the *Magnus Liber Organi*," *Computers and the Humanities* V/2 (November): 111.

Tokumaru, Yoshihiko. 1970. "Joho-riron to ongaku-kodo," *Arima daigoro sensei koki kinen ronbunshu* [*Daigoro Festschrift*], edited by Kunitachi Ongaku Daigaku. Tokyo: Kunitachi Music College. pp. 195-212.

Trowbridge, Lynn Mason. 1970. "The Burgundian Chanson: An Index and Analysis of Incipits," *Computers and the Humanities* IV/5 (May): 343-344.

Walker, Thomas. 1970. "The computer and music (Review of)," *Notes: Quarterly Journal of the Music Library Association* 27/2 (December): 178-183.

Wenker, Jerome R. 1970. "A Computer Oriented Music Notation Including Ethnomusicological Symbols," *Musicology and the Computer: Three Symposia*, edited by Barry S. Brook. New York: The City University of New York Press. pp. 91-129.
Youngblood, Joseph E. 1970. "Root Progressions and Composer Identification," *The Computer and Music*, edited by Harry B. Lincoln. Ithaca: Cornell University Press. pp. 172-178.

1971

Anonymous. 1971a. "Directory of Scholars Active," *Computers and the Humanities* V/5 (May): 291-320.
Anonymous. 1971b. "Directory of Scholars Active," *Computers and the Humanities* VI/2 (November): 114-124.
Ashton, Alan Conway. 1971. Electronics, Music and Computer. Ph.D. dissertation. Salt Lake City, UT: University of Utah.
Baron, John H. 1971. "First Report on the Use of Computer Programming to Study the Secular Solo Songs in France from 1600 to 1660," *Bericht über den internationalen musikwissenschaftlichen Kongress: Bonn 1970*, ed. by Carl Dahlhaus et al. Kassel: Bärenreiter. pp. 333-336.
Bengtsson, Ingmar. 1971. "Analysis of Rhythmic Performance," *Computers and the Humanities* V/5 (May): 310.
Böker-Heil, Norbert. 1971a. "Programmierte Musikanalyse," *Computers and the Humanities* V/5 (May): 314.
__________. 1971b. "DODEK - Eine Computerdemonstration," *Zeitschrift für Musiktheorie* II/2: 2-14.
Borris, Siegfried. 1971. Review of *Musikalische Stilanalyse auf der Grundlage eines Modelles für Lernprozesse* by Hermann Gerhard Rohrer, *Musik und Bildung* III/11 (November): 567-568.
Byrd, Donald Alvin. 1971. "Humanities Programming for Creative Work," *Random Bits* VI/5 (January): 1, 8-12.
Cantor, Don. 1971. "A Computer Program that Accepts Common Musical Notation," *Computers in the Humanities* VI (November): 103-109.
Charnassé, Hélène, and Henri Ducasse. 1971. "De l'emploi de l'ordinateur pour la transcription des trablatures," *Revue de Musicologie* 57/2: 107-133.
Chenoweth, Vida, and Darlene Bee. 1971. "Comparative-Generative Models of a New Guinea Melodic Structure," *American Anthropoligist* 73: 773-782.
Ciamaga, Gustav. 1971. "The Training of the Computer in the Use of New technological Means," *Music and Technology*. Paris: La Revue Musicale. pp. 143-150.
Deihl, Ned C. 1971. Computer-Assisted Instruction and Instrumental Music: Implications for Teaching and Research," *Journal of Research in Music Education* XIX/3 (Fall): 299-306.
Erickson, Raymond F. 1971a. "Rhythmic Problems and Melodic Structure in Organum Purum: A Computer-Assisted Study," *Computers and the Humanities* V/5 (May): 312-313.
__________. 1971b. "DUPACK (DARMS Utility Package)," *Computers and the Humanities* V/5 (May): 313.
__________. 1971c. The Ford-Columbia Music Representation (DARMS). [New York: IBM Systems Research Institute].

Frisbie, Charlotte J. 1971. "Anthropological and Ethnomusicological Implications of a Comparative Analysis of Bushmen and African Pygmy Music," *Ethnology* X/3 (July): 265-290.
Haefer, John Richard. 1971. Selected Cantatas of Alan Hovhaness: A Linear Analysis. M.M. thesis. Tucson, AZ: University of Arizona.
Heckmann, Harald. 1971. "Katalog 'Deutsches Tenorlied des 16. Jahrhunderts," *Computers and the Humanities* V/5 (May): 313-314.
Heller, Jack J., and Warren C. Campbell. 1971. "Music Performance Analysis," *Council for Research in Music Education Bulletin* 24 (Spring): 1-9.
Helm, Everett. 1971. "UNESCO Report on the Stockholm Meeting," *Music and Technology*. Paris: La Revue Musicale. pp. 193-206.
Hessert, Norman Dale. 1971. The Use of Information Theory in Musical Analysis. Ph.D. dissertation. Bloomington, IN: Indiana University.
Howe, Hubert S. 1971. "Two Parameters of Melodic Line as Stylistic Discriminants by David Sheldon Lewis; Some Techniques for Computer-Aided Analysis of Musical Scores by Donald Margedo Pederson [Review]," *Perspectives of New Music* 9-10/2-1 (Spring/Summer-Autumn/Winter): 350-355.
Kaegi, Werner. 1971. "Music and Technology in the Europe of 1970," *Music and Technology*. Paris: La Revue Musicale. pp. 9-31.
Kostka, Stephan M. 1971. "Recent Developments in Computer-Assisted Musical Scholarship," *Computers and the Humanities* VI/1 (September): 15-21.
Longuet-Higgins, H. Christopher, and Mark J. Steedman. 1971. "On Interpreting Bach," *Machine Intelligence 6*, edited by Bernard Meltzer and Donald Michie. Edinburgh: Edinburgh University Press. pp. 221-241.
Marillier, Cecil Glyn. 1971. Tonal Structure in the Symphonies of F. J. Haydn. M.A. thesis. North Dunedin, New Zealand: University of Otago.
Maser, Siegfried. 1971. *Numerische Ästhetik. Neue mathematische Verfahren zur quantitativen Beschreibung und Bewertung ästhetischer Zustände*, 3rd edition. Stuttgart: Krämer.
Moore, F. 1971. "Musica ed elaboratori elettronici," *Scienza & Tecnica: Annuario della EST, Enciclopedia della Scienza e della Tecnica*: 490-498.
Patrick, Robert Lee. 1971. A Computer-Based Thematic Index to the Works of Heinrich Schütz. D.M.A. dissertation. Lexington, KY: University of Kentucky.
Prerau, David S. 1971. "Computer Pattern Recognition of Printed Music," *AFIPS Conference Proceedings* 39: 153-162.
Rohrer, Hermann G. 1971. *Musikalische Stilanalyse auf der Grundlage eines Modelles für Lernprozesse*. Berlin: Siemens AG.
Rothgeb, John. 1971a. "Musical Research by Computer: Some Current Limitations [Review of Harry B. Lincoln, ed., *The Computer and Music*]," *Computers and the Humanities* V/3 (January): 178-182.
__________. 1971b. "Some Early Efforts in Computational Musicology," *Computers and the Humanities* VI/1 (September): 56-58.
__________. 1971c. Harmonizing the unfigured bass: a computational study. Ph.D. dissertation. New Haven, CT: Yale University.
Sands, Alyce E., et al. 1971. "Annual Bibliography for 1970," *Computers and the Humanities* V/4 (March): 215-238.
Scherrer, Deborah K., and Philip H. Scherrer. 1971. "An Experiment in the Computer Measurement of Melodic Variation in Folksong," *Journal of American Folklore* 84/332 (April-June): 230-241.

Schiødt, Nanna. 1971. "A Computer-Aided Analysis of Thirty-Five Byzantine Hymns," *Studies in Eastern Chant II*, edited by Miloš Velimirović. London: Oxford University Press. pp. 129-154.

Shamos, Michael Ian. 1971. "Computer Investigation of Highland Bagpipe Music," *Computers and the Humanities* V/5 (May): 311-312.

Smoliar, Stephen William. 1971a. A Parallel-Processing Model of Musical Structures. Ph.D. dissertation. Boston, MA: Massachussetts Institute of Technology.

_________. 1971b. *A Parallel-Processing Model of Musical Structures*. Cambridge, MA: Project Mac, Massachusetts Institute of Technology.

Štědroň, Miloš. 1971. "Možnosti intervalové a melodické analýzy," *Opus Musicum* [Czechoslovakia] III/7 (July): 202-208.

Stephan, Claudio. 1971. "Harmonic and Phraseologic Computer Aided Music Analysis," *Computers and the Humanities* VI/2 (November): 123.

Suchoff, Benjamin. 1971. "The Computer and Bartók Research in America," *Journal of Research in Music Education* XIX/1 (Spring): 3-16.

Suchoff, Benjamin, and Jack Heller. 1971. "Studies Relating to Automatization of Bartók Archives," *Computers and the Humanities* V/5 (May): 309-310.

Trowbridge, Lynn Mason. 1971. "An Analytical and Indexing System for Incipits of Renaissance Polyphonic Compositions," *Computers and the Humanities* V/5 (May): 310.

Vercoe, Barry L. 1971. Reviews of *The computer and music*, ed. Hary B. Lincoln; *Musicology and the computer*, ed. Barry S. Brook, *Perspectives of New Music* IX/X (Spring/Summer-Autumn/Winter): 323-330.

Warburton, Thomas. 1971. Review of *The Opening Sonata-Allegro Movements in a Randomly Selected Sample of Solo Keyboard Sonatas Published in the Years 1742-1774* by Roger Jaques Kamien, *Current Musicology* XI: 118-121.

Wittlich, Gary E. 1971. "Music as Information," *Your Musical Cue* VII/3 (December-January): 3-9.

Xenakis, Iannis. 1971. *Formalized Music. Thought and Mathematics in Composition*. Bloomington: Indiana University Press.

Zaripov, Rudolf K. 1971. *Kibernetica i Muzyka*. Moscow: Nauka.

1972

Anonymous. 1972a. "Directory of Scholars Active," *Computers and the Humanities* VI/5 (May): 301-320.

Anonymous. 1972b. "Directory of Scholars Active," *Computers and the Humanities* VII/2 (November): 111-128.

Böker-Heil, Norbert. 1972a. "Weiße Mensuralnotation als Computer-Input und -Output," *Acta Musicologica* XLIII/1-2 (January-June): 21-33.

_________. 1972b. "Ein algebraisches Modell des Dur-Moll-Tonalen Systems," *Bericht über den 1. Internationalen Kongress für Musiktheorie Stuttgart 1971*, ed. by Peter Rummenhöller, Friedrich Christoph Reininghaus, and Jürgen Habakuk Traber. Stuttgart, Germany: Ichthys-Verlag. pp. 64-107.

Broeckx, Jan L., and Walter Landrieu. 1972. "Comparative Study of Style, Based on Five Liedmelodies," *Interface* I/1 (April): 29-92.

Burns, Betty Beryl Remy. 1972. An Electronic Data Processing System for the Organization and Documentaion of the 16th Century Motet. Ph.D. dissertation. Cincinnati, OH: University of Cincinnati.

Delalande, François. 1972. "L'analyse des musiques electro-acoustiques," *Musique en Jeu*: 50-56.

Elscheková, Alica. 1972. "Klasifikacie Kratkych Motivickych Usekov Netrofickych i Strofickych Piesni Tradicnymi a Netradicnymi Technikami," *Lidová písen a samostatný pocítac I*, edited by Dušan Holý and Oldrich Sirovátka. Brno: Klub uživatelů MSP. pp. 219-243.

Erickson, Raymond F. 1972a. "The Computer and Music," *Journal of the American Musicological Society* XXV/1 (Spring): 102-107.

_________. 1972b. Abstract of *Rhythmic Problems and Melodic Structure in Organum Purum: A Computer-Assisted Study* by R. F. Erickson, *Computers and the Humanities* VI/4 (March): 254.

_________. 1972c. "The Uses of Computers in Music: A State of the Art Report," *First USA-Japan Computer Conference Proceedings: October 3-5, 1972, Tokyo, Japan.* Montvale, NJ: American Federation of Information Processing Societies. pp. 124-129.

Fink, Michael. 1972. Music Analysis: An Annotated Bibliography. Los Alamitos: Southwest Regional Laboratory for Educational Research and Development. Technical Report Vol. 43.

Fornůsek, Jaroslav. 1972. "Aplikace zkusenosti z projektovani uloh na samocinnem pocitaci pro oblast lidove pisne," *Lidová písen a samostatný pocítac I*, edited by Dušan Holý and Oldrich Sirovátka. Brno: Klub uživatelů MSP. pp. 11-18.

Gasparov, Boris M. 1972. "Strukturnyj metod v muzykozananii," *Sovetskaya Muzyka* 4: 42-51.

Greussay, Patrick. 1972. "Un modèle informatique de description de structures musicales," *Recherches linguistiques* 1: 89-128.

Gutknecht, Dieter. 1972. *Untersuchungen zur Melodik des Hugenottenpsalters*. Regensburg: Bosse.

Heckmann, Harald. 1972. "Informationstheorie und Computer," *Informatik. Vorträge anläßlich der Jahresversammlung vom 14. bis 17. Oktober 1971 zu Halle (Saale)*, edited by Jocahim-Hermann Scharf. Nova Acta Leopoldina vol. 37/1, no. 206. Leipzig: Barth. pp. 619-627.

Heller, Jack J., and Warren C. Campbell. 1972. Computer Analysis of the Auditory Characteristics of Musical Performance. Final Report, Project No. 9-0546A, Grant No. OEG-0-9-160546-4439 (010). Washington: U.S. Dept. of Health, Education and Welfare, Office of Education, Bureau of Research.

Herndon, Marcia. 1972. "The computer and music (Review of)," *Ethnomusicology: Journal of the Society for Ethnomusicology* 16/2 (May): 290-292.

Hofstetter, Fred T. 1972. "A Computer System for Musical Description," *Journal of the Graduate Music Students at the Ohio State University* 3: 4-42.

Holý, Dušan, Antonin Bartošik, and Stanislav Zabadal. 1972. "Cíle úkoly postupy perspektivy. Za studium lidovych pisni pomoci samočinneho počítač," *Lidová písen a samostatný pocítac I*, edited by Dušan Holý and Oldrich Sirovátka. Brno: Klub uživatelů MSP. pp. 19-42.

Holý, Dušan, and Oldrich Sirovátka. Eds. 1972. *Lidová písen a samostatný pocítac I.* Brno: Klub uživatelů MSP. Mimeographed.

Karkoschka, Erhard. 1972. "Letzter Schreck: der Computer," *Melos* 39/5: 285-288.

Kassler, Michael. 1972. "Optical Character-Recognition of Printed Music: A Review of Two Dissertations," *Perspectives of New Music* XI/1 (Autumn-Winter): 250-254.

Kupper, Hubert. 1972. "GEASCOP - Ein Kompositionsprogramm," *Informatik. Vorträge anläßlich der Jahresversammlung vom 14. bis 17. Oktober 1971 zu Halle (Saale)*, edited by Jocahim-Hermann Scharf. Nova Acta Leopoldina vol. 37/1, no. 206. Leipzig: Barth. 629-655.

Laske, Otto. 1972. "On Musical Strategies With a View to a Generative Grammar for Music," *Interface* I/2: 111-125.
Leng, Ladislav. 1972. "O niektorych možnostiach využitia SP pri klasifikácii ozdobovanych ludovych instrumentalnych melodii," *Lidová písen a samostatný pocítac I*, edited by Dušan Holý and Oldrich Sirovátka. Brno: Klub uživatelů MSP. pp. 207-213.
Lincoln, Harry B. 1972a. "Uses of the Computer in Music Composition and Research," *Advances in Computers*, edited by Morris Rubinoff, vol. 12. New York: Academic Press. pp. 73-114.
_________. 1972b. "A Fortran Computer Program for Transcribing Franconian Rhythm," (Review of)," *Bulletin of the Council for Research in Music Education* 29 (Summer): 39-41.
Lönn, Anders. 1972. "Trends and Tendencies in Recent Swedish Musicology," *Acta Musicologica* 44/1: 11-25.
Mathews, Max V. 1972. Review of *The Computer and Music* by Harry B. Lincoln, *Computer Studies in the Humanities and Verbal Behavior* III/4 (November): 224-225.
Maultsby, Portia Katrenia. 1972. "Afro-American Music, 1619-1861: An Analytical Study," *Computers and the Humanities* VII/2 (November): 125.
Miller, Alyce Sands, et al. 1972. "Annual Bibliography for 1971," *Computers and the Humanities* VI/4 (March): 235-251.
Nattiez, Jean-Jacques. 1972. "Is a Descriptive Seomiotics of Music Possible?" *Language Sciences* 23: 1-7.
Ravnikar, Bruno. 1972. "Nekaj rezultatov proucevanja glasbene folklore z metodami matematicne statistike," *Rad XVII Kongresa Saveza udruzenja folklorista Jugoslavije, Porec, 1970*, edited by Vinko Zganec. Zagreb, Jugoslavia: Savez udruzenja folklorista Jugoslavije, Drustvo folklorista Hrvatske. pp. 271-286.
Ryžov, L. 1972. *Točnyje metody i muzykalnoje iskusstvo*. Rostov na Donu: Rostov University Press.
Scharf, Joachim-Hermann. 1972. "Einführung in 'Computer und Musikwissenschaft'," *Informatik. Vorträge anläßlich der Jahresversammlung vom 14. bis 17. Oktober 1971 zu Halle (Saale)*, edited by Jocahim-Hermann Scharf. Leipzig: Barth. pp. 563-572.
Smoliar, Stephen William. 1972a. "Music Theory – A Programming Linguistic Approach," *Proceedings of the ACM 25th Annual Conference*. New York: Association for Computing Machinery. pp. 100-114.
_________. 1972b. Music Theory – A Programming Linguistic Approach. Technical Report # 15. Haifa, Israel: Israel Institute of Technology.
Stroh, Wolfgang Martin. 1972. "Über Schwierigkeiten bei der mathematischen Darstellung musikalischer Sachverhalte," *Neue Zeitschrift für Musik* X: 567-572.
Suchoff, Benjamin. 1972a. "A National Science Computer Network: A Report on the First Working Seminar," *Computers and the Humanities* VII/2 (November): 96-97.
_________. 1972b. "Recent Developments in Computer-Assisted Musical Scholarship [Review of]," *Computing Review* 13/2 (February): 68-69.
Urup, Henning. 1972. Danske Folkedanse. En beskrivelse og undersogelse af det danske folkelige melodistof med hertil horende dansebeskrivelser. M.A. thesis. Kobenhavn, Denmark: University of Kobenhavn.
Wenker, Jerome R. 1972a. "A Music Compiler for Musicologists and Ethnomusicologists," *Computers and the Humanities* VII/2 (November): 124.
_________. 1972b. "An Analytic Approach to Folk Music," *Computers and the Humanities* VII/2 (November): 124-125.

_________. 1972c. "MUSTRAN II - An Extended *MUS*ic *TRAN*slator," *Computers and the Humanities* VII/2 (November): 125.

Wolff, Anthony B. 1972. "Development of a DARMS-to-Canonical DARMS Translator," *Computers and the Humanities* VI/5 (May): 316.

Zoch, Josef. 1972. "Vztah mezi vokaly a melodii v lidove pisni," *Lidová písen a samostatný pocítac I*, edited by Dušan Holý and Oldrich Sirovátka. Brno: Klub uživatelů MSP. pp. 215-219.

1973

Anonymous. 1973. "Directory of Scholars Active," *Computers and the Humanities* VII/5 (May): 295-318.

Avenary, Hanoch. 1973. "Analysis of Musical Modes on a Quantitative Base," *Computational Musicology Newsletter* I/1: 13.

Baroni, Mario, and Carlo Jacoboni. 1973. "Four-part Choral Generation," *Computational Musicology Newsletter* I/1: 10.

Bent, Ian D. 1973. "Analysis of Melodic Structure," *Computers and the Humanities* VII/5 (May): 314.

Boggs, Beverly. 1973. "Analysis of Ethnomusicological Transcritions," *Computational Musicology Newsletter* I/1: 14.

Boggs, J. K. 1973. "Music Ancoding," *Computational Musicology Newsletter* I/1: 3.

Böker-Heil, Norbert. 1973. "Plotting Conventional Music Notation," *Journal of Music Theory* XVI/1-2 (Spring-Winter): 72-101.

Boroda, Moisej G. 1973. "K voprosu o metroritmiceski elementarnoj edinice v muzyke," *Bulletin of the Academy of Science of the Georgian SSR* 71/3: 745-748.

Bridgman, Nanie. 1973. "Catalogue par incipit musicaux," *Informatique et Sciences Humaines* 19 (December): 33-38.

Campos, Arthur Nogueira. 1973. "Music Analysis," *Computational Musicology Newsletter* I/1: 14.

Charnassé, Hélène. 1973. "Musicologie et Informatique: Les grands axes de recherche," *Informatique et Sciences Humaines* 19 (December): 19-31.

Clifton, Thomas. 1973. "Music and the a priori," *Journal of Music Theory* 17/1: 66-85.

Ducasse, Henri. 1973a. "Introduction," *Informatique et Sciences Humaines* 19 (December): 7-15.

_________. 1973b. "Compte-rendu de Journees d'Etudes d'Informatique Musicale," *Informatique et Sciences Humaines* 19 (December): 67-70.

Entwisle, Jeffrey Lynn. 1973. Visual Perception and Analysis of Musical Scores, B.S. thesis. Boston, MA: Massachusetts Institute of Technology, Department of Humanities.

Forte, Allen. 1973. *The Structure of Atonal Music*. New Haven: Yale University Press.

Greussay, Patrick. 1973a. "Procédures LISP d'analyse de relations harmoniques," *Artinfo-Musinfo* 13: 1-7.

_________. 1973b. Modèles de descriptions symboliques en analyse musicale. Ph.D. dissertation. Paris, France: University of Paris VIII.

Gross, Dorothy Susan. 1973. "Music Department," *Computational Musicology Newsletter* I/1: 14.

Halmos, István. 1973. "Automation of Analysis and Classification of Folk Tunes. Part One: Comparison Note by Note," *Computational Musicology Newsletter* I/1: 15.

Heckmann, Harald. 1973a. "Musik - Dokumentation, Musik - Information," *Neue Zeitschrift für Musik* 134/8: 479-482.

_________. 1973b. "Musikwissenschaft, Dokumentation, Information," *Musicae Scientae Collectanea. Festschrift Karl Gustav Fellerer zum 70. Geburtstag*, edited by Heinrich Hüschen. Köln. pp. 219-224.
Hofstetter, Fred T. 1973. "Computer Applications to Music at OSU," *Computational Musicology Newsletter* I/1: 2.
Iglickij, M. A. 1973. "Rodstvo tonalnostej i zadaca ob otyskanii modulajacionnych planov," *Muzykalnoje Iskusstvo i Nauka* II: 192-205.
Knowlton, Prentise H. 1973. "Capture and Display of Keyboard Music," *Datamation*: 56-60.
Laske, Otto. 1973a. "On the Methodology and Implementation of a Procedural Theory of Music," *Computational Musicology Newsletter* I/1: 15-16.
_________. 1973b. "Toward a Musical Intelligence System: OBSERVER," *Numus West* IV: 11-16.
Lidov, David, and Jim Gabura. 1973. "A Melody Writing Algorithm Using a Formal Language Model," *Computer Studies in the Humanities and Verbal Behavior* XIV/3-4: 138-148.
Mendel, Arthur, and Thomas Hall. 1973. "Princeton Computer Tools for Musical Research," *Informatique et Sciences Humaines* 19 (December): 39-59. French translation: "Usage de l'ordinateur dans la recherche musicale à Princeton," pp. 61-65.
Moles, Abraham A. 1973. *Kunst & Computer*. Köln: M. DuMont Schauberg.
Moomaw, Charles J. 1973. A PL-1 Program for the Harmonic Analysis of Music by the Theories of Paul Hindemith and Howard Hanson. M.M. thesis. Cincinnati, OH: University of Cincinnati.
Moorer, James Anderson. 1973. "Segmentation and Analysis of Continuous Musical Sound," *Computational Musicology Newsletter* I/1: 3-4.
Morton, Ian A. 1973. "Analysis of Tonal Music at the Level of Perception," *Computational Musicology Newsletter* I/1: 16.
Nattiez, Jean-Jacques. 1973a. "Musical Semiotics," *Computational Musicology Newsletter* I/1: 17.
_________. 1973b. "Linguistics: A New Approach for Musical Analysis?" *International Review of the Aesthetics and Sociology of Music* IV/1 (June): 51-69.
Nelson, Gary Lee. 1973. "COMPOSE: A Program for Musical Composition," *Computational Musicology Newsletter* I/1: 11.
Patrick, Philip Howard. 1973. A Computer Study of a Suspension Formation in the Masses of Josquin Desprez. Ph.D. dissertation. Princeton, NJ: Princeton University.
Raskin, Jeffrey F. 1973. "On Keyboard Input of Music to the Computer," *Computational Musicology Newsletter* I/1: 4.
Rojterstejn, Mihail I. 1973. "Graf i matrica kak instrumenty ladovogo analiza," *Muzykalnoje Iskusstvo i Nauka*. Moskva: Muzyka. pp. 175-189.
Scherrer, Deborah K. 1973. "Computer-Aided Music Analysis," *Computational Musicology Newsletter* I/1: 17.
Shatzkin, Merton. 1973. "Bach Chorales," *Computational Musicology Newsletter* I/1: 17.
Smoliar, Stephen William. 1973. Systemic Aspects of Musical Activity. Technical Report # 28. Haifa, Israel: Israel Institute of Technology.
Suchoff, Benjamin. 1973a. "An Application of GRIPHOS to Bartók's Turkish Folk Music Materials," *Computational Musicology Newsletter* I/1: 18.
_________. 1973b. "Toward a Computer Typography for Music Research: A Progress Report (Review of)," *Computing Review* 14/5 (May): 224-225.
_________. 1973c. "The Computer and Bartók Research in America," *Magyar zenetörténeti Tanulmányok: Mosonyi Mihály és Bartók Béla emlékére* [Studies on the History of

Hungarian Music in Memory of Mihály Mosonyi and Bela Bartók], edited by Ferenc Bonis. Budapest: Zeneműkiadó. pp. 313-327.
Tänzer, Peter. 1973. "Musik und Kybernetik," *Neue Zeitschrift für Musik* 134/8 (1973): 483-492.
Tischler, Hans. 1973. "Parisian Two-Part Organa," *Computational Musicology Newsletter* I/1: 18.
Wagner, Christoph, Ernst Piontek, and Ludwig Teckhaus. 1973. "Piano Learning and Programmed Instruction," *Journal of Research in Music Education* XXI/2 (Summer): 106-22.
Waite, Stephen V. F., et al. 1973. "Annual Bibliography for 1972 and Supplement to Preceding Years," *Computers and the Humanities* VII/4 (March): 229-252.
Wenker, Jerome R. 1973a. "Music Encoding - Keypunch," *Computational Musicology Newsletter* I/1: 6-7.
_________. 1973b. "Editorial Forword," *Computational Musicology Newsletter* I/1: 1-2.
Wittlich, Gary E. 1973a. "Project Score," *Computational Musicology Newsletter* I/1: 6.
_________. 1973b. "Pattern Structure Studies," *Computational Musicology Newsletter* I/1: 19.
_________. 1973c. "Scale Index," *Computational Musicology Newsletter* I/1: 19.

1974

Addison, Don. 1974. "Elements of Style in Performing the Chinese *P'i-p'a*," *Selected Reports in Ethnomusicology* II/1: 118-139.
Alphonce, Bo H. 1974a. The Invariance Matrix. Ph.D. dissertation. New Haven, CT: Yale University.
_________. 1974b. "The Invariance Matrix as an Analytical Tool," *International Musicological Society: Report of the Eleventh Congress, Copenhagen 1972*, edited by Henrik Glahn, Søren Sørensen, and Peter Ryom. Copenhagen: Edition W. Hansen. pp. 228-235.
Anonymous. 1974a. "Directory of Scholars Active," *Computers and the Humanities* VIII/1 (January): 40-55.
Anonymous. 1974b. "Directory of Scholars Active," *Computers and the Humanities* VIII/4 (July): 250-257.
Aranovskij, Mark G. 1974. "Myslenije, jazyk, semantika," *Problemy muzykalnovo myslenija.* Moskow: Muzyka. pp. 90-128.
Baggi, Denis L. 1974. Realization of the Unfigured Bass by Digital Computer. Ph.D. dissertation. Berkeley, CA: University of California.
Barbaud, Pierre. 1974. "Methodes d'analyse de textes harmoniques," *Informatique musicale: Journées d'etude 1973. Textes des conférences E.R.A.T.T.O.*, edited by Hélène Charnassé and Henri Ducasse. Paris: Centre de documentation sciences humaines. pp. 165-176.
Barth-Wehrenalp, Renate. 1974. Studien zu Adan de le Hale. Ph.D. thesis. University of Vienna.
Bauer-Mengelberg, Stefan. 1974. "Digital Alternate Representation of Musical Scores (DARMS)," *Computers and the Humanities* VIII/4 (July): 255.
Bernard, Jean J. 1974. "Sciences exactes et musicologie," *Informatique musicale: Journées d'etude 1973. Textes des conférences E.R.A.T.T.O.*, edited by Hélène Charnassé and Henri Ducasse. Paris: Centre de documentation sciences humaines. pp. 115-124.
Böker-Heil, Norbert. 1974a. "Der Zustand polyphoner Strukturen: Ein Beispiel Automatischer Stilbeschreibung," *International Musicological Society: Report of the Eleventh*

Congress, Copenhagen 1972, edited by Henrik Glahn, Søren Sørensen, and Peter Ryom. Copenhagen: Edition W. Hansen. pp. 108-120.

_________. 1974b. "Musikalische Stilanalyse und Computer. Einige grundsätzliche Erwägungen," *International Musicological Society: Report of the Eleventh Congress, Copenhagen 1972*, edited by Henrik Glahn, Søren Sørensen, and Peter Ryom. Copenhagen: Edition W. Hansen. pp. 45-50.

Boroda, Moisej G. 1974. "O castotnoj strukture muzykalnych soobscenij," *Bulletin of the Academy of Science of the Georgian SSR* 76/2: 178-202.

Byrd, Donald Alvin. 1974. "A System for Music Printing by Computer," *Computers and the Humanities* VIII/3 (May): 161-172.

Castman, Bernt, and Lars Elve Larsson. 1974. Ett dataprogram (RHYTHMSYVARD) för bearbetning av rytmiska duraionsvärden. Mimeographed. Uppsala, Sweden: Instutionen för Musikvetenskap.

Charnassé, Hélène. 1974. "Transcrition Automatique de Tablatures," *Informatique musicale: Journées d'etude 1973. Textes des conférences E.R.A.T.T.O.*, edited by Hélène Charnassé and Henri Ducasse. Paris: Centre de documentation sciences humaines. pp. 25-47.

Charnassé, Hélène, and Henri Ducasse. Eds. 1974. *Informatique musicale: Journées d'etude 1973. Textes des conférences E.R.A.T.T.O.* Paris: Centre de documentation sciences humaines.

Chenoweth, Vida. 1974. *Melodic Perception and Analysis: A Manual on Ethnic Melody.* Ukarumpa: Summer Institute of Linguistics.

Cohen, Dalia, and Ruth Katz. 1974. "Quantitative Analysis of Monophonic Music: Towards a More Precise Definition of Style," *Orbis Musicae* III-IV: 83-96.

Couturier, Marcel. 1974. "L'emploi du langage forcod en collecte et traitement d'inventaires après deces," *Informatique musicale: Journées d'etude 1973. Textes des conférences E.R.A.T.T.O.*, edited by Hélène Charnassé and Henri Ducasse. Paris: Centre de documentation sciences humaines. pp. 104-114.

Demorgon, Jacques. 1974. Une communication de masse: la chanson a succes. Essai d'une premiere systematisation de son etude en France de 1946 a 1966. Ph.D. dissertation. Paris, France: Department of Sociology. University of Paris V.

Ducasse, Henri. 1974. "Un problem de saisie de l'information," *Informatique musicale: Journées d'etude 1973. Textes des conférences E.R.A.T.T.O.*, edited by Hélène Charnassé and Henri Ducasse. Paris: Centre de documentation sciences humaines. pp. 48-65.

Egeland Hansen, Finn. 1974. "Tonality in Gregorian Chant Based on an Investigation of the Melodies in Codex H 159, Montpellier," *[IMS] Report of the Eleventh Congress, Copenhagen, 1972*, edited by Henrik Glahn, Søren Sørensen, Peter Ryom. Copenhagen: Edition W. Hansen. pp. 425-431.

Feld, Steven. 1974. "Linguistic Models in Ethnomusicology," *Ethnomusicology* XVIII/2 (May): 197-217.

Frankel, Robert E., Stanley J. Rosenschein, and Stephen W. Smoliar. 1974. The Modeling of Musical Perception on a Digital Computer Via Schenkerian Theory. Music Report No. 4, April 1975. Philadelphia: Moore School of Electrical Engineering, University of Pennsylvania.

Fraser, Robert. 1974. "Computer Implementation of Musical Linguistics," *Computers and the Humanities* VIII/1 (January): 49-50.

Gasparov, Boris M. 1974a. "O nekotorych principach strukturnogo analiza muzyki," *Problemy muzykalnogo myshlenija.* Moskow: Muzyka. 129-152.

_________. 1974b. "Nekotorye Deskriptivnye Problemy Muzykal'noj Semantiki," *Acta et Commentationes Universitatis Tartuensis, Trudy po Znakovym Sistemam* 8: 120-137.

Greussay, Patrick. 1974. "Structures de controle en description symbolique d'analyses musicales," *Informatique musicale: Journées d'etude 1973. Textes des conférences E.R.A.T.T.O.*, edited by Hélène Charnassé and Henri Ducasse. Paris, France: Centre de documentation sciences humaines. pp. 177-203.

Hofstetter, Fred T. 1974. A Quantitative Method for the Study of Musical Style Applied to National Differences and Similarities in the Use of Melodic Intervals During the Mid-Nineteenth to Early Twentieth Centuries. Ph.D. dissertation. Columbus, OH: The Ohio State University.

Huber, Alfred. 1974. "Informationstheorie und Musikanalyse," *Melos* XLI/4 (July-August): 207-210.

Huglo, Michel. 1974. "Le classement par ordinateur des listes de repons liturgiques: les problemes musicologiques," *Informatique musicale: Journées d'etude 1973. Textes des conférences E.R.A.T.T.O.*, edited by Hélène Charnassé and Henri Ducasse. Paris: Centre de documentation sciences humaines. pp. 125-134.

Huglo, Michel, and Knud Ottosen. 1974. "Le classement par ordinateur des listes de repons liturgiques, *Informatique musicale: Journées d'etude 1973. Textes des conférences E.R.A.T.T.O.*, edited by Hélène Charnassé and Henri Ducasse. Paris: Centre de documentation sciences humaines. pp. 125-143.

Jansen, Paule. 1974. "Emploi de l'ordinateur pour le depouillement des periodiques litteraires," *Informatique musicale: Journées d'etude 1973. Textes des conférences E.R.A.T.T.O.*, edited by Hélène Charnassé and Henri Ducasse. Paris: Centre de documentation sciences humaines. pp. 93-103.

Kluge, Reiner. 1974a. *Faktorenanalytische Typenbestimmung an Volksliedmelodien*. Beiträge zur musikwissenschaftlichen Forschung in der DDR 6. Leipzig: Deutscher Verlag für Musik.

_________. 1974b. "Was kann die Kybernetik der Musikwissenschaft helfen?," *Report of the Eleventh Congress, Copenhagen*, 1972, edited by Henrik Glahn, Søren Sørensen, and Peter Ryom. Copenhagen: Edition W. Hansen. pp. 486-495.

Kostka, Stephan M. 1974. *A Bibliography of Computer Applications in Music*. Hackensack, NJ: Joseph Boonin.

Labussiere, Annie. 1974. "Codage des structures rythmo-melodiques a partier de creations vocales," *Informatique musicale: Journées d'etude 1973. Textes des conférences E.R.A.T.T.O.*, edited by Hélène Charnassé and Henri Ducasse. Paris: Centre de documentation sciences humaines. pp. 66-92.

Laske, Otto. 1974a. "In Search of a Generative Grammar for Music," *Perspectives of New Music* XII/1-2 (Autumn-Summer): 351-378. Reprinted in *Machine Models of Music*, edited by Stephen M. Schwanauer and David A. Levitt. Cambridge, MA: The MIT Press, 1993. pp. 214-240.

_________. 1974b. "Toward a Center for Studies in Musical Intelligence," *Numus West* V: 44-46.

_________. 1974c. "The Information Processing Approach to Musical Cognition," *Interface* III/2 (December): 109-136.

_________. 1974d. "Musical Acoustics (Sonology): A Questionable Science Reconsidered," *Numus-West* 6: 35-40.

Leipp, Emile, and Moncef Mlouka. 1974. "Apports de l'acoustique musicale a l'etude digitale des musiques ethniques," *Informatique musicale: Journées d'etude 1973. Textes des *conférences E.R.A.T.T.O.*, edited by Hélène Charnassé and Henri Ducasse. Paris: Centre de documentation sciences humaines. pp. 144-164.

Lincoln, Harry B. 1974. "Use of the Computer in Music Research: A Short Report on Accomplishments, Limitations, and Future Needs," *Computers and the Humanities* VIII/5-6 (September-November): 285-289.

Ludvová, Jitka. 1974. "The Application of Analytical Methods of Information Theory to Tonal Music," *De musica disputationes Pragenses* II/4: 72-85.

Maultsby, Portia Katrenia. 1974. Afro-American Religious Music: 1619-1861. Historical Development and Computer Analysis of one Hundred Sprituals. Ph.D. dissertation. Madison, WI: The University of Wisconsin.

McMullen, Patrick T. 1974. "Influence of Number of Different Pitches and Melodic Redundancy on Preference Responses," *Journal of Research in Music Education* XXII: 198-204.

Mermet, Jean, and Denis Jaeger. 1974. "Un peripherique d'ordinateur a l'usage des musiciens," *Informatique musicale: Journées d'etude 1973. Textes des conférences E.R.A.T.T.O.*, edited by Hélène Charnassé and Henri Ducasse. Paris: Centre de documentation sciences humaines. pp. 204-218.

Meylan, Raymond. 1974. "Limites de l'objectivite dans les ecritures instrumentales de la Renaissance," *Informatique musicale: Journées d'etude 1973. Textes des conférences E.R.A.T.T.O.*, edited by Hélène Charnassé and Henri Ducasse. Paris: Centre de documentation sciences humaines. pp. 1-9.

Morse, Margaret Beverly. 1974. A Quantitative Stylistic Analysis of the Agnus Dei Mass Movements of Guillaume Dufay Supporting the Doubtful Authenticity of the Missa Caput. M.M. thesis. West Hartford, CT: Hartt College of Music.

Morton, Ian A. 1974a. "Analysis of Tonal Music at the Level of Perception," *Computers in the Humanities*, edited by J. L. Mitchel. Minneapolis: University of Minnesota Press. pp. 261-266.

__________. 1974b. "Judgmental Factors in the Perception of Tonal Music," *Computers and the Humanities* VIII/1 (January): 51.

Nake, Frieder. 1974. *Ästhetik als Informationsverarbeitung. Grundlagen und Anwendungen der Informatik im Bereich ästhetischer Produktion und Kritik.* Wien: Springer.

Nelson, Gary Lee. 1974a. Anton Webern's 'Five Canons' op. 16: A Test Case for Computer-Aided Analysis and Synthesis of Musical Style. Ph.D. dissertation. St Louis, MO: Washington University.

__________. 1974b. "Pattern Recognition in Musical Score," *Computers and the Humanities* VIII/1 (January): 50-51.

Patrick, P. Howard. 1974. "A Computer Study of a Suspension Formation in the Masses of Josquin Desprez," *Computer and the Humanities* VIII/5-6 (September-November): 321-331.

Piotrowski, Zbigniew. 1974. "O zastosowaniu komputerow w muzyce mowi Lejaren Hiller," *Ruch Muzyczny* [Poland] IV (February): 3-4.

Pletka, Vaclav. 1974. "Methodologische Probleme der Arbeiterliedforschung," *Arbeiterklasse und Musik: theoretische Positionen in der deutschen Arbeiterklasse zur Musikkultur vor 1945: Eine Dokumentation des Arbeiterliederarchivs*, edited by Charlotte Albrecht, Inge Lammel, Ilse Schütt, and Marlene Weller. Berlin: Akademie der Künste der Deutschen Demokratischen Republik. pp. 32-35.

Rader, Gary M. 1974. "A Method for Composing Simple Traditional Music by Computer," *Communications of the ACM* November 1974: 631-638. Reprinted in *Machine Models of Music*, edited by Stephen M. Schwanauer and David A. Levitt. Cambridge, MA: The MIT Press, 1993. pp. 242-260.

Riotte, Andre. 1974. "Informatique musicale: jonction nouvelle entre art et science," *Euro-Spectra* XIII/1 (March): 2-15.

Rojterstejn, Mihail I. 1974. "'Muzykalnye' structury v poezii Bloka," *O Muzyke. Problemy analiza: k semidesiatiletiiu so dnia rozhdeniia i piatidesiatiletiiu nauchno-pedagogicheskoi deiatel'nosti zasluzhennogo deiatelia iskusstv RSFSR, doktora iskusstvovedeniia professora Viktora Abramovicha TSukkermana*, edited by V. P. Bobrovskii and G. L. Golovinskii. Moskow: Sovetskij Kompozitor. pp. 323-343.

Silverman, Faye-Ellen. 1974. "Report from New York City: Computer Conference, June 1973," *Current Musicology* 17 (January): 77-80.

Smoliar, Stephen William. 1974a. "Process Structuring and Music Theory," *Journal of Music Theory* XVIII/2 (Autumn): 308-336. Reprinted in *Machine Models of Music*, edited by Stephen M. Schwanauer and David A. Levitt. Cambridge, MA: The MIT Press, 1993. pp. 188-212.

_________. 1974b. "An Interactive Computer Music Facility," *Computers and the Humanities* VIII/4 (July): 254-255.

Smoliar, Stephen W., and M. Joseph Willson. 1974. "Proposal for an Interactive Computer-Music Facility," *Numus-West* V: 39-43.

Vercoe, Barry L. 1974. "Music computation conference: a report and summary," *Perspectives of New Music* XIII/1 (Fall): 234-238.

Waite, Stephen V. F., et al. 1974. "Annual Bibliography for 1973 and Supplement to Preceding Years," *Computers and the Humanities* VIII/2 (March): 99-113.

Wenker, Jerome R. 1974. "MUSTRAN II: A Foundation for Computational Musicology," *Computers in the Humanities*, edited by J. L. Mitchell. Edinburgh: Edinburgh University Press. pp. 267-280.

Zwink, Eberhard. 1974. *Paul Hindemiths "Unterweisung im Tonsatz" als Konsequenz der Entwicklung seiner Kompositionstechnik. Graphische und Statistische Musikanalyse.* Göppingen: Alfred Kümmerle.

1975

Adamčiak, Milan. 1975. "Die semiotische Analyse des Musikwerkes," *Methoden der ethnomusikologischen Analyse*, edited by Oskár Elschek. Bratislava : Sekcia hudobnej vedy-etnomuzikológia, Umenovedný ústav, Slovenská akademia vied. p. 12.

Anonymous. 1975a. "Directory of Scholars Active," *Computers and the Humanities* IX/1 (January): 30-35.

Anonymous. 1975b. "Directory of Scholars Active," *Computers and the Humanities* IX/4 (July): 187-196.

Baroni, Mario, and Carlo Jacoboni. 1975. "Analysis and Generation of Bach's Choral melodies," *Actes du 1er congress international de semiotique musicale*, edited by Gino Stefani. Pesaro: Centro di iniziativa culturale. pp. 125-134.

Bartmiński, Jerzy. 1975. "Komputery w badaniach nat pieśnią ludową," *Literatura Ludowa* 19 (January-February): 54-56.

Bielawski, Ludwik. 1975. "Ähnlichkeiten und Zusammenhänge – System und Syntagma in der ethnomusikologischen Analyse," *Methoden der ethnomusikologischen Analyse*, edited by Oskár Elschek. Bratislava: Sekcia hudobnej vedy-etnomuzikológia, Umenovedný ústav, Slovenská akademia vied. pp. 32-33.

Boody, Charles George. 1975. Non-Compositional Applications of the Computer to Music Published in America Through June of 1972. Ph.D. dissertation. Minneapolis, MN: University of Minnesota.

Braun, Hartmut. 1975. "Das Problem der Zeilenbegrenzung," *Methoden der ethnomusikologischen Analyse*, edited by Oskár Elschek. Bratislava: Sekcia hudobnej vedy-etnomuzikológia, Umenovedný ústav, Slovenská akademia vied. pp. 40-41.

Byrd, Donald Alvin. 1975. "Music Programs at Indiana University," *Computational Musicology Newsletter* II/1: 2-4.

Chalupka, Lubomír. 1975. "Kybernetik und EDV im Dienste der Musikanalyse," *Methoden der ethnomusikologischen Analyse*, edited by Oskár Elschek. Bratislava : Sekcia hudobnej vedy-etnomuzikológia, Umenovedný ústav, Slovenská akademia vied. pp. 7-8.

Charnassé, Hélène, and Henri Ducasse. 1975. "Automated Tablature Transcription," *Computational Musicology Newsletter* II/1: 9-10.

Elschek, Oskár, et al. 1975a. "Protokoll der Schlußsitzung des ethnomusikologischen Seminars," *Methoden der ethnomusikologischen Analyse*, edited by Oskár Elschek. Bratislava: Sekcia hudobnej vedy-etnomuzikológia, Umenovedný ústav, Slovenská akademia vied. pp. 53-57.

Elschek, Oskár, et al. 1975b. "Protokoll der geschlossenen Sitzung der Study Group of Folk Music Systematisation of Folk Music des IFMC (26. September 1974)," *Methoden der ethnomusikologischen Analyse*, edited by Oskár Elschek. Bratislava: Sekcia hudobnej vedy-etnomuzikológia, Umenovedný ústav, Slovenská akademia vied. pp. 59-62.

Elscheková, Alica. 1975a. "Systematisierung, Klassifikation und Katalogisierung von Volksliedweisen," *Handbuch des Volksliedes*, edited by Rolf Wilhelm Brednich, Lutz Röhrich and Wolfgang Suppan, vol. 2. München: Fink. pp. 549-582.

_________. 1975b. "Die Entwicklung der ethnomusikologischen Analyse," *Methoden der ethnomusikologischen Analyse*, edited by Oskár Elschek. Bratislava : Sekcia hudobnej vedy-etnomuzikológia, Umenovedný ústav, Slovenská akademia vied. pp. 20-21.

Erickson, Raymond F. 1975a. "'The DARMS Project': A Status Report," *Computers and the Humanities* IX/6 (November): 291-298.

_________. 1975b. "'The Darms Project': A Status Report," *Computational Musicology Newsletter* II/1: 7-8.

Ermedahl, Gunnar. 1975. "Notskrift och inspelning som underlag for musikalisk analys," *Svensk Tidskrift for Musikforskning* LVII/2: 65-66.

Galko, Ladislav. 1975. "Die musikalische Liedanalyse für einen Inzipienkatalog," *Methoden der ethnomusikologischen Analyse*, edited by Oskár Elschek. Bratislava: Sekcia hudobnej vedy-etnomuzikológia, Umenovedný ústav, Slovenská akademia vied. pp. 38-39.

Gomberg, David Aaron. 1975. A Computer-Oriented System for Music Printing. D.Sc. dissertation. Saint Louis, MO: Washington University.

Gross, Dorothy Susan. 1975a. A Set of Computer Programs to Aid in Music Analysis, Ph.D. dissertation. Bloomington, IN: Indiana University.

_________. 1975b. "A Computer Package for Music Analysis," *Proceedings of the 2nd Indiana University Computer Network Conference on Instructional Computer Applications*. [s.l.]: Indiana University Computing Network. pp. 6-10.

_________. 1975c. "A Set of Computer Prtograms to Aid in Music Analysis," *Computational Musicology Newsletter* II/1: 16.

Hall, Thomas B. 1975. "Some computer aids for the preparation of critical editions of Renaissance Music," *Tijdschrift van de Vereniging voor Nederlandse Muziek Geschiedenis* 25/1: 38-53.

Halmos, István, Miklós Havass, and György Köszegi. 1975. Experiments in Automation of Analysis, Systematization, and Listing of Monodic Folk Tunes. Budapest, Hungary: Institute of Musicology, Hungarian Academy of Sciences.

Hinderer, Drew Elliott. 1975. Music Analysis and the Genuine Instance Problem. PhD thesis, The University of Michigan.

Hoshovskyj, Vladimir. 1975. "Katalogisierungsanalyse – Algorithmus einer umfassenden formalisierten Beschreibung," *Methoden der ethnomusikologischen Analyse*, edited by Oskár Elschek. Bratislava: Sekcia hudobnej vedy-etnomuzikológia, Umenovedný ústav, Slovenská akademia vied. pp. 28-29.

Imberty, Michel. 1975. "Sémantique musicale: Approche structural, approche expérimentale," *Actes du 1er congress international de semiotique musicale*, edited by Gino Stefani. Pesaro: Centro di iniziativa culturale. pp. 225-244.

Kassler, Michael. 1975a. "Explication of Theories of Tonality," *Computational Musicology Newsletter* II/1: 17.

_________. 1975b. Proving Musical Theorems I: The Middleground of Heinrich Schenker's Theory of Tonality. Technical Report No. 103. Sydney: The University of Sydney, Basser Department of Computer Science.

_________. 1975c. "Explication of Theories of Tonalities," *Computers and the Humanities* IX/4 (July): 192-193.

Kawano, Hiroshi. 1975. "The Informational Analysis of Musical Communication," *Computational Musicology Newsletter* II/1: 15.

Laske, Otto. 1975a. *Introduction to a Generative Theory of Music*. Sonological Reports. Utrecht: Institute for Sonology.

_________. 1975b. "Musical Semantics: A Procedural Point of View," *Actes du 1er congress international de semiotique musicale*, edited by Gino Stefani. Pesaro: Centro di iniziativa culturale. pp. 214-224.

_________. 1975c. "Sufficiency Analysis of Music-Syntactic Composition," *Computers and the Humanities* IX/1 (January): 33.

_________. 1975d. "Studies in Musical Problem Solving," *Computers and the Humanities* IX/4 (July): 192.

Levy, Morten. 1975. "On the Problem of Defining Musical Units," *Actes du 1er congress international de semiotique musicale*, edited by Gino Stefani. Pesaro: Centro di iniziativa culturale. pp. 135-149.

Lidov, David. 1975. *On Musical Phrase*. Montréal: Les Presses de l'Université.

Moorer, James Anderson. 1975. On the Segmentation and Analysis of Continuous Musical Sound by Digital Computer. Ph.D. dissertation. Stanford, CA: Stanford University.

Nattiez, Jean-Jacques. 1975. "From Taxonomic Analysis to Stylistic Characterization: Debussy's Syrinx," *Actes du 1er congress international de semiotique musicale*, edited by Gino Stefani. Pesaro: Centro di iniziativa culturale. pp. 83-110.

Pawlak, Aleksander. 1975. "Die Analyse und Klassifikation der Melodien aus der Region Kujawa," *Methoden der ethnomusikologischen Analyse*, edited by Oskár Elschek. Bratislava: Sekcia hudobnej vedy-etnomuzikológia, Umenovedný ústav, Slovenská akademia vied. pp. 36-37.

Peterson, Don Laurel. 1975. Tonal Characteristics in the Kyrie and Sanctus Sections of Twelve L'homme arme Masses: A Computer-Assisted Study. Ph.D. dissertation. Madison, WI: University of Wisconsin.

Prerau, David S. 1975. "DO-RE-MI: A Program that Recognizes Music Notation," *Computers and the Humanities* IX/1 (January): 25-29.

Rader, Gary M. 1975. "A Method for Composing Simple Traditional Music by Computer," *Computational Musicology Newsletter* II/1: 14.
Smoliar, Stephen William. 1975a. "Proposal for an Interactive Computer-Music Facility," *Computational Musicology Newsletter* II/1: 5-6.
_________. 1975b. "Process Structuring and Music Theory," *Computational Musicology Newsletter* II/1: 17.
Štědroň, Miloš. 1975. "K analýze vokální melodiky Janáčkovy opery Věc Makropulos s využitím samočinného počítače," *Hudebni Veda* [Czechoslovakia] XII/1: 46-64.
Sundberg, Johan, and Björn Lindblom. 1975. "A Generative Theory of Swedish Nursery Tunes," *Actes du 1er congress international de semiotique musicale*, edited by Gino Stefani. Pesaro: Centro di iniziativa culturale. pp. 111-124.
Victor, Michele. 1975. "L'Informatique musicale," *Musique En jeu* (France) XVIII (April): 45-62.
Völz, Horst. 1975. "Beitrag zur formalen Musikanalyse und -synthese," *Beiträge zur Musikwissenschaft* XVII/2-3: 127-154.
Waite, Stephen V. F., et al. 1975. "Annual Bibliography for 1974 and Supplement to Preceding Years," *Computers and the Humanities* IX/3 (May): 127-144.
Winckel, Fritz. 1975. "Das Wirkgefuge von Musikstrukturen in der Analyse durch Computer und Kybernetik," *Festschrift Kurt Blaukopf*, edited by Irmgard Bontinck and Otto Brusatti. Wien: Universal Edition. pp. 156-163.

1976

Adams, Charles R. 1976. "Melodic Contour Typology," *Ethnomusicology* XX/2 (May): 179-215.
Allen, John R. Ed. 1976. "Directory of Scholars Active," *Computers and the Humanities* X/1 (January-February): 41-55.
Ballová, Luba. 1976a. "Methoden der Quantifizierung von Melodieähnlichkeiten," *Hudobná klasifikácia a samocinné pocitace: predbezná zpráva 6. Etnomuzikologického seminára = Musikklassifikation und elektronische Datenverarbeitung: Vorbericht des 6. Ethnomusikologischen Seminars, Kocovce, 6.-10. Október 1975*, edited by Oskár Elschek. Bratislava: Sekcia hudobnej vedy-etnomuzikológia, Umenovedný ústav, Slovenská akademia vied. 2 p.
_________. 1976b. "Štruktúra testovacích súborov pre výskum podobnosti" ["The structure of test sets in the investigation of similarities"], *Lidová píseň a samočinný počítač III: Sborník materiálů ze 3. semináře o využití samočinného počítače při studiu lidové písně (Brno 15.-16.10.1974)*, ed. by Dušan Holý, Karel Pala, and Miloš Štědroň. Praha: Státni pedagogické nakladatelstvi. pp. 211-218.
Baroni, Mario, and Carlo Jacoboni. 1976. *Verso una grammatica della melodia*. Bologna, Italy: Università Studi di Bologna, 1976.
Bartmiński, Jerzy, et al. 1976. "Diskuse," *Lidová píseň a samočinný počítač III: Sborník materiálů ze 3. semináře o využití samočinného počítače při studiu lidové písně (Brno 15.-16.10.1974)*, ed. by Dušan Holý, Karel Pala, and Miloš Štědroň. Praha: Státni pedagogické nakladatelstvi. pp. 357-411.
Bauer, Hans-Joachim. 1976. "Statistik, eine objektive Methode zur Analyse von Kunst?" *International Review of the Aesthetics and Sociology of Music* VII/2 (December): 249-263.
Blombach, Ann Kariger. 1976. A Conceptual Framework for the Use of the Computer in Music Analysis. Ph.D. dissertation. Columbus, OH: Ohio State University.

Böker-Heil, Norbert. 1976. "Die maschinenverständliche Darstellung musikalischer Sachverhalte," *Hudobná klasifikácia a samocinné pocitace: predbezná zpráva 6. Etnomuzikologického seminára = Musikklassifikation und elektronische Datenverarbeitung: Vorbericht des 6. Ethnomusikologischen Seminars, Kocovce, 6.-10. Október 1975*, edited by Oskár Elschek. Bratislava: Sekcia hudobnej vedy-etnomuzikológia, Umenovedný ústav, Slovenská akademia vied. 2 p.

Byrd, Donald Alvin. 1976. "Music Notation by Computer," *Computers and the Humanities* X/1 (January-February): 51-52.

Chalupková, Viera, and Lubomír Chalupka. 1976. "Die Bearbeitung von Volksliedern aus dem Záhorie auf einer EDV-Anlage," *Hudobná klasifikácia a samocinné pocitace: predbezná zpráva 6. Etnomuzikologického seminára = Musikklassifikation und elektronische Datenverarbeitung: Vorbericht des 6. Ethnomusikologischen Seminars, Kocovce, 6.-10. Október 1975*, edited by Oskár Elschek. Bratislava: Sekcia hudobnej vedy-etnomuzikológia, Umenovedný ústav, Slovenská akademia vied. 2 p.

Charnassé, Hélène. 1976. "La transcription automatique des tablatures: le language d'entree," *Proceedings of the Second Annual Music Computation Conference: November 7-9, 1975 at the University of Illinois at Urbana-Champaign*, compiled by James Beauchamp and John Melby. Urbana, IL: Office of Continuing Education and Public Service in Music, University of Illinois. pp. 13-27.

Cinková, Irena. 1976. "Využití informačního szstému asti pro analýzu a třídění lidových písní," *Lidová píseň a samočinný počítač III: Sborník materiálů ze 3. semináře o využití samočinného počítače při studiu lidové písně (Brno 15.-16.10.1974)*, ed. by Dušan Holý, Karel Pala, and Miloš Štědroň. Praha: Státni pedagogické nakladatelstvi. pp. 183-195.

Ducasse, Henri, and Denys Pages. 1976. "Un systeme de constitution et d'exploitation de donnees pour l'identification et l'analyse de textes musicaux," *Revue de Musicologie* [France] LXII/2: 292-293.

Elschek, Oskár. Ed. 1976a. *Hudobná klasifikácia a samocinné pocitace: predbezná zpráva 6. Etnomuzikologického seminára = Musikklassifikation und elektronische Datenverarbeitung: Vorbericht des 6. Ethnomusikologischen Seminars, Kocovce, 6.-10. Október 1975*. Bratislava: Sekcia hudobnej vedy-etnomuzikológia, Umenovedný ústav, Slovenská akademia vied.

_________. 1976b. "Die Anwendungsbereiche der gegenwärtigen Musikklassifikation," *Hudobná klasifikácia a samocinné pocitace: predbezná zpráva 6. Etnomuzikologického seminára = Musikklassifikation und elektronische Datenverarbeitung: Vorbericht des 6. Ethnomusikologischen Seminars, Kocovce, 6.-10. Október 1975*, edited by Oskár Elschek. Bratislava: Sekcia hudobnej vedy-etnomuzikológia, Umenovedný ústav, Slovenská akademia vied. 2 p.

Elschek, Oskár, et al. 1976. "Protokoll der Schlußsitzung des ethnomusikologischen Seminars," *Hudobná klasifikácia a samocinné pocitace: predbezná zpráva 6. Etnomuzikologického seminára = Musikklassifikation und elektronische Datenverarbeitung: Vorbericht des 6. Ethnomusikologischen Seminars, Kocovce, 6.-10. Október 1975*, edited by Oskár Elschek. Bratislava: Sekcia hudobnej vedy-etnomuzikológia, Umenovedný ústav, Slovenská akademia vied. 6 p.

Elscheková, Alica. 1976a. "Klasifikácia krátkych motivických úsekov nestrofických i strofických piesní tradičnými i netradičnými technikami," *Lidová píseň a samočinný počítač III: Sborník materiálů ze 3. semináře o využití samočinného počítače při studiu lidové písně (Brno 15.-16.10.1974)*, ed. by Dušan Holý, Karel Pala, and Miloš Štědroň. Praha: Státni pedagogické nakladatelstvi. pp. 219-243.

__________. 1976b. "Entwicklung der ethnomusikalischen Klassifikation," *Hudobná klasifikácia a samocinné pocitace: predbezná zpráva 6. Etnomuzikologického seminára = Musikklassifikation und elektronische Datenverarbeitung: Vorbericht des 6. Ethnomusikologischen Seminars, Kocovce, 6.-10. Október 1975*, edited by Oskár Elschek. Bratislava: Sekcia hudobnej vedy-etnomuzikológia, Umenovedný ústav, Slovenská akademia vied. 3 p.

Erickson, Raymond F. 1976. DARMS: A Reference Manual. New York: Department of Music, Queens College.

Fornůsek, Jaroslav. 1976. "Vyžití existujících projectů pro spraování dat o lidové písni," *Lidová píseň a samočinný počítač III: Sborník materiálů ze 3. semináře o využití samočinného počítače při studiu lidové písně (Brno 15.-16.10.1974)*, ed. by Dušan Holý, Karel Pala, and Miloš Štědroň. Praha: Státni pedagogické nakladatelstvi. pp. 45-55.

Frankel, Robert E., Stanley J. Rosenschein, and Stephen W. Smoliar. 1976a. Schenker's Theory of Tonal Music: Its Explication Through Computational Processes. Music Project Report No. 7. Philadelphia: University of Pennsylvania, Department of Computer and Information Science.

Frankel, Robert E., Stanley J. Rosenschein, and Stephen W. Smoliar. 1976b. "A LISP-Based System for the Study of Schenkerian Analysis," *Computers and the Humanities* X/1 (January-February): 21-32.

Gelnár, Jaromír. 1976. "Die Beziehungen zwischen dem Musikmaterial und dem Klassifikationssystem," *Hudobná klasifikácia a samocinné pocitace: predbezná zpráva 6. Etnomuzikologického seminára = Musikklassifikation und elektronische Datenverarbeitung: Vorbericht des 6. Ethnomusikologischen Seminars, Kocovce, 6.-10. Október 1975*, edited by Oskár Elschek. Bratislava: Sekcia hudobnej vedy-etnomuzikológia, Umenovedný ústav, Slovenská akademia vied. 2 p.

Gelnár, Jaromír, and Lubomír Šváb. 1976. "Analýza Rytmického průběhu ve folklórních nápěvech pmocí matematických metod," *Lidová píseň a samočinný počítač III: Sborník materiálů ze 3. semináře o využití samočinného počítače při studiu lidové písně (Brno 15.-16.10.1974)*, ed. by Dušan Holý, Karel Pala, and Miloš Štědroň. Praha: Státni pedagogické nakladatelstvi. pp. 245-252.

Halmos, István. 1976. "Experiments in Automation of Analysis, Systematization and Listing of Monodic Folk Tunes," *Hudobná klasifikácia a samocinné pocitace: predbezná zpráva 6. Etnomuzikologického seminára = Musikklassifikation und elektronische Datenverarbeitung: Vorbericht des 6. Ethnomusikologischen Seminars, Kocovce, 6.-10. Október 1975*, edited by Oskár Elschek. Bratislava: Sekcia hudobnej vedy-etnomuzikológia, Umenovedný ústav, Slovenská akademia vied. 2 p.

Henriksen, Jon Petter. 1976. Satsteknisk analyse ved hjelp av datamaskin. En musikologisk vinning? M.A. thesis. University of Oslo.

Henry, Edward O. 1976. "The Variety of Music in a North Indian Village: Reassessing Cantometrics," *Ethnomusicology* XX/1 (January): 49-66.

Holý, Dušan. 1976a. "Projekt der Dokumentation und Klassifikation des Volksliedes auf der Grundlage des ASTI Informationssystems," *Hudobná klasifikácia a samocinné pocitace: predbezná zpráva 6. Etnomuzikologického seminára = Musikklassifikation und elektronische Datenverarbeitung: Vorbericht des 6. Ethnomusikologischen Seminars, Kocovce, 6.-10. Október 1975*, edited by Oskár Elschek. Bratislava: Sekcia hudobnej vedy-etnomuzikológia, Umenovedný ústav, Slovenská akademia vied. 3 p.

__________. 1976b. "Dosavadní postupy a výsledky studia lidové písně pomocí smočinného počítače na půdě ČSSR," *Lidová píseň a samočinný počítač III: Sborník materiálů ze 3. semináře o využití samočinného počítače při studiu lidové písně (Brno 15.-*

16.10.1974), ed. by Dušan Holý, Karel Pala, and Miloš Štědroň. Praha: Státni pedagogické nakladatelstvi. pp. 25-35.

_________. 1976c. "Glosy k dokumentačnímu záznamu, segmentaci a popisu tematické výstavby lidové písně," *Lidová píseň a samočinný počítač III: Sborník materiálů ze 3. semináře o využití samočinného počítače při studiu lidové písně (Brno 15.-16.10.1974)*, ed. by Dušan Holý, Karel Pala, and Miloš Štědroň. Praha: Státni pedagogické nakladatelstvi. pp. 155-182.

Holý, Dušan, Karel Pala, and Miloš Štědroň. Eds. 1976. *Lidová píseň a samočinný počítač III: Sborník materiálů ze 3. semináře o využití samočinného počítače při studiu lidové písně (Brno 15.-16.10.1974)*. Praha: Státni pedagogické nakladatelstvi.

Kaden, Christian. 1976. "Strukturelle Segmentierung von Musik - Probleme, Schwierigkeiten, Möglichkeiten," *Beiträge zur Musikwissenschaft* 18: 149-162 and 293-334.

Kluge, Reiner. 1976a. "Anmerkungen zur Rolle des Rechenverfahrens im musikwissenschaftlichen Experiment," *International Review of the Aesthetics and Sociology of Music* VII/1: 5-42.

_________. 1976b. "Über typologische Klassifikation von Melodien und elektronische Datenverarbeitung bei der Melodie-Analyse und -Klassifikation," *Hudobná klasifikácia a samocinné pocitace: predbezná zpráva 6. Etnomuzikologického seminára = Musikklassifikation und elektronische Datenverarbeitung: Vorbericht des 6. Ethnomusikologischen Seminars, Kocovce, 6.-10. Október 1975*, edited by Oskár Elschek. Bratislava: Sekcia hudobnej vedy-etnomuzikológia, Umenovedný ústav, Slovenská akademia vied. 3 p.

Lincoln, Harry B. 1976. "Tablature pour les luths," *Computers and the Humanities* X/6 (November-December): 360-361.

Lomax, Alan. 1976. *Cantometrics: An Approach to the Anthropology of Music*. Berkeley, CA: The University of California Press.

Longuet-Higgins, H. Christopher. 1976. "Perception of Melodies," *Nature* 263: 646-653. Reprinted in H. Christopher Longuet-Higgins, *Mental Processes: Studies in Cognitive Science*. Cambridge, MA: MIT Press, 1987. pp. 105-129.

Melkus, Ilja. 1976. "Některé Příklady Vyžití Samočinného počíytače v zahraniční muzikologii," *Lidová píseň a samočinný počítač III: Sborník materiálů ze 3. semináře o využití samočinného počítače při studiu lidové písně (Brno 15.-16.10.1974)*, ed. by Dušan Holý, Karel Pala, and Miloš Štědroň. Praha: Státni pedagogické nakladatelstvi. pp. 333-338.

Mendel, Arthur. 1976a. "Towards Objective Criteria for Establishing Chronology and Authenticity: What Help Can the Computer Give?" *Josquin des Prez. Proceedings of the international Josquin festival-conference held at The Juilliard School at Lincoln Center in New York City, 21-25 June 1971*, edited by Edward E. Lowinsky. London: Oxford University Press. pp. 297-308.

_________. 1976b. "Critical Editions of Josquin Desprez," *Computers and the Humanities* X/1 (January-February): 52.

Móži, Alexander. 1976. "Pokus o harmonickú analýzu inštrumentálnej hudby pomocou numerického kódového systému," *Lidová píseň a samočinný počítač III: Sborník materiálů ze 3. semináře o využití samočinného počítače při studiu lidové písně (Brno 15.-16.10.1974)*, ed. by Dušan Holý, Karel Pala, and Miloš Štědroň. Praha: Státni pedagogické nakladatelstvi. pp. 287-309.

Pala, Karel. 1976. "Poznámy k popisu tematické stavby lidové písně," *Lidová píseň a samočinný počítač III: Sborník materiálů ze 3. semináře o využití samočinného počítače při studiu lidové písně (Brno 15.-16.10.1974)*, ed. by Dušan Holý, Karel Pala, and Miloš Štědroň. Praha: Státni pedagogické nakladatelstvi. pp. 197-210.

Reier, Ellen Jane, and Warren Reier. 1976. "The Introit Trope Repertory at Nevers," *Nordiskt Kollokvium III. I Latinsk Liturgiforskning*, edited by Knud Ottosen. HelsinkiL Helsingfors University. pp. 97-110.

Remmel, M. Ed. 1976. *Towards a Monographical Analysis of Some Folk-Song Arrangements*. Tallin: Academy of the Sciences of the Estonian S.S.R., Department of Social Sciences.

Ševčíková, Marie. 1976. "Tematická Výstavba lidové písně," *Lidová píseň a samočinný počítač III: Sborník materiálů ze 3. semináře o využití samočinného počítače při studiu lidové písně (Brno 15.-16.10.1974)*, ed. by Dušan Holý, Karel Pala, and Miloš Štědroň. Praha: Státni pedagogické nakladatelstvi. pp. 145-153.

Sirovátka, Oldřich. 1976. "Členění písňového textu," *Lidová píseň a samočinný počítač III: Sborník materiálů ze 3. semináře o využití samočinného počítače při studiu lidové písně (Brno 15.-16.10.1974)*, ed. by Dušan Holý, Karel Pala, and Miloš Štědroň. Praha: Státni pedagogické nakladatelstvi. pp. 107-119.

Smoliar, Stephen William. 1976a. "Music Programs: An Approach to Music Theory Through Computational Linguistics," *Journal of Music Theory* XX/1 (Spring): 105-131.

__________. 1976b. Schenker: A Computer Aid for Analysing Tonal Music. Music Project Report No. 6. [Philadelphia]: Department of Computer and Information Science, University of Pennsylvania.

Solomon, Larry. *Music Analysis System*. Software 1976, 1982, 1984.

Stech, David. 1976. A Computer-Assisted Approach to Micro-Analysis of Melodic Lines. Ph.D. dissertation. East Lansing, MI: Michigan State University.

Štědroň, Miloš. 1976. "K intervalovým charakteristikám jednotlivých rolí v Janáčkově opeře Věc Makropulos," *Lidová píseň a samočinný počítač III: Sborník materiálů ze 3. semináře o využití samočinného počítače při studiu lidové písně (Brno 15.-16.10.1974)*, ed. by Dušan Holý, Karel Pala, and Miloš Štědroň. Praha: Státni pedagogické nakladatelstvi. pp. 263-285.

Štědroň, Miloš, et al. 1976. "Kriticky o možnostech hudební analýzy," *Lidová píseň a samočinný počítač III: Sborník materiálů ze 3. semináře o využití samočinného počítače při studiu lidové písně (Brno 15.-16.10.1974)*, ed. by Dušan Holý, Karel Pala, and Miloš Štědroň. Praha: Státni pedagogické nakladatelstvi. pp. 339-356.

Steinbeck, Wolfram. 1976a. "The Use of the Computer in the Analysis of German Folksongs," *Computers and the Humanities* X/5 (September/October): 287-296.

__________. 1976b. "Die Liederbank Kiel," *Jahrbuch des Staatlichen Instituts for Musikforschung* 1976: 94-108.

__________. 1976c. Review of *Faktorenanalytische Typenbestimmung an Volksliedmelodien* by Reiner Kluge, *Jahrbuch für Volksliedforschung* 21: 217-218.

Sundberg, Johan, and Björn Lindblom. 1976. "Generative Theories in Language and Music Descriptions," *Cognition* IV: 99-122. Reprinted in *Machine Models of Music*, edited by Stephen M. Schwanauer and David A. Levitt. Cambridge, MA: The MIT Press, 1993. pp. 262-286.

Tesař, Stanislav. 1976. "K možnostem využití SP v hymnologii," *Lidová píseň a samočinný počítač III: Sborník materiálů ze 3. semináře o využití samočinného počítače při studiu lidové písně (Brno 15.-16.10.1974)*, ed. by Dušan Holý, Karel Pala, and Miloš Štědroň. Praha: Státni pedagogické nakladatelstvi. pp. 253-261.

Toncrová, Marta. 1976. "Zur Frage der individuellen und normalisierten Fassung des Volksliedes vom Gesichtspunkt der Klassifikation," *Hudobná klasifikácia a samocinné pocitace: predbezná zpráva 6. Etnomuzikologického seminára = Musikklassifikation und elektronische Datenverarbeitung: Vorbericht des 6. Ethnomusikologischen Seminars, Kocovce, 6.-10. Október 1975*, edited by Oskár Elschek. Bratislava: Sekcia hudobnej vedy-etnomuzikológia, Umenovedný ústav, Slovenská akademia vied. 1 p.

Vos, Piet G. 1976. Identification of Metre in Music. Bericht Nr. 76 ON 06. Nijmegen, Netherlands: University of Nijmegen.

Wagner, Günther. 1976. "Exaktwissenschaftliche Musikanalyse und Informationsästhetik." *International Review of Aesthetics and Sociology of Music* VII/1 (June): 63-76.

Waite, Stephen V. F., et al. 1976. "Annual Bibliography for 1975 and Supplement to Preceding Years," *Computers and the Humanities* X/2 (March-April): 101-121.

Wenker, Jerome R. 1976. "On the Indexing of Melodies," *Hudobná klasifikácia a samocinné pocitace: predbezná zpráva 6. Etnomuzikologického seminára = Musikklassifikation und elektronische Datenverarbeitung: Vorbericht des 6. Ethnomusikologischen Seminars, Kocovce, 6.-10. Október 1975*, edited by Oskár Elschek. Bratislava: Sekcia hudobnej vedy-etnomuzikológia, Umenovedný ústav, Slovenská akademia vied. 1 p.

1977

Allen, John R. Ed. 1977. "Directory of Scholars Active," *Computers and the Humanities* XI/1 (January-February): 24-46.

Avenary, Hanoch. 1977. "The Northern and Southern Idioms of Early European Music: A New Approach to an Old Problem," *Acta Musicologica* XLIX/1: 27-49.

Barenholtz, Jerry, Z. Wolofsky, I. Ganapathy, Thomas W. Calvert, and P. O'Hara. 1977. "Computer Interpretation of Dance Notation," *Computing in the Humanities: Proceedings of the Third International Conference on Computing in the Humanities*, edited by Serge Lusignan and John S. North. Waterloo, Ontario: The University of Waterloo Press. pp. 235-240.

Baroni, Mario, and Carlo Jacoboni. 1977. "A Grammar of Melody," *Computers and the Humanities* XI/1 (January-February): 42.

Bent, Ian D. 1977. "Analysis of Melodic Structure," *Computers and the Humanities* XI/1 (January-February): 41.

Boroda, Moisej G. 1977. "O melodiceskoj elementarnoj edinice," *MAAFAT'75 1 vsesoûznyj seminar po masinnym aspektam algoritmiceskogo formalizovannogo analiza muzykal'nyh tekstov. (Erevan-Dilizan, 27.10.-1.11.1975 g.): materialy*, edited by Vladimir Leonidovic Gosovskij. Erevan: Izdat. Akad. nauk Armânskoj SSR. pp. 112-120.

Boroda, Moisej G., I. Sch. Nabareyshvili, Jurij K. Orlov, R. Ja. Tshitashvili. 1977. "O Karaktere raspredelenija informatcionnuych edinic maloj tshastotyu v chudoshestvennych tekstach," *Semiotika i Informatika* IX: 23-35.

Brantley, Daniel Lawrence. 1977. Disputed Authorship of Musical Works: A Quantitative Approach to the Attribution of the Quartets Published as Haydn's Opus 3. Ph.D. dissertation. Iowa City, IA: University of Iowa.

Byrd, Donald Alvin. 1977. "An Integrated Computer Music Software System," *Computer Music Journal* I/2 (April): 55-60.

Charnassé, Hélène, Raymond Meylon, and Henri Ducasse. 1977. "Transcription automatique de notations musicales en tablatures," *Computers and the Humanities* XI/1 (January-February): 41-42.

Cohen, Dalia, and Ruth Katz. 1977. *The Israeli Folk Song: A Methodological Example of Computer Analysis of Monophonic Music*. Jerusalem: The Magnes Press.

Czekanowska-Kulinska, Anna. 1977. "Comparative and quantitative methods in international research projects on folk music," *Ethnologia Slavica* VIII-IX (1976-77): 307-18.

Erickson, Raymond F. 1977. "MUSICOMP 76 and The State of DARMS," *College Music Symposium* XVII/1 (Spring): 90-101.
Holtzman, Steven R. 1977. "A Program for Key Determination," *Interface* VI/1: 29-56.
Hughes, Matt. 1977. "A Quantitative Analysis," *Readings in Schenkerian Analysis*, edited by Maury Yeston. New Haven: Yale University Press. 144-164.
Kassler, Michael. 1977. "Explication of the Middleground of Schenker's Theory of Tonality," *Miscellanea Musicologica* IX: 72-81.
Laske, Otto. 1977a. *Music, Memory and Thought: Explorations in Cognitive Musicology*. Ann Arbor: University Research Press.
__________. 1977b. "Toward a Process Model of Musical Structures," *Proceedings of the International Workshop on the Cognitive Viewpoint*, edited by Marc T. De Mey, R. Pinxten, M. Poriau, F. Vandamme. Ghent, Belgium: Communication and Cognition. pp. 295-304.
Lerdal, Fred, and Ray Jackendoff. 1977. "Toward a Formal Theory of Tonal Music," *Journal of Music Theory* 21/1 (Spring): 111-171.
Lincoln, Harry B. 1977. "Indices of the Italian Madrigal, 1530-1550," *Computers and the Humanities* XI/1 (January-February): 41.
Narmour, Eugene. 1977. *Beyond Schenkerianism: The Need for Alternatives in Music Analysis*. Chicago: University of Chicago Press.
Paszkowska, Elzbieta. 1977. "Struktura napiecia w klasyoznej formie sonatowej," *Muzyka* [Poland] XXII/4: 14-37.
Remmel, Mart N. Ed. 1977. *Problemy taksonomii estonskich runiceskich melodij*. Tallin: Academy of Science.
Smoliar, Stephen William. 1977. "SCHENKER: A Computer Aid for Analyzing Tonal Music," *SIGLASH Newsletter* X/1-2: 30-61.
Starr, Daniel, and Robert Morris. 1977. "A General Theory of Combinatoriality and the Aggregate (Part 1)," *Perspectives of New Music* XVI/1 (Autumn-Winter): 3-35.
Steedman, Mark J. 1977. "The Perception of Musical Rhythm and Metre," *Perception* VI: 555-569.
Stephan, Claudio. 1977. "Computer Aided Music Analysis," *Computers and the Humanities* XI/1 (January-February): 42.
Suchoff, Benjamin, and Jack Heller. 1977. "Computer Oriented Music Materials Permuted for User Transformation or Exchange (COMMPUTE)," *Computers and the Humanities* XI/1 (January-February): 42.
Ulrich, John Wade. 1977. "The Analysis and Synthesis of Jazz by Computer," *Proceedings of the 5th International Joint Conference on Artificial Intelligence 1977 (IJCAI-77)*, vol. 2. Pittsburgh, PA: Carnegie-Mellon University. pp. 865-872.
Waite, Stephen V. F., et al. 1977. "Annual Bibliography for 1976 and Supplement to Preceding Years," *Computers and the Humanities* XI/2 (March-April): 100-118.
Whitney, Thomas G. 1977. "Music analysis: SLAM simplified or how the computer compares 16th century Bourgeois with eighteenth century Bach," *Creative Computing* III/2: 88-89.
Wolff, Anthony B. 1977. "Problems of Representation in Musical Computing," *Computers and the Humanities* XI/1 (January-February): 3-12.

1978

Ballo, Igor. 1978. "FIS, metóda triedenia melódií z hlàdiska podobnosti," *Musicologica Slovaca* VI (1978): 175-182.

Ballová, Luba. 1978. "Algoritmizácia Vyhodnocovania Podobnosti Melódií," *Musicologica slovaca* VI: 167-174.

Baroni, Mario, and Carlo Jacoboni. 1978. *Proposal for a Grammar of Melody. The Bach Chorales*. Montreal: Les presses de l'Université de Montral.

Battier, Marc, and Jacques Arveiller. 1978. *Musique et informatique: une bibliographie indexée*, réédition augmentée. Paris: Elmeratto.

Bengtsson, Ingmar, Alf Gabrielsson, and Barbro Gabrielsson. 1978. "RHYTHM-SYVARD, A Computer Program for Analysis of Rhythmic Performance," *Svensk Tidskrift for Musikforskning* LX/1: 15-24.

Bent, Ian, and John Morehen. 1978. "Computers in the Analysis of Music," *Proceedings of the Royal Musical Association* CIV (1977-78): 30-46.

Bertoni, Alberto, Goffredo Haus, Giancarlo Mauri, and Mauro Torelli. 1978a. "A Mathematical Model for Analyzing and Structuring Musical Texts," *Interface* VII: 31-43.

Bertoni, Alberto, Goffredo Haus, Giancarlo Mauri, and Mauro Torelli. 1978b. "Analysis and Compacting of Musical Texts," *Journal of Cybernetics* 8: 257-272.

Boody, Charles George. 1978. The Micro-Computer as an Input Device for Music Analysis or Composition by Computer. Ann Arbor, MI: MPublishing, University of Michigan Library.

Boroda, Moisej G. 1978. "Ob opredelenii informacionnoj melodiceskoj edinicy tipa frazy v muzyke," *Bulletin of the Academy of Science of the Georgian SSR* 89/1: 57-60.

Boroda, Moisej G., and Jurij K. Orlov. 1978. "O sravnenii skorostej vosprijatija informacijonnych edinic v muzyke i reci," [*Proceedings of the Conference "The Functioning of Communication Systems"*]. Erevan: Academy of Science. pp. 58-62.

Brinkman, Alexander R. 1978. Johann Sebastian Bach's Orgelbüchlein: A Computer-Assisted Analysis of the in Fluence of the Cantus Firmus on the Contrapuntal Voices. Ph.D. dissertation. Rochester, NY: University of Rochester, Eastman School of Music.

Chalupka, Lubomír, and Viera Chalupková. 1978. "Spracovianie Suboru L'udovych Piesni na SP MSP 2A," *Musicologica slovaca* (Czechoslovakia) VI: 203-208.

Chalupková, Viera. 1978. "Tonalna Analyza Suboru Piesni a Jej Vyhodnotenie," *Musicologica slovaca* (Czechoslovakia) VI: 209-215.

Chmurny, Rudolf. 1978. "DIS, metoda Vyhodnocovania Podobnosti Melodii," *Musicologica slovaca* [Czechoslovakia] VI: 183-186.

Clauß, Günter and Heinz Ebner. 1978. *Grundlagen der Statistik für Psychologen, Pädagogen und Soziologen*, 7th ed. Berlin: Technik Verlag.

Elschek, Oskár. 1978. "Ludová piesen a samocinny pocítac 2," *Musicologica slovaca* VI: 163-308.

Elscheková, Alica. 1978. "Metoda Vyhidnocivania Melodickych Podobnosti Pomocou Klasifikacnych Tabuliek," *Musicologica slovaca* [Czechoslovakia] VI: 217-234.

Frankel, Robert E., Stanley J. Rosenschein, and Stephen W. Smoliar. 1978. "Schenker's Theory of Tonal Music - its Explication through Computational Processes," *International Journal of Man-Machine Studies* X: 121-138.

Grey, John M. 1978. "Timbre Discrimination in Musical Patterns," *Journal of the Acoustical Society of America* 64: 467-472.

Grey, John M., and John W. Gordon. 1978. "Perceptual Effects of Spectral Modifications on Musical Timbres," *Journal of the Acoustical Society of America* 63 (May): 1493-1500.

Halperin, David. 1978. A Structural Analysis of Troubadour Music. M.A. thesis. Tel Aviv, Israel: Tel Aviv University.

Hanzelin, Fred Lee. 1978. The Software for Computer Assisted Graphical Representation of Single Instrument Melodic Lines and Harmonic Spectra Using DARMS Encoding and Acoustical Data. Ph.D. thesis, University of Illinois at Urbana-Campaign.

Hasty, Christopher F. 1978. A Theory of Segmentation Developed from Late Works of Stefan Wolpe. Ph.D. dissertation. New Haven, CT: Yale University.

Kaden, Christian. 1978. "Ludwig van Beethoven, Sinfonie Nr. 8, zweiter Satz, Allegretto scherzando. Ansätze zu einer statistischen Strukturanalyse." *Bericht über den Internationalen Beethoven Kongreß 20. bis 23. März 1977 in Berlin*, edited by H. Goldschmidt, K.-H. Köhler, and K. Niemann. Leipzig: Deutscher Verlag für Musik. pp. 113-130.

Kasem-Bek, Jan. 1978. "Informationstheorie und Analyse musikalischer Werke," *Archiv für Musikwissenschaft* 35: 62-75.

Knopoff, Leon, and William Hutchinson. 1978. "An Index of Melodic Activity," *Interface* VII/4 (December): 205-229.

Kolata, Gina Bari. 1978. "Singing Styles and Human Cultures: How are They Related?" *Science* CC/4339 (April): 287-288.

Lande, Tor Sverre. 1978. "Musikkanalyse med Datamskin," *Studia Musicologica Norvegia* IV: 47-60.

Longuet-Higgins, H. Christopher. 1978. "The Perception of Music," *Interdisciplinary Science Reviews* 3 (June): 148-156. Reprinted as "Grammars of Music" in H. Christopher Longuet-Higgins, *Mental Processes: Studies in Cognitive Science*. Cambridge, MA: MIT Press, 1987. pp. 130-149.

Lord, Charles Hubbard. 1978. An Explication of Some Recent Mathematical Approaches to Music Analysis. Ph.D. dissertation. Bloomington, IN: Indiana University.

Morehen, John, and Ian Bent. 1978. "Computers in the Analysis of Music," *Proceedings of the Royal Musical Association* CIV (1977/78): 30-46.

Patrick, P. Howard, and Karen Strickler. 1978. "A Computer-Assisted Study of Dissonance in the Masses of Josquin Desprez," *Computers and the Humanities* 12/4: 341-364.

Sentieri, Alfred Richard. 1978. A Method for the Specification of Style Change in Music: A Computer-Aided Study of Selected Venetian Sacred Compositions from the Time of Gabrieli to the Time of Vivaldi. Ph.D. thesis. Ohio State University.

Sørensen, Av Olve. 1978. "Metoder og Metodeproblemer ved Harmonisk Analyse med EDB," *Studia Musicologica Norvegica* IV: 201-216.

Srinivasan, R. 1978. "Studies on Indian Musical Scales. Part I: Computer Analysis of Venkatamakhi's Melakarta Scheme," *Journal of the Sangeet Natak Academy* [India] 49 (July-September): 33-42.

Starr, Daniel, and Robert Morris. 1978. "A General Theory of Combinatoriality and the Aggregate (Part 2)," *Perspectives of New Music* XVI/2 (Spring-Summer): 50-84.

Štědroň, Miloš. 1978. "Zjistovani Typicnosti Nekterych Melodickych Struktur ve Vokalni Melodice Janackovy Opery Věc Makropulos Zapomoci SP," *Musicologica slovaca* [Czechoslovakia] VI: 187-198.

Steinbeck, Wolfram. 1978. "Zur Methodik der Analyse deutscher volkstümlicher Lieder mit Hilfe elektronischer Rechenanlagen," *Beiträge zur Musikgeschichte Nordeuropas. Kurt Gudewill zum 65. Geburtstag*, edited by Uwe Haensel. Wolfenbüttel: Möseler. pp. 323-341.

Tenney, James C., and Larry Polansky. 1978. Hierarchical Gestalt Perception in Music: A 'Metric Space' Model. Mimeographed. Toronto: York University Music Department.

Vikis-Freibergs, Vaira, and Imants Freibergs. 1978. “Formulaic Analysis of the Computer-Cccessible Corpus of Latvian Sun-Songs,” *Computers and the Humanities* XII/4: 329-339.

Wenker, Jerome R. 1978. A Computer-Aided Analysis of Anglo-Canadian Folktunes. Ph.D. dissertation. Bloomington, IN: Indiana University.

Wittlich, Gary, Donald Byrd, and Rosalee Nerheim. 1978. “A System for Interactive Encoding of Music Scores Under Computer Control,” *Computers and the Humanities* XII/4: 309-319.

Zimmerly, John David. 1978. A Computer-Assisted Study of Selected Kyries from the Parody Masses of Clemens non Papa. M.A. thesis. East Lansing, MI: Michigan State University.

1979

Anonymous. 1979a. “Directory of Scholars Active,” *Computers and the Humanities* XIII/1 (January-March): 43-63.

Anonymous. 1979b. “Directory of Scholars Active,” *Computers and the Humanities* XIII/3 (July-September): 247-267.

Anonymous. 1979c. “Annual Bibliography for 1977 and Supplement to Preceding Years,” *Computers and the Humanities* XIII/2 (April-June): 172-183.

Askenfelt, Anders. 1979. “Automatic Computer Notation of Played Melodies,” *Computers and the Humanities* XIII/1 (January-March): 58-59.

Baroni, Mario, and Carlo Jacoboni. 1979. “Formal Analogies in Different Phrases of a Monodic Composition,” *The Third Colloquium on Musical Informatics*, April 1-2, 1979, Padua University, Italy. See abstract in *Computers in the Humanities* XVI/4 (1982): 264.

Berrett, Joshua. 1979. “Alan Lomax: Some Reconsiderations,” *Journal of Jazz Studies* VI/1 (Fall-Winter): 54-63.

Böker-Heil, Norbert, and Harald Heckmann. 1979. “Elektronische Datenverarbeitung,” *Die Musik in Geschichte und Gegenwart*, vol. 16. Kassel: Bärenreiter. pp. 36-51.

Boroda, Moisej G. 1979. Principy Organizacii Povtorov na Microurovne Muzykalnovo Teksta. Dissertation. Tiblissi.

Brinkman, Alexander R. 1979. “A Computer-Assisted Analysis of Melodic Borrowing from the Cantus Firmus in the Chorale Preludes in Bach’s ‘Orgelbüchlein’,” *Proceedings of the 1978 International Computer Music Conference*, compiled by Curtis Roads. [Menlo Park, CA]: Computer Music Journal. pp. 732-760.

Calvert, Thomas W. 1979. “Computer Interpretation of Dance Notation,” *Computers and the Humanities* XIII/1 (January-March): 58.

Colquhoun, Daryl George. 1979. “Computer Piano Concertos,” *Computers and the Humanities* XIII/3 (July-September): 261.

Cuddy, Lola L., Annabel J. Cohen, and J. Miller. 1979. “Melody Recognition: The Experimental Application of Musical Rules,” *Canadian Journal of Psychology* XXXIII/3: 148-157.

Gadviev, Shamil Allgedar. 1979. “Statistic Analysis of Structure of Azerbaijzan Folk Songs,” *Proceedings of the 1978 International Computer Music Conference*, compiled by Curtis Roads. [Menlo Park, CA]: Computer Music Journal. pp. 761-774.

Haus, Goffredo. 1979. “Musical Text Transformations by Operators,” Paper presented at The Third Colloquium on Musical Informatics, April 1-2, 1979, Padua University, Italy. See abstract in *Computers in the Humanities* XVI/4 (December): 264.

Hofstetter, Fred T. 1979. "The Nationalistic Fingerprint in Nineteenth-Century Romantic Chamber Music," *Computers and the Humanities* XIII/2 (April-June): 105-119.
Karkoschka, Erhard. 1979. "On the Analysis of Melodic Activity," *Interface* VIII/2 (October): 117-127.
Krumhansl, Carol L., and Roger N. Shepard. 1979. "Quantification of the Hierarchy of Tonal Functions Within a Diatonic Context," *Journal of Experimental Psychology: Human Perception and Performance* V/4: 579-594.
Longuet-Higgins, H. Christopher. 1979. "The Perception of Music," *Proceedings of the Royal Society of London* Series B 205: 307-322. Reprinted in H. Christopher Longuet-Higgins, *Mental Processes: Studies in Cognitive Science*. Cambridge, MA: MIT Press, 1987. pp. 169-187.
Meehan, James R. 1979. "An Artifical Intelligence Approach to Tonal Music Theory," *Proceedings of the ACM*. New York: Association for Computing Machinery. pp. 116-120.
Mendel, Arthur. 1979. "Recension of the Sources of the Works of Josquin Dezpres," *Computers and the Humanities* XIII/3 (July-September): 260.
Morehen, John, and Ian Bent. 1979. "Computer Applications in Musicology," *The Musical Times* 120/7 (July): 563-566.
Nakamura, Yasuaki, and Seiji Inokuchi. 1979. "Music Information Processing System and Its Applications to Comparative Musicology," *Proceedings of the Sixth International Joint Conference on Artificial Intelligence, Tokyo, August 20-23, 1979* [*IJCAI-79*]. [s.l.]: IJCAI, 1979. pp. 633-635.
Piszczalski, Martin B., and Bernard A. Galler. 1979. "Computer Analysis and Transcription of Performed Music: a Project Report," *Computers and the Humanities* 13/3 (July-September): 195-206.
Polansky, Larry. 1979. "A Hierarchical Gestalt Analysis of Ruggles' Portals," *Proceedings of the 1978 International Computer Music Conference*, vol. 2, edited by Curtis Roads. Evanston: Northwestern University. pp. 790-852.
Rabson, Carolyn. 1979. "National Tune Index," *Computers and the Humanities* XIII/3 (July-September): 261.
Roads, Curtis. 1979. "Grammars as Representations for Music," *Computer Music Journal* III/1 (March): 48-55.
Rothgeb, John. 1979. "Simulating Musical Skills by Digital Computer," *ACM/CSC-ER: ACM Annual Conference / Annual Meeting* (January): 121-125. Revised in *Computer Music Journal* 4/2 (Summer 1980): 36-40. Reprinted in *The Music Machine*, edited by Curtis Roads. Cambridge, MA: MIT Press, 1989. pp. 657-662.
Snell, James Loftin. 1979. Design for a Formal System for Deriving Tonal Music. Master's thesis. Binghamton, NY: State University of New York at Binghamton.
Steinbeck, Wolfram. 1979. "Die Liederbank Kiel," *Computers and the Humanities* XIII/3 (July-September): 263.
Stoffer, Thomas H. 1979. *Aspekte einer generativen Syntax zur Beschreibung musikalischer Strukturen für eine kognitive Musikpsychologie*. Berichte des Psychologischen Instituts der Ruhr-Universität Bochum, Arbeitseinheit Kognitionspsychologie, Nr. 11, 1979.
Suchoff, Benjamin. 1979. "The COMMPUTE Program," *Computers and the Humanities* XIII/3 (July-September): 262.
Sward, Rosalie La Grow. 1979. "The Computer Assists in Attempting to Solve a Problem of Twentieth Century Music," *Proceedings of the 1978 International Computer Music Conference*, vol. 2, edited by Curtis Roads. Evanston, IL: Northwestern University. 853-872.

Tadeusiewicz, Ryszard, and Aleksander Sodo. 1979. "Kompozycje muzyczne z komputera," *Problemy* (Poland) XII (December): 25-30.

1980

Alphonce, Bo H. 1980. "Music Analysis by Computer – A Field for Theory Formation," *Computer Music Journal* IV/2 (Summer): 26-35.

Arom, Simha. 1980. "Structuration du Temps dans les Musiques d'Afrique Centrale: Periodicité, Mètre, Rhythmique et Polyrhythmie," *Revue de Musicologie* 70 (1984): 5-36.

Bailey, Robert Lee. 1980. Music and Mathematics: An Interface in the Writings of Leonhard Euler. EDD thesis, State University of New York at Buffalo.

Bent, Ian D. 1980. "Analysis," *The New Grove Dictionary of Music and Musicians*, edited by Stanley Sadie, vol. 1. London: Macmillan. 340-388.

Bersano, James Richard. 1980. Formalized Aspect Analysis of Sound Texture. PhD thesis, Indiana University.

Boroda, Moisej G. 1980. "Häufigkeitsstrukturen musikalischer Texte," *Glottometrika 3*, edited by Wolfhart Matthäus. Bochum: Studienverlag Dr. N. Brockmeyer. pp. 36-96.

Brinkman, Alexander R. 1980. "The Melodic Process in Johann Sebastian Bach's *Orgelbüchlein*," *Music Theory Spectrum* II (Spring): 46-73.

Duisberg, Robert Adamy. 1980. A digital representation of musical samples and a calculation thereon of autocorrelation as a function of frequency. D.M.A. dissertation. Seattle, WA: University of Washington.

Ellis, Mark. 1980. Linear Aspects of the Fugues of J. S. Bach's "The Well-Tempered Clavier": A Quantitative Survey. Ph.D. dissertation. Nottingham, UK: University of Nottingham.

Gross, Dorothy Susan. 1980. "A Project in Computer-Assisted Harmonic Analysis," *Proceedings of the International Computer Music Conference*, edited by. Hubert S. Howe. San Francisco: Computer Music Association. pp. 525-533.

Halperin, David. 1980. "Distributional Structure in Troubadour Music," *Orbis Musicae* VII (1979-80): 15-26.

Kassler, Michael, and Hubert S. Howe Jr. 1980. "Computers and Music," *The New Grove Dictionary of Music and Musicians*, edited by Stanley Sadie, vol. 2. London: Macmillan. pp. 603-615.

Sørensen, Olve. 1980. "Musikkanalyse med datamaskin II," *Nordisk musik och musikvetenskap under 1970-talet: en rapport från 8:e Nordiska musikforskar-kongressen, Ljungskile folkhögskola 25-30 juni 1979*, edited by Anders Carlsson and Jan Ling. Göteborg: Musikvetenskapliga institutionen, Göteborgs universitet. pp. 177-192.

Srinivasan, R. 1980. "Studies on Indian Musical Scales. Part II: On the Degree of Relatedness of Ragas and Application to 72 Melas," *Journal of the Sangeet Natak Academy* [India] 58 (October-December): 27-38.

Steinbeck, Wolfram. 1980. "ANTOC. Ein neues Verfahren zur Aufzeichnung von Melodien durch den Computer," *Bericht über den Internationalen musikwissenschaftlichen Kongress Berlin 1974*, edited by Hellmut Kühn and Peter Nitsche. Kassel: Bärenreiter. pp. 546-553.

After 1980

Alphonce, Bo H. 1989a. "Computer Applications: Analysis and Modeling," *Music Theory Spectrum* XI/1 (Spring): 49-59.

_________. 1989b. "Computer Applications in Music Research: A Retrospective," *Computers in Music Research* I (Fall): 1-74.

_________. 1989c. "[Review of] Deta S. Davis, Computer Applications in Music: A Bibliography," *Computers in Music Research* I (Fall): 133-159.

Aranovskij, Mark G. 1991. *Sintaksiceskaja struktura melodii: issledovanie*. Moskva, Russia: Muzyka.

Barth-Wehrenalp, Renate. 1982. *Studien zu Adan de le Hale*. Tutzing, Germany: H. Schneider, 1982.

Bent, Ian D. 1987. *Analysis*, with a glossary by William Drabkin. London: Macmillan.

Blombach, Ann Kariger. 1981. "An Introductory Course in Computer-Assisted Music Analysis: The Computer and the Bach Chorales," *Journal of Computer-Based Instruction* 8 (February): 70-77.

_________. 1982. "Harmony vs. Counterpoint in the Bach Chorales," *Computing in the Humanities*, edited by Richard W. Bailey. Amsterdam: North-Holland Publishing Company. pp. 79-88.

Böker-Heil, Norbert. 1981. "Computer-Simulation eines musikalischen Verstehensprozesses," *International Musicological Society: Report of the Twelfth Congress, Berkeley 1977*, edited by Daniel Heartz and Bonnie C. Wade. Kassel: Bärenreiter. pp. 324-329.

Boody, Charles George. 1989. Review of Fred T. Hofstetter's *Computer Literacy for Musicians, Computers and Music Research* I: 123-131.

Byrd, Donald Alvin. 1984. Music Notation by Computer. Ph.D. dissertation. Bloomington, IN: Indiana University.

Cope, David. 1991. *Computers and Musical Style*. Madison, Wisconsin: A-R Editions.

Cope, David. 1996. *Experiments in Musical Intelligence*. Wisconsin: A-R Editions.

Cope, David. 2008. *Hidden Structure: Music Analysis Using Computers*. Wisconsin: A-R Editions.

de la Motte, Diether. 1987. *Musikalische Analyse*. Kassel: Bärenreiter.

Dunsby, Johnathan, and Arnold Whittall. 1988. *Music Analysis in Theory and Practice*. London: Faber Music.

Feld, Steven. 1990. "Linguistic Models in Ethnomusicology," *Ethnomusicological Theory and Method*, edited by Kaufman Shelemay. New York: Garland. pp. 183-203.

Gross, Dorothy Susan. 1981. "A Computer Project in Music Analysis," *Computing in the Humanities*, edited by Peter C. Patton and Renee A. Holoien. Lexington: Lexington Books. pp. 299-313.

Gross, Dorothy Susan. 1984. "Computer Applications to Music Theory: a Retrospective," *Computer Music Journal* VIII/4 (Winter): 35-42.

Jesser, Barbara. 1988. "Rechnergestützte Melodieanalyse - Sackgasse oder Inspiration für die Volksliedforschung" *Musikpädagogische Forschung* IX: 213-228.

Jesser, Barbara. 1991. *Interaktive Melodienanalyse. Methodik und Anwendung computergestützter Anaylseverfahren in Musikethnologie und Volksliedforschung: typologische Untersuchung der Balladensammlung des DVA*. Studien zur Volksliedforschung 12. Bern: Peter Lang.

Kassler, Michael. 1981. "Transferring a tonality theory to a computer," *International Musicological Society: Report of the Twelfth Congress, Berkeley 1977*, edited by Daniel Heartz and Bonnie C. Wade. Kassel: Bärenreiter. pp. 339-347.

Kostka, Stephan M. 1984. The M-PARC System for Musical Encoding (Mnemonic Pitch and Rhythm Code, Version 3). Unpublished Manuscript. Austin, TX: The University of Texas at Austin, Department of Music.

Locke, David. 1981. "Cantometrics: An Approach to the Anthropology of Music by Alan Lomax [Book Review]," *Ethnomusicology* XXV/3 (September): 527-529.